Dostoevsky and the Riddle of the Self

SRLT

NORTHWESTERN UNIVERSITY PRESS
Studies in Russian Literature and Theory

SERIES EDITORS
Caryl Emerson
Gary Saul Morson
William Mills Todd III
Andrew Wachtel
Justin Weir

Dostoevsky and the Riddle of the Self

Yuri Corrigan

NORTHWESTERN UNIVERSITY PRESS / EVANSTON, ILLINOIS

Northwestern University Press
www.nupress.northwestern.edu

Copyright © 2017 by Northwestern University Press. Published 2017. All rights reserved.

An earlier version of chapter 1 appeared as "Interiority and Intersubjectivity: The Vasia Shumkov Paradigm" in *Dostoevsky beyond Dostoevsky: Science, Religion, Philosophy*, ed. Svetlana Evdokimova and Vladimir Golstein (Academic Studies Press, 2016), 250–65. An earlier version of chapter 2 appeared as "Amnesia and the Externalized Personality in Early Dostoevsky" in *Slavic Review* 72, no. 1 (Spring 2013): 79–101. Parts of chapter 6 appeared under the title "The Hiding Places of the Self in Dostoevsky's Adolescent" in *Russian Writers at the Fin de Siècle: The Twilight of Realism*, ed. Katherine Bowers and Ani Kokobobo (Cambridge University Press, 2015), 33–51. Reprinted here with permission of the publishers.

Printed in the United States of America

10 9 8 7 6 5 4 3 2 1

Library of Congress Cataloging-in-Publication Data

Names: Corrigan, Yuri, 1979– author.
Title: Dostoevsky and the riddle of the self / Yuri Corrigan.
Other titles: Studies in Russian literature and theory.
Description: Evanston, Ill. : Northwestern University Press, 2017. | Series: Northwestern University Press studies in Russian literature and theory | Includes bibliographical references and index.
Identifiers: LCCN 2017000991 | ISBN 9780810135703 (cloth : alk. paper) | ISBN 9780810135697 (pbk. : alk. paper) | ISBN 9780810135710 (e-book)
Subjects: LCSH: Dostoyevsky, Fyodor, 1821–1881—Criticism and interpretation. | Self in literature.
Classification: LCC PG3328.Z7 S4536 2017 | DDC 891.733—dc23
LC record available at https://lccn.loc.gov/2017000991

Contents

Acknowledgments		vii
Introduction		3
Chapter One	On the Dangers of Intimacy (The Vasia Shumkov Paradigm)	16
Chapter Two	Amnesia and the Collective Personality in the Early Works	30
Chapter Three	Transparency and Trauma in *The Insulted and Injured*	51
Chapter Four	Beyond the Dispersed Self in *The Idiot*	68
Chapter Five	On the Education of Demons and Unfinished Selves	86
Chapter Six	The Hiding Places of the Self in *The Adolescent*	104
Chapter Seven	The Apprenticeship of the Self in *The Brothers Karamazov*	120
Conclusion		142
Notes		151
Bibliography		215
Index		231

Acknowledgments

This book was initially conceived while I was teaching at the College of Wooster, and I'd like to thank Matthew Mariola, Beth Ann Muellner, Mareike Herrmann, and Peter Pozefsky, among many others, for their warm collegiality and friendship. It was completed over three years in the department of World Languages & Literatures at Boston University, where I've had the great fortune to be mentored and befriended by William Waters, who has helped this book along with advice, encouragement, and keen editorial suggestions. I am very grateful to my departmental colleagues who make our sixth-floor hallway a joy and inspiration, especially Peter Schwartz, Margaret Litvin, Sarah Frederick, J. Keith Vincent, Abigail Gillman, Yoon Sun Yang, Roberta Micallef, Sunil Sharma, Catherine Yeh, Irena Katz, Wiebke Denecke, Gisela Hoecherl-Alden, Robert E. Richardson, Olga Livshin, Svitlana Malykhina, Ines Garcia de la Puente, and Anna Zielinska-Elliott. Thank you also to the invigorating intellectual community of the Core Curriculum, especially Stephanie Nelson, Diana Wylie, Sassan Tabatabai, and Kyna Hamill, and to the Boston University Center for the Humanities.

Although this book was not derived from my dissertation, it owes a great deal to the Slavic department at Princeton where I was fortunate to do my graduate work. I'd like to thank Caryl Emerson who professes dialogism not only in theory but in practice (which is much, much harder to do), and who shows through example how scholarship can be as much an ethical enterprise as it is an intellectual one; and Ellen Chances, whose life and work are an embodied and elegant protest against conformity and who is extraordinarily kind to fragile thoughts. Thank you also to Michael Wachtel, Olga Hasty, and Ksana Blank, the best mentors and teachers one could ask for. I am very grateful also to my colleagues and friends, Sasha Spektor, Anna Berman, Timothy Portice, Dennis Yi Tenen, Thomas G. Marullo, Nina Tumarkin, Simon Rabinovitch, Robert Chodat, and Robin Feuer Miller; and to the members of the North American Dostoevsky Society for their support and encouragement, especially Deborah Martinsen and Carol Apollonio. I'd

Acknowledgments

like to express my gratitude to the readers at Northwestern University Press, both of whom made this a better book, and to Mike Levine, Maggie Grossman, and Anne Gendler, the editorial team, and to Gary Saul Morson.

I owe an enormous debt of gratitude to Larisa Leites and Sergei Bukalov, who took me on as a personal project during several years in Moscow, and to Alexander, Emma, and Dmitry Kouzov. Thank you also to friends Tarik Dessouki, Bryce Janssens, Mikael Rechtsman, Jim Hanson, Scott Gordon, Elaine Sokyrka, Jolene Shif, and Jaime Kirzner-Roberts. Thank you to my uncle Gregory Glazov and his family, to my uncle Jamie Glazov, to my uncles Francis and Sean Corrigan, and to Aunties Anne-Marie Purvis, Angela Ball, Eileen Michaels, and their families. I am deeply grateful to my mother- and father-in-law, Susan and Stuart Doneson, and to my brothers-in-law Daniel Doneson and David Doneson, for their support and love and for our many conversations. It is my great privilege to have three siblings who are constant friends and interlocutors, each of whom contributed to this project in very different ways: thank you to my brother John, and to my sisters Maria and Sarah.

I'd like to express some of my overwhelming gratitude to my mom and dad, Elena Glazov-Corrigan and Kevin Corrigan, whose advice and wisdom have made every page of this book possible. Much more should be said here.

Most of all, I thank my wife, Arielle, for her inexhaustible love and support, for her patience and wisdom, and for her compass-like hold on what it all means. Thank you to my son, Rafael, for presenting so many glorious obstacles to the writing of this book, and to my daughter, Natasha, who only just came into the world as it went to press.

This book is dedicated to the memory of my dear friend and grandfather Yuri Glazov who didn't just read, but lived and breathed Dostoevsky, who forced me to read *The Brothers Karamazov* when I was sixteen, and who helped bring its every corner to life through a series of soul-stirring and life-altering conversations which have managed somehow to continue unabated almost two decades after his death. The book is dedicated in equal measure to my step-babushka Marina Glazova who explained to me when I was fourteen why two times two might equal five and who has been a bedrock of wisdom and integrity for the life of my whole family. One of my grandfather's many pet theories about Dostoevsky had to do with his belief in the magical quality of numbers. I note to my grandpa that this book has seven chapters (which I remember to be a good number according to his theory), and that with the introduction and conclusion that makes nine (three threes, also good), a fact that I hope will have an auspicious effect upon its content.

Dostoevsky and the Riddle of the Self

Introduction

DOSTOEVSKY WAS FASCINATED by the dynamics of human closeness. His characters are known for their participation in convulsive, irrational, and even supernatural forms of intimacy that often surpass the bounds of love or friendship in any traditional sense. In the midst of a dramatic scene, they suddenly freeze and gaze into each other's eyes silently for extended periods of time; they echo and adopt each other's ideas and intonations; they sense each other's presences within themselves; and, in apparent violation of the rules of psychological realism (to which Dostoevsky continually professed his faithfulness), they seem to possess access to each other's private thoughts, feelings, and memories. The boundaries between selves appear strangely fluid and nonbinding: a gentleman-tutor wakes his pupils up multiple times in the night to embrace them and tearfully confide his secrets; a young novelist becomes so emotionally connected to an orphan girl he has saved from ruin that he can hear her heart beating from several feet away; a troubled dreamer finds himself unable to distinguish his own memories from those of his new landlady; a murderer prostrates himself before a prostitute he hardly knows, asking her to make his most important decisions for him; a brilliant young intellectual is disconcerted to feel the presence of his father's servant taking up residence within him; two friends lie down next to a corpse embracing each other so closely that the tears of one fall onto the cheeks of the other.

Behind such examples of feverishly intersecting personalities looms the foundational riddle of Dostoevsky's writing, perhaps the most confusing, contradictory, and agonized aspect of his philosophical worldview, namely, his simultaneous advocacy for and rejection of the notion of an individual self. As an enemy of individualism, Dostoevsky categorically rejected the concept of a self that was not inherently integrated into other selves. He conceived of the Christian ideal as the overcoming of the "I," the development of an ability "to annihilate this I, to give it wholly to all and everyone, undividedly and selflessly" (20:172), and he persistently criticized the European bourgeois conception of selfhood, which he described disparagingly as "the principle of the detached place of residence" (5:79).[1] "In Christianity," he once remarked in his notebook, the attempt to "determine where your personality ends and another begins [. . .] is unthinkable" (27:49). The crux of Dostoevsky's psychology, however, lies in his passionate reverence for the irreducible and inviolable nature of the individual personality. In the very same passages where he espouses the annihilation of the "I," he fervently advocates the necessity of *"becoming a personality*, even at a much more elevated level than that which has now been defined in the West" (5:79; emphasis added). The "annihilation" of the "I," for Dostoevsky, depends, in fact, upon the "very highest development of the personality," the "fullest realization of one's I" (20:172), and the possession of such an "abundance" of self that one has no anxiety over its preservation and is free to renounce it entirely (5:79).

How these attendant ideals—"annihilating the I," on the one hand, and "becoming a personality," on the other—are meant to coexist is never explained in Dostoevsky's theoretical writings, though the yoking together of these concepts leads directly to numerous practical and theoretical problems.[2] In what, one wonders, should this "abundance" of personality consist? What does it mean, in concrete terms, to possess a highly developed personality but to "annihilate" one's "I"? For a deeper and more embodied meditation on the question of selfhood than his theoretical writings provide, we can look to his art and, more specifically, to the unusually intimate and intersecting personalities that populate his stories and novels. In this book I explore the comprehensive and coherent meditation on the nature of the self that takes shape over the course of the evolution of Dostoevsky's fictional writing. I argue that Dostoevsky gradually conceived of a solution to the apparent paradox of the self as both individually distinct and open-endedly plural through a study of human intimacy that began in his early work and developed, over the course of his career, into an innovative and synthetic topography of the personality, a metaphysical psychology by means of which he attempted to rescue spiritual notions of self and soul for a secular age.

The problem of the self in Dostoevsky's writing evokes a multitude of critical perspectives. Mikhail Bakhtin's notion of a dialogical self, for instance, was born out of his reading of Dostoevsky. Sigmund Freud recognized the underpinnings of psychoanalysis in Dostoevsky's examination of the unconscious. Albert Camus formulated his notion of the absurd with constant reference to Dostoevsky's "creatures of fire and ice."[3] The list of prominent theoreticians of the ethics, psychology, metaphysics, and poetics of selfhood who identify Dostoevsky as a decisive interlocutor includes Friedrich Nietzsche, Vladimir Solovyov, Lev Shestov, Jean-Paul Sartre, Emmanuel Levinas, and René Girard, not to mention numerous other modernist artists and literary theorists (Marcel Proust, Thomas Mann, Georg Lukács, Virginia Woolf) who address Dostoevsky as a formative influence, nor of course the vibrant contemporary world of Dostoevsky studies, both East and West. With so many scrupulous readers having walked this ground, why the need for this book?

Ironically, it is the very richness of this interpretative tradition that blurs our understanding of Dostoevsky's conception of personality and leaves a somewhat chaotic notion of the Russian novelist's philosophical legacy. Indeed, it would be difficult to find another modern writer so unanimously celebrated by mutually hostile schools of thought: by those for whom the self is a radically social phenomenon, and those for whom it is a solitary one; those who reject or deemphasize the importance of the unconscious mind, and those who are its champions; those who interpret Dostoevsky as a romantic defender of the inviolate indwelling soul, and those who approach him as a postmodern pioneer of social and relational conceptions of selfhood. While this plurality testifies to an extraordinary breadth of vision in the writer, it also impedes his ability to speak to the major resurgence of literature on the self in the last few decades.[4] The general impression of Dostoevsky as an advocate of the "extinction of self within the Christian fold," while reflecting an important aspect of his worldview, cannot on its own account for the immense fertility of the Russian author's legacy as a theorist of the personality, nor for the complex, contradictory, inconsistent, even tormented expression that his meditation on the human being assumes in his fictional writings.[5] On the other hand, the inclination of many critics simply to accept the complexity of Dostoevsky's views on the self as constituting an unresolvable and "fatal" paradox does not, I will argue, do justice to the coherence of his worldview.[6]

Attempts to interpret Dostoevsky's convulsively embracing personalities come in two kinds, the philosophical and the psychological. In classical Dostoevsky scholarship (the realm of commentary where we find the most sustained effort to understand his concept of the personality), Dostoevsky appears as a philosophical experimenter, and his characters tend to be viewed as embodiments of ideas or as allegorical pieces of a larger collective phenomenon, rather than as reflections of "real people."[7] The Russian religious philosopher Nikolai Berdiaev, for example, envisioned Dostoevsky's novels as dramatizations of the journey of "a single human spirit, revealed from different sides and various moments of its path."[8] Such a way of reading is inherently friendly to psychoanalytic perspectives, which conceive of these whirling chains of personalities as allegorical reconstructions of one central extended psyche with its vast landscape of embodied selves, drives, thoughts, and instincts.[9] Along the same avenue of interpretation, Dostoevsky's novels readily come to be taken as medieval morality plays in which a

Introduction

central character battles between good and evil embodiments (in others) of his own thoughts and desires.[10]

At the other end of the theoretical spectrum, sensing the insufficiency of such allegorical accounts in explaining Dostoevsky's memorable, vivid, and "living" characters, psychologically minded critics approach Dostoevsky as himself a prescient psychologist preoccupied with attempting to portray "real people." Here the agitated and intimate embraces are evidence not of cosmic or national allegory but rather of pathological inclinations among Dostoevsky's characters—projective identification, schizoid mechanisms, morbid codependency, personality disorders. If the philosophical Dostoevsky presents us with bloodless "carriers of ideas" instead of people, the psychological Dostoevsky gives us fully embodied characters who carry little but their own anguish, thus causing us to lose sight of the philosophical substance that is so central to the Russian author's artistic project.[11]

I aim, in this book, to bring together philosophical, theological, and psychological perspectives by exploring the practical meditation on the formation and integration of the self that comprises Dostoevsky's fictional works. Dostoevsky spent his career, I shall argue, searching for a psychological way of conceiving of the social and metaphysical ideals of *sobornost'* (organic collective unity) and *tsel'nost'* (wholeness of personality) that had been advanced but never sufficiently elaborated by thinkers of a preceding generation. In so doing Dostoevsky invented both a new kind of psychology that would help lay the groundwork for the emergence of psychoanalysis and a new approach to metaphysics that was informed by his own specific understanding of pathology and interiority. Dostoevsky was interested in characters terrified of interior space (of memory, of the unconscious, of the indwelling energies that underlie the experience of subjectivity). I explore how this terror of interiority and erasure of memory in Dostoevsky's characters leads to an extraordinary outwardness: a compulsive clinging to others as substitutions for avoided and atrophied internal faculties and a desperation to dissolve oneself within larger collective unities and selves; and I trace the gradual emergence of Dostoevsky's theological psychology through his protagonists' attempts to overcome the loss of self in the other by means of a harrowing and perilous journey inward through the uncharted territory of thought, emotion, memory, and unconscious experience toward the destabilizing and terrifying divine sources that underlie the self.[12] Thus I challenge the canonical distinction in scholarship that separates an early "psychological," "humanist" Dostoevsky from a later "dialectical," "idea-driven" Dostoevsky, a distinction which ignores both the philosophical potential of his early works and the psychological coherence of his later novels.[13] I argue instead for a continuity and gradual evolution of Dostoevsky's view of personality, with the religious conversion that occurred during his imprisonment and exile in Siberia constituting not a breach but an expansion.[14]

The book approaches Dostoevsky as a theorist of the self who thought primarily in images and characterizations, and whose works can be read as one extended text, or rather, as a vast experimental canvas on which the problem of selfhood is continuously explored over the course of four decades through the use of specific recurring images and dramatic paradigms. Dostoevsky "the thinker," who believed in Russian Orthodoxy, *sobornost'*, *pochvennichestvo* (return to the soil), nationalism, and who dreamed of Russia's great gift to the world, bears an indirect relation to Dostoevsky the artist/philosopher of the self and thus takes a secondary position in this study.[15] Perhaps more surprisingly, a secondary position is also given here to the prodigiously literary-minded Dostoevsky who experimented ingeniously with form, genre, and narrative technique, and who expanded the possibilities of the novel in order to address the mounting crises of self and society that were his subject matter.[16] In devoting less attention than is customary to both the formal considerations and shifts in political and philosophical worldview that distinguish Dostoevsky's works from each other, I do not mean to deny the significance of the changes in Dostoevsky's approach to art, politics, and religion over the course of his long and turbulent career. Rather, I place the focus upon the underlying continuity in Dostoevsky's project from earliest to latest in order to open up a less familiar perspective: to tell the story of his gradual development of a theory of the self, initially semiconscious and highly experimental, through the steady accumulation of a symbolic vocabulary for the depiction of personality formation, a vocabulary that acquired more determinate meanings as the author became increasingly aware of the nature of his project and of its far-reaching consequences. Dostoevsky referred to himself as "more a poet than an artist" in that he tended to "adopt themes" that were "beyond [his] own powers" (29.1:145) and to embrace images and paradigms in his fiction that he himself had grasped only intuitively. It is this feature, I believe, that makes it possible to read his works, for all their rich diversity of formal innovation and ideological motivation, as distinctive drafts or complementary parts of one decisive literary examination of the personality.

In exploring the fictional personalities that populate Dostoevsky's works, my guiding assumption is that his approach to characterization is mimetic and referential, that his characters are not merely allegorical vehicles, disembodied voices, or representatives of ideas, but also implied human beings. As Dostoevsky noted in his preparatory notebooks for *The Demons*, "it is possible to create these characters *in the flesh*, and *not just as ideas*" (11:96; emphasis added). The fact that, as Bakhtin observed, Dostoevsky's characters seem to possess almost none of the memories or personal histories that realist authors bestow on implied human persons does not, I shall argue, testify to a nonpsychological or non-realist poetics on Dostoevsky's part. When Ivan Karamazov equates his own personal "essence" with a philosophical "thesis" (14:215), this does not indicate that he is in fact simply the carrier of an idea, but rather that he wishes to be flattened and reduced to a mere vehicle in order to continue to avoid the suppressed memories and unacknowledged sensations that "seethe" and "boil up" from within him and that constitute the evaded content of his personality (15:54). At the same time, in examining the haunting presence of unwanted memory and the unspoken narrative prehistories that lie at the epicenter of Dostoevsky's approach to characterization, I do not mean to treat these characters as living beings enjoying the full scope of human experience in some imagined parallel universe.[17] Rather, I argue that Dostoevsky, being heavily preoccupied with questions of repression and collapsed interiority, had the breadth of imagination to think beyond his characters' circumscribed activity within the narrative proper by endowing them with the imprint and trace of potent memories that are themselves scrupulously elided and felt as specific absences in the text.[18]

In addressing the structure of the psyche in Dostoevsky, I attempt to use as a guide the paradigms that the works themselves provide for us. For this reason, I have been careful throughout not to conflate Dostoevsky's conceptions with other psychoanalytic vocabularies. Jung's notions, for example, of the captive anima, the projective shadow, and the collective unconscious, are elements that emerge from the same European romantic tradition as did Dostoevsky's writing, as does also Freud's nonmystical conception of the psyche. It is tempting, too, to see Dostoevsky's psychology through the lens of twentieth- and twenty-first-century psychoanalysis, dynamic psychiatry, and cognitive psychology. While I draw on these fields for theoretical context, I place the emphasis upon Dostoevsky's own searching paradigmatic formulations of the self. Thus, when I refer to such phenomena as the "unconscious," or "collective unconscious," or "projection," I do not, unless indicated, have in mind the psychoanalytic, psychological, or clinical concepts in their strict terminological senses.

The book is comprised of seven core chapters. Chapter 1 develops a paradigm of the collective self from the little-known early story "A Weak Heart" (1848). The story provides a foundational vocabulary for describing the conflation of self and other and the problem of collapsed interiority that will resonate throughout Dostoevsky's career and thus throughout all the chapters of this book. Chapter 2 explores, in Dostoevsky's early writings, the conditions of trauma and violent shock that create a barrier in the mind and propel the personality outward to unravel itself in external relationships. Through readings of *The Double* (1846), "The Landlady" (1847), and *Netochka Nezvanova* (1849), I approach the clusters formed by compulsively intersecting characters as projective maps of the psyche. The chapter also locates Dostoevsky's developing model of a triadic collective personality in the context of various traditions of doubling and dualism. Chapter 3 looks closely at Dostoevsky's notion of wounded memory in *The Insulted and Injured* (1861) and its connection to the emergence of a metaphysical dimension in the personality. In the novel's implicit attack on the Enlightenment virtue of personal transparency, Dostoevsky champions the psychic wound as an opaque aperture in the self that allows for the formation of a more capacious and potentially robust personality. In each of these three initial chapters, which trace the problem of the splintering and externalizing of the self, I use *Crime and Punishment* (1866) as a touchstone for my discussion of the early works. In this way, I hope to emphasize, at each juncture, the continuity of Dostoevsky's project at its various stages.

Chapter 4 initiates a shift of focus to Dostoevsky's philosophical exploration of the self in his later works. Chapter 4 investigates the buried but potent presence of unwanted memory that exists beneath the surface of *The Idiot* (1869), haunting the novel's protagonists and prompting them, in their attempts to escape, erase, or preserve facets of their personalities, to dissolve themselves into a larger, collective unity. In reading Prince Myshkin as the apotheosis of Dostoevsky's wounded heroes, I approach his journey in the novel as an attempt to discover a principle outside of the self—a transcendental anchor for selfhood—so as to rebuild the personality from its projective dispersal into others and to liberate others, in turn, from their confined status as aspects of his own psyche. Chapter 5 reads *Demons* (1872) to investigate Dostoevsky's innovative demonology as a study of collapsed selfhood. I argue that the novel's examination of *bezlichnost'* (impersonality or facelessness) and of rickety selves that succumb helplessly to foreign agencies finds its center in the vampiric pedagogical activity of an unlikely, tragicomic demon, Stepan Verkhovensky, and in his concerted attack upon the development of interior personal space among the members of the younger generation. This context allows us to see *The Adolescent* (1875), in chapter 6, as an exploration of the attempt to recover the interior space of the self. The novel's seemingly scattered plot, I argue, becomes strikingly coherent when viewed as an examination of the various strategies of the displacement of the "soul" into exterior space, and of the search for a theory of personality that would redeem the body as the dwelling place of the I. Chapter 7 brings the lines of inquiry together to explore the depictions of personality formation in *The Brothers Karamazov* (1880) through a series of parallel apprenticeships in which the pupil is subsumed into the personality of the master. The novel, I argue, presents us with an extensive topography of the interior space of the self through the inward journeys of its protagonists—Alyosha, Mitya, Ivan—upon their respective dislocations from a larger collective experience of personhood. In my "Conclusion," I recapitulate the book's findings through a

Introduction

discussion of "The Dream of a Ridiculous Man" (1877) and situate Dostoevsky's project within the broader context of the problem of the "inner life" as it emerged in the cultural discourse of prerevolutionary Russian society.

As this brief outline shows, my own approach diverges from the canonical path to the question of the self in Dostoevsky, which finds its fulcrum and point of departure in *Notes from Underground* (1864) and *Crime and Punishment* (1866). In teaching Dostoevsky, I have found these mid-career masterpieces to be the central and indispensable texts for grasping the author's examination of the emergence of modern subjectivity in late imperial Russia, of the splintering of subject and object, and of the interior plight of the deracinated St. Petersburg intellectual, "torn from the dark ages" by Russia's accelerated enlightenment and thoroughly unequipped for the furious dialectic of self-consciousness that accompanies his cultural adolescence. Among its many riches, *Notes from Underground* presents us with Dostoevsky's most concentrated and decisive portrait of the unhappy "I" in all of its intensity, broken and paralyzed by self-consciousness, desperately at odds with its own embodiment, desiring freedom and self-mastery while depending begrudgingly on others for existence, and thus compelled to affirm its freedom from the laws of nature and from the reductive eyes of others by means of self-destruction and industrious solipsism.[19] From here, it takes only one short step to arrive at Raskolnikov's duality in *Crime and Punishment*, his self-enmity, his psychological collapse, and subsequent quasi-religious conversion as illustrative of Dostoevsky's artistic attempts to rescue the modern mind from self-destruction and to minister to a broader cultural impasse in Russia's encounter with the perils of enlightenment. But I have also found in my teaching that the exegetical narrative of the personality broken and unraveled by heightened consciousness, compelling as it is, nevertheless leaves us in some perplexity when it comes to the looser, baggier masterpieces—*The Idiot*, *Demons*, *The Adolescent*—that inform and lead the way to *The Brothers Karamazov*. This current project was born in part from the desire to devise an alternate, complementary path through Dostoevsky's examination of the divided self, a path that would reach farther back in Dostoevsky's artistic evolution and thus present a more holistic picture of his career-long struggle with the "mystery" of the human being. Thus, I have intentionally displaced *Notes from Underground* and *Crime and Punishment* from the center of my discussion as a way of defamiliarizing Dostoevsky's artistic journey, and I engage these works not as guides to the problem of selfhood in Dostoevsky, but rather as touchstones for assessing the rightness of our course, with *Crime and Punishment* as constant counterpoint to the analysis of the early works in chapters 1, 2, and 3, and the underground man appearing in the conclusion (next to his near relative, the ridiculous man), illumined, I hope, in a new way in the context of the argument as a whole.

Introduction

Indeed, the canonical Dostoevsky as he often appears in criticism, is, much like his characters, strangely disconnected from his past. Just as Myshkin appears on a train to Petersburg already fully formed, with no distinct memories from before the age of twenty-four, so studies of Dostoevsky's writing tend to begin in the writer's forties, sometimes with the tacit assumption that his experiences in prison and exile were so utterly transformative as to render his earlier works all but extraneous. By fashioning an interpretive lens through readings of the early works, I hope to offer a more integrated and complete understanding of Dostoevsky's project, according to which his earliest driving intuitions as a writer remain active forces in his later work, even if the form of their expression has grown dramatically in its complexity and effectiveness. I do not champion "A Weak Heart" or "The Landlady" as misunderstood masterpieces but rather as somewhat hastily conceived and aesthetically imperfect stories, which, whether despite or because of these qualities, provide us with considerable insight into the unconscious or semiconscious workings of Dostoevsky's artistic imagination and allow us to glimpse in greater relief the shaping principles of the later, and far more harmonious, formal successes.

My hope is that these readings offer not only a coherent account of the evolution of the concept of the personality in Dostoevsky but also new and useful interpretations of the works themselves. The core of this book is new readings of Dostoevsky's works, with special emphasis on the significance of his early works—both in themselves as examinations of personality and as illuminative guides to Dostoevsky's major novels. I do not provide a complete study of all of Dostoevsky's writings, as will be readily apparent. I hope this book will appeal to specialists as well as to nonspecialist readers interested more generally in Dostoevsky or the problem of the self. I assume familiarity with the basic plot elements and characters only of Dostoevsky's most famous works (*Crime and Punishment*, *The Idiot*, *Demons*, and *The Brothers Karamazov*). For other works, I provide synopses.

In what remains of the introduction, I shall offer some brief context in nineteenth-century Russian culture, first, for the vocabulary of selfhood, and then for the discussion of trauma, since it is the thesis of this book that these two concepts are inextricably linked in Dostoevsky's writing.

DEFINING TERMS: SELF, PERSONALITY, SPIRIT, MIND, CONSCIOUSNESS, SOUL

For the study of Russian intellectual history, the question of the "self" is inherently problematic in that the word itself has no single equivalent in Russian. Terms exist for soul (*dusha*), personality (*lichnost'*), person (*chelovek*;

litso), individual (*osoba*), and selfhood in the more negative sense (*samost'*). But there is no direct equivalent for the "self," *soi*, or *selbst* of European cultural traditions, apart from the first-person pronoun, *ia*—which Dostoevsky does frequently employ in his writings on the topic. The absence of such a term has been attributed to Russia's unique history in which the concept of individualism emerged later, and with many more attendant difficulties, than in Europe.[20] I use the term "self" throughout this book as roughly equivalent to the concept of "personality" or *lichnost'*, with the caveat that "self" is generally narrower than "personality." This imperfect comparison reflects Dostoevsky's own ambiguity regarding the problem of *lichnost'*, since he used that term sometimes as a synonym and sometimes as an antonym for the "I." When he opposes the two terms, the "I" or "self" (*ia*) denotes the site of consciousness, while "personality" (*lichnost'*) includes the more expansive terrain that underlies and transcends the activity of being aware.[21] When he uses the terms as synonyms, *lichnost'* tends to take on the more negative quality of a self-enclosed individual consciousness. More determinate for Dostoevsky is the opposition of *bezlichnost'* (facelessness, impersonality) to *samootverzhenie* (selflessness): the first is an intensely negative and detrimental state of being and the other a desirable Christian ideal. For Dostoevsky, it is a bad thing to lose one's personality, but a good thing to lose one's self. Our purpose in this book is to discover, in practical terms, how Dostoevsky conceived of the expansion of a *self*—as a rickety, enclosed phenomenon, helpless against annexation from without—into a capacious, robust, open-ended, and integral entity, or *personality*.

In our exploration of the inner topography of the human being in Dostoevsky, the traditional romantic landscape of selfhood can serve as a helpful backdrop. According to the neo-romantic and mystical Russian philosophical tradition that emerged toward the end of the nineteenth century, the terrain of the personality can be charted by means of the terms "self," "soul," and "spirit" (*ia, dusha,* and *dukh*). Here the term "self" or the "I" refers to the experience of subjectivity, the center of consciousness and awareness;[22] soul is the innermost, unconscious domain that underlies the I; and "spirit" is the realm of abstraction and idea toward which the I extends itself in thought. Thus "mind" (*um*, in Russian, equivalent to Greek *nous*) can be seen as approximately synonymous with "spirit" (*dukh*). All of these three elements—mind (or spirit), consciousness, and soul—constitute the elements of *lichnost'* in its expansive form.[23] It is worth noting that Bakhtin's non-essentialist view of the "soul"—born at least in part from his reading of Dostoevsky—can serve as a direct counterpoint to the mystical romantic landscape of the self.[24] For Bakhtin, soul cannot be hidden somewhere beneath consciousness in the individual as something "already present-on-hand."[25] "In my relationship to myself," he argues, "I have nothing to do with

Introduction

the soul." The soul, rather, "is bestowed upon me" from the outside, from another person, who is capable of seeing and making sense of me from without.[26] Parsing the tension in Dostoevsky's writing between "soul" as inwardly abiding essence and as intersubjective activity will be a significant aspect of this book's project.

BEFORE "TRAUMA"

There is a potential anachronism in arguing that Dostoevsky's experimental engagement with the concept of the personality draws on his study of the wounds of the mind. Indeed, the point of origin for our contemporary notion of trauma is generally located in the years surrounding and following Dostoevsky's death.[27] For some scholars, this period (the 1870s and 1880s) simply marks the beginning of the scientific study of a phenomenon that had always existed and that may have been commented upon previously outside the realm of medical inquiry.[28] A strong current in the historiography of trauma, however, maintains that the very "idea that intensely frightening or disturbing experiences could produce memories that are concealed in automatic behaviors, repetitive acts over which the affected person exercised no conscious control" was "literally unthinkable" before the late nineteenth century.[29] The principal explanation of trauma's specific historical locality lies in the convergence, within medical research during this period, of two fields of inquiry: in neurology, the understanding of how painful experience could cause bodily illness, and, in psychology, the discovery that repressed or suppressed memories could affect the health of the mind.[30]

The notion, however, that something very like these forms of insight could have been intuitively available to intelligent people before this date seems to be all but self-evident. We have to look no further than the personal correspondence of Vissarion Belinsky, the fabled literary critic and erstwhile champion of Dostoevsky, to establish the concept's circulation, in an implicit, untheorized form, in mid-nineteenth-century Russian culture. In a letter from 1840, Belinsky conceived his own debilitating social awkwardness, his "wild strangeness," as resulting from psychic wounds accrued in the distant, long-forgotten past. He points to childhood experiences which continue to overpower his present behavior in the form of unconscious physiological reactions. The remarkable passage is worth quoting at some length as indicative of the understanding of the wounds of the mind in Dostoevsky's time:

> I can't show myself among people: my mug flares up, my voices shakes, my arms and legs quiver, I am afraid that I'll fall down. [. . .] What is the meaning of this wild strangeness? I remembered my mother's story. [. . .] As

a nursing infant, I stayed with the nanny [. . .]: she suffocated and beat me so that I wouldn't bother her with my crying. Maybe that's the reason. Moreover, I never nursed: I was born deathly ill, never took to the breast and didn't know it (that's why now I love it doubly), I sucked a bottle, and so, if the milk was sour and foul, I couldn't get fresh milk. Later, my father couldn't stand me, he would tell me off, put me down, find fault with me, he would beat me mercilessly and coarsely—eternal memory to him! I was an alien in the family. Here, perhaps, lies the reason for this wild phenomenon. [. . .] But if I see a nice female face: I perish, fog falls onto my eyes, my nerves fall apart, as upon seeing a boa constrictor or a rattlesnake, my breath breaks, I am on fire. [. . .] I am ill, my friend, with a terrible illness—have pity on me.[31]

Belinsky's description of his "terrible illness" is useful in grasping the pre-psychoanalytic concept of the psychic wound. On the one hand, Belinsky's description matches our contemporary notion of trauma in that highly distressing experiences are thought to endure as a form of somatic memory unavailable to consciousness, exerting a potent, debilitating impact upon present behavior. Coming into contact with certain seemingly innocuous stimuli ("a nice female face") revives physically encoded reactions to long-forgotten distressing experiences (the nanny's cruelty, foul milk, etc.) and evokes an insidious, automatic behavioral pattern in the sufferer ("as upon seeing a boa constrictor or rattlesnake"). The description, however, can also be seen as characteristic of the pre-psychoanalytic perspective in the sense that Belinsky's traumatic experiences have not been repressed; they are either preconscious (nanny's cruelty) or possibly even available to memory (father's beatings). One could argue that there is little indication here that these memories are preserved in an unintegrated form somewhere in the brain and psyche, but rather that bad memory and distressing experience are simply understood as formative for the personality. Dostoevsky, as we shall see, builds on such an understanding in a pioneering and prescient manner in his study of unintegrated and banished memory.

Dostoevsky's own personal traumas from childhood have been debated over the years. Alexei Suvorin, perhaps sensing the importance of this theme in Dostoevsky's life and work, surmised (contentiously) that "something terrible, enduring, and torturous happened to Dostoevsky in childhood, the result of which would be the falling sickness."[32] Dostoevsky's brother Andrei objected to this idea and wrote to Suvorin, protesting that "what precisely the 'something terrible, enduring and torturous' is I do not understand."[33] Stepan Yanovsky, Dostoevsky's longtime doctor and friend, expressed to Anna Grigorievna, Dostoevsky's widow, his thought that "it was precisely in childhood that something gloomy and burdensome seized hold of Fyodor Mikhailovich."[34] In this study I avoid entering into this speculative territory, since my focus is simply upon the importance of the psychic wound within the context of personality formation in Dostoevsky's fictional writings. I mention these aspects at the outset as an indication that the themes themselves were evidently relevant and available to Dostoevsky, both in his writing and in his life.

Chapter One

On the Dangers of Intimacy (The Vasia Shumkov Paradigm)

> And it happened [. . .] that Jonathan's very self became bound up with David's, and Jonathan loved him as himself. [. . .] And Jonathan, and David with him, sealed a pact because he loved him like himself. And Jonathan took off the cloak that was on him and gave it to David, and his battle garb, and even his sword and his bow and his belt.
> —1 Samuel 18:1–4

> People receive nourishment from one another [. . .] through the soul, through sensing and imagining one another; otherwise, what can they think about, where can they spend the tender, trusting strength of life, where can they scatter their sorrow and find comfort, where can they die an unnoted death? With only the imagination of his own self to nourish him, a man soon consumes his soul, exhausting himself in the worst of poverties and dying in mindless gloom.
> —Platonov, *Soul*

> We like subsisting on someone's else mind . . . that's what we like!
> —Dostoevsky, Crime and Punishment

INDWELLING SELF / RELATIONAL SELF

Among studies of Dostoevsky's conception of personality, two largely incompatible and equally influential schools of thought can be discerned. On the one hand, Dostoevsky has been read as a neo-romantic "expressivist" who situated the roots of the personality, and of the world itself, in the inexhaustible depths of the "human soul."[1] The elder Zosima's teaching in *The Brothers Karamazov* on the organic nature of the personality whose roots "touch other worlds" provides an illustration of this view: Zosima describes our "secret innermost sensation" of a "connection with [. . .] a celestial and higher world," and the sense that "the roots of our thoughts and feelings are not here, but in those other worlds" (14:291). It was in this mystical romantic vein that Vladimir Solovyov spoke of Dostoevsky's belief in "the divine power in the soul" and in its "divine origin."[2] The personality, understood in this way, becomes not only a repository for divinity but also an "all-encompassing," "microcosmic" universe within itself.[3] Various traditions of selfhood stand behind this notion of personality, among them, the Neoplatonic Augustinian self that turns inward to discover the presence of the divine in its depths, and the German romantic self that reaches, in its dark inscrutable basis, into the very sources of nature and of the universe.[4]

In observing the radically social, relational nature of Dostoevsky's characters, however, readers have questioned whether this apparent belief in the infinite inward capaciousness of the self extends to his active psychological portraits.[5] Thus, a second school of thought finds its center in what can be described as Bakhtin's Dostoevsky: a remarkably contemporary, potentially postmodern, writer who reconceived traditional notions of self in intersubjective space. This is the Dostoevsky who, according to Tzvetan Todorov, "rejects an essentialist conception of man," and for whom "the human being has no existence prior to the other or independent of him."[6] Bakhtin called attention to the absence of a psychologized and naturalized sense of self in Dostoevsky's characters, who lack the detailed interiority or personal biography of realist literature, and whose radical inner formlessness abates only in the activity of interpersonal dialogue.[7] These characters, Bakhtin observed, are always on the "threshold," looking outward, existing fully in the "living *present*," never determined or limited by unconscious lives or biographical pasts.[8] Bakhtin's perspective helps to illuminate the relational nature of personhood in Dostoevsky whose characters apprehend their depths *outside* of themselves, "in the souls of *others*."[9] From this perspective, if the self is rooted in other worlds, as Zosima espouses, then those other worlds are not transcendent essences but rather the worlds of other consciousnesses.

Thus, the personality in Dostoevsky is thought of, on the one hand, as an *essence*, a bottomless depth, encompassing and expressing the entire universe, and on the other, as an *activity*, *event*, or *point of view* that constitutes itself outwardly through relationships. The present chapter engages this duality in commentary by examining the tension between interiority and intersubjectivity already distinctly evident in one of Dostoevsky's early stories,

"A Weak Heart" ("*Slaboe serdtse*"), published in 1848. Both the indwelling and relational models of selfhood are evoked in the story's depiction of how two personalities of significant interior complexity become merged into one extended self.

INTIMATE FRIENDSHIP AND THE COLLECTIVE SELF

"A Weak Heart" depicts the anxious travails and gradual descent into madness of one Vasia Shumkov, a humble, ardent, slightly disfigured clerk who has been entrusted with a large amount of copying work by his superior and benefactor, Yulian Mastakovich. Because of a newly formed engagement with his beloved Liza, whom he has fervently pursued for weeks, Vasia has egregiously neglected his work. His roommate and best friend, Arkady Nefedevich, tries to help him finish the copying, attempting at all costs to shore up his friend's sanity, but Vasia is ultimately beyond saving, overwhelmed as he is by the emotions of his newfound happiness, and tormented by his own professional negligence and apparent "ingratitude" before his benefactor. Vasia undergoes a pitiful public collapse, is removed to an asylum, and Arkady is left alone without his friend in the cold and ghostlike city of St. Petersburg.

The work has been consistently read, for good reason, as "a story of social protest"[10] in its illustration of how a lowly civil servant is crushed by the hierarchical rank and file nature of imperial Russia.[11] According to this traditional reading, the meek Vasia Shumkov, in his wrenching psychological collapse, is a representative of Dostoevsky's "downtrodden" (the focus of his early, socially oriented writing), and the hero's breakdown is the result of his having utterly internalized his subordinate social status.[12] Vasia, it follows, is so terrified of his superiors that he loses his mind as he suffers convulsive and devastating bouts of gratitude and anxiety before them.

When read in the context of Dostoevsky's extended inquiry into the notion of relational personhood, however, the passionate, intimate attachment between Vasia and his roommate, Arkady, seems less a facet of Dostoevsky's social commentary and more the emerging kernel of a larger philosophical and psychological project. The destructive consequences of the pair's loving friendship vividly express the dangers of intimacy in Dostoevsky's world, as the friends' closeness leads directly to the replacement of aspects of the self with the activities of the other. In this sense, the friends' interdependence provides a depiction of intersubjective selfhood notably different from, and considerably more pathological than, the dialogical model espoused by Bakhtin: in Vasia and Arkady we see an overwhelming need for the other as a completion of one's own unfinished personality, a personality that degenerates as it becomes gradually subsumed and supplanted by its loving but overpowering counterpart. As we shall see, the images surrounding Vasia's escape from assimilation by Arkady's personality directly prefigure scenes and paradigms from the later works in which characters struggle to be released from their imprisonment within collective personalities, while encountering within themselves only atrophied potentialities which have been replaced and supplemented by the tireless activity of another person.

The friendship between Arkady and Vasia enacts a complementary distribution of faculties between adjacent personalities, of a vigilant administrative mind (Arkady) which binds itself to a subordinate, largely irrational, intensely emotional, obedient nature, or "weak heart" (Vasia). Arkady plays the role of the friends' collective superego, having "loved [Vasia] so, watched over him, instructed him at every step with saving advices" (2:28). As Vasia's external conscience, he takes on full responsibility for his friend's work deadline, beseeching Vasia to look to him for guidance: "Just make sure you hold onto me, [. . .] and I will stand over you with a stick today and tomorrow, and all night, and I will torment you in your work: finish up! Finish up faster, brother!" (2:29). Arkady's zealous solicitude at times resembles an invasion, or annexation, of his friend's agency. He consistently bemoans the fact that he cannot take over for Vasia entirely, that he cannot save his friend by simply occupying his place: "How annoying that I cannot help you," he exclaims to Vasia, "or else I would have taken it and would have written it all for you . . . Why don't you and I have the same handwriting?" (2:29).[13] In his urgent desire to substitute himself for Vasia, Arkady emphasizes his ability, for example, to sign Vasia's name: "I sign your name terribly similarly and make the same curl [. . .] Who would notice!" (2:31). Vasia, in turn, repeatedly conceives of his own existence as directly dependent on Arkady's: "Really, Arkasha, I love you so that, if it were not for you, it seems to me, I wouldn't even be living in this world altogether" (2:18, 2:26). The weaker of the two men, Vasia is generally inclined to accept Arkady's administration, looking at his friend "ever so timidly [. . .] as if his decision [. . .] depended on him" (2:22), his pathetic "feeble" (2:17) physicality repeatedly overwhelmed by Arkady's "leonine," (2:22) "powerful greedy [. . .] embraces" (2:33) and "strong arms" (2:17).

As co-joined personalities, Arkady and Vasia exhibit an extreme degree of intimacy. They constantly throw themselves into each other's passionate embraces (2:17, 18, 36, 42, 44, 47), which often evoke a parent-child bond. Early in the story, Arkady lifts Vasia up and carries him around the room like a child, "pretending that he was lulling him to sleep" (2:17).[14] Later on, "Arkady throws himself upon [Vasia], like a mother whose kindred child is being taken away" (2:44). At times, the friends are so intimately connected that they appear to share a nervous system, as when Vasia "held Arkady by

Chapter One

the shoulders, looked into his eyes and moved his lips as if he himself wanted to say the words for him" (2:22). Their intimacy extends equally beyond the physical. Arkady claims to have special insight into Vasia's inner processes ("I understand you; I know what is happening within you" [2:37]), and Vasia wonders at his friend's uncanny powers of perception: "for a long time now I've wanted to ask you: how is it that you know me so well?" (2:39).

Like Ivan with Smerdiakov in the (much later) *Brothers Karamazov*, Arkady sees Vasia's actions as realizations of his own private intentions. At first surprised by Vasia's decision to get married, he then recalls the impulse in himself: "'I myself, brother, thought about getting married; and now suddenly you're getting married, so it's all the same'" (2:19). He then quite suddenly discovers in himself the same passionate love for the same woman (he "was in love, fatally in love with Liza"): "just as she looks after you, let her look after me too. Yes, friendship for you and friendship for her; you are indivisible now; only I will have two beings like you instead of one" (2:29); to which Vasia, "terribly pleased" with Arkady's plan to invade his marriage, "pointed out that this was just how it should be and that now they will be even greater friends" (2:28–9).[15] For her part, Vasia's fiancée intuitively understands the bizarre fluidity between the friends' identities when she cries out, "in the most naïve rapture," her hope for the future: "'We will be the three of us like one person!'" (2:28).

In this portrait of intimate friendship, we encounter another curious detail: the two heroes, utterly preoccupied with their shared concerns over Vasia's predicament, have no tangible pasts, except for some intentionally obscured details—for example, Arkady and Vasia are both orphans, and Vasia, unlike Arkady, is initially presented without patronymic, a detail the author promises to explain but then never does. Concerning Arkady's past, the narrator promises to recount an episode ("once it even happened that . . . But this can wait until later" [2:26]), and again conspicuously fails to deliver on his promise. These references to the past, appearing as obvious ellipses in the text, emphasize a lack within these characters, a blank space where memory or personal biography fails to reside, and we begin to suspect that this interior absence is somehow connected to the peculiar intensity of their intimacy.

This intimate extension into the other recalls elements of the doppelgänger tradition (to be discussed in chapter 2), and in fact replays many of the scenes from Dostoevsky's *The Double*, which was published two years earlier: we think of Goliadkin Senior when Arkady rushes through the streets of Petersburg, trying to anticipate and to reverse preemptively the self-destructive behavior of his emancipated counterpart; or when he suddenly runs into the guilty Vasia, "nose to nose," like Goliadkin with his double on the street, and Vasia stops "like one caught in a crime" (2:35); or especially in the public scandal at the end, when Vasia appears before his superiors in a deluded, incoherent, and trembling state and, like Goliadkin, is removed to an asylum. "A Weak Heart," however, represents a distinct departure from *The Double*, in that, unlike Goliadkin, who encounters a perfect replica of himself, Arkady and Vasia are unmistakably two separate individuals.[16] In reincorporating the events and images of *The Double*, Dostoevsky indicates his growing interest in the psychology of two, discrete, sovereign individuals who come to enact the behavior of a single self.[17]

PRETENDING TO SLEEP: ESCAPE FROM THE OTHER

As mentioned above, the story dramatizes a crisis in the friendship, in which Vasia, as the result of some nascent and concealed inner anguish, begins to refuse Arkady's administrative instructions. We discover that Vasia, by the time the story begins, has recently begun nurturing a sense of privacy. Just as he keeps the shameful secret of his neglected, unfinished work ("five of the thickest notebooks" [2:37]) hidden from Arkady in a box, he has told Arkady nothing of his engagement to Liza, and when Arkady teasingly holds his friend down, trying to force the confession out of him, Vasia insists on the dignity of his personal interior space, exclaiming that "if you had gone to ask me 'what's her name?' I swear I would have killed myself before answering you" (2:18). Vasia's secrecy is symptomatic of a larger transformation in his character, a change that he himself does not understand. He tries to explain his newfound inner complexity to Arkady, vaguely describing a growing consciousness of the division between self and other, with an attendant longing for personal dignity and responsibility:

> It seems to me that I didn't know myself before [. . .] and I only discovered others yesterday too. I [. . .] didn't feel, didn't value fully. The heart . . . in me was callous. . . . Listen, how did it happen that I hadn't done any good to anyone on the earth, because I was incapable, [. . .] And so many have done good to me! Take you first: do you think I don't see. I was [. . .] only keeping quiet! (2:39)

The experience of being loved and recognized by his fiancée has evidently shaken Vasia, forcing him to evaluate himself as a discrete personality. "I am undeserving of this happiness!" he protests to Arkady, "what have I done that was special, tell me! [. . .] And I! Such a woman loves me, me . . . [. . .] She came to love me as I am" (2:25). A distinct moral ambiguity, therefore, attends the emergence of the interior life, since it is connected, on the one hand, with the discovery of self-worth at being loved and, on the other, with vague but intense feelings of guilt and criminal secrecy.

Arkady perceives grave danger in his friend's emergent complexity. He beseeches Vasia to "reveal [his concealed] torments," so that he can take responsibility upon himself. He repeatedly offers to act as intermediary between Vasia and his "benefactor," Vasia's section head, Yulian Mastakovich, who is, to Vasia, a divine, omnipotent being. "I'll save you!" he offers Vasia, "I'll go to Yulian Mastakovich . . . don't shake your head, no, listen! . . . I'll explain [. . .] how you're destroyed, how you're tormenting yourself. [. . .] I'll sacrifice myself for you [. . .] don't contradict me!" (2:38). Vasia, however, determined to free himself from Arkady's government, "cries out, turns white as a wall," and protests vehemently: "Do you know that you're killing me right now?" (2:37). He is especially anxious about Arkady's helpful plan to sign Yulian Mastakovich's visitors' books for him (in other words, to subsume his identity), afraid that his benefactor will notice "that it's a different hand" (2:31). In Arkady's presence, he appears to accept his friend's orders docilely and agrees to stay home to copy the neglected work. When Arkady leaves, however, Vasia's agency awakens. As Arkady rushes to the benefactor's residence to sign, he notices that Vasia has secretly escaped to sign his own name ("imagine his surprise when before him appeared Vasia Shumkov's very own signature!" [2:35]); Vasia thus insists upon the inviolability of his own un-annexable personality. The awakening of the self is portrayed in Vasia through these irrepressible desires: to sign one's own name, to atone for one's crimes, to feel the full weight of one's "guilt" before "God," to repent and to pray for divine mercy, to "tell him myself," to "go myself": "I'll explain everything myself [. . .] he'll see my tears, he'll be moved by them" (2:38–40).

The story provides us with a clear vantage point onto one of Dostoevsky's most ubiquitous leitmotifs of the emergence and concealment of interiority (and thus of the instability of the intersubjective self): the action of pretending to sleep. In Arkady's dream, he sits over a sleeping Vasia, symbolically enacting the structure of their relationship, with Arkady as a vigilant consciousness to Vasia's supine, malleable, unconscious body. The dream—an important moment in Dostoevsky's early conception of the collective personality—dramatizes Vasia's transformation:

> His dream was anxious and strange. It seemed that he [Arkady] was not sleeping and that Vasia, as before, was lying on the bed. But the strangest thing! It seems Vasia is pretending, that he is even deceiving Arkady and is now getting up ever so quietly, observing him out of the corner of his eye and stealing to the desk. A burning pain seizes Arkady's heart; it was vexing, sad and difficult to see that Vasia doesn't trust him, that he's hiding and concealing from him. He wanted to grab him, to cry out and carry him to the bed . . . Then Vasia screamed out in his arms, and Arkady was carrying a lifeless corpse to the bed. (2:43)

On the Dangers of Intimacy (The Vasia Shumkov Paradigm)

The events of the dream vividly portray Vasia's attempt to emancipate himself from Arkady's will, to overcome his role as the sleeping body, passive to Arkady's administrative mind. Still pretending to be subdued, Vasia has secretly awakened to his own agency, and Arkady attempts to reverse the process, to seize control of his friend and to force him into unconsciousness, even by destroying him—reducing him to a "lifeless corpse"—in the process. This image of pretend sleep, as a motif of the unstable intersubjective self, extends throughout Dostoevsky's writing—for example in *The Demons*, in Stepan Trofimovich's attempt to escape Varvara Petrovna's vigilant administration (10:502) or in Maria Timofeevna's flight from Stavrogin (10:219), and later, in Smerdiakov's feigned seizure in *The Brothers Karamazov*, during which he purports to realize Ivan's suppressed intentions.

SELF WITHOUT SOUL

The story's final passage—in which Arkady, lamenting his friend's demise, experiences a vision of the unearthly city of Petersburg, as though "a new city were taking shape in the air"—presents a fascinating description of the severed collective self. The episode has received a great deal more commentary than the rest of the story as an autobiographically derived epiphany that Dostoevsky extracted from the story thirteen years later (in 1861) and inserted into a journalistic feuilleton. Since Dostoevsky himself tore the passage from its original context, criticism has followed suit and has weighed it on its own merits. Readers have argued that Arkady's glimpse into "the fantastical, magical reverie" of the city "that will disappear in its turn and waft into steam to the dark blue sky" (2:47–48) is an early presentiment of Dostoevsky's program of "fantastic realism," of his separation from quotidian, earthly reality and his discovery of another, spiritual world.[18] In treating Arkady's experience as a form of mystical initiation into an otherworldly spiritual realm, readers overlook the implicit emphasis upon Arkady's *bereaved* status, since he encounters this ethereal vision of the city melting into the air when he has lost Vasia, that is, after an element of his own personality has collapsed and vanished. Arkady's flight into disembodied modes of perception occurs in the context of Vasia's demise. As Arkady approaches the Neva, we are told that although he had been "fatally in love" with Liza, he could no longer speak to her ("he didn't want to visit them, indeed he could not" [2:48]), as though he could only be bound to her through Vasia's mediation. Arkady no longer possesses the external physical conduit for his sensations and passions, and the story ends with a description of the experience of an incorporeal consciousness that can only behold the world as fantastical and unreal.

Perhaps as a result of reading the scene outside of its narrative context, critics consistently gloss over the strangest part of the passage—the peculiar

Chapter One

physiological reaction that Arkady suffers as he looks out over the Neva. We are told that he shudders and feels "the surge of some powerful and hitherto unknown sensation" as a "spring of blood" fills his "heart." Together with this physical sensation, he is visited by a sudden spontaneous insight into Vasia's experience:

> Some kind of strange thought visited the orphaned comrade of poor Vasia. He gave a start, and his heart was as if filled in this moment with a hot spring of blood, which suddenly boiled up from the surging of some powerful sensation, hitherto unknown to him. It was as if he only now [. . .] discovered why his poor Vasia, who had not been able to bear his happiness, had lost his mind. His lips quivered, his eyes blazed, he grew pale, and it was as if his eyes were opened to something new in this moment. (2:48)

The bizarre description suggests that, in the absence of Vasia as cathected object, as externalized bearer of Arkady's suppressed emotional life, Arkady painfully feels the upsurge of the atrophied faculties within himself that had formerly been replaced externally by his friend's activity. Vasia too, when he attempted to escape Arkady's protection, felt stricken and overwhelmed by the new burden of thought that the absence of Arkady awakened in him, a sensation he experienced physically: "he ran his hand over his forehead as if wanting to remove from himself some kind of heavy, oppressive weight that had lain on his entire being" (2:43). Arkady's vision on the Neva in this context can be seen as a depiction of the anguish of the disembodied personality, which has used the other as a substitution for its own interior life, and is now forced, quite suddenly, to encounter these dimensions within.

One is tempted to venture a Bakhtinian reading of Arkady's predicament on the Neva—his lonely disembodied existence in the wake of Vasia's demise—as a natural consequence of the dialogical nature of selfhood. In Bakhtinian terms, Arkady's bereft status as I-for-myself, his sensation of ghostly semi-existence or soullessness could be read as a result of the "dialogical need for the other." Since the fullness of being exists only within human relationships, Vasia, as a beloved other, acted as "bestower" of "soul" upon Arkady.[19] In Vasia's absence, the lonely consciousness is reduced to a "spurious and scattered subjectivity" that can have no soul on its own.[20] Such an argument, however, would dramatically contradict the tenets of Bakhtin's thought, since Bakhtin, who tended not to see the darker aspects of dialogue in Dostoevsky, saw dialogical interaction as taking place between "unmerged" and "sovereign" consciousnesses.[21] Arkady's sudden interior sensations (the surges of blood from an unknown source) that emerge in the absence of the other indicate that there is another level of complexity underlying Arkady's radical solitude—that his need to enact his personality intersubjectively is the result of pathologically suppressed or erased interior life. As we shall see, Dostoevsky's return to this paradigm almost two decades later in *Crime and Punishment* (1866) points to the collapse of the intersubjective self as a moment of central and sustained importance in his thought.

FEAR OF THE INTERIOR

For good reasons, Raskolnikov's lineage is most often traced to the radical idealists of Dostoevsky's earlier prose, the "dreamers" of his stories from the 1840s (Ordynov of "The Landlady," or the protagonist of "White Nights"), who long to "transform the world and bring it into conformity with [their] visionary longings" and the intellectual rebels, from Goliadkin to the underground man, who attempt to stage a "revolt against the established social-moral order."[22] Innumerable explications of Raskolnikov's internal divisions have refined for us his image as an exacerbated intellect, testing out the postulates of ideological theories while hindered by his inescapable status as a "trembling creature" subject to natural laws and impulses.[23] Raskolnikov's connection with Vasia Shumkov, however, opens up a markedly different aspect of his character: through this lens we see Raskolnikov as a weak, damaged, and incomplete personality who attempts hysterically to escape domination by external administrative minds while incapable of self-government. A brief examination of some of the resonances between *Crime and Punishment* and the early, little-studied story "A Weak Heart" helps us further grasp the tension between interiority and intersubjectivity that underlies both texts and defines the problem of selfhood in Dostoevsky.

The first, most apparent repetition from the earlier template lies in the description of Raskolnikov and Razumikhin's friendship. When in Raskolnikov's presence, Razumikhin reminds us distinctly of Arkady in his struggle to annex and take over his friend's functioning; his "powerful arms" (6:150), like Arkady's (2:33), grasp hold of Raskolnikov and forcefully direct him toward health, prudence, and recuperation.[24] Razumikhin's surname (formed from *razum*, "reason") takes on a much more literal meaning in this context since, like Arkady, he enacts the faculty of the executive mind externally for the incomplete self.[25] We see him "taking charge at once," deftly "grasping" Raskolnikov's "head with his left hand, regardless of the fact that [Raskolnikov] would have been able to get up himself," and bringing soup and tea to the latter's lips (6:95). He also immediately takes over Raskolnikov's finances and personal appearance, buying clothes for his helpless friend, "because," he explains, "we need to make a human being out of you," and even overcomes indignant opposition ("Leave me be! I don't want it!") in changing Raskolnikov's undergarments, while the latter, defeated and humiliated,

Chapter One

eventually complies (6:101–2). The struggle of wills concerning the problem of signature (the desire to annex the identity of the other) is repeated from the earlier story. When Raskolnikov refuses to sign for his mother's gift of money, Razumikhin, attests to his ability to "direct" the invalid ("we will direct him, that is simply guide his hand"), and, we are told, "was seriously getting ready to guide Raskolnikov's hand" before Raskolnikov, like Vasia, insists on signing himself (6:94).

In "A Weak Heart," Dostoevsky closely follows Arkady in his agony as he gradually loses all control over his counterpart; in the later novel, by contrast, the entire emphasis is not upon Razumikhin but upon the fugitive self, Raskolnikov, who is protecting an interior personal realm in which is concealed, among other, more deeply buried memories, a horrific crime. As Raskolnikov attempts to escape Razumikhin's vigilant surveillance, he, like Vasia, has no defined intention of his own—only a suppressed and now insurgent sense of agency that fuels disorganized, frenzied activity. In the absence of external surveillance, he is unable to stay in his room and sleep, unable to fulfill the very sensible command of his external superego, but "leaps up, half crazed, from bed" as soon as he is left alone, "with burning impatience" to do something: "But to what business? It was as if he had forgotten" (6:99). The descriptions of Raskolnikov released from Razumikhin's supervision emphasize simultaneously a desperate desire to exert agency and an utter incapacity for thought or self-administration: "He didn't know and didn't think about where to go; he knew one thing: 'that it was necessary to end all *this* today, in one go, at once [. . .]' How to end it? With what? About this he didn't have any idea, and he didn't want to think" (6:121). Raskolnikov's hysterical bustling about the city directly repeats Vasia's. When Arkady leaves, Vasia simply cannot stay at home, for all the good it would do him. Instead, he feels a frantic compulsion to go directly to the authorities, to confess his "crime," though he can give no rational explanation for his impulse. Arkady's desperate, agonized search for Vasia, who has run away from his incarceration in their room, is replayed here as well, as Razumikhin and Raskolnikov collide suddenly, like Arkady and Vasia, on the street ("Neither had caught sight of the other up to the last step, so that they almost collided heads" [6:129]), and Razumikhin scolds his disobedient friend ("I'm going to take you up under my arm, tie you up in a knot, and carry you home, then lock you in!" [6:129]), implying a real sense of ownership over him.

In *Crime and Punishment*, the pathology of the collective personality is still more pronounced than in "A Weak Heart." For all of Raskolnikov's attempts to evade Razumikhin, we see that he exhibits a desperate, compulsive need for the other as a result of his own incapacity for self-administration. From the beginning, despite himself, he is deeply, actively embroiled in the collective self that his friendship with Razumikhin enacts. Upon receiving

On the Dangers of Intimacy (The Vasia Shumkov Paradigm)

the devastating news of his sister's intended marriage, he seeks out Razumikhin compulsively, in a state of despair, as if hypnotized, crying out for his friend's surveillance, though unaware of it himself:

> "And where am I going?" he thought suddenly. "Strange. I had set off for a reason. As soon as I read the letter, I set off . . . [. . .] to Razumikhin I set off, that's where, now [. . .]. But why, after all. And how did the idea to go to Razumikhin fly into my head now? This is remarkable." [. . .] The question, why had he now set off to see Razumikhin bothered him more than it even seemed to him; [. . .] "Could I really have wanted to fix the whole business through Razumikhin alone and find the solution to everything in Razumikhin," he asked himself in surprise. (6:43–45)

The murder is committed in that moment, when Raskolnikov, panicked and distraught, overcomes his mysterious compulsion to visit Razumikhin, and attempts to assume responsibility himself for his family dilemma. The crime is committed outside of Razumikhin's purview, as an expression of Raskolnikov's own hysterical, secret attempt at self-direction. We discover later in the novel that Raskolnikov cannot survive for long without an external mind; when he finally shirks Razumikhin's supervision, he immediately binds himself to other kinds of administrative minds and agencies, most prominently to Svidrigailov and Sonya. In this sense, the novel comes to explore not only the suppressed interior life of the incomplete personality but also the ways in which this atrophied self succumbs to various external sources of intellection.

The image of pretend sleep as a symbol of concealed interiority (or of the collective self's instability) finds immense resonance in the novel. Vasia's pretend sleep in Arkady's dream, as examined above, dramatized an externalized relationship of malleable body to executive mind: the subdued self feigned docility while hiding a secret, interior life, planning its escape and bid for independence. Pretending to be a compliant limb of Razumikhin's administrative will, Raskolnikov, like Vasia, "conceals his power" from his friend with a "feral cunning" (6:95–96), "closing his eyes and pretending to be asleep" as he hears Razumikhin entering the room (6:210). As Raskolnikov falls under the administration of Svidrigailov, the nature of their relationship is quickly established (as if by shorthand) by use of this image (6:214, 219). Later, we discover that Svidrigailov (who incidentally has the same name and patronymic—Arkady Ivanovich—as Vasia Shumkov's friend and mentor) comes to suicidal despair after his dream in which he is confronted by the image—"horrific" to him—of a child, pretending to sleep, concealing depravity and mockery under closed eyelids: "her long dark eyelashes seem to shiver and wink, and from under them looks out a sly, sharp, unchildlike-winking little eye, as if the little girl is not sleeping and is pretending." When the child's eyes finally open, we infer from Svidrigailov's acute terror that he sees something from his own much-avoided unconscious life in the "boundlessly ugly and offensive [. . .] filth" that no longer conceals itself under the winking eyelids. In each of these instances, the unconscious interior life—that which is hidden behind closed eyelids—is a region of shame, ugliness, disgust, of unwanted, criminal memory. It is the shame and avoidance of what is hidden beneath the veneer of this pretend sleep that propels the personality beyond the threshold of the self into a world of frantic intersubjective activity. In each case these hateful interior phenomena are placed outside of the self, grafted onto another person, until that other person refuses to be subsumed, awakens covertly from an enforced sleep, and launches a rebellion against the colonizing other.

POINTS OF DEPARTURE

The intersecting personalities of Vasia and Arkady testify to the brokenness of dialogic interaction in early Dostoevsky and to the pathologies inherent in his conception of the open-ended, relational self. Whether we prefer a diagnosis of "morbid codependency" or "projective identification,"[26] or whether we suspect subliminal sexual anxieties or desires in Arkady and Vasia, it is clear that Dostoevsky is describing disturbed characters who suffer from some form of collapsed interiority, and that the deficiency of the interior dimension causes them to cling to each other with greater convulsive energy. Even Razumikhin, the most refreshingly level-headed of all of Dostoevsky's characters, nevertheless exhibits all the insatiable hunger for the other of a disturbed psyche. Though Pulkheria Alexandrovna and Dunya do not "want to notice these eccentric details," still he grasps onto their hands "as if in a vise," pressing them "to the point of pain," grasping them "even more firmly" if they attempt to "tear their hands from his enormous and bony hands" as they realize that it is "impossible to run away from him" (6:154). In the context of these ravenous, colonizing personalities, both the early story and the later novel approach the question of introspection—of stepping back from the threshold through the attempt to discover and acknowledge what is concealed within: whether in Vasia's passionate desire to confess his "crime" to Yulian Mastakovich, or in Raskolnikov's urgent impulse to confess his murder and to atone for it. Both crimes, though obviously very different in their degree of seriousness, can be understood as metaphors for the recognition of interior, personal space, especially since the crimes themselves, we suspect, point to the presence of earlier, more deeply buried memories in these characters whose personal biographies and "former past," rarely mentioned, are glimpsed, if at all, from afar, in the waters of the Neva, "in some depths, below, somewhere barely visible" (6:90).[27]

Vasia Shumkov's interior awakening sheds some light on the tension between interiority and intersubjectivity in Dostoevsky, since it suggests that if the self is simply the site of consciousness, a point of view, or an activity of addressivity directed toward the other, then the gulf between selves cannot be preserved: the self falls into and becomes annexed by the other. As Ivan's formulation goes in *The Brothers Karamazov*, "if there is no immortality of the soul, then all is permitted, even anthropophagy" (14:65). The example that occurs to Ivan—*anthropophagy*—is significant, and suggests mutual consumption as the direct consequence of the disappearance of an essential indwelling principle.[28] In early Dostoevsky, we are left with a depiction of the need to recover an interior space in the self as a psychological quandary. In the next chapter we approach the problem of reconstituting the personality by looking at the speculative map of the self that emerges from Dostoevsky's exploration of how the personality extends itself into others. The outwardly constituted personality expresses itself most often in early Dostoevsky not as a dualism (as we have examined it here), but as a triadic relationship. Our next step is to look more deeply into the conditions of amnesia and self-obliteration that unravel the personality into the passionate and intimate bonds of a larger, collective, intersubjective phenomenon.

Chapter Two

Amnesia and the Collective Personality in the Early Works

> Our memories do not go back beyond yesterday; [. . .] We resemble children who have not been taught to think for themselves, and who, having become adults, have nothing of their own; all their knowledge lies on the surface of their existence, their whole soul exists outside themselves.
> —Chaadaev, "First Philosophical Letter"

> How different it is with us moderns! With us too the image of the human species is projected in magnified form into separate individuals—but as fragments, [. . .] with the result that one has to go the rounds from one individual to another in order to be able to piece together a complete image of the species.
> —Schiller, "Letters on the Aesthetic Education of Man"

> He attached his memories and mind to every external object, and he liked doing this: he kept wanting to forget something, something present, urgent . . .
> —Dostoevsky, *The Idiot*

GUARDING THE THRESHOLD

When Bakhtin noted the absence of memory in Dostoevsky's characters, he was describing a new form of poetics: the bestowal of unprecedented freedom upon fictional characters, the refusal to barge into a protagonist's unconscious life or to constrain that character's discourse with the manacles of social typology or personal biography.[1] Standing always on the "threshold," in the "living present," Dostoevsky's characters, for Bakhtin, are remarkably free from the influences of "external forces," among which he included the unconscious mind, with its distant memories and deterministic drives.[2] Bakhtin's description of the amnesia and outwardness of Dostoevsky's characters holds true, however, in a very different, unintended sense in early Dostoevsky where the pervasive presence of amnesia emerges not as an aspect of a liberating poetics, but as an illness. Having experienced some intense but vaguely defined distress or terror in the narrative prehistory, Dostoevsky's early protagonists are intent upon forgetting, and they guard their interior space against any intrusions, even from their own inquiries, preferring instead to remain forever on the thresholds of their own personalities. The protagonist of "White Nights," for example, is utterly mortified when a visitor attempts to enter his private room. The young man describes how he "takes wing, [. . .] becomes embarrassed, [. . .] blushes" (2:117), how he "meets [his acquaintance] in such a disconcerted way [. . .] as if he had just committed a crime within his four walls" (2:112). Feelings of shame, self-disgust and an undefined sense of interior criminality propel these characters outward, to encounter others on the public square, away from the compromising inner rooms of dreams, desires, and memories.[3]

In this chapter I explore the phenomenon of amnesia in Dostoevsky's early works as directly connected to the compulsion to displace elements of one's personality into others and thus to become part of a collective self. I examine the phenomenon of interior personal emptiness in Dostoevsky's initial studies of the self by tracing a pattern through his works of the 1840s in which characters are bound to each other as interacting aspects of a larger personality. There is significant evidence in the works from this period—specifically, *The Double*, "The Landlady," and *Netochka Nezvanova*—to suggest that Dostoevsky was fascinated with the obliteration of personal memory as a result of early, suppressed childhood trauma. My intention in introducing the notion of trauma is not to diagnose Dostoevsky's characters according to contemporary manuals of psychiatry, but rather to illuminate the author's early preoccupation with the suppression of interiority and the consequent confusion that arises between self and other.[4] In connection with Dostoevsky's concept of the personality as enacted externally among complementary selves, the present chapter also provides an account of Dostoevsky's creative transformation of the doppelgänger tradition. At the end of the chapter I shall explore how the depictions of amnesia and doubling in the early works help to illuminate the treatment of memory and the collective self in *Crime and Punishment*.

Chapter Two

TWO KINDS OF DOUBLING: PSYCHIC AND COGNITIVE EMANATIONS

We can begin our discussion of Dostoevsky's method of externalizing personality by outlining two general tendencies in the scholarly reception of his treatment of the double. From one perspective, Dostoevsky's doubles (in their many varieties, from the two Goliadkins to Ivan and his Devil) have been interpreted as a development of the romantic paradigm of the doppelgänger, which has been described as "a projection of the unconscious [. . .] self as a physical [being], apparent to the senses."[5] In this regard, Dostoevsky's doubles can be said to represent explorations of *unconscious* elements in the personality. Within the framework of this narrative, critics have provided accounts of how Dostoevsky inherited Neoplatonic and romantic models of inward dualism (Franz Mesmer's "night-side of the mind," Carl Gustav Carus's "night of the unconscious," among many other reverberations and echoes) and, in his own creative formulation of the dynamism of the unconscious, prefigured key aspects of twentieth-century psychoanalytic theory.[6] Dostoevsky's exploration of doubles and the unconscious mind continues to resonate in contemporary psychology, especially in the field of object-relations, in which accounts of the schizoid mechanism of "projective identification" illuminate how a repressed unconscious inner self can become projected onto an object or person in the outside world.[7]

This reading of Dostoevsky as a neo-romantic psychologist who stands roughly between Hoffmann and Freud has, with the rise of Bakhtin, lost considerable ground to yet another Dostoevsky, namely, the dramatizer of *self-consciousness*. For Bakhtin, Goliadkin Junior is not a dark, irrational, unconscious element of Goliadkin's personality, as Hoffmann might have conceived of such a character, but quite the opposite: he is a much-observed external self that Goliadkin is desperate to shirk in his desire to exist in a free and disembodied state.[8] For Bakhtin, Dostoevsky's conception of personality focuses not on the sleeping mind, but on the mind that is remarkably, radically, awake to its potential manifestations. In other words, if the romantic doppelgänger evokes a dualistic relationship between the conscious mind and the unconscious soul, the Kantian-Bakhtinian conception represents a cognitive divide between the conscious mind aware of its unlimited potential and the self as an embodied, perceived thing.

Each of these conceptions of doubling—the psychic and the cognitive—has its limits as an all-encompassing model of Dostoevsky's theory of the externalized personality. When considered together, their resonance is fuller and more complex. As we approach Dostoevsky's early narratives, we can observe the emergence of two kinds of doubles, or emanations, with relation to one protagonist, prompted in turn by two conflicting impulses of the psyche toward self-annihilation. On the one hand, Dostoevsky's early characters desire to erase their internal dimensions, to stifle their memories, and to avoid introspection. On the other hand, there is a strong impulse to erase the outward self, to distance oneself from and rid oneself of the embodied creature that occupies space in the perceptions of others. Each of these impulses leads to the formation of relationships that, together, reveal the outlines of a broader, more multifaceted conception of personality in a state of acute imbalance.

GOLIADKIN'S OTHER EMANATION AND MR. SMITH'S HOWLING SOUL

In the case of *The Double*, Bakhtin's conception of the cognitively divided self powerfully illuminates Goliadkin Senior's relationship with his "twin." As Bakhtin's reading suggests, Goliadkin panics under the gaze of others as he perceives himself through their eyes, and he defends himself by obliterating the world that limits him, by directing his "all-destroying gaze" against anyone who challenges his sovereignty (1:125).[9] For Goliadkin, the distance between the self as a free limitless consciousness and the embodied self mercilessly scrutinized by others generates an excruciating dissonance, which expands in the novel into the actual separation between two individuals. "Goliadkin's intrigue with his double," Bakhtin argues, "unfolds as the dramatized crisis of self-consciousness," and consequently the entire novel is caught within the bounds of Goliadkin's self-consciousness, between his "'I for myself'" and his "fictitious 'I for the other.'"[10] "In the narration," Bakhtin insists, "we do not find a single element that exceeds the bounds of Goliadkin's self-consciousness, not a single word or a single tone that could not have been part of his interior dialogue with himself."[11]

Bakhtin's persuasive reading of *The Double*, however, overlooks some singular occurrences in the narrative, for there appears to be at least one element of personality that exceeds the bounds of Goliadkin's self-consciousness, one that subtly evokes an unconscious depth of character in Goliadkin and resonates with the psychic, rather than the cognitive, tradition of doubling. As Goliadkin chases his double through the streets of St. Petersburg, another emanation, or projective identity, follows the unfortunate character and "links" itself to him:

> Some kind of forsaken little dog, all wet and shivering, linked itself to Mr. Goliadkin and also ran around his side, hurriedly, [. . .] looking at him shyly and intelligently from time to time. Some kind of far-off, long ago forgotten idea—a remembrance of some long ago occurring circumstance—came into

Chapter Two

his head now, knocked as if with a little hammer in his head, bothered him, would not unlink itself from him. "Ah, this nasty little dog," whispered Mr. Goliadkin, not understanding himself. Finally, he saw his stranger at the corner of Ital'ianskaia Street. (1:142)

While Goliadkin chases his hated external manifestation through the streets of Petersburg, this second projective emanation stirs some hidden memory and, as a result, a "remembrance of some long ago occurring circumstance" begins to resurface. Here we encounter the novel's only reference to personal memory that does not touch immediately upon Goliadkin's situation, and it is externalized as a "forsaken," "shivering," "intelligent" creature, which appears for a moment and then is easily outrun.

Yet, for all the brevity of its appearance in *The Double*, this psychic echo that attaches itself to the divided self—the dog at the heels who carries a memory from the unconscious realm—is to reappear persistently in Dostoevsky's early works. To jump ahead in time for a moment, Goliadkin's dog, as the carrier of suppressed memory, appears prominently in Dostoevsky's post-Siberia writing. In *The Insulted and the Injured* (1861), the old Mr. Smith, who has attempted to annihilate his feelings for his daughter, to the point of morbid psychological disturbance, is inseparable from his dog, Azorka: "From where did he get this hideous dog," asks the narrator, "which is always at his side, as if together they constitute something whole, indivisible, and which looks so much like him?" (3:170–71). The narrator emphasizes "something fantastical, enchanted" in this relationship, and recognizes a parallel with classical German literature, in Faust's entanglement with Mephisto (who first appears to Faust as a poodle):[12] "from the first time I saw [the dog], it immediately came into my head that this dog could not be like all dogs; that it is an extraordinary dog; [. . .] that perhaps this is some kind of Mephistopheles in a dog's form and that her destiny is united with the destiny of her master in some mysterious unknown paths" (3:171). Dostoevsky fleshes out Smith's relationship to Azorka as a carrier of suppressed memory to a point that risks losing all subtlety, especially in the scene where Nellie recalls the encounter between Smith, Azorka, and Smith's beloved and shunned daughter:

Mama cried out "Azorka! Azorka!" and suddenly a big dog [. . .] ran up to Mama, howled and threw herself at her [. . .]. [Grandfather] grew completely pale, and when he saw how Mama was lying before him and embracing his feet, he broke away, pushed Mama, hit his stick against the stone street and quickly walked away from us. Azorka stayed behind, howling and licking Mama, then ran to Grandfather, grabbed him by the edge of his coat and pulled him back, but Grandfather hit him with the stick. Azorka wanted to run to us again, but Grandfather called to her and she ran after Grandfather and kept howling. (3:411)

The relationship between Smith and Azorka can hardly be considered to illustrate the doubling of self-consciousness that we observe in the two Goliadkins. Rather, it dramatizes the individual's relationship with his suppressed unconscious life, which is externalized into a living creature, as a result of the erasure of memory.

On the whole, however, the two traditions of doubling, psychic and cognitive (as in the case of Goliadkin), tend to appear simultaneously in Dostoevsky's early works; rarely does a character have only one kind of double. Consequently, the notion of personal division entailed by the concept of "doubles" becomes further complicated by the multiple roles that the externalized personality assumes and embodies. As we follow this pattern in more detail through some of the early works, we can observe Dostoevsky's movement from the depiction of the individual with two projected manifestations toward a coherent triadic conception of a collective self.

"THE LANDLADY": ENTERING INTO THE COLLECTIVE SELF

Dostoevsky's "The Landlady" (1847) offers an intricate depiction of the process through which one intermediary personality finds itself overpoweringly drawn to two different kinds of projective interlocutors. The story, an experimental work which remains, to this day, a critical failure,[13] begins with its protagonist, Ordynov, a young Petersburg intellectual, searching for new living quarters. After some tormented wandering through the city, he finds himself in a church where he sees a beautiful young woman praying tearfully before the icon. The woman is accompanied by an old man who watches over her possessively. Overwhelmingly and mysteriously drawn to this couple, Ordynov follows them, and eventually takes up residence in their apartment. He falls ill, and Katerina, the young landlady, cares for him, caresses him, and tells him about her past, in a semi-coherent story through which we discover that the old man, her husband, Murin, was also her mother's lover— thus potentially her father as well—and that Katerina has committed some terrible, unspeakable crime in the past, which is perhaps connected to the death of her family and the burning down of her childhood home. Living in the room adjacent to theirs, Ordynov observes Murin's cruel tyranny over Katerina, and he attempts, futilely, to liberate her, before Murin finally succeeds in ejecting him from the apartment.

On the surface, "The Landlady" is an investigation into the solipsistic idealism of the romantic dreamer, the perils of *mechtatel'nost'* (dreamerness), which preoccupied Dostoevsky in the late 1840s.[14] A Victor Frankenstein figure, devoted exclusively to disembodied intellectual concerns, the protagonist, Ordynov, is forced to encounter his neglected emotional and bodily faculties externally, not in the form of a vengeful monster, but as a weeping woman, a "landlady," enslaved by a calculating tyrant. Because of the evident analogy between Ordynov's divided inner state and the two characters who begin to dominate his life, critics have often read the events of the story as allegorical enactments of the dynamism of a single psyche.[15] In observing the interactions of his landlords, Murin and Katerina, Ordynov is horrified by the power that a calculating intellect wields over a "weak heart," a relationship that reflects and externalizes Ordynov's own inner predicament as a modern fragmented intellectual: "The old man grasped her with his mighty arms and almost crushed her on his chest. But when she hid her head on his heart, every feature on the old man's face laughed with such naked shameless laughter that Ordynov's whole being was seized with horror. Deceit, calculation, cold jealous tyranny and terror over a poor torn heart—this is what he understood in this shameless, already unconcealed, laughter" (1:311). Repeatedly, his hosts appear to Ordynov in the form of disjointed agencies of a single personality, with Katerina pressed uncomprehendingly against the chest of the shamelessly ironic master, together enacting the intellect's "sly" "tyranny" over the "soul" (1:319). In this context, Ordynov's attempts to liberate Katerina from Murin possess potential allegorical significance as the ego's impulse to liberate his own soul, or anima ("the image of a weeping woman" that "overwhelms his imagination" [1:269]) from the cold tyranny of Reason.[16] Thus, the psychodrama that Dostoevsky captures can be described as derivatively romantic, and in this sense is largely indebted, as critics have pointed out, to the works of such earlier precursors as Hoffmann and Gogol.[17]

Numerous details in "The Landlady," however, suggest that Dostoevsky was not so much imposing a romantic allegory of mind and soul upon his characters, as examining instead how a traumatized personality can, in a very real sense, become drawn into a larger collective personality. Indeed, the more unusual and innovative aspect of the story lies in Dostoevsky's examination of the convulsive relationships that form among three central characters—the circumstances in which an individual at odds with his interior life finds himself spasmodically attached to two other people: the first of whom seems to reflect elements of the hero's suppressed unconscious life, and the second, a form of extension of his own self-consciousness.

The clearest indication that Ordynov is not simply the traditional romantic dreamer suggested by the narrator and genre is that Ordynov, in fact, has no palpable inner life. Rather, he is introduced as an amnesiac who is unable to make any sense of his thoughts and impressions, and who behaves throughout as if shattered by some vaguely defined interior force. Emphasis is placed continually on the unbearable pain associated with Ordynov's efforts at reflection, and upon his desperate unwillingness to remember:

> He couldn't reason and was even afraid to [. . .] Walking at random, not seeing the road, he tried with all his might, as much as he could to concentrate his spirit, to direct his fractured thought and at least to reason a little bit about his situation. But the exertion only brought him to suffering, to torment [. . .] "No, death would be better," he thought, "better death," he whispered. (1:273–74)

When Katerina asks Ordynov about his past, his answer manifests both avoidance and suppression: "There is no one; I am alone . . . it doesn't matter, let it be! Now it's better . . . It's good now!" (1:276). Upon wandering into the church and prostrating himself on the ground, sobbing and feeling "crushed," he does not pray, but only falls into a state of "oblivion" (1:267, 270). It is in this moment, as he collapses "into oblivion" from "an attack of profound anxious anguish and some kind of trampled feeling," that he attaches himself to his future landlords as a way of avoiding his interior agony. "He came to," we are told, "when the measured, muffled sound of two arriving parishioners sounded under the domes of the temple," and, seized by an "inexpressible curiosity," he obeys the "mysteriously sweet and persistent feeling" that commands him to follow them, though "his fascination seemed strange even to himself" (1: 267–68).

In the context of the protagonist's refusal to reflect or to remember, the only glimpse we are offered into his psyche comes in the form of a dream, in which Ordynov is being tormented as a child:

> But here [among idyllic images of childhood] began to appear one being, which disturbed him with some kind of unchildlike terror [. . .]. While Ordynov was asleep, the evil old man sat down at the head of his bed . . . He chased away swarms of light spirits [. . .] and began, for whole nights on end, to whisper a long, marvelous fairy tale to him, which was unintelligible to the child's heart, but which tore at him, upset him with terror and unchildlike fear. (1:278–79)

Though it is possible to read the "old man" in the dream in terms of romantic allegory as the force of Reason which robs the Imagination of its capacity to perceive the "swarms of light spirits," Orydnov's convulsive terror and amnesia in his waking state prompts us to read the dream more literally, as the fragment of a recollection in which an actual child is being tormented. The descriptions of the child's agony in the dream are terrifying and vivid. The "spiteful" or "evil" old man "follows him everywhere." When, at his bedside, Ordynov begs the man to stop his terrible whispering, the old man "does not heed his sobbing and entreaties" and continues until Ordynov falls into "stupor, into oblivion" (1:278–79).

These vague memories suggest that Ordynov is not simply a romantic dreamer, ruined by excessive attention to ideal things and intellectual pursuits, but a wounded individual who has barred himself from any relationship with his unconscious life. Ordynov latches onto Katerina as an external substitution for these erased internal dimensions, as she is constantly associated in his eyes with the life of "the soul": "as if in answer to his despair, in answer to his trembling heart, the familiar, thick, silver voice of Katerina sounded like that internal music known to a person's soul" (1:302). As an auxiliary unconscious, Katerina becomes not only the "voice of the soul" but the bearer of his memory. When she begins to tell him of her memories, the tormenting and almost incoherent recollections of a shameful crime for which she can never atone, Ordynov comes to recognize the barely coherent events she describes, her own imprisonment and torment at the hands of an "old man," as his own memories:

> Her story was incoherent, the soul's storm could be heard in her words, but Ordynov understood everything, since her life had become his life, her sorrow his sorrow and since he could already see his enemy standing before him, taking form and growing before him in every word [. . .]. The evil old man of his dream (Ordynov believed it) was in reality before him. (1:294)

As part of their seemingly uncanny connection, Ordynov and Katerina appear, strangely enough, to possess the same memories of a tormented childhood. Or rather, in what will become a constant refrain throughout Dostoevsky's writing, the protagonist appropriates his interlocutor's memories as a form of replacement for his own erased interior life.

As Ordynov takes on Katerina's memories as his own, the two characters simultaneously enact a mysterious and bizarre form of intimacy of which we saw elements in "A Weak Heart" and which will become prominent in Dostoevsky's later novels. The intensity of their sudden intimacy is unlikely, even impossible. When Ordynov first visits the house, he can hear Katerina's heart beating from two steps away (1:272). In the vivid descriptions of their interactions, Dostoevsky uses an image that will become a recurrent signifier in his works of the extended self, namely, the shedding of tears upon each other's skin: "[she] placed her cheek to his cheek; her warm, humid breath fluttered along his face . . . Suddenly Ordynov felt that her hot tears poured from her eyes in a torrent and fell, like molten lead, on his cheeks" (1:277).

A similar image is used much later in *The Idiot*, in the mysterious communion between Myshkin and Rogozhin at the end of the novel: "tears flowed from his eyes onto Rogozhin's cheeks, but perhaps he already didn't feel his own tears" (8:507). In "The Landlady," the sensation of warm foreign tears as an image of self-reconciliation is enhanced when, as Ordynov sleeps, the tears that fall onto his cheeks are from an ambiguous source, perhaps even from his own eyes: "someone's scalding tears burned his inflamed cheeks" (1:278).[18] Yet another peculiarity of the intimacy between these characters lies in Dostoevsky's constant use of the term *vzdragivat'/vzdrognut'* ("to shudder" or "to give a start") in the interactions among the three characters, suggesting a pathological undercurrent to these ties of extension.[19] Ordynov "starts" (1:301, 308) when his eyes meet Murin's, and Murin, in turn, "starts" (1:305) at Ordynov's rebellious gaze. The convulsive shuddering extends to Katerina; Ordynov "starts" when he first sees her in the church (1:269), and Katerina "starts" when Ordynov rushes into her room to save her, as she does when she tells Ordynov of Murin's entry into her life, and when she meets Ordynov's gaze (1:281, 297, 299). One senses that this shuddering, which will later become perhaps the most strangely and widely used verb of Dostoevsky's novels, emerges from the convulsive ties of extension that exist among these characters and from the recognition of something inwardly suppressed that they evoke in each other.

If Ordynov relates to Katerina as to a projective substitution for his own unconscious life, he is simultaneously drawn to another extension of himself, Murin, who stares at him "fixedly" throughout (1:272). "Not taking his eyes from Ordynov," Murin enacts the process of self-consciousness externally for him, thus taking on the form of an external mind. While Ordynov struggles toward intimacy with his psychic double, he constantly senses Murin's gaze upon him, a gaze that debilitates the young man's overtures toward Katerina and exerts an uncanny administrative power over him. Ordynov moves to embrace her, but "the cursory, momentary gaze of the old man again bound him to his place. Some kind of strange mixture of disdain, contempt, impatient, irritated concern and [. . .] spiteful, sly curiosity gleamed in his cursory, momentary gaze, from which every time Ordynov gave a start and which every time filled his heart with bile, irritation and impotent malice" (1:307–8). When Ordynov follows them from the church, seized by a desire to apprehend Katerina, "the old man turned and glanced at Ordynov with impatience. The young man stopped as if rooted to the spot" (1:268).

Murin and Katerina are not simply allegories for conflicting agencies in Ordynov's mind. Dostoevsky gives them lives and histories that have nothing to do with Ordynov. We discover, for example, at the end of the story, that they are somehow implicated in a band of smugglers. In this image of the tyrant who "slyly" clips the "wings" of the subdued "soul" so that she

Chapter Two

cannot escape "into real life," we can observe a more disturbing depiction in the landlord and landlady of Arkady and Vasia as one extended personality, with a vigilant consciousness holding the "weak heart" in forced subjugation. As fragmented pieces of a collective personality themselves, Murin and Katerina are drawn in as convulsive extensions of Ordynov's collapsed personality.[20] Dostoevsky returns directly to this paradigm—of the collapse of interiority leading to the compulsive need to extend oneself into others—as we shall see, in his next major work, *Netochka Nezvanova*.

NETOCHKA NEZVANOVA: THE CREATURE, THE BEAUTY, AND THE AMNESIAC

In *Netochka Nezvanova* (first published in 1849, but never completed), Dostoevsky continues to refine these mechanisms of doubling and provides a more focused investigation of the tripartite relationship that he had explored with little aesthetic success in "The Landlady." The novel, which was never completed before Dostoevsky was arrested and sent to Siberia, follows the life of a young girl, nicknamed "Netochka" (derived from Annetochka [little Annete] and meaning roughly "little nothing"), through her mother's death, her subsequent abandonment by her megalomaniacal stepfather who dies in a state of madness, her adoption by an altruistic prince, her intense friendship with his daughter, Katia, and finally, her forced separation from Katia after which she is sent to live with Katia's half-sister.

The plan for the novel, according to the stated intentions of its narrator, was to include three protagonists of approximately the same age: Netochka, Laria (a boy she meets unexpectedly in the prince's house), and Katia. The sections that Dostoevsky completed before his arrest establish the pathologically intimate relationships that bind the three figures. Netochka, the central figure, transforms the other two children into extensions of her personality, which, on its own, is marked by a sense of absence, as her nickname suggests.[21] When she encounters these two interlocutors, Netochka is in the midst of an intense effort to suppress her terrifying thoughts and memories in the wake of her parents' death. In our discussion here of the unfinished novel, we shall focus entirely upon these relationships formed during this moment of crisis in the life of the heroine.

While the mechanism of amnesia appears more subtly in "the Landlady," in *Netochka Nezvanova* it takes center stage. Netochka's inability to remember is essential to the narrative and is described at length:

> But such a strange thing happened! It was as if I'd forgotten the ending of what had happened to me with my parents, and the whole terrible story.

[. . .] It was true, I remembered everything—the night, the violin, and my papa, I remembered how I got the money for him; but I somehow wasn't able to make sense of or clarify all these events to myself . . . *It only became heavier on my heart, and when I came up in my remembrance to that moment when I was praying next to my dead mother, then frost would suddenly run across my limbs; I would shiver, cry out lightly, and then it would become so difficult to breathe that my whole breast would ache and my heart would thump so powerfully that I would run out of the corner in fright.* (2:191; emphasis added)[22]

Ordynov's memories were warped and unrecoverable; an old man tormenting a child with fairy tales suggests a screen image of fictitious accounts, overshadowing and concealing real events. In Netochka's case, we encounter the suppressed events directly, as they are narrated to us earlier in the novel. Feelings of terror surround two adjacent images in Netochka's mind: the corpse of her recently deceased mother and the icon of the Mother of God:

[My stepfather] led me to the corner where the icon was and told me to kneel. "Pray, my child, pray! You'll feel better! [. . .]" he whispered to me, pointing to the icon [. . .]. I threw myself on my knees, clasped my hands, and full of horror [. . .] fell on the floor and lay there for some minutes as if lifeless. I strained all my thoughts and all my feelings to pray, but fear overwhelmed me. [. . .] "Papa," I said, in a flood of tears, "[. . .] Where is Mama?" [. . .] Finally he took me by the hand, led me to the bed [. . .] and opened the blanket. My God! She was lying dead, having already grown cold and blue. As if unconscious, I threw myself on her and embraced her corpse. Father placed me on my knees. "Bow to her, child!" he said, "say farewell to her . . ." I bowed. (2:185–86)

In the description of Netochka's traumatic experience, Dostoevsky conflates the images of the dead mother and the icon, so that the image of the icon evokes terror by association. Attempts to recover these images lead Netochka either into serious illness or into relationships of passionate extension. Later, her guardian asks her to pray before the icon, thereby drawing her into a fit of near-fatal anxiety: "The Prince hurriedly placed me on my knees before the icon of the mother of God and he knelt down beside me. But I could not pray; I was stricken, even frightened; I recalled the words of my father on that final night, at the body of my mother, and I was overcome by a nervous fit" (2:194).

Two relationships pull her away from these terrifying memories. The first interlocutor Netochka encounters is a boy, Laria, so deeply traumatized by his own memories that he has been reduced to a semi-coherent, hysterical, constantly weeping and trembling "creature": "a creature who was hiding from me, terrified and who almost cried out when I approached him. It was a boy, about eleven years-old, pale, skinny, red-headed, who was squatting and whose whole body was trembling" (2:440).[23] Netochka recognizes "instinctively" that there is an implicit connection between them as she questions him about his past: "Who was he and where had he been before? But at my question his face changed . . . I remember that my heart contracted as I looked at him, perhaps because I instinctively felt that his grief was akin to my grief, which I felt at times painfully in my soul, but which I still hadn't fully comprehended: some kind of fear would descend upon me whenever I would begin to think of myself" (2:441). Here we can observe an almost exact parallel to Ordynov's intense identification with Katerina, and to his recognition of her memories as his own. Netochka comments explicitly on the inexplicable connection between her own inner confusion and Laria's visible agony.[24] Unable to look inward, she can only approach her memories by externalizing them, that is, by encountering them in Laria:

> And it was Laria who was chosen to explain to me all my grief with his story! [. . .] listening to his story, I made sense of almost all my past. I myself was in some kind of frenzy from grief, from terror, from everything that had so suddenly risen from my heart, but that had long been accumulating in him. [. . .] When Laria finished his story, I was weeping violently, I embraced him and already didn't try to comfort or dissuade him. I myself was under the influence of that very same impression that was destroying the poor child, and some kind of enthusiasm of sympathy for him enveloped my entire soul. (2:445)

As was also the case with Ordynov and Katerina, the impression is mutual; Laria recognizes himself in Netochka too as she tells him about her parents, and he clings to her passionately, becoming actively subsumed into, and conquered by, her personality: "He pressed himself to me and began ardently to kiss my cheek, shoulders, dress. He was in a state of intense anxiety. An indescribably pleasant feeling overtook me. I understood that I had finally overcome his fear, his distrust, and had obtained his love. [. . .] I became calm while he was kissing me, and a sweet confusion enveloped my heart" (2:442). As in the earlier story, the act of remembering takes on a mysteriously communal form and binds the two figures together into a compound personality. Connected by their remarkably similar pasts, the characters entwine themselves together as fragmented faculties of a larger, extended self.

This mutual recognition, however, does not take the place of actual recollection. As with Ordynov and Katerina, the convulsive relationship leads to an intense deterioration in both individuals. The collective personality, we discover, is highly unstable: "We didn't part for the whole week, we only existed for each other; but the more tightly connected we became, the more wild and unsociable we became to everything around us. As for me, I had already completely assimilated his manner of thinking and was thus perishing just as he was" (2:446). We are told that Laria had "developed abnormally, developed in a sensory manner [*chuvstvenno*], as a heart, while his mind was more and more obscured in dreams" (2:445). Netochka, as the administrative mind, tries to take control of this emotional creature, while finding herself pulled into its sphere of unintelligibility. Laria's sudden disappearance from the house thus evokes a crisis in Netochka, when, in the absence of her projective addressee, she begins to search for her dead mother in external space, and ultimately finds herself in front of the icon of the mother of God, an experience that, as mentioned above, sends her into a dangerous illness.

As the primary trauma is restaged, a second relationship of extension is immediately formed. She awakens to see a young girl "just like me" ("*takaia zhe devochka, kak i ia*" [2:189]), "the same age as me," and "my first movement was to stretch my hand towards her" (2:197). Netochka's identification with this new counterpart is again immediate and encompasses the whole of her inner life: "From my first glance upon her *my entire soul* was filled with some kind of happiness [. . .]. My first idea was to never again be separated from Katia. Something uncontrollable pulled me to her" (2:197–99). If the first emanation appeared as a trembling creature, whose memories were somehow the same as Netochka's, this second interlocutor is aloof, unknowable, even sublime: "Imagine an ideally beautiful little face, an astonishing, blazing beauty, before whom you would suddenly stop as if pierced, in sweet confusion, shuddering from rapture" (2:197). In Katia, Netochka encounters a remote, detached, ideal self that watches her, and to which she aspires, whose ideal beauty "awakens" Netochka's "aesthetic feeling" (2:207).

Like Ordynov's relationship with Murin, Netochka's convulsive attachment to Katia dramatizes the awakening of self-consciousness. To Netochka, Katia assumes the status of a transcendent, imperious, perfect being, who observes Netochka with ironic detachment, as she "trembles with all [her] members" under this scrutiny (2:203) and strives to look at herself constantly through Katia's eyes. Dostoevsky persistently calls attention to Katia's fixed gaze upon the heroine: "The Princess would usually sit down across from me [. . .] and would begin to look me over with her black eyes [. . .] she constantly looked me over from head to foot with the most naïve amazement"; "she looked me over for a very long time [. . .] as if solving a new problem that had suddenly arisen in her mind"; "she glowered at me [. . .] and for half an hour didn't take her gaze from me"; "more and more often, she would sit across from me in order to scrutinize me more comfortably" (2:198, 199, 202, 206). Under Katia's gaze, Netochka becomes intensely aware of herself as an awkward and imperfect creature: "I wanted with all my strength for

Chapter Two

her to like me and thus I was afraid of my every word, of my every action" (2:197); "my failures [to make Katia like me] hurt me to the point of pain, and I was ready to cry from Katia's every strict word, from her every distrustful look" (2:199). From her powerful vantage point of pure perception, Katia observes the sluggish and infuriating creature across from her, is annoyed at Netochka's awkwardness and inability to recover from her illness, and is irritated by the unflattering mirror that follows her around. When their governess compares them to each other, Katia uses Goliadkin's solipsistic mechanism of the "all-destroying gaze" to obliterate her embodied counterpart, looking "at me as if she wanted to burn me with her gaze" (2:202). In response to Katia's imperious observational distance and her "disgust" (2:200), Netochka's obsession with Katia becomes the sole substance of her inner life. The rapturous identification fills her mind entirely, erasing all other potential thoughts and gradually "dislodging" the "memories of [her] sad past":

> At first Katia's indifference tormented me to the point of offense; but now everything in me grew dim, and I had no awareness of my sensations. Thus, new impressions little by little dislodged the old ones, and the memories of my sad past lost their painful force and were replaced in me by a new life. (2:210)

In this way, memory becomes displaced through the intensity of intersubjective identification. Hidden grief or terror becomes externalized, and, when Netochka steals Katia's ribbon and kisses it, "the whole night through, drenched in tears" (2:210), she has found an external object on which to focus all her anguish, longing, spiritual devotion, all the aspects of her collapsed interior life: "I didn't take my eyes off of her, and when she would go away, I would continue to look, as if enchanted, at where she had stood. She began to appear in my dreams. And when I was awake, when she wasn't there, I composed whole conversations with her" (2:197).

Katia is not a mere aspect of Netochka's personality. On her own, as a character, she exhibits a wide range of emotional and psychological complexity. The intensity of Netochka's attachment, however, gradually destabilizes Katia, drawing both girls into the sphere of pathology so that they become reduced to aspects of a collective personality: "Little by little I observed— since I already hadn't taken my eyes from her all month—that Katia was daily becoming more lost in thought, her character was beginning to lose its evenness" (2:210).[25] The erotic intimacy of their relationship expresses itself in a gradually intensifying mirroring, or an extension of faculties into the other person, a desire for mutual substitution. Their first loving exchange involves Katia's tying Netochka's shoes for her, then tying her kerchief (2:211). The climactic act of substitution between them occurs when Netochka takes the blame for Katia's mischief and is punished in her stead (2:215). In their intense physical embraces, their interactions continue to express a wish for mutual substitution. They fantasize about being each other's slaves: "Katia thought up that we will live in this way: she would order me around for one day, [. . .] and the next day would be the opposite—I would give orders, and she would obey unquestioningly; and then we would both equally give each other orders" (2:221). Again, the description of their intimacy is accompanied by the image of the tears on each other's faces ("Several drops from her tears fell on my cheeks" [2:219]), and Netochka can hear "every thump" of Katia's heart (2:217). As in the case of Netochka and Laria, their shared personality is quickly collapsing; the governess notices "that we were both in some kind of frenzy, already three days we didn't separate from each other, constantly kissing, crying, guffawing like crazy people—like crazy people chattering endlessly" (2:221). In both cases, the personality that has been extended into two people is extremely unstable.

The relationship between Katia and Netochka provides us with insight into the missing personal histories of Vasia and Arkady. When Netochka, asked by Katia what she is thinking of, replies, "I think about you" (2:198), we are reminded of Vasia whose interior life is also utterly saturated with the image of the other: "I always," he tells Arkady, "think about you when I'm falling asleep" (2:39). Indeed, like Arkady, dramatizing the distance from her own unconscious life, Netochka sits above Katia at night, watching her friend sleep (as Arkady did with Vasia in his dream), discovering only later that, like Vasia, Katia was in fact only pretending to sleep (2:220). In these images of pretend sleep, the shedding of tears upon the other, and the convulsive shuddering or "starting" of the two friends (2:206, 212), we can trace the emergence of a core imagistic vocabulary surrounding the phenomenon of the shared self in Dostoevsky's early writing.

These initial sections of the unfinished *Netochka Nezvanova* indicate that, already in the 1840s, Dostoevsky was writing a novel about a collective personality. With Netochka as an intermediary between her sublimely beautiful friend, Katia, and her terrified, trembling double, Laria, we can observe a vague precursor of those later novelistic arrangements in which, for example, Myshkin, Nastasia Filippovna, and Rogozhin, while separate individuals, are simultaneously aspects of one extended self.

AMNESIA AND THE CRIES OF RASKOLNIKOV'S LANDLADY

The notion that Raskolnikov's psyche is reflected and externalized among the dramatis personae of *Crime and Punishment* is, to say the least, a commonplace in criticism. Scholarship has shown repeatedly and in great detail how Raskolnikov's personality constitutes the entire landscape of the novel. As with "The Landlady," the protagonist's extension into others in *Crime and Punishment* is generally read as a form of allegory, a facet of Dostoevsky's dynamic moral or metaphysical symbolism (i.e., Raskolnikov struggles between "good" and "evil" impulses within himself, as dramatized through his relationship with Sonia and Svidrigailov; or Raskolnikov, in committing murder, destroys both sides of his personality, the proud and meek, as reflected in the victims, Alyona Ivanovna and her sister, Lizaveta).[26] By approaching the novel through the lens of our discussion of the earlier works, we can see how the wounded, extended personalities in the early writings help to shed light on how Dostoevsky turns the novel into a map of the self while remaining within the realm of psychological realism.

Perhaps because of the rich philosophical, political, and allegorical meanings with which Raskolnikov's crime is textured, readers have largely overlooked what is perhaps one of its most obvious motivations: that it is the behavior of a traumatized individual who is compulsively reenacting some form of suppressed or unintegrated memory. The depiction of Raskolnikov's amnesia is very much in keeping with that of Ordynov and Netochka. From the outset, he is engaged in an active attempt to forget: "it was difficult in general for him in that minute to think about anything. He wanted to fall into utter oblivion, to forget everything, then to awaken and to start altogether from the beginning" (6:43). To this portrait of a semi-deliberate amnesia, we add Dostoevsky's evident awareness, in depicting Raskolnikov, of the repetition compulsion, which has, more recently, come to be seen as a defining characteristic of post-traumatic stress disorder.[27] After the murder, we are told that an "incontrovertible and inexplicable longing drew him" (6:132–33) to the scene of his distress, that he is compelled irrationally to repeat his former actions, even deriving pleasure from satisfying the compulsion:

> Suddenly, it was as though someone had whispered into his ear. He raised his head and saw that he was standing at *that* very house, at the very gates [. . .] he grasped onto the bell and pulled. The very same bell, the very same tinny sound! He pulled a second time, a third time; he listened and remembered. A former, tormentingly terrifying, awful feeling began to recall itself to him in an ever more vivid and lively way, he gave a start with every ring, and it became more and more pleasant to him. (6:134)

While this passage portrays Raskolnikov suffering from the memory of his crime and drawn overpoweringly to repeat the former sequence of events, it is important to emphasize that the notion of trauma applies to Raskolnikov equally *before* the murder. In the opening pages of the novel, when Raskolnikov rings the bell to visit the pawnbroker, the action evokes an earlier, more deeply buried memory, which is left unnamed: "this particular ring as if suddenly reminded him of something and clearly presented something to him . . . He gave a start, his nerves having become so weak" (6:8). The murder, in fact, serves to reinforce Raskolnikov's amnesia, covering over the deeper memories that Raskolnikov suppresses, and providing him with a violent break from his "former past," which he sees after his crime as if from afar, in the waters of the Neva, "in some depths, below, somewhere barely visible below his feet" (6:90). The descriptions of compulsion and "determinism" (6:55) surrounding the crime itself, the sensation that "he no longer had any freedom of reason or will" (6:52), as if "he had gotten a piece of his clothing stuck in the wheels of a machine and was being drawn into it" (6:58) add to the impression of a need to repeat something unavailable to consciousness, especially since these feelings stem from an irrational and overpowering visceral reaction at the sight of Lizaveta: "When Raskolnikov suddenly saw her, some kind of strange sensation, resembling deep astonishment grasped hold of him, although in this meeting there was nothing astonishing." The compulsion that she awakens within him reminds us of Ordynov's behavior in the church upon seeing Katerina, a comparison strengthened by the fact that Lizaveta, like Katerina, is also "completely enslaved" (6:51) to a cruel tyrant whom Raskolnikov plans to murder.

The earlier descriptions of amnesia—particularly of Ordynov's in "The Landlady"—provide further insight into the nature of the suppressed memories that Raskolnikov is prompted to reenact. As we have seen, Ordynov's personality was dramatized externally as three inhabitants of an apartment—a cruel abuser (Murin), a suffering victim (Katerina), and a powerless witness (Ordynov), brought together in the central paradigm of Murin tormenting Katia, while Ordynov watches with horror through a hole in the wall. These three archetypal figures, captured within these gestures, form the substance of Raskolnikov's nightmares. The child-observer's futile attempt to rescue the horse from the peasant's abuse in Raskolnikov's first dream constitutes the first repetition of the Ordynov paradigm.[28] Raskolnikov's second nightmare in which he listens in terror from up in his tiny room as the police inspector beats his landlady on the stairs is even more closely aligned with Ordynov's predicament. Again, we encounter the apartment as a symbolic portrait of the wounded personality, and again the landlady and her abuser appear as elements of the self somehow adjacent to, but separate from, the protagonist's sphere of awareness. Like Ordynov, observing the "inescapable tyranny" over the "soul" from his helpless vantage point, Raskolnikov finds himself in the role of powerless observer:

> To his utmost astonishment, he suddenly heard his landlady's voice. She was howling, screeching and lamenting, [. . .] begging for them to stop beating her, because someone was beating her mercilessly on the stairs. Her assailant's voice had become so horrible, already hoarse, from spite and fury [. . .] [Ilya Petrovich] was kicking her, was striking her head against the steps [. . .] a crowd gathered around the staircase, voices could be heard [. . .]. He wanted to lock himself in by the hook, but he could not lift his arm . . . and it was useless in any case! Fear, like ice, surrounded his soul, tormented him, numbed him [. . .] he lay for about half an hour in such suffering, with such an unbearable sensation of limitless horror, the like of which he had never known before. (6:90–91)

If we take the building, with all its inhabitants, as an image of the personality, we can perceive in Raskolnikov's dream a depiction of consciousness, enclosed on the top floor in its tiny sphere of awareness, but terrified of other insidious, palpable presences to which it has no direct access, and from which, in fact, it wants to lock itself away. Raskolnikov's "limitless horror" and frustrated desire to lock the door constitute a vivid symbolic depiction of his incomplete amnesia.

In the novel, Dostoevsky continues to develop the imagery from the earlier story according to which Ordynov associated his landlady with the suppressed elements of the unconscious. Raskolnikov's landlady, Praskovia, lives just below him, a reclusive, "unnecessarily shy" (6:93) character whom we almost never see, but of whose presence we are nevertheless constantly aware. The first thing we discover about Raskolnikov is that he is afraid of meeting his landlady, but that he does not understand the reasons for his fear (6:5). Just as we encounter glimpses of Raskolnikov's memories, we see his landlady only for brief moments in the novel as her eyes "peep in through the half-opened door" before she quickly "closes the door and hides" (6:92–93).[29] Thus, Raskolnikov's landlady, like Ordynov's, becomes an external soul for the inwardly collapsed personality—the quiet, unseen, but ever-present, ever-active subliminal proprietor of the edifice.[30] In his most intense states of emotional anguish the protagonist can hear her screaming from the stairs below, but he is incapable of encountering her directly.

The remembering sequence from "The Landlady," in which Katerina semi-coherently relates her memories to Ordynov while Murin's presence looms ominously from behind the partition, is also replayed as one of the novel's central scenes. Raskolnikov's first visit to Sonia elicits an echo from the earlier story, with Raskolnikov and Sonia engaging in unusually sudden emotional intimacy while Svidrigailov takes up Murin's position, listening to them ironically from just behind the thin wall. The form of memory shared between Raskolnikov and Sonia suggests that Dostoevsky's concept of interiority has evolved in the intervening decades. The deeply private space that Sonia, with great trepidation, reveals to Raskolnikov, is not personal memory in the literal sense (as was the case with Katerina and Laria), but rather the Gospel passage recounting the raising of Lazarus. When Raskolnikov commands Sonia to read, he recognizes from her "feverish trembling" that the text itself occupies the most intensely private and innermost region of her personality:

> He understood how difficult it was for her now to yield and reveal everything that was *hers*. He understood that these feelings truly constituted her real and perhaps long-vested *secret*, maybe even from her youth, while still with her family, next to her unfortunate father and stepmother who was crazy from grief, among hungry children, hideous cries and reproaches. (6:250)

When Sonia finally reads "loudly and triumphantly, trembling and growing cold, as if she were seeing it with her own eyes" (6:251), "as if she herself were confessing it for all to hear" (6:250), Dostoevsky is portraying a deeper layer of memory, which has a revelatory, and perhaps even healing, power.[31] The images they encounter in the text—of the dead man, Lazarus, rotting, and locked in a cave, revived, and brought out into the daylight—emphasize the concealed nature of the unconscious life, hidden, left for dead, and miraculously restored. The innermost room, so protected and feared in Dostoevsky, in this case contains not personal memory in the literal sense, but the images that take up residence in the mind "next to" (as was the case with Sonia [6:250]) painful and traumatic experience.

From a careful reading of these early works, we see that Bakhtin's argument for the absence of memory in Dostoevsky's characters as a prerequisite for existential freedom is intensely problematic. Indeed, the amnesia that allows for such freedom is also a major symptom of the illness that Dostoevsky confronts in his writing. At the heart of Dostoevsky's concept of the person is an unnamable psychic wound that provides the ground for the vast intersecting constructions of character that will constitute his later novels. The "forsaken little dog" that links itself to Goliadkin, stirring the "remembrance of some long ago occurring circumstance," is no textual anomaly. Its presence indicates the unconscious survival of unwanted memories that prompt these individuals to disperse themselves into others. As we have seen, these emanations coalesce gradually into a recurrent tripartite paradigm for the self, in the gestures of calculating tyrant, imprisoned soul, and powerless witness. These archetypes present us with a dynamic reformulation in exterior space of the faculties of mind, soul, and consciousness (which develop

Chapter Two

throughout Dostoevsky's career into the gestures of watchman, prisoner, and redeemer). In his later work, Dostoevsky will portray the endeavors of these characters to recover this terrain as *interior* space, to become more than a helpless, convulsive figure on the threshold, dispersed and dissolved into a collective self, and to encounter the other as more than a personal emanation of oneself.

Chapter Three

Transparency and Trauma in *The Insulted and Injured*

> I have always regarded as the worthiest of men that Roman who wanted his house to be built in a way that whatever occurred within could be seen [by all].
> —Rousseau, *Julie, or the New Heloise*

> In any person's memories there are such things that he will reveal not to everyone, but only to his friends. There are also things he won't reveal to his friends either, and really only to himself, and even then as a secret. But there are, finally, such things that he is afraid to reveal even to himself, and any honest person will have accumulated a good portion of these. One could even say that the more decent a person, the more of these he will have.
> —Dostoevsky, Notes from Underground

"THE CONCEALED SIDE"

Prior to the emergence of the scientific study of trauma in Europe in the 1870s and 1880s, Dostoevsky had spent decades exploring the effects of distressing and frightening memory upon the self. He articulated some of his thoughts on this topic in his *Diary of a Writer* for 1877, where he described the impact of "unhealed" childhood "wounds" upon the life and art of the then recently deceased poet Nikolai Nekrasov. During intimate conversations with Nekrasov in the early days of their literary careers, Dostoevsky, according to his account, had managed to observe the "most essential and concealed [or suppressed, *zataennyi*] side" of the "enigmatic" poet's "spirit," namely, "a heart that had been wounded at the very beginning of his life." Nekrasov's "hideous" childhood experiences, Dostoevsky claimed, had exerted a guiding and fortifying influence upon the poet throughout his life, while also catalyzing certain "dark, uncontrollable attractions" and unconscious "impulses" in him:

> This wound of his, which never healed, was the foundation and source of all of his passionate, suffering poetry [. . .]. If there was to be something sacred in his life, something that could save him and serve as a beacon, a guiding star, [. . .] then it could only be this primary childhood impression of a child's tears, of a childish sobbing together [with his mother], embracing, somewhere in secret, so they wouldn't be seen. [. . .] I think that no single attachment in his life could have so influenced and overpoweringly acted on his will and on other dark uncontrollable attractions of his spirit which pursued him all his life as did this one. (26:111–12)

Dostoevsky's reflections drew a sharp response from his long-standing ideological nemesis, Nikolai Chernyshevsky, who expressed objections on two fronts.[1] First, evoking his own canonical concept of the human being as a rational and transparent phenomenon, Chernyshevsky insisted that there was "absolutely nothing 'enigmatic'" about Nekrasov. "He was," on the contrary, "a very straightforward person" who could "always" give a "clear" and "direct" account of his "motives" and "actions." Second, as Chernyshevsky pointed out, Nekrasov's childhood memories were not at all "concealed." Not only did the poet "share the painful impressions of his childhood with the entire Russian public in so many of his lyrical plays and [. . .] poems," but he would even "recount them in detail to any acquaintance who wished to listen." How then, Chernyshevsky asked with some irritation, could these memories possibly constitute "the most 'concealed side' of this 'enigmatic' person's spirit"?

The dispute over Nekrasov points to a largely unexplored dimension of Dostoevsky's artistic campaign against the tenets of radical materialism: that is, his complex, innovative, and idiosyncratic conception of traumatic memory. In the years directly following his inward religious conversion and return to St. Petersburg (in 1859) from imprisonment and exile, as he was attempting to conceive of a compelling refutation to the materialist and determinist models of the human being that had become so prevalent in Russian society (and whose leading proponent was Chernyshevsky himself), Dostoevsky turned to an exploration of the psychic wound in his first major novel, *The Insulted and Injured* (1861). Chernyshevsky's appraisal of Nekrasov as a transparent and "straightforward person" restates the very position against which Dostoevsky had initially formulated his concept of the wound in this, his highly readable, but aesthetically uneven, and critically shunned, novel. *The Insulted and Injured* presents a sustained critique of the moral emptiness, weakness, and even villainy of the transparent personality, and depicts the opaque and traumatized self as a moral counterweight, as not only broken but expanded by the lasting effects of wounding memory. In this chapter I shall examine Dostoevsky's exploration of the concept of trauma in *The Insulted and Injured* in his critique of personal transparency and in his portrayal of two opposing reactions to violent shock and distress—the preservation and concealment of memory, on the one hand, and its suppression and erasure, on the other. By bringing together two kinds of wounded personalities in his novel—one who remembers and one who forgets—Dostoevsky develops a concept of trauma that encompasses the alternately debilitating, curative, fortifying, and even revelatory properties of the psychic wound upon the self.

REVEALING "EVERYTHING"

The Insulted and Injured presents us with a forceful critique of the notion of personal transparency. The constant refrain of the novel's characters is the intention to reveal all the contents of their minds—"To pour out [one's] soul" (3:306), to "open the whole heart" (3:366), to "express oneself decisively" (3:356), to "say *everything*" (3:314, 411), a preponderance not generally noted by critics who are otherwise sensitive to the central role of the confession in Dostoevsky's writing.[2] Among the numerous confessions of the novel, two instances stand out as definitive, divergent paradigms for the act of becoming transparent to others—of revealing "everything." I begin simply by recounting them.

The first paradigmatic act of self-revelation occurs in the impromptu confession of the novel's villain, Prince Valkovsky. The Prince, desirous of financial and social advancement, does not wish his son Alyosha to marry the penniless Natasha, the daughter of his estate manager, Ikhmenev. But the two young people, Alyosha and Natasha, have run away together against the Prince's wishes and to the great distress of Natasha's family. For the Ikhmenevs, the loss of their daughter's honor is worsened by the fact that their family is in the midst of a legal battle with the Prince who has unjustly accused Ikhmenev of swindling him as his estate manager and also of engineering Alyosha's alliance with Natasha. Prince Valkovsky, for his part, has conceived of a devious plan for preventing his son's marriage: vocally encouraging the young couple to get married, and so lifting the taboo, and thus deflating the romantic intensity of Alyosha's rebellion. Valkovsky hopes his plan will encourage Alyosha to cast aside the ruined Natasha and to form a more advantageous union. Having invited Vanya—the novel's hero and narrator, and a devoted defender of the Ikhmenevs—to dine with him in a restaurant, the Prince drinks, grows expansive, and then suddenly decides to "express [himself] definitively." He candidly discloses the full nature of his scheme, and, largely out of contempt for his idealistic interlocutor's prudish astonishment, adds details of his own past crimes, mocks the Ikhmenevs for having trusted him, and muses sardonically on the topic of Natasha's ruined honor. By way of explanation for these unsolicited "confidences," Valkovsky declares that "there is a special sensual delight in the sudden tearing off of the mask, in the cynicism with which a person suddenly reveals himself before another in such a way that he doesn't even consider it necessary to feel shame before him" (3:362).

As a counterpoint to the Prince's impulsive confession, the novel's climactic scene presents an altruistic and excruciating act of self-disclosure. By now the Ikhmenevs are in the midst of a family crisis. Natasha, duly abandoned by Alyosha Valkovsky, is afraid to come home because her father has vowed never to forgive her. Wishing to reunite the family at all costs, Vanya brings his protégée, Nellie, an abused child whom he has saved from ruin, to speak to the Ikhmenevs, husband and wife. His plan is to have Nellie tell them of her own family experiences, which are directly analogous to the current torments of the Ikhmenevs. Like Natasha, Nellie's mother was spurned by her father for running away with a capricious egoist (unbeknownst to all, the seducer was in fact Alyosha's father, Prince Valkovsky). When the latter absconded, Nellie's hard-hearted grandfather, Jeremiah Smith, refused to forgive his daughter, who died in a state of poverty and madness, all of which Nellie witnessed firsthand. While he encourages her to speak of her memories, Vanya knows that Nellie's heart has a defect and that any excitement could kill her. Thus, to recall publicly the horrific events of her mother's death, and in such a dramatic context, is perilous to Nellie's survival. At Vanya's request, Nellie, trembling all over, and with great reluctance, begins to relate her memories to the Ikhmenevs. As she tells her story, the thirteen-year-old girl, who, until now, has been resolutely silent about the horrors of her past, becomes carried away and decides, we are told, to reveal *"everything"* (3:411). Her impassioned testimony meets with unqualified success: it pierces Ikhmenev's heart, bringing about a complete conversion in him (one which never occurred in Nellie's own grandfather). It even seems as if her story, at its grand finale, brings Natasha (as though magically) to the front door of the apartment. In speaking, Nellie heals the shattered family, but also overtaxes her heart, so that she in fact sacrifices her life in telling her story.

Apart from the very different moral attitudes that characterize these contrasting confessions (the Prince's sadistic self-exposure, on the one hand, and Nellie's tormented, self-sacrificial recollection of the buried past, on the other), the respective treatments, as we shall see, underlie a more extensive meditation on the nature of transparency and of the effects of traumatic memory on the self.[3]

THE DOCTRINE OF THE "UNWRAPPED EGO"

Dostoevsky's investigation of personal transparency and openness is centered in his depictions of the Valkovskys: Prince Valkovsky, the corrupt egoist, who delights in revealing his sordid secrets, and his son, Alyosha, the naive idealist who, like Rousseau's Emile, is constitutionally incapable of concealment.[4] For all their many differences (e.g., the son's idealism, the father's cynicism, the son's youthful candor, the father's extreme duplicity), father and son are united in their shared belief in the essential transparency of the personality. Alyosha, "in [whom] nothing was concealed" (3:202), constantly expresses his eagerness to unfold his depths entirely in the present moment, to "tell everything," to "pour out my soul before you all" (3:306). Alyosha's belief in personal transparency, moreover, extends equally to his ideological convictions. Together with his allies among the utopian socialists, Alyosha preaches the abolition of privacy and secrecy: "We gave each other our word to be absolutely open with one another and to say everything about ourselves straightforwardly to each other without embarrassment. Only openness, only straightforwardness will attain the goal" (3:310). "How much evil," Alyosha enthuses, "can be avoided with openness!" (3:311).[5]

Prince Valkovsky, like his son, believes that the self can be made transparent, although in his case this practice takes on a more perverse expression. While Alyosha's candor flows from naive sincerity, Prince Valkovsky, as mentioned above, derives "special sensual pleasure" from the "sudden tearing off of the mask" (3:362), or what he ironically describes as the "pouring out of the soul" (3:359) or the "opening of the whole heart" (3:366). He prides himself on his courageous ability to make himself transparent. "You accuse me," he tells Vanya, "of vice, debauchery, immorality, and I am perhaps only guilty in that I am *more open* than others and that's all, that I don't hide that which others hide from themselves" (3:362). Though Valkovsky does not share his son's longing for a transparent utopia, he agrees that such a state of universal transparency, though undesirable, is nevertheless possible. "If it could only be," he muses, "that each of us described all of his innermost secrets [*vsiu vsoiu podnogotnuiu*], [. . .] then such a stench would arise on the earth that we would all have to suffocate" (3:361). Thus, while each bears a drastically dissimilar understanding of what lies within, father and son share a conception of the self whose full revelation is impeded merely by social norms and external constraints.

Prince Valkovsky's declarations on the nature of the self (e.g., "at the foundation of all human virtue lies the deepest egoism" [3:365]) are informed to a large degree by the German philosopher Max Stirner's book *The Ego and Its Own* (*Der Einzige und sein Eigentum*), which exerted a profound, even sensational, impact upon Dostoevsky and his contemporaries after its publication in Russia in the 1840s.[6] Like Valkovsky's, Stirner's egoism precludes any notion of hidden depths, of attempts to defer the principle of the self beyond the conscious present into "ghostly" essences or interior realms.[7] Stirner's attempt to conceive of the personality, quite radically, as presence ("I—am present!") and his hostility to notions of essence, immanence, or deferral provide a vital philosophical backdrop to the notion of transparency in the novel.[8] "I can never take comfort in myself," Stirner declares, "as long as I think that I have still to find my true self, [. . .] that not I but Christ or some other spiritual, ghostly, self (the true, the essence of man, and the like) lives in me." Remarkable in his prescience as a forerunner of existentialist thought, Stirner proposed a worldview in which instead of going "toward myself, [. . .] I start from myself."[9] For Stirner, the conscious and immediate "I" is the tangible core of the personality, "the kernel that is to be delivered from all wrappings and—freed from all cramping shells. What is to be left," asks Stirner, "when I have been freed from everything that is not I? Only I, and nothing but I."[10]

As Valkovsky dramatizes his own conception of the fully disclosed self, he employs two parables that closely echo the Stirnerian position. The first parable (which he relates to a scandalized Vanya) develops the image, drawn from Rousseau's *Confessions*, of peep show or indecent exposure, a concept that would preoccupy Dostoevsky's imagination for decades (and which will resurface later in *The Adolescent*). He tells the story of a "madman" in Paris who would walk through town naked but covered in a raincoat: "With the most serious and profoundly thoughtful look, he would suddenly stop before [some passerby], open up his raincoat, and show himself in all . . . his pureheartedness [or frankness, *chistoserdechie*]. [. . .]. Then he would wrap himself up again and, silently, without moving a single facial muscle, would walk past the astonished viewer" (3:362–63). Valkovsky interprets the "madman's" game in an implicitly Stirnerian light as a parable for the "unwrapping" of the "I," the discarding of its superfluous accessories (the interior life, memory, the recesses of the "soul") by opening them up suddenly to the astonished other.[11] If there is a ghostly essence that lurks behind the world of appearance, it is in fact only a naked body, which can be revealed by a simple act of will, just as Valkovsky himself chooses suddenly to reveal "all" to his unwilling interlocutor. To portray more vividly his conception of the revealable self, Valkovsky supplements the above image with a second parable in which a respected countess conceals a life of boundless debauchery behind a morally severe, "majestic and inaccessible" outward persona. Valkovsky recalls the "inner diabolical laughter" that motivated her deceit, the sudden "guffawing, as if in a frenzy [. . .] in the fervor of the hottest pleasures" (3:364).[12] Here the countess's frenzied laughter offers yet another conceit of the "kernel" of the self—as the ironic, ever-vigilant consciousness hiding beneath the multiple covers of self-righteousness. In both of his parables, then, Valkovsky pursues an attack on essentialist conceptions of selfhood by conceiving of the "mystery" within the self as a scandalous, but entirely determinate, secret.[13]

In his portraits of the Valkovskys, Dostoevsky depicts the moral effects of this doctrine of transparent selfhood upon the personality, particularly in the peculiar forms of moral amnesia exhibited among its proponents. Alyosha's doctrine of personal transparency is accompanied by a remarkable receptivity to the intensity of the present moment. As Natasha points out, Alyosha is powerless against "the very first impression, the first external influence" (3:198) that he encounters. In response to the forceful "impressions" of the present, he immediately forgets all of his most cherished desires and convictions.[14] His broken promises, Natasha explains, are not lies ("he is incapable of lying"); rather his moral fickleness arises from an actual inability to remember the past, an inability which renders him effectively conscienceless:

> He has no character. Now he'll make a vow to you, and then the very same day, just as truthfully and sincerely, he'll give himself over to another; [. . .] He's even capable of self-sacrifice [. . .], but only until some new impression comes along: here he'll forget everything again. *And he'll forget me too, if I am not constantly in his presence.* [. . .] He'll forget about me and fall in love with another, and then as soon as he sees me, he'll be at my feet again. [. . .] *If I am not with him always, constantly, every moment, he will stop loving me, will forget and abandon me.* (3:198–99; Dostoevsky's emphasis)

In Alyosha's unusual form of amnesia, we encounter a morally sinister version of Bakhtin's concept of the personality on the "threshold," the memoryless, outwardly oriented consciousness that, in Bakhtin's view, emerges from the nature of Dostoevsky's poetics. According to this model, the personality, free from temporal limitations, does not experience the determining influence of the past and thus, together with shifting states of consciousness, is given radically to the possibility of transformation.[15] After his conversion to utopian socialism, Alyosha proclaims (as is characteristic of him throughout) that "I have changed absolutely, to the tips of my fingers, [. . .] I'm a different person" (3:307–8). As in the case of his father, the past is available to consciousness and yet does not exert any effect upon it. Prince Valkovsky, for his part, is delighted to revisit his past crimes indifferently and without compunction, like the "madman in the raincoat" (3:369) as Vanya observes.[16] In the Valkovskys, therefore, transparency and egoism are inextricably linked; both qualities emerge from an underlying anti-essentialist conception of self, in which the kernel of the personality refuses to be relegated to a ghostly elsewhere, and proclaims itself fully in the present moment, in the activity of consciousness.

THE PATHOGENIC SECRET

As a conceptual counterweight to the idea of the unwrapped ego, Dostoevsky develops in *The Insulted and Injured* the contrasting notion of a secret, opaque region that emerges in response to the experience of being wounded. Obsessive concealment, we discover, is one of the principal characteristics of the novel's titular characters. "Tender and subtle" Ikhmenev, for example, is characterized by a "chaste unwillingness to express [himself] or to show his tenderness even to his beloved, and not only in front of others, but even in private" (3:214). "'I show no one the interior of my heart,'" he tells Vanya (3:290), while agonizingly concealing the wounded love he bears for his daughter. The most powerful representative of this phenomenon is the novel's heroine, the orphaned and abused Nellie who exhibits a "strange stubbornness of heart, which chastely concealed itself [. . .] more stubbornly and sternly the more the need to pour itself out, to express itself" (3:296–97). Vanya is continually astonished by Nellie's "inaccessibility," by her "somberness and silence" in concealing the past (3:299, 379), and by the immense tension between her longing to speak and unwillingness to reveal her secrets (3:379–80). Her stubborn policy of secrecy with regard to memory exerts a devastating effect upon Nellie's psyche, and, it seems, upon the lives of others around her as they unwittingly replay patterns from her memories while she looks on silently and helplessly. Ikhmenev, for example, unknowingly becomes an embodiment of her dead grandfather (3:383), Natasha a manifestation of her mother (3:379), and Vanya a reincarnation of her mother's former helper and confidant (3:185); all are somehow connected to the concealed narrative pattern that exists already in the child's past.

In his study of the wounded psyche, which occupies the central focus of the novel, Dostoevsky thus initiates a realm of inquiry—the study of trauma—which, in 1861, was still more than a decade away from its debut in European scientific culture. At first glance, his descriptions of wounded personalities seem to belong to a traditional conception of psychological disturbance. The portrait of the novel's emotionally scarred heroine, Nellie, for example, differs markedly from the later psychoanalytic conception of trauma (as involving "forgotten memory") in that Nellie does not repress her memories; rather (much like Nekrasov in Dostoevsky's depiction of him), she guards her wounds fastidiously, anxious to preserve them intact as a perceived sacred duty to the memory of her dead mother. Her attraction to patterns of abuse—which "aggravate" the "open wound" in the mind and keep it alive (3:373, 385)—and her refusal to speak about her past arise from a stubborn policy of secrecy and of devotion to wounded memory, a behavior the narrator describes as the "the egoism of suffering" (3:386). For this reason, in Dostoevsky's portrayal of his heroine, a clear distinction can be made between "trauma" (which involves the unconscious repression, or at least active suppression, of memory) and "pathogenic secrecy"—the latter concept having preceded and played a role in the genealogy of the former.[17]

The notion of the festering personal secret is of course by no means Dostoevsky's unique discovery (it has a long history—reaching, for example, into Christian practices of confession), and the depiction of Nellie's pathogenic secrecy is in keeping with (if slightly ahead of) European scientific thought of the early 1860s. In fact, a few years after the publication of *The Insulted and Injured*, scientists began, as a prelude to the study of trauma, to explore the thesis that a "painful secret" could be the cause "of many cases of hysteria and other neuroses" and that "many patients could be cured by the confession of their pathogenic secrets and by the working out of the related problems."[18] As we look more closely at the novel's depictions of the psychic wound, however, we see that Nellie's "pathogenic secrecy" is only the most detectable aspect of a more extensive study of wounded memory, one which reaches beyond the heroine into other, neighboring personalities. The novel's plot, we discover, brings together two wounded characters—the child, Nellie, who guards her memories, and her protector, the narrator, Vanya, who, unlike Nellie, is wounded in unnamed, indeterminate ways. Vanya's unfathomably opaque personality (with his wounds buried under a deceptive aura of transparency) provides us with another dimension of Dostoevsky's conception of the psychic wound: that of the suppressed psyche that binds itself hungrily to the contents of other people's minds as a form of substitution.

VANYA'S EXPANDING ROOM

The characterization of Vanya, the novel's protagonist and narrator, has prompted conflicting critical evaluations as a consequence of the unusual combination that he embodies of extraordinary goodness and frail ineffectuality. On the one hand, Vanya has often been embraced as an ideal, a forerunner of such later selfless and compassionate protagonists as Prince Myshkin and Alyosha Karamazov. Since the novel's villain, Prince Valkovsky, embodies the principle of egoistic Western selfhood, readers have been inclined to interpret Vanya, in his radical selflessness, as Dostoevsky's antidote to egoism, his representation of the Christian ideal.[19] Others have perceived greater complexity both in the character and in the novel. Sensing Dostoevsky's dissatisfaction with his protagonist's ineptitude and futility, these readers have seen the novel as reflecting an ideological crisis in the author: while repudiating Valkovsky's egoism, Dostoevsky, it has been argued, equally rejects his own former idealism as embodied in his protagonist, without yet wielding any positive philosophical outlook with which to oppose either of these phenomena.[20] As yet on the verge of discovering the tenets of his mature moral philosophy, Dostoevsky, according to this perspective, succumbs by means of a generic inertia to the sentimental cliché of pitting a radically sincere hero (Vanya) against a masked and duplicitous villain (Valkovsky).[21] I would maintain that these readings overlook the traumatic wound that underlies the protagonist's characterization. His moral and physical frailty, I shall argue, comes not from an ideological commitment to idealism (though his idealism is perhaps a symptom of his condition), but from a tormented longing to discard his submerged memories and to become dispersed entirely in relational space.

As a personality, Vanya, appears, at first glance, to resemble Alyosha Valkovsky in his extraordinary quality of transparency. Not only is he openhearted, ever eager to relate all that he knows (3:215, 228), selfless, and strikingly sincere, but he also often appears to be transparent even in the literal sense.[22] Ikhmenev, alone with Vanya, "would forget sometimes that he was not alone in the room and would talk to himself" (3:211); Katia feels that speaking with Vanya is like "talking with herself" (3:257); Alyosha thinks nothing of the fact that Vanya spends long hours alone with Natasha in the apartment (3:233); and the lovers, Alyosha and Natasha, interact before him in extremely intimate ways as if he were not there (3:216–17). We find that others continually "launch into the strangest confidences" with him (3:215), at times because they "have no one else" (3:215), at other times because they "do not consider [him] a person" (3:369). Others marvel at his capacity to erase his own wants and needs, to become a passive mediator in the service of other people, to become merely the "eyes" of others (3:322), their messenger and the medium through which they communicate (3:224–25).[23] As a result of his capacity for selflessness, Vanya becomes a structurally convenient nexus in the novel, a mediational presence through which other characters coalesce into interactions constitutive of a coherent plot.[24]

Careful scrutiny of Vanya's characterization, however, reveals that his transparency is an elaborate illusion that conceals a subtly elided interior realm. Like the heroes of Dostoevsky's early prose (Ordynov, Netochka, Goliadkin), Vanya is characterized by an intense desire to erase and escape some form of indeterminate memory. Apart from a sketch of the basic events of his biography, the following passage is the only indication we are given of the protagonist's personal past:

> It also occurred to me that it would be good if by means of some magic or miracle I could absolutely forget everything that had been, that I had lived through in recent years; to forget everything, to refresh my head and begin again with new strength. Then I still dreamed about this and hoped for resurrection. (3:207)

Unlike Nellie, who lives with her distressing memories constantly before her, Vanya sees the suppression of memory as the key to his future moral and physical survival. Although, unlike Alyosha Valkovsky, Vanya does not belong entirely to the transparency of the present, nevertheless he wishes to rid himself of those elements of his personality that render him opaque and that impede his regeneration.

The symbolic vocabulary of the emptied, collapsed, and externalized self that we have assembled in the previous two chapters resonates emphatically with Vanya's characterization. The novel begins as a recasting of "The Landlady," with the hero, like Orydnov, looking for a new apartment. As Vanya wanders the streets of Petersburg, he, like Ordynov, is compulsively and mysteriously entranced by the phenomenon of one personality broken and externalized into two selves. This time instead of Murin and Katerina praying in the cathedral (the tyrant mind and the captive soul; or watchman and prisoner), he perceives yet another externalized personality: master and dog, Smith and Azorka. As we noted in chapter 2, the relationship between Smith and Azorka enacts a form of collective selfhood. The old man looks ahead "all eyes, but with such a dull, lifeless gaze" (3:171), "as if there were almost no body on him" (3:170), while the sentient dog remembers the past, carrying the painful memory of Smith's beloved daughter after Smith has torn her violently from his heart.[25] Vanya's overwhelming attraction to the pair is described with striking similarity to Ordynov's attraction to his landlord and landlady. Vanya, we are told, "suddenly stopped as if shackled," visited by a mysterious "premonition" when he apprehends the master and dog, overwhelmed by an utterly unfathomable physical compulsion, a "strange, morbid, [. . .] extremely unpleasant sensation, [though] I myself couldn't decide what kind of sensation it was" (3:170–72). At length, Vanya ponders the incomprehensibility of his irresistible fascination with the pair: "Why did I come in here, when [. . .] I am ill [. . .]? Can I really be here simply to scrutinize this old man? [. . .] Why this fantastical frame of mind?" (3:172).

Chapter Three

While Dostoevsky leaves Vanya's irresistible attraction to Smith and Azorka as an open question in the novel, from "The Landlady," we recognize the impulse as the projective event of a partially collapsed personality.[26]

The motif of the apartment as the image of the personality that we examined in both "The Landlady" and *Crime and Punishment* is central to Vanya's characterization. As Vanya takes over residence of the dead man's apartment, the old man and his dog become his ghostly landlords, the projective inhabitants of the dreaded interior realm of his personality. As he sits in the apartment, longing to "forget everything," he desires simultaneously to escape the room itself, thus instinctively conflating the dark space around him with the interior personal memories he wishes to erase: "to forget everything, to refresh my head and begin again [. . .] I wanted as soon as possible to tear myself out of my apartment, to go anywhere, even into the rain, into the mire" (3:207). As the room grows darker, we are told it becomes "more expansive, as though it had grown wider" (3:207). Vanya's fear of the interior dimensions of the self, projected onto the dark, expanding room, is described in great detail as "a state of soul which [. . .] I call *mystical horror*," a severe dread of the unconscious dimensions of the personality that plague the wounded amnesiac. Vanya experiences "the heaviest tormenting fear of [. . .] something ungraspable" and "indefinite," of something that "will become an inescapable fact before me, a terrible, hideous and inexorable fact, as if in mockery of all the arguments of reason," and he is seized by an overwhelming agony as his mind, "in a fearful agony of expectation," is gradually "deprived of any ability to resist these sensations": "It seems to me that such is partly the agony of people who are afraid of dead bodies" (3:207–8). Though the passage has often been read as a philosophical meditation on the "dark mysteries of human existence," the description of debilitating, agonizing terror and "danger," likened to a fear of dead bodies, actually focuses upon the protagonist's attempts to forget, or rather to continue to suppress, an unknown and highly "indefinite" series of memories.[27]

In keeping with the protagonists of the earlier works, Vanya displaces these "inexorable" terrors into external personalities, for example, into the "apparition" of Smith and his dog that he constantly expects "every night and in every corner" of his expanding apartment (3:207). As Vanya sits contemplating the terrifying darkness around him, and attempting meanwhile to suppress the "terrible, hideous, inexorable fact" that haunts him, Nellie visits him for the first time and thus enters directly into the projective landscape of his personality as a "strange creature" appearing "suddenly on the threshold": "someone's eyes, as far as I could make out in the darkness, were scrutinizing me fixedly and intently. A shiver ran over all my limbs. To my great horror, I saw that it was a child, a little girl" (3:208).[28] In this context, the suffering, wounded child, though a separate character, becomes immediately inscribed into the projective landscape of the self that expands around the protagonist so terrifyingly and against his will. As Nellie, terrified, flees Vanya's questioning scrutiny, he pursues her down the stairs, groping in the darkness to find her hiding in a shadowy corner of the staircase (prefiguring Myshkin's later near-fatal encounter with Rogozhin). The wounded child who does not want to be seen, who flees inquiry and weeps "soundlessly" (3:210) in the darkness on the stairs, becomes in this context a projective image of wounded interiority fleeing consciousness, hiding somewhere below (as consciousness gropes toward it, sensing its presence) in the unknown reaches of the personality. In the strange, pathological intensity of the relationship that subsequently forms between the two characters, Vanya becomes Nellie's savior and protector, while Nellie, in turn, becomes both an embodiment of and a replacement for Vanya's unconscious mind, offering a repository of memories and a concealed interiority that are less threatening than his own. The relationship of extension between Vanya and Nellie employs the full range of Dostoevsky's vocabulary for the shared self, from the uncannily intense nature of their intimacy, to Vanya's conquering of Nellie (like Netochka's of Laria) as she relates her memories to him, and to her "pretending to sleep" as she attempts to escape his benevolent tyranny over her.[29]

THE REMEMBERING SCENE

The mechanism of shared memory that draws Vanya and Nellie together is developed from Dostoevsky's early writing where wounded characters encounter their own distressing and suppressed memories in the minds of others. As we have seen, Dostoevsky repeatedly brings together the wounded who remember with the wounded who actively suppress and erase their memories, and who then search for their own obliterated memories in adjacent minds. The first emphatic appearance of the mutual attraction of two characters, each bearing a different form of wounded memory (obliterated, forgotten, on the one hand; preserved and concealed, on the other), occurs, as we saw in chapter 2, in "The Landlady" in which the troubled protagonist, Ordynov, beseeches his landlady to share her memories with him; as she relates the tormenting events of her horrific, destroyed childhood, Ordynov recognizes the events she describes as his own memories (1:294). Likewise, in *Netochka Nezvanova*, the heroine who represses the memory of her mother's dead body discovers traces of her memories in another child, a trembling, traumatized creature to whom she finds herself clinging impulsively ("I instinctively felt that his grief was akin to my grief, which I felt at

Chapter Three

times painfully in my soul" [1:441]) and from whom she draws out memories that are remarkably similar to the ones she finds it too painful to acknowledge in herself.

In *The Insulted and Injured,* Dostoevsky begins to adapt the collective remembering scenes (instances when remembering occurs vicariously through the confession of the other) into the central events of his novelistic structure. Nellie's cathartic and melodramatic confession, like the episode in "The Landlady," takes part in a lineage of personal confessions leading up to Sonya's reading of Lazarus's resurrection. In all of these sequences—each representing in some way the emotional core of the work in which it appears—the heroine is compelled to share her deepest secret in response to the protagonist's insistent request (with the genders reversed in the case of *Netochka Nezvanova*). In Nellie's case, when Vanya brings her to the Ikhmenevs to resolve the family crisis, she begins to reveal her memories to the group under duress, "breathing unevenly and with difficulty, [. . .] whispering jerkily and fearfully [. . .] in the most extreme anxiety." Then, gradually, "stirred" by the force of her memories, her "eyes begin to glitter," and she becomes resolute and forceful in telling her story: "She was very pale, but resolution flashed in her gaze. It was obvious that she had made up her mind, finally, to tell everything. There was even something defiant in her in that moment" (3:407–11). The description closely prefigures Sonya's initial "gasping for breath" in the Lazarus episode where Sonya's "voice broke, her breath failed and her chest contracted," until, deeply moved by the events of the Gospel story, "as if she herself were confessing it herself for all to hear," she is "overtaken by a feeling of great triumph" and begins to read "loudly and triumphantly, trembling and growing cold, as if she were seeing it with her own eyes" (6:250–51).

By looking at Nellie's confession as a precursor to Sonya's, we see that Dostoevsky initially represents the salvific force (the power capable of dissolving entrenched patterns of suffering and egoism) not as a religious text, but as a personal memory. The contents of the two confessions—Nellie's and Sonya's—also share a more essential likeness in that both prominently feature the late arrival at the sickbed of a loved one and the shocking discovery of that loved one's corpse. In the Lazarus scene that Sonya presents to Raskolnikov, Christ, arriving four days late, is told by the bereaved family that "if you had been here my brother would not have died" (6:251).[30] In her story, Nellie recalls how she brought her estranged grandfather to see her perishing and despairing mother, only to find that she had died before they arrived:

> But Mama was already lying dead. When Grandpa saw her he threw up his hands, trembled, and stood over her, but himself said nothing. Then I went up to my dead mama, grasped Grandpa by the hand and screamed at him:

"Well, cruel and evil man, look! . . . look!" Here Grandpa cried out and fell onto the floor like a dead man. (3:420)

In this, the wrenching and climactic moment of her confession, Nellie finds herself in the position of Mary and Martha, grieving over the corpse of Lazarus, furious with her grandfather who has arrived too late and who is powerless to revive the dead body. In Nellie's case, however, the content of the memory and the act of confession itself begin to merge. As Vanya commands Nellie to reveal her memories, to lift the stone, as it were, and call forth the corpse of the mother into the open, Nellie in fact performs an action akin to the miracle of raising Lazarus by (indirectly) bringing the dead body of her mother to life and redeeming the events of her past. Indeed, as soon as Nellie has revealed her tale, her mother (in the dissociated, allegorical embodiment of Natasha) appears at the door, very much alive, and falls into the forgiving embrace of Nellie's grandfather (in the form of Ikhmenev).

If we are not distracted by the sentimentality of this "highly emotional and embarrassingly bathetic climax," we can perceive an early expression of Dostoevsky's search for a revelatory principle within the realm of wounded memory.[31] Indeed, it is worth noting that the disclosure of Nellie's memories, which have been concealed and preserved behind a strictly enforced taboo, constitutes the only effective force of redemption in the novel, where decent but weak individuals watch helplessly while their fates are determined by merciless egoists and while they themselves are captured within patterns of recrimination and separation by the "egoism of" their own "suffering." In fact, situated among a cast of characters subject to a pervasive amnesia, whether in the literal (Vanya) or moral (Prince Valkovsky, Alyosha) senses, Nellie, as the bearer of memory, becomes the "savior" by dint of her unique, morbid obsession with her devastating past. Nellie's remembering scene indicates the manner in which the religious dimension emerges from within the pathological in Dostoevsky's early meditation on the self. The confession is construed as a quasi-religious moment in the narrative, replete with echoes of Christ's death on the cross: "Nellie, angel!' said [Vanya], 'would you like to be our salvation? Would you like to save us all? [. . .] Tell them, Nellie, everything [. . .] everything, simply and without concealing anything" (3:406). For all its melodrama, the scene in which the heroine is destroyed by the articulation of her memory constitutes an important moment in the development of Dostoevsky's psychological theology. Through the movement into the closed inner room of the mind, the heroine releases forces that lead simultaneously to the triumph over patterns of determinism and to the destruction of the self. This notion of the fatal danger of entering into the inner rooms of the mind for the unprepared consciousness will become, as we shall see, one of the central themes of Dostoevsky's later novels.

Chapter Three

THE CORPSE AT THE END OF THE MIND

The novel's hero, Vanya, reflects the ambivalent and complex treatment of the wounded psyche in Dostoevsky's early writing: unlike the Valkovskys, he is broken by memory, pierced and haunted by his experiences, but is meanwhile so terrified of these interior dimensions that he displaces the contents of his psyche into others. Thus, although he wills the salvation of the Ikhmenevs, Vanya has no inner content of personality upon which he can draw for strength. The utopian idealist reverts to child-sacrifice not because of the failure of his theories (as has sometimes been argued), but rather because of the psychological fragility of the non-introspective consciousness, or in other words, because of an unwillingness to overcome the "presentness" of a transparent and ultimately powerless self.[32] The miracle of the raising of Lazarus is wrought instead by Nellie, who, through her fastidious "pathogenic secrecy," has nurtured a secret interior source of power. While exerting a debilitating effect on the health of the personality, the wounding memory thus also generates an alternate interior dimension which points beyond the self. As Vanya observes, even after all of Nellie's secrets had been revealed, "after everything has passed and everything is known, even now I don't know the whole mystery of this ill, tormented and insulted little heart" (3:371).

None of this, of course, invalidates Chernyshevsky's principal objection to the description of Nekrasov's wound. Nekrasov was evidently much more forthcoming than Nellie and did not require a family crisis to "open his heart." For Dostoevsky, however, as we shall see, the wound leads to an awareness of a farther room in the self, something beyond memory, of which traumatic experience becomes only the first intimation.

The image of the corpse buried deeply in the heroine's mind—an image that is to play a formidable role in the symbolic vocabulary and plot lines of Dostoevsky's major novels—is, in *The Insulted and Injured*, the point of intersection for all the novel's characters—as Nellie's sacred memory, Valkovsky's crime, Smith's trauma, and Natasha's fate (barring intervention from Nellie). This corpse over which Nellie keeps vigil is also connected to the presences that Vanya fears in his own suppressed memories—the "dead bodies" from his own past, which haunt him while he is alone, but which he is unwilling to approach in himself. In the Gospel story of Lazarus, when Christ arrives, the others in fact do not want the corpse to emerge from behind the stone since it is already in a state of decay. The Christian miracle of reawakening and redeeming the rotting corpse behind the stone is linked directly in both *Insulted and Injured* and *Crime and Punishment* with the problem of reviving memory as a dangerous but potentially redemptive endeavor. The dual activity of the wound in *The Insulted and Injured*—as establishing, on the one hand, a prohibitive limit in the mind which causes the self to become dispersed in relational space, and, on the other, as generating an aperture in the self and thus opening consciousness toward a deeper form of interiority—will be crucial for the development of Dostoevsky's metaphysical psychology in his later works. The image of the corpse in the depths of the mind, as we shall see in the next chapter, will be developed into the central motif of *The Idiot*, a novel which depicts the terror of religious experience in the harrowing, introspective journey into the nether region of unintegrated memory.

Chapter Four

Beyond the Dispersed Self in *The Idiot*

> "Spirit! [. . .] Shew me no more! Conduct me home. Why do you delight to torture me? [. . .] No more. I don't wish to see it. Shew me no more!" [. . .] But the relentless Ghost pinioned him in both his arms, and forced him to observe what happened next.
> —Dickens, "A Christmas Carol"

> I too with my soul and body,
> We, a curious trio, picking, wandering on our way . . .
> —Whitman, "Pioneers! O Pioneers!"

THE SPHINX

Of all Dostoevsky's protagonists, Prince Myshkin appears to be the one who most mystified his creator. Having decided "to portray a positively beautiful (or good) person" (28.2:251), Dostoevsky, during the difficult and constrained conception process of *The Idiot*, continually deferred reckoning with his hero's psychology. In March 1868, after publishing the first part of the novel, Dostoevsky toyed in his notebooks with the idea of "convey[ing] the prince's personality [*litso*] enigmatically *throughout the whole novel*" and then "suddenly explain[ing] his personality at the end" (9:220; Dostoevsky's emphasis). A month later, after struggling to send out two more chapters, he seems to have given up on the prospect of deciphering the riddle at all. "Why not," he asked himself, "present the Prince as a continuous sphinx?" (9:242).[1]

While it is tempting to ascribe perceived deficiencies or inconsistencies in Myshkin's character to a hurried conception, it is nevertheless evident that the figure of the Prince emerged from a gestation period extending over several decades. In experimenting with a new kind of personality—one that was unprecedentedly compassionate, magnetic, wise, meek, and selfless—but without having managed to discern the underlying psychological conditions from which these virtues emerged, Dostoevsky relied instinctively on the extensive blueprints developed in his earlier writing. In the context of Dostoevsky's examinations of trauma and amnesia in his earlier works, Prince Myshkin emerges in fact as the apotheosis of Dostoevsky's traumatized protagonists. The rich allegorical and poetic texture of Myshkin's characterization has persistently deflected readers' attention away from this aspect of his personality.[2] Critics have explained the extreme faintness of the protagonist's biographical history before the age of twenty-four by means of his status as a "heavenly emissary," wounded, like Lermontov's angel, by the beauty of the eternal forms.[3] In this sense, his illness, which is said to cause memory loss (8:48), adds to the aura of the saintly figure, providing a screen from the mysteries of an ostensibly divine origin.[4] Alternately, critics have dealt with the lack of memory or personal biography in Myshkin by approaching him as a thoroughly selfless, ethical, and dialogical personality whose biographical past is obscured as a result of his utter immersion in the concerns of those around him, his fierce dedication to the "perpetual present," and his radical, unswerving responsiveness to the face of the other.[5]

The Prince's amnesia, however, is persistently linked in the novel to a debilitating fear of something that lies within and that is constantly rising up toward the sphere of conscious awareness. When, for example, the Prince is reminded of himself as a "ten or eleven year-old" boy who was beaten with birch rods, his lack of memory concerning that time ("I don't remember anything!" [8:447]) suggests the presence of a submerged memory system, especially as the mention of his childhood evokes a convulsive and dangerous state of nervous overexcitement and leads ultimately to an epileptic seizure: "The prince trembled all over. Why he had suddenly become so agitated, why he went into such emotional rapture, [. . .] not at all, it seemed, in measure with the subject of conversation, would have been difficult to decide" (8:448). Though the narrator expresses bewilderment as to Myshkin's sudden nervous eruption, those around him recognize his state as having been brought on by the unexpected reference to his childhood. As one guest notes, the mention of the Prince's "benefactor has already shocked you too much [. . .] you are inflamed" (8:452). Touching here momentarily upon an emotionally charged and sensitive childhood memory, we begin to suspect the existence of a more expansive system of buried memories that underlies the novel's events and that exerts an influence on its principal characters, each of whom bears some relation to what has been erased and forgotten.

In this chapter, I read the novel through the lens of distressing memory, through the buried, damaging, and haunting past experiences that can be said to prevail intensely upon the novel's protagonists—especially Myshkin, Rogozhin, and Nastasia Filippovna—prompting them, in their attempts to escape, erase, or preserve facets of their personalities, to dissolve themselves into a larger, collective unity. More explicitly than with many of his earlier protagonists, Dostoevsky, in his depiction of Myshkin, imagines a wounded individual who struggles to distinguish between a projective world, populated with reflections of his own psyche, on the one hand, and the actual world of other people, on the other. I shall argue that Dostoevsky, in *The Idiot*, significantly expands on his meditation of the collective self from the earlier works by depicting Myshkin's attempts to overcome the pathological dispersal of self into others, to escape the darkness of his projective psychic terrain into the "real" world of others. Thus, the central problem of the novel is one that Dostoevsky has prepared over the course of his writing leading up to *The Idiot*: namely, the question of how to rebuild the personality from its projective dispersal into others; and how to liberate others from their confined status as extensions of one's own personality.[6] In this context, the hero's mysteriously undefined quest in the novel becomes, I shall argue, the need to discover a principle outside of the self—to find an anchor for the personality in something that has not been compromised by the all-annexing solipsism of the damaged psyche.

THE BEARER OF MEMORY

In depicting the collective personality in *The Idiot*, Dostoevsky draws extensively upon the symbolic vocabulary of collapsed interiority developed in the earlier works. Myshkin's recognition of Nastasia Filippovna from her portrait, for example, draws on a number of previous manifestations; most strikingly it recalls Ordynov's convulsive astonishment upon seeing Katerina (in "The Landlady"), whose face "cuts into the youth's memory" with an "obscure, unbearable pain" (1:270) and sends him into a state of uncontrollable sobbing. Just as Ordynov sensed "traces of [. . .] mysterious horror" and a "terrible crime" concealed in Katerina's memory (1:268–70), so Myshkin is entranced by the impression on Nastasia's face of "repentance and horror" (8:352) and the traces of guilt for a vague but "horrific crime" (8:69). The Ordynov template directly informs Myshkin's characterization: that of a personality tormented by some sequence of painful, submerged memories which he confronts outside of himself in the arresting face of a suffering woman. Attempting to "decipher something concealed in this face," Myshkin sees yet another face, a hidden, "familiar face" that "calls" to him (8:142), a note of apparent resonance from his own inaccessible past.[7] In conflating Nastasia with aspects of his own remote memory, the prince experiences a concatenation of "oppressive" emotions upon encountering her portrait. "In the very face of this woman," we are told, "there was always something tormenting for him; [. . .] he hadn't found words to express the horror; yes, the horror!" (8:289). To Radomsky, he explains his seemingly bizarre behavior in relation to Nastasia Filippovna as a compulsion that stems from a visceral sense of terror at the face he "cannot bear" to apprehend: "I'm afraid of her face!" (8:484). Radomsky, a rationalist with no inkling of the submerged unconscious life of his interlocutor, naturally throws up his hands at the illogicality of Prince's explanation: "It seems you're getting married from some kind of fear? [. . .] what does it mean, this face which he fears and loves so much!" (8:484–85).[8] What Myshkin tries and fails to explain, however, is that his horror consists of the fact that, for him, Nastasia's face is not the face of the other.[9]

As in his earlier studies of traumatic memory, Dostoevsky conceives of Myshkin as an amnesiac who latches onto another wounded person's memories as a form of compensation for his own interior absence. In contrast to Myshkin (and much like Nellie from *The Insulted and Injured*), Nastasia Filippovna has carefully preserved her memories. Her own horrific childhood story, of a mother and family home burned in a fire (memories very similar to Katerina's in "The Landlady"), a father who lost his sanity and died in delirium, a sister who died of illness (all this by the age of approximately seven years old), and finally her sexual defilement at the hands of an "inveterate sensualist" (8:40), are very much alive both in the narrative exposition and in the heroine's psyche. In the culminating scene of the first part of the novel, she (apparently unwittingly) restages the destruction of her childhood as she places a package containing a hundred thousand rubles in the fire, forcing those around her to watch the flames in agony ("'it's burning, it's burning!' all cried in one voice, almost everyone straining toward the fireplace" [8:146]). The package, we are told, after she has ordered for it to be taken out, is "burned and smoldered, but it was immediately evident that the inside was not touched" (8:146). The description of the package resonates directly with Myshkin's portrayal of Nastasia several pages earlier as having "emerged pure from such hell" (8:138); both descriptions evoke the notion of an inviolate interior self preserved despite intense traumatic experience.[10] As with Vanya and Nellie in *The Insulted and Injured*, it is the secret, unspoken memory in Nastasia Filippovna—the interior fortune apparently undefiled within the tightly wrapped and smoldering package—that draws Myshkin, the amnesiac, to attach himself to her so inexorably.

Though it is difficult to determine precisely how intentional Dostoevsky was in building the plot of *The Idiot* around the compulsive attraction of an amnesiac to an embittered and vengeful carrier of memory, nevertheless, this approach helps us understand the numerous passages in the novel devoted to the Prince's active suppression of thought, emotion, and memory, which in each case leads him compulsively to search out Nastasia so as to protect her from herself. Throughout, Myshkin is incapable of considering the reasons for his overpowering attraction to the heroine.[11] When he asks

Chapter Four

himself about the causes of his attachment, he experiences the onslaught of deeper, more terrifying questions which force him to desist from any further reflection:

> "What will he do there and why is he going?" He decidedly couldn't find a reassuring answer to this question [. . .]. Yet another undecided question presented itself, one so crucial that the Prince was even afraid, even unable, to think about it, didn't dare to permit it, didn't know how to formulate it, and blushed and trembled at the mere thought of it. (8:114)

Attempting to explain to himself the compulsion to see Nastasia, Myshkin is arrested by the uprising of painful memory: "[her face] inspires suffering, it grasps hold of the whole soul, it . . . and a burning, tormenting memory suddenly passed through the prince's heart" (8:191).[12] Like Ordynov with Katerina, the Prince is desirous to explore Nastasia's memories, to attempt to "disperse her darkness" by helping her to come to terms with her past, as a way, it seems, of displacing or distracting himself from the memories and impressions that are constantly welling up within him against his will.[13] Nastasia, indeed, is a highly appropriate bearer of memory (or cathected object) for the Prince since—as in the case of Ordynov and Katerina ("her life had become his life, her sorrow his sorrow" [1:294]), or Netochka and Laria ("I instinctively felt that his grief was akin to my grief, which I felt at times painfully in my soul" [1:441])—Myshkin's and Nastasia's pasts are structurally parallel; both lost their parents at the age of six or seven under mysterious circumstances and were adopted afterward by "benefactors."[14]

A wounded personality susceptible to annexation, Nastasia has, in turn, long dreamed of losing herself within the capable administration of another person. "I kept imagining someone like you," she tells the Prince, "who would suddenly come and say: 'You are not to blame [. . .] and I adore you!'" (8:144).[15] Varya points out the mysterious "influence" that the Prince immediately wields over Nastasia (8:101), as she instinctively begins to defer her agency to him ("As you say, so I shall do" [8:130]). Just as in the earlier works that describe the relationship between the amnesiac and the carrier of memory, the Prince's influence, for all his intense compassion, has a destructive effect upon Nastasia, and we see that it is in fact his appearance as a savior that pushes the heroine into a state of insanity (8:140).[16] Later in the novel, in the midst of her increasingly erratic interactions with Myshkin and Rogozhin, the "damaged and half-witted" heroine (8:192) expresses the impression that her being has become utterly subsumed by others: "I already almost do not exist and I know this; God knows what lives in me instead of me" (8:380).

The novel depicts the process by which the intense mutual recognition of two wounded personalities exerts a debilitating effect on both parties and captures each within a fixed posture: an archetype as it were from one's own imagination, projected onto and overpowering the real other.[17] Though she first appears in the novel as a complex, unpredictable, self-possessed, and socially ingenious personality, Nastasia, through her interactions with Myshkin (and Rogozhin, as we shall see), is gradually reduced to the status of an "extraordinary apparition" (8:390), limited to primitive gestures of repentance and rebellion: the iconic "weeping woman" of Ordynov's imagination in "The Landlady."[18] As Myshkin's "heart overflows and moans with pain" upon seeing her, the generic quality of her gestures corresponds directly to those from his dreams, though he reminds himself that "this is not a vision!": "she went down on her knees [. . .] grasped for his hand in order to kiss it and, *precisely as earlier in his dream*, tears glistened now on her long eyelashes" (8:381–82; emphasis added). Not only do Nastasia's image and behavior correspond to those of the Prince's unconscious life, but her letters, one of the few occasions in the novel in which the heroine's voice emerges at length, also "resemble a dream" (8:377), expressing something that (like the witty remarks of the devil in *The Brothers Karamazov* for Ivan) already existed somewhere within Myshkin's mind:

> It even seemed to him as though he had already read this all, sometime long long ago, and everything about which he had suffered since that time, everything about which he was tormented and what he feared—all this was contained in these letters which he had read already long ago. (8:378)

In her letter to Aglaya, moreover, Nastasia behaves as an extension of the Prince's emotional life, taking on his feelings of love ("For me you are the same as you are for him") and becoming the bearer and expresser of his emotion. "I love you," she writes to Aglaya, "If it were possible, I would kiss your footprints" (8:379). Thus, in the relationship between Myshkin and Nastasia, Dostoevsky explores the imposition of one's own collapsed interiority upon that of another, who initially agrees, out of weakness and brokenness, to be annexed into a shared self, to give up administration of her own personality and to become an external expression of another person's suppressed unconscious life.

THE STATIONS OF THE SELF: WATCHMAN, PRISONER, REDEEMER

If Dostoevsky had once planned to write a novel about three children—Netochka, Laria, and Katia—all suffering from wounded or forgotten pasts, all of approximately the same age, and all of whom experience profound pathological, mutual recognition with regard to one another, he finally achieves this plan (over twenty years later) in *The Idiot* in the intersecting figures of Myshkin, Rogozhin, and Nastasia Filippovna, all of whom bear a complex relationship to a traumatic, haunted, or buried past and who, together, come to enact a collective self.[19] After the six months that they spend mysteriously together in Moscow between the novel's first and second parts, the three characters return to Petersburg as reduced, simplified beings. In their interactions, they are condensed as it were to specific gestures or aspects of their former selves, each locked into a particular dimension of one extended personality that envelops them all.[20]

The abrupt degeneration that characterizes Nastasia Filippovna under Myshkin's influence—into a weeping woman, an iconic *anima*—is even more strongly pronounced in Rogozhin who becomes (like Murin in "The Landlady," or Katia in *Netochka Nezvanova*, or Mr. Smith in *The Insulted and Injured*) a pure gesture of looking, an extension as it were of the hero's self-consciousness—a pair of eyes that exerts an uncanny administrative power over him. As has been noted, after Rogozhin's return from Moscow, his "intensely physical presence [. . .] is replaced by a phantom, a shadowy figure in the park, the product of a dream or hallucination."[21] In his initial interactions with Nastasia Filippovna we witness his gradual reduction to a pair of eyes, or to a personality which expresses itself entirely in relational space.[22] When Nastasia first suggests the possibility of choosing him from among her suitors, Rogozhin "simply gave a start and *gazed, all eyes,* as though not believing himself" (8:142; emphasis added). Later, as she vaguely enacts her own childhood trauma with the wrapped bundle of money in the fire, Rogozhin's transformation intensifies: "Rogozhin *himself turned into a single immovable gaze*" (8:146; emphasis added). Rogozhin's state of utter oblivion seems, at first glance, to be a form of generic hyperbole, an example of the sensual, romantic intensity of the "passionate character" or of the "Russian soul." "Everything else stop[s] existing for him" when he sees his beloved; he turns "pale" and his "heart beats terribly"; he begins to "stagger," "as if having lost all his reason," bumping up against others without noticing or apologizing, "completely stupefied, as though from a terrible blow to the head" (8:135, 142). Beneath the veneer of romantic clichés of emotional intensity, however, Rogozhin's mysterious and unreasoning compulsive behavior (which echoes Myshkin's state) reminds us of those projective episodes from Dostoevsky's earlier writing, since, as in the case of Netochka and Katia, for example, the compulsive need for the other drives all else from Rogozhin's mind, blotting out and replacing his entire interior life with "only one thing [that] remained constantly in his sight, in his memory and heart, every moment, every instant" (8:134).[23] He admits to Myshkin that he has no thoughts, and in Nastasia's absence only "remember[s] her every little word and [. . .] tone," while in her presence "I thought of nothing, I just listened to how she breathed in her sleep" (8:176). Like Netochka in Dostoevsky's earlier work, he rarely sleeps, and, when he does, he "dreams about her every night" (8:174). In Myshkin's presence too, Rogozhin compulsively assumes the gesture of a watchman, looking "extremely fixedly [. . .] observing every change, every fleeting expression on the Prince's face" (8:178), and he appears to the Prince constantly in the form of "the strange, burning gaze of someone's two eyes" (8:158).

Like Myshkin, Rogozhin is characterized by an absence of memory, though in a different sense. Rogozhin's house, whose very "physiognomy" is said to be an image of Rogozhin himself (not to mention of his "entire family and of [his] entire Rogozhin life" [8:171–72]), represents a veritable poetic treatise on the notion of buried and forgotten—rather than suppressed—memories. A "graveyard" (8:338), "with thick walls and extremely few windows," in which "both outside and inside [. . .] everything as though conceals itself and hides," the cavernous house is filled with depictions of indistinct and enshrouded memories: faces of dead people in picture frames which "it was very difficult to decipher" (8:172) since their features are covered in dirt and grime, "portraits of bishops and landscapes, of which it was impossible to make anything out" (8:181), the "suspicious, secretive and mournful" gaze of his severe and abusive father, looking out from among the blurry images on his walls and, locked away "somewhere under the floorboards" (or so it seems to Nastasia Filippovna), the remnants of a dead body which has been buried and forgotten. "He has a dark, dull house," Nastasia explains to Myshkin, "and there is a secret in it" (8:380). The corpse buried under the floorboards, she speculates, is part of the larger "secret" of his ever-watchful eyes (8:380), a secret that is concealed somewhere within Rogozhin's unconscious life. As we shall note later in this chapter, it is among these faint memory-images that Dostoevsky situates Hans Holbein's *Dead Christ*, the image of a divine corpse which haunts the novel's principal characters, and which Rogozhin refers to as the only image of value from among all the "trash" that covers the walls of the house (8:181). If Myshkin's memories are discarded and suppressed, and Nastasia Filippovna's bitter past is carefully guarded and preserved, Rogozhin's ignorance and inability to understand the significance of any of the images that surround him turn him into an unconscious agent of a burial ground, engendering in him, as we shall see, a need to re-create these images in the present.

As the three protagonists lose their breadth of character in each other's presence, they degenerate into the archetypal gestures of the self that constituted the topography of the externalized personality over the course of Dostoevsky's career—the tyrannical watchman (Murin, Rogozhin), the suffering prisoner (Katerina, Nastasia), and the helpless liberator (Ordynov, Myshkin)—or, to use a more traditional romantic vocabulary, mind, soul, and consciousness, but in a degraded and dispersed state.[24] If in Nastasia Filippovna's madness, Myshkin perceives a woman "on a chain behind an iron fence, under the stick of a watchman" (8:289), the state of her psyche draws Rogozhin into the posture of a cruel warden, compelled repeatedly, like Murin from "The Landlady," to "appear suddenly, [. . . to] take Nastasia Filippovna by the hand and [to lead] her away" (8:291, 382).[25] Myshkin, for his part, while also dreaming of a greater wholeness, finds himself trapped within a single gesture in his relations with both Rogozhin and Nastasia Filippovna, compelled continually to take on the futile attitude of the deliverer who dreams of liberating the soul from its imprisonment.

The problem Dostoevsky explores in the novel is the healing and untangling of these wounded selves, and thus Myshkin's own undefined quest becomes inseparable from his compulsion to assist in the reconstitution of the reduced and shattered personalities he recognizes as his own. Myshkin's aspirations in this regard are not unrealistic. He hopes, for example, that Rogozhin can be freed from the obsessive and reductive gesture of watchman, interestingly, through a study of the past. In his delight upon seeing Sergei Solovyov's "Russian History" on Rogozhin's table, Myshkin feels suddenly hopeful when he hears how Nastasia Filippovna had insisted on Rogozhin's education. Rogozhin himself, we discover, has sensed the potential expansion of his personality in this prospect: "for the first time I breathed like a living human being" (8:179). In the case of Nastasia Filippovna, her dueling instantiations—as the projective "soul" and the real other—exist in a state of constant tension, and her willful self-destruction (like Vasia Shumkov's bid for independence in "A Weak Heart") is her only line of defense in resisting her annexation by the Prince's personality.[26] In this struggle, even her face resists assimilation, never completely corresponding to the image Myshkin carries within; though "he knew her [. . .] to the point of suffering," yet "it was as though hers was altogether not the same face that he had always known" (8:352). For all his compassionate desire to save her, the Prince too senses the dangerous pathology of his compulsion, understanding that "here is something else, and not love!" "I know *for certain*," he tells Aglaya, "that she will perish with me, and that is why I am leaving her" (8:363). Thus, in a significant departure from the earlier works, Myshkin attempts to decipher the psychic force underlying his compulsive longing for Nastasia Filippovna, as he begins to suspect that in marrying her, he would in fact be marrying a "corpse" (8:492), something, in other words, ultimately inseparable from the darkness of his own personal memories.[27]

BEYOND THE SELF: ASCETIC IDEAL / INNER LIGHT

In this context, the Prince's quest can be described as an attempt to find a point *outside of the self*, uncompromised by projection, an anchor or a foundation of sorts that exists beyond the pervasive "darkness" of the solipsistic, pathological compulsion of mutual recognition. At first, the Prince comes to associate this quest with his romantic feelings for Aglaya Epanchina, who appears to him "in [his] darkness" as "a new dawn" (8:363) and whose existence allows him to experience "moments of full life" and "extreme hopes" for the future (8:264).[28] Nastasia Filippovna observes to Aglaya that "he remembered you as the 'light'" (8:379).[29] Aglaya (whose name, from the Greek, means literally "light," "shining," or "beauty") comes to represent, for Myshkin, at least three interconnected realities, all implicit in the Russian word *"svet"*—a bright light, the external world itself, and the community of high society. The promise of happiness with Aglaya makes life in the "real" world accessible to the Prince, and yet she represents simultaneously a transcendent ideal, an uncompromised principle of divine beauty, which the Prince, who keenly feels the anxiety of attempting to live in the world of others without the necessary psychological resources, hopes might sustain him and anchor his fragile being: "to think about one thing alone—oh! All his life only about this—and it would be enough for a thousand years! [. . .] Sometimes suddenly he would begin to peer at Aglaya and for five minutes not tear his gaze from her face" (8:287).[30] Aglaya herself articulates the Prince's desire to anchor his existence through allegiance to an "image of pure beauty" in Myshkin's attraction to the "enormous concept of some pure and lofty knight's medieval knightly platonic love," an "ideal" which Myshkin has "taken to the very final degree, to the point of asceticism" (8:207).[31]

This notion of the ideal (of devotion to and reliance upon a transcendent principle) proves ineffective in the novel as a means of anchoring the self, since it offers merely a form of temporary escape from the unwanted contents of the psyche and is ultimately powerless to counteract the unshakable hold of unintegrated memory upon the ascetic, idealistic lover.[32] The feelings of joy and forgetfulness that characterize Myshkin's love for Aglaya are admixed continually with an unwilling allegiance to the darker undercurrents of his being, which are personified in the discomfiting appearances of Rogozhin and Nastasia Filippovna who invariably bring "darkness" with them. As he delights in his feelings for Aglaya, "grasping her note from his pocket and kissing it," Myshkin finds himself wandering unwittingly into the "thick, shadowy alley" where "it was already completely dark" and where Rogozhin lies in wait, evoking through his "sudden appearance [. . .] a tormenting sensation [. . .] in [Myshkin's] heart" (8:301). As Myshkin attempts to live in the uncompromised world of "light," his moments of estrangement, confusion, and despair are tied likewise to the apparitions of Nastasia's "pale face, with curly dark hair, with a [. . .] very familiar smile and gaze" (8:287–88). The depiction of the amnesiac attempting to fortify himself by means of a transcendent ideal, but meanwhile bound steadfastly to the unwanted undercurrents of being, is ultimately crystallized in the tormenting confrontation scene between Aglaya and Nastasia Filippovna. Here Aglaya demands that the Prince abandon Nastasia without suspecting the extent to which Nastasia is indistinguishably tied to the Prince's own unconscious personality. As the ultimatum is placed, the Prince "only saw before him the despairing, insane face, from which [. . .] his 'heart had been forever pierced'" (8:474–75). In this sense, the confrontation between Myshkin, Aglaya, and Nastasia Filippovna is not the denouement of a tragic love triangle, as has often been supposed, but rather a depiction of the failure of ascetic self-transcendence since such a trajectory represents a mere escape from, or a disavowal of, the psychological "darkness" underlying the self.[33]

As a conceptual counterpoint to the external ideal of "pure beauty," Dostoevsky presents another source of light (of a place beyond the self) in the novel as internally beheld, a light approached not by extricating oneself from the weeping prisoner within, but which rather dwells beneath the most agonizing memories, which are too terrifying even to approach. This meditation upon a light beneath memory is situated in the Prince's interactions with Rogozhin that lead to Myshkin's epileptic seizure—pages that are perhaps the most opaque, mysterious, and difficult to read of Dostoevsky's entire body of work.[34] The chapter portrays Myshkin wandering the streets of Petersburg after his visit to Rogozhin's house, troubled by the feeling that Rogozhin is watching him. He boards a train to Pavlovsk, then leaves the train, goes instead to Nastasia Filippovna's house, and finally returns to his hotel, where Rogozhin confronts him on the stairs and is about to stab him with a knife when the Prince collapses into a seizure.

The episode focuses upon Myshkin's struggle to suppress a distressing series of impressions, feelings, and memories which he displaces and projects onto the figure of Rogozhin.[35] The description of projective identification, which is established explicitly in the text, constitutes perhaps the most straightforward exposition of this phenomenon in the whole of Dostoevsky's writing. As Myshkin walks through the streets of Petersburg, tormented by vague, suppressed thoughts, he discovers, as a means of temporary relief, a method of "attaching" his "memories" to objects in the external world:

> He attached his memories and mind to every external object, and he liked doing this: he kept wanting to forget something, something present, urgent, but in his first glance around him he immediately recognized his dark thought again, a thought from which he so wanted to untie himself. (8:189)

This remarkable passage offers a precise description of the transformation of the outside world into a projective map of the personality. The Prince, we are told, "attaches" his "mind" and "memories" to "every object" and finally "recognizes" his "dark thought" in the space behind him—in the very spot where Rogozhin is standing.[36] "Every object" becomes a dissociated signifier of something from the Prince's unconscious that he refuses to encounter as indwelling. Descriptions of the agony of struggling to suppress memory abound throughout the episode. "With disgust," we are told, the Prince "didn't want to solve the questions that rushed at his heart and soul"; he "suddenly as though remembered something, as if suddenly understood something, something very strange, something that had already bothered him for a long time." Rather than decipher the nature of this "something," Myshkin searches it out in the present moment: "he would forget even for a long time, for half an hour, and suddenly would look around again with anxiety and look for something around him." Having generated a shadowy projective world of the mind—as with the apparitions of Nastasia Filippovna—the Prince struggles to understand whether the landscape before him "really exists." To distinguish between the real world and the projective world, however, would require confronting his own thoughts and memories, and he finds himself incapable of such a course of action, as "some overpowering inner disgust again got the upper hand: he did not want to think anything over; he did not think anything over" (8:186–87).

Thus, both of Myshkin's seizures—the seizure at the end of this scene and the later seizure at the party that follows upon the mention of Myshkin's childhood floggings—are incited by exposure to unwanted memory that never quite surfaces.[37] In the scene with Rogozhin in Petersburg, the darkness associated with the memory that Myshkin is actively suppressing (and that he is in the constant process of "attaching" instead to the "objects" around him) finally consumes the outside world utterly, as the "storm cloud engulfs the evening light." Instead of recollecting "something that had already bothered him for a long time" (8:186), Myshkin sees the dim figure of Rogozhin in the "depths of the gates, in the semi-darkness, [. . .] a man [who . . .] quickly flitted by and disappeared." As with the blurry memory-images on the walls of Rogozhin's house, the Prince "could not make out clearly and of course could not at all say for certain who it was" (8:194). Here Dostoevsky draws on the earlier scene from *The Insulted and Injured* where Vanya, having banished his memories, sees Nellie in the darkness on the stairs, weeping—as a projective expression of his own unintegrated memory (3:210). At first the Prince, in keeping with his impulse to suppress, wants to avoid the figure in the darkness, "wanted to walk past and not look" (8:195), but then, "suddenly," and devastatingly for him, he confronts the figure directly: "the prince grasped him by the shoulders and turned back to the staircase, closer to the light: he wanted to see the face more clearly" (8:195).

In Myshkin's sudden and disastrous confrontation with his memory we begin to discern Dostoevsky's innovative adaptation of the Neoplatonic Augustinian notion of the divine presence that lies "beyond memory," namely, the metaphorical conception within numerous forms of Christian mysticism (both Eastern and Western) that the journey toward God is a "journey inward":[38] "it was as though something opened up before him": "an extraordinary *inner* light lit up his soul" before "his consciousness went out momentarily and complete darkness set in" (8:195).[39] Dostoevsky adapts the mystical notion of indwelling divinity by placing the "inner light" beyond a distinctly traumatic and horrifying memory. We are told that the Prince "could not allow for doubt" that what this principle revealed to him in his moments of collapse was "really 'beauty and prayer,' that this really was the 'highest synthesis of life'" (8:188). He is at the same time deeply uncomfortable with the seemingly pathological nature of revelation, the notion that the journey toward God, the flash of "extraordinary light" that magnifies the "sensation of life almost tenfold" and that illuminates "the mind and the heart," emerges from deep within the "sadness" and "pressure" of the "soul's darkness" (8:188).[40] The episode with "the man" beyond "the gates" (that is, Rogozhin; 8:194) illustrates the danger of approaching the sources that underlie memory, especially for a personality that is unaccustomed to the practice of introspection: for these sources have the power to destroy and overwhelm the self, as we see in Myshkin's near-fatal epileptic experience.[41] In the context of the failure of the ascetic ideal, however, the Prince's only hope in his quest to escape the all-annexing power of the self (and to release Nastasia and Rogozhin from their destructive bond to him) lies, it seems, in this harrowing "journey of inwardness."

INSIDE THE TOMB

The journey toward the innermost realm of the psyche underlies the novel's climactic scene, for the sake of which Dostoevsky once claimed to have written the entire novel (28.2:38). As Myshkin attempts to acquire access to Rogozhin's locked house (already vaguely aware of what lies inside—that is, Nastasia Filippovna's murdered corpse), he is in the process of trying yet again to remember something: "a feeling that was torturously striving to realize itself in some kind of idea; but he couldn't figure out what constituted this new thought that was thrusting itself upon him" (8:498). The windows of Rogozhin's house mirror the blurriness of Myshkin's memories in that they are "so dingy and so long unwashed that it [was] difficult to discern" anything "through the glass" (8:498). As Myshkin looks up at the shuttered windows of the house in which an image, the figure of Rogozhin himself, suddenly flickers and then disappears, the silhouette is difficult to distinguish, much like the blurry paintings on Rogozhin's walls:

The prince [. . .] stopped to look at the windows: not only were they closed but almost everywhere white shades had been drawn. He stood for a minute, and—strangely—it suddenly seemed to him that the edge of one blind was raised and Rogozhin's face flickered—flickered and disappeared in the same moment. (8:496)

In Myshkin's predicament on the sidewalk in front of the shuttered house, as he discerns only a flickering image in the window, we observe the hero's determination to remember (though this journey is enacted in external space), to encounter the almost imperceptible images in the edifice of his personality and the festering memory, or corpse, that lies within. We also see Dostoevsky's return, now with greater artistic power, and now in a more fertile philosophical context, to the figure of Ordynov desperate to find his way into the apartment where Murin and Katerina will enact the confusion of his own collapsed and dispersed personality.

As a reservoir of collective memory, Rogozhin's house evokes wider, civilizational implications, and thus the motif of the corpse in the shuttered house extends beyond the sphere of the protagonist's personal memory. Rogozhin, as has often been argued, is conceived as an image of the Russian people—he sits obliviously inside the "darkness" of his house (8:172), which is presented as a symbol of his "entire family and of [his] entire Rogozhin life" [8:171–72]).[42] The blurry portraits on the walls are also memories that extend into a collective past, all of which are almost wiped out but still vaguely present, even to the uneducated mind ("portraits of bishops and landscapes, of which it was impossible to make anything out" [8:181]).[43] It has been pointed out that Rogozhin's murder of Nastasia Filippovna is in fact the "acting out of a sectarian ritual," a reenactment of historical memory that abides in Rogozhin's family history, embedded deeply as the family is in Russia's religious past, and, more broadly, in the history of Christian civilization.[44]

Among all the blurred and indistinct images on the walls, all of which exert little effect upon Rogozhin, the one of greatest power and value (according to Rogozhin) is Holbein's image of Christ as a corpse.[45] Without understanding its significance, Rogozhin is nevertheless attracted to the painting. The Prince, for his part, does not want to look at the painting, and his revulsion is described again as a reluctance to confront a painful memory. We are told that, encountering the image of the dead Christ, "as if remembering something [. . .] he felt very oppressed and wanted to leave the house as soon as possible" (8:181). While the fact of a dead body, or of an unredeemed decaying corpse belongs, perhaps, to the Prince's own suppressed traumatic history (as it did to Katerina's from "The Landlady" and Nellie's in *The Insulted and Injured*), here it is also presented as a memory underlying and festering within the civilization as a whole. The placement of the Holbein painting in Rogozhin's house suggests Dostoevsky's response to Pyotr Chaadaev's highly influential description of the absence of any sustaining images within the collective memory of Russian culture, which has become cut off from the "sources of life," to use Lebedev's words in *The Idiot* for the great "connecting idea" (8:315), which he maintains has been lost in the contemporary world.[46] According to Dostoevsky, the emptiness and stagnation pervasive in Russian culture are not attributable to an absence of history (as Chaadaev maintains), but rather to an omission in the collective memory—namely, the death of Christ at the hands of the world. Because of an unwillingness to perceive the dead body within the "darkness" of the collective psyche, the killing of Christ is continually reenacted on multiple levels, from the contemporary Zhemarin murders that surface in the newspapers, to the murder of Nastasia Filippovna, whose body lies, like the image of Christ's corpse, in the deepest reaches of the tomb.[47] In Rogozhin's compulsion to kill Nastasia Filippovna, and in Myshkin's compulsion to save her, the two are not only ostensibly reenacting submerged patterns from their own personal memories, but also those of the forgotten history of the civilization as a whole.

The novel's climactic scene—the hero's entry into Rogozhin's house to encounter the corpse at its heart—is therefore also the hero's journey into the depths of the personality, both individual and collective. As Myshkin enters this tomb, Dostoevsky returns to the motif—that we saw in *The Insulted and Injured* (in Nellie's memory of her dead mother), and in *Crime and Punishment* (in Sonya's reading of the Lazarus episode)—of the deliverer arriving *too late* at the tomb and encountering a body that is already dead and festering.[48] Myshkin's attempt to face the content of the tomb is akin to his last effort to remember, a process enacted as the Prince journeys, led by Rogozhin, into the shuttered house (where no candles can be lit) into a dark room, where "it was possible to discern faces, but very indistinctly" (8:502), and he discovers, behind the thick curtain, the image of the dead body, barely discernible in the darkness. The conscious apprehension of an indwelling traumatic image (of Nastasia's corpse), however vaguely visible, in the depth of the tomb, entails the final disintegration of Myshkin's personality into its constitutive parts. Now the self, scattered among adjacent selves, appears in its utterly degraded gestures—a dead body, a shivering and babbling idiot, and an "absolutely open and motionless" set of eyes (8:506): the pieces of Myshkin's own mutilated personality (body, consciousness, and mind) which cling to each other in a kind of meaningless unity, now that the underlying connective principle of soul, the bearer of memory, has been destroyed.

Can one bring the body behind the stone to life and overcome the sense of a festering absence at the core of the self?[49] In subsequent chapters, I shall argue that the image of unredeemed memory will motivate Dostoevsky's theological inquiries throughout the rest of his career. By placing both Nastasia's corpse and the image of the dead Christ at the deepest reach of the unconscious, Dostoevsky dramatizes the despair that comes with the loss of the sources of life that underlie the self: "beyond memory" rather than in a living divine source, is the murdered corpse of a divine being, a source that no longer gives light—neither to the collective life of the civilization nor to the individual personality.[50] With all of Myshkin's intimations of the "divine light" within, Dostoevsky formulates a despairing image of the self in *The Idiot*, one which contains at its heart unillumined memory that will ultimately, if not attended to, poison, and destroy even the most "positively beautiful person" of whom his author could conceive.

DEMONS AND UNRAVELED SELVES (LOOKING AHEAD)

Dostoevsky's moral universe has often been described as essentially dualistic. Mitya's portrait of the morally divided self in *The Brothers Karamazov*—namely, that "the devil struggles with God, and the battlefield is the hearts of human beings" (14:100)—has been widely accepted as a precise formulation of Dostoevsky's own metaphysical psychology. Dostoevsky's protagonists have been perceived in this light as figures "out of a medieval mystery-play, standing between a good and an evil angel," and his supporting characters as anthropomorphized manifestations of good and evil, dramatizing the internal moral divisions of the protagonist.[51] Sonya and Svidrigailov, for example, have been read, respectively, as the good and evil impulses of Raskolnikov's personality, just as Alyosha and Smerdiakov have been interpreted as embodying the moral polarities of Ivan Karamazov's interior struggle.[52] This interpretation of Dostoevsky as a medieval "Manichaean" thinker tends to draw most emphatically upon the juxtaposition of Myshkin and Rogozhin, developed in such a pronounced manner in *The Idiot*. From the novel's first pages, when these "spiritual brothers" appear facing each other on a train, one light in complexion, the other dark, Dostoevsky, it is often claimed, asks us to envision these characters against the background of a dualistic philosophical canvas.[53] Rogozhin has accordingly been read as a "demon of death," an "embodiment of chaos and non-being," a "personification of fate," or a dead body from the underworld who pulls the angelic Myshkin into the darkness.[54] In their mutual opposition, Myshkin and Rogozhin, according to this prevalent reading, embody the interior moral polarizations of the figures who are drawn to them—for instance, Nastasia Filippovna and Ippolit—

Chapter Four

figures whose experience of the absolute dialectic of light and dark, spirit and matter, good and evil is dramatized through this attraction.[55]

Problems with such a view of Dostoevsky's moral universe are immediately evident. To accept a medieval anthropology and, thus, to approach any character as an embodiment of evil not only greatly reduces the complexity of Dostoevsky's moral philosophy and psychology, but also present a rather incoherent conception of evil, since each of these figures associated with "evil"—Svidrigailov, Rogozhin, Smerdiakov—represents a highly specific moral and psychological orientation. If, however, we approach the light/dark motif through the lens of the dispersed personality in *The Idiot*, we come to see the notions of light and dark as reflecting not absolute or abstract moral categories, but visceral, psychologically realized states of being.[56] As we have seen, the pervasive imagery of light and dark provides a backdrop to the hero's attempt to find a way out of the projections and extensions of his own psyche.

Dostoevsky's view of evil, in this sense, possesses a distinct psychological foundation.[57] In his study of the personality collapsed and dispersed into others, Dostoevsky draws a persistent parallel between the notion of demonic possession and the imprisonment of the self in the imagination of another person. The parallel between collective selfhood and demonic possession is especially striking in the bizarre scene leading up to Myshkin's epileptic seizure under Rogozhin's knife. Perhaps the most puzzling aspect of this episode lies in Myshkin's compulsion to behave in a manner so much at odds with his character. Indeed, by boarding a train, then exiting suddenly, and, feigning sneakiness, visiting Nastasia Filippovna's house, though he knows that she is not home and that Rogozhin is watching him, he knowingly acts in such a way as violently to inflame Rogozhin's morbid imagination. Here we observe a process by which, while fleeing his own memories, and falling under Rogozhin's ever-watchful, ever-pursuant gaze, Myshkin becomes so susceptible to Rogozhin's will that he becomes identical with Rogozhin's image of him. Thus Myshkin absurdly steals toward Nastasia Filippovna's house as if seeking out a romantic tryst, obeying the "sudden idea" that "came into his head," the "extreme incontrovertible desire, almost a temptation, [that] suddenly took over his entire will," from a "strange and terrible demon" that "attached itself to him definitively" (8:189, 193). Succumbing to the "revolting whisperings of his demon" (8:193), Myshkin arrives at the house, and realizes that his "convulsive desire" to act according to his "sudden idea" was prompted by the power of Rogozhin's eyes upon him (8:192–93). The scene dramatizes, therefore, not an essential conflict between good and evil, but the process by which the suppression of memory leads to a state of possession by others—or to a helpless compulsion to enact and reenact patterns suggested and imposed by the minds of other people.

Demonic possession is reformulated here as a relinquishing of self and an agreement to be subsumed by the will of another person.

It appears, then, that a demon, for Dostoevsky, at least in *The Idiot*, is neither a supernatural being that preys on the energies of the living, nor a bestial walking corpse from the beyond.[58] Myshkin's demon is a hollowed-out self, who, because of an interior emptiness, has the need to colonize and annex (or to be colonized and annexed by) other adjacent personalities. These uncannily possessive and invasive qualities of the self can be observed in Rogozhin's compulsion to play the role of the dark, menacing figure that rises out of Myshkin's own imagination or, in Myshkin's uncharacteristic compulsion to enact Rogozhin's thoughts and expectations, to become congruent with the phantasm that exists in Rogozhin's imagination. A similar transposition occurs during Myshkin's mortifying introduction into high society, when, becoming drawn into Aglaya's imagination, the Prince inexorably fulfills the action she has already prescribed of destroying her mother's vase. As Myshkin performs the scene precisely as Aglaya imagined it, he falls into a seizure that is described as a kind of demonic possession (they heard "the wild shriek of the 'spirit, which had shaken and thrown down' the unfortunate man" [8:459]). If Nastasia Filippovna's personality was embodied in the tightly wrapped fortune smoldering in the fire, Myshkin's personality acquires the very different incarnation of the beautiful, priceless vase, hollow and susceptible to being suddenly shattered. The hollowness of the possessed or possessing self is not its intrinsic state, but the result of an inability to turn inward, a consequence of the fragility of a self that has been chased by unwanted memory into the prison of a "perpetual present."[59]

Chapter Five

On the Education of Demons and Unfinished Selves

> Within the human being there is a permanent revolutionary tribunal [and . . .] there is a guillotine. Sometimes the judge dozes, the guillotine gets rusty, all that is false, of the past, romantic, weak raises its head and takes root, and suddenly some wild shock wakens the negligent court, the sleeping executioner; and then the fierce carnage begins. [. . .] We have not been called to harvest the past but to be its executioners, to execute, persecute, and recognize it in all its guises and to offer it up as a sacrifice to the future.
> —Herzen, *From the Other Shore*

> The devil's despair is the most intensive despair, for the devil is sheer spirit and hence unqualified consciousness and transparency; there is no obscurity in the devil that could serve as a mitigating excuse.
> —Kierkegaard, *The Sickness Unto Death*

"TWO NOVELS"

Demons (1871–72) has often been read as the most dramatic example of Dostoevsky's inclination to "sacrifice verisimilitude" in pursuit of a more expansive, metaphysical subject matter.[1] The impression noted in criticism of the novel's "mythical," "otherworldly" space-time conditions emanates principally from the figure of Nikolai Stavrogin and from the host of seemingly mesmerized interlocutors who encircle him as extensions or echoes of his being. In his depiction of Stavrogin's enchanted circle, Dostoevsky has been said to push beyond the limits of psychological realism, dismantling all boundaries between interior and exterior space, and thus widening his compass to portray not mere individuals but the collective tragedy of the "fate of the [. . .] Russian soul."[2] In this highly evocative allegorical conceit (of one collective personality which envelops the landscape of an entire novel), critics have perceived the strongest ground for distinguishing the author's earlier psychological realism from his later "metaphysical symbolism."[3]

It has also been noted, however, that this apocalyptic allegory does not seem to extend to the novel as a whole. Other dimensions of the narrative appear to fit comfortably within the tradition of European realism, especially those anchored in the comical, and fully embodied, portrayal of the tutor and liberal scholar Stepan Verkhovensky. Readers have accounted for this dissonance by emphasizing Dostoevsky's merging of two very different plans—a "political pamphlet" and a "metaphysical drama"—into one novel.[4] In the "pamphlet," the Verkhovenskys, father and son, are said to illustrate the relentless movement from liberalism to nihilism that characterizes the period between the 1840s and 1860s in Russia, with Stepan as the source of malignant socialist ideas that radicalize the younger generation.[5] The "metaphysical drama," by contrast, so it has been argued, offers a symbolic canvas upon which the novel's characters—shadowy fragments of a collective whole—clash and coalesce as embodiments of the ideas, desires, and unresolvable juxtapositions that Dostoevsky perceived in the Russian "national psyche."[6]

In this chapter I shall argue for a more integrated reading of the novel by looking closely at the peculiar nature of Stepan Trofimovich's pedagogy and the critical role it plays in the "metaphysical drama" of the collective self.[7] In the often ridiculous figure of Stepan (the "empty, empty, [. . .] eternally empty person" [10:502], as Varvara Petrovna calls him), we can discern a template for Dostoevsky's idiosyncratic notion of demonism, a template that helps illuminate the bizarre insubstantiality and interconnectivity of the novel's cast of characters. I shall argue that Dostoevsky's study of demonology in the novel emerges from his depiction of the flimsy, depthless, possessive and possessed personality of the tutor, who in his hunger to dissolve himself in others, develops a pedagogical practice with destructive consequences for the wounded, ravenous, and "unfinished" selves that grow up in his care. While Dostoevsky initially conceived of Stepan's culpability for the radicalization of the young as a consequence of his liberal idealism, the real Stepan, as he acquires life in the novel, has remarkably little interest in political ideology.[8] Closer scrutiny of his pedagogy reveals that Stepan's prevailing impact upon the youth lies not in the transmission of ideas, but rather in the concerted invasion of the self that he both pursues and embodies. Exploring the demonic qualities of the apparently innocuous "gentleman tutor" sheds significant light on the psychological underpinnings of Dostoevsky's metaphysical worldview and on his utterly unique and innovative concept of the demon.

THE SEEKER OF OBLIVION

One of the most informative portraits of Stepan in the novel is provided by the "poem" he once composed in his youth. Though presented only in a mocking paraphrase by the narrator, who emphasizes Stepan's vainglorious Faustian or even Christlike conception of himself as the protagonist of his own composition, the poem, nevertheless, calls our attention to a distinctive characteristic of the hero in his youth—an urgent desire to forget the past, a trait that links Stepan to so many of Dostoevsky's earlier protagonists:

> Between the cliffs wanders one civilized young man who tears and sucks some kinds of herbs, and to the question of the fairy as to why is he sucking these herbs, he answers that, feeling a surplus of life within himself, *he is seeking oblivion* and finds it in the juice of these herbs; but that *his main desire is to lose his mind as soon as possible* (a desire that is perhaps superfluous). (10:10; emphasis added)

This urgent desire to forget ("to lose one's mind as soon as possible"), it turns out, is Stepan's enduring feature in his later life, a longing he fulfills by habitually burying his secrets in the minds of others. The narrator describes, for example, how Stepan is "feverishly [. . .] compelled" to write the most humiliatingly candid confessional letters to Varvara Petrovna, insisting on baring everything to his benefactor ("I will die if I do not confess everything to her, everything!"). Upon receiving these communications, and reading them "always in the most attentive way," Varvara, we are told, stores Stepan's confessions not only "in a special drawer" but by "putting them away in her heart" (10:13), thus allowing Stepan to fall immediately into a state of lighthearted forgetfulness:

> She would never forget anything, and he would forget often altogether too quickly and, encouraged by her calm, often in the same day would laugh and behave like a schoolboy over champagne if his friends would come by. With what venom she must have looked at him in those moments, but he didn't notice a thing! (10:13)

This detail—of Varvara burying Stepan's revelation "in her heart," and thus allowing him to forget—is symptomatic, as we shall see, of a more essential union in which the two friends become extensions of each other's personalities.

As an illustration of the blurring of the self within a larger, collective unity, the narrator painstakingly elucidates the "most subtle and delicate of connections" that binds Stepan to Varvara, the "strange" friendship in which "both friends are on the verge of eating each other, [. . . but] cannot part," since one would "fall ill and possibly die" without the other (10:12).[9] According to the structure of their friendship, Varvara, like Arkady in "A Weak Heart," plays the role of governmental mind for both of them. Apart from supporting Stepan financially, she exerts a "fundamental [. . .] twenty-year influence [. . .] on her poor friend" (10:12), who behaves, in turn, like a "hysterical [. . .] fifty-year-old infant" (10:13). As a "nanny," she anxiously "guards" Stepan "from every speck of dust" and "from every trivial inclination" (10:16). Her investment in the creation and sustenance of her friend's identity goes far beyond guardianship, toward a visceral merging of selves as complementary aspects of one extended personality. Stepan becomes not merely Varvara's dependent companion, but her homunculus-like invention, a concentrated expression of her secret dreams:

> He had become finally her son, her creation, even, one can say, her invention, *became the flesh of her flesh* [. . .]. She had thought him up and she, first and foremost, believed in her invention. He was something akin to her dream . . . But for this she demanded a very great amount from him, sometimes even slavery. (10:16; emphasis added)

Varvara, we discover, dresses up her invention in clothing modeled after a portrait she "had fallen in love with" as a young girl and which she still kept among "her most intimate precious things" (10:19); and, perhaps as a result of Stepan's status as an extension or phantasmic projection of her innermost self, Varvara is extraordinarily sensitive to how Stepan is viewed by the world and disproportionately furious when he humiliates himself in the eyes of others. Treating him as an extension of herself, moreover, Varvara controls him by issuing "quick and mysterious" (10:47) executive orders that "astonish and torment [his] timid heart," but which he feels compelled to obey.[10]

Stepan's extreme dependency upon an external mind is reflected throughout his various relationships, since he, as a subordinate fragment of a personality, is not bound exclusively to one master.[11] In moments of disconnection from Varvara, he (much like Raskolnikov when separated from Razumikhin) immediately attaches himself to other, temporary hosts, most often the narrator, G—v. We are told that on these occasions, Stepan "throws himself greedily upon" the narrator (10:72), waits for him "in a state of hysterical impatience" (10:96), "conceals nothing" from him (10:53), and "needs" him "like water or air": "he couldn't be two hours without me" (10:66). The narrator notes Stepan's "inability to bear solitude" and his "constant thirst" for other people: "If no one would appear for a long time, then he would roam his rooms miserably, would go up to the window [. . .] would sigh deeply and finally all but whimper" (10:52). As we eventually discover, however, this personality, unraveled into relational space, possesses, nevertheless, stores of interior, atrophied agencies that, in the greatly undesired state of solitude, flicker and begin to come to life. These flarings-up of memory and self-consciousness, though fleeting, are invariably devastating (10:26), and express themselves in hysterical fits, convulsive longings for "independence," and crushing sensations of shame and despair. Stepan, we are told, "would suddenly burn from shame" in recalling "some expression of one of these letters, and then the whole letter," and be taken ill (10:13).

AN INVASIVE PEDAGOGY

In the limited glimpse we are given of the past before the events of the novel, we can observe that Stepan's overwhelming need to unravel his personality into relational space—that is, to insert himself as a fragment into other personalities and to draw energy from them for emotional sustenance—is equally pronounced in his relationships with the younger generation, especially with Liza, Pyotr, and Stavrogin. In each case, we are provided with a vivid description of Stepan's "embraces." If there is a pedagogical principle at work here, it seems to consist rather exclusively of a passionate, hungry, and tactile intimacy, a peculiar form of vampirism, which involves the transmission of all one's innermost secrets to one's pupils in order to awaken in them genuine and deep-seated emotions of empathy and grief. "It was amazing," the narrator observes, "how children became attached to him!" (10:59), the key to his success, we are told, being his "constant need for a true friend" (10:35), or, in other words, his perpetual hunger for others. In the case of Stavrogin, whose "education and moral development" was "fully entrusted" to Stepan (10:35), the embraces are all that is related of Stepan's "pedagogical" activity.[12] Dostoevsky is altogether uninterested in the content of Stepan's lessons and focuses instead on the unmistakable sense of trauma the pupil experiences when he is woken up in the middle of the night, embraced, and initiated, just as Varvara is by Stepan's habitual letters, into the tutor's secrets:

> It somehow naturally came about that there turned out to be not the smallest distance between them. More than once he would wake his ten or eleven-year-old friend up in the night, merely to unpour before him in tears his insulted feelings or to disclose some domestic secret to him, without noticing that this was already completely impermissible. They threw themselves into each other's arms and wept. (10:35)

These intimate nocturnal sessions are apparently traumatic for the child. We are told that "one must think that the pedagogue upset his pupil's nerves somewhat" (10:35), and that, when the two friends are finally separated, the intervention comes too late: "But in any case it was good that the pupil and the tutor, though not soon enough [*khot' i pozdno*], were parted in separate directions" (10:35).[13]

We can discern a similar pattern in Stepan's relationship with Liza Drozdova, in the description of how Stepan "fell in love with the delightful child," and of how they were constantly "throwing themselves into each other's arms" (10:59). Liza recounts to Stepan how "you used to throw yourself into my embraces [. . .], and I would comfort you and weep." Liza, for her part, becomes "ill and [is] taken to Petersburg at the age of eleven." Whether or not this repeats the pattern of Stepan's effect upon Stavrogin is unclear; we are only told that "in her illness [Liza] was somehow crying and asking for Stepan Trofimovich" (10:87). Stepan immediately puts his pedagogy into effect with his son, Pyotr, though the little boy was only in his presence for a very short period of time. "He would wake me up twice in the night," Pyotr relates, "embrace me and cry like a woman, and what do you think, what was he telling me about at night? Those very lewd anecdotes about my mother!" (10:240). This repeated image of interrupted sleep, accompanied by a constant demand for emotional support, provides a concise illustration of Stepan's educational activity. As a fragmented personality, desperate to "lose [his] mind as soon as possible," he exists by means of a kind of vampirism: a nightly activity ascribed to mythical beings who drink the blood of the hosts they assault. Ever hungry for empathy and human warmth, Stepan compulsively invades the private, as yet unformed unconscious interior realms of his pupils, tearing them from their sleep in order to puncture their dreams with the elements and details of his own unwanted interior life.

It would be hasty to conclude from these details that Stepan sexually abused a whole generation of children.[14] Rather, the pedagogical practices themselves are shown to be intrinsically harmful to these developing personalities: that is, the repeated invasion of the interior space of the other in order to fill that space with one's own secrets. These invasions throw the child's interior life into a state of imbalance and allow the tutor to feed off of the energy emitted from this process. Indeed, there is a striking disproportion between the emptiness of Stepan's personal secrets and the spiritual hunger, left unnourished, that they stimulate within the pupil:

> It was not only about some little domestic anecdotes that the friends wept, throwing themselves into each other's embraces. Stepan Trofimovich knew how to touch upon the very deepest strings of his friend's heart and to call forth in him the first, still indefinite sensation of that eternal, holy yearning,

Chapter Five

which any chosen soul, once it has tasted and known, will already never exchange afterward for cheap satisfaction. (10:35)

In Stepan's stirring of an "eternal, holy yearning" in Stavrogin, we recognize an echo of the earlier description of childhood trauma in "The Landlady,"[15] of an old man who tortures a child by whispering an "unchildlike [. . .] fairy tale" to him at the head of his bedside:

> While Ordynov was asleep, the evil old man sat down at the head of his bed [. . .] and began, for whole nights on end, to whisper a long, marvelous fairy tale to him, which was unintelligible to the child's heart, but which tore at him, upset him with terror and unchildlike fear [. . .]. (1:278)

As we saw in "The Landlady," the old man's whispering induces a state of interior collapse in the child. While Stepan's waking of Stavrogin possesses none of the Gothic terror of its precursor, it nevertheless exerts a lasting impression on the boy, who is "frail and pale, strangely quiet and thoughtful" (10:35) when he is finally sent away from his tutor. Stepan's hungry embraces and excessive intimacy, moreover, comprise the only element that is related from the childhood of a character who, as he appears in the novel, seems, as we shall see, to be suffering from a lost traumatic memory. When Stavrogin, in turn, embraces the childlike Matriosha, we are given the detail that he "kept whispering something to her" (11:16), a mysterious action that is somehow connected to the old man whispering to the tormented child in Ordynov's dream, and to the tutor at the young boy's bedside waking him in the middle of the night to tell him all of his innermost secrets.

While Stepan's pedagogy, at first glance, appears to have little to do with the sinister and violent activities of the younger generation, a closer look reveals a direct connection between his intrusions into his students' psyches and the subsequent explosion of destructive activity in the town. It is noteworthy, for instance, that all three children who experience Stepan's embraces grow up eager to annex and overpower other personalities.[16] Liza, referred to in the notebooks as the "Horsewoman" ("Naezdnitsa"), appears in the novel "as a conqueror." "Ill" and suffering from "morbid, nervous, constant anxiety," her personality ever in a state of "chaos" (10:88), she "reveres, loves and respects" the compliant Mavrikii Nikolaevich (10:259–60), while "aggressively, inexorably demanding" that he bow down at her bidding: "kneel without fail, I want to see how you will kneel" (10:259). As she capriciously imposes her will upon him, she imagines him as a potential extension of her wounded body, that is, her legs (10:157). Likewise, Pyotr, who first encountered Stepan's embraces as "a nervous boy [. . .] very sensitive and . . . fearful" (10:75), resurfaces as an administrative agency wielding dominion over whole groups of people. Indeed, Pyotr's constant occupation is the active conquering and assimilating of other personalities as he discerns and assumes vacancies in others, for example, in Erkel' "from [whose] head the tsar was missing," or, in other words, who has no capacity for self-administration but who has "enough of little, submissive sense" (10:439). Liputin, for his part, realizes that under Pyotr's influence, he himself is "only a coarse, senseless body, an inert mass [. . .] moved by a terrible extraneous force" (10:430). The scene of Shatov's murder, moreover, an act with which Pyotr intends to bind the conspirators to his will forever, involves dramatic and passionate embraces, of which Stepan's were, by comparison, benign echoes. When Liamshin embraces Virginsky, screaming, and then "firmly grasps [Pyotr] in his embraces, pressing himself to his breast with his head" (10:461), the bizarre demonic intimacy bears a distinct relation to Stepan's tactile nocturnal lessons.[17]

As far as Stavrogin is concerned, he inherits from his tutor both the desire for oblivion and the need to shed the unbearable internal "surplus of life" through the external embrace of the other. Thus, as with the habitual practices of his "eternally empty" teacher in whose vigorous embraces he came to consciousness, Stavrogin's defining characteristic is his desire to "discard" his "memories," a feat which he believes can be achieved by a simple act of will: "I discarded them all at once in a mass, and the entire mass obediently vanished each time as soon as I wished it" (11:21). The sleeping Stavrogin appears to his mother as "a soulless wax figure," "too motionless," "almost without breath" (10:182). Readers—describing Stavrogin as "innerly stagnant," "vacuous," "empty," "pure nothingness," even "terribly, ominously, hellishly absent"—have often treated this decisive trait in the protagonist as an aspect of Dostoevsky's conception of evil, with Stavrogin as "the incarnation of that zero point, the pure nothingness of absolute pride."[18] These critical appraisals of Stavrogin's character, however, present an incomplete picture. When we encounter him in the novel, he is not "pure emptiness," but is suffering rather from a growing inability to erase and suppress the interior dimensions that he senses within himself. These interior elements take on the form of at least two projective apparitions (in other words, elements of his psyche that he displaces into external space): the first "some kind of malicious being, contemptuous and 'reasonable,' which assumes 'various faces and characters'" (11:9); and the second, the "almost daily" apparition of the abused Matryosha, "wasted away and with feverish eyes, precisely as she was when she stood on the threshold and [. . .] raised her tiny little fist toward" him (11:22).[19] Finding it unbearable to keep the latter image within, Stavrogin desires, in vain, to make it somehow external. "If only, if only it had been a real apparition!" he exclaims to Tikhon, "oh, if only I could see her once in reality, even if only in a hallucination!" (11:22). His desire, expressed only semi-coherently, is not to return Matryosha to life (he wishes even for a hallucination), but to have the vision occur outside of himself.[20]

If Stavrogin's activities consistently reflect the endeavor to project outward unwanted interior memories by finding an appropriate "burden" in external space (10:228), his "crimes" occur according to a strict template, involving, in each case, the sudden intimate embrace of an uncomprehending and astonished other: either in grasping suddenly onto Gaganov's nose (10:39), or in sending the "terribly timid" Madame Liputina "into a faint" by "clutching her by the waist and kissing her on the lips" (10:41) or again in propelling the "lovely, gentle Ivan Osipovich" into a "fit" from "mortal terror" when Stavrogin "suddenly clasps onto the upper part of his ear with his teeth and quite firmly clenches down on it" (10:37, 43). With these actions, performed hypnotically, as though "lost in thought" (10:39), Stavrogin, in each case, imposes the image of a helpless, terrified, and invaded creature onto yet another person in the outside world.[21] Through his bizarre embrace of Matryosha, moreover, Stavrogin comes to externalize his suicidal self-hatred: "the sensation was tormenting [. . .] I started to hate her to the point that I decided to kill her" (11:17).[22] These embraces, moreover, have consequences which allow the images of Stavrogin's interior life to project themselves outward into the world. Matryosha's menacing fist, for example, so unbearable as an internal memory, appears recurrently in the "child's little fist" of hair on his wife's head (10:114), and later in Shatov's "fist" that strikes him unexpectedly (10:164). If Stavrogin thus turns the world of the novel into an externalized map of his personality, we can also see that this process begins not as a poetic allegory, but as a visceral and compulsive need to extend the self into others, to colonize others by puncturing the boundaries of other selves: a need that characterizes the very essence of his childhood lessons.

THE EPIDEMIC OF *BEZLICHNOST'*

While it would be an overstatement to identify Stepan Trofimovich as the main cause of the epidemic of *bezlichnost'* (impersonality or facelessness) in his provincial town, he is at least the most discernible and psychologically fathomable exemplar of the condition, and provides the reader with a key for understanding the loss of self that Dostoevsky detects in the younger generation. Indeed, the violation or invasion of personal privacy and the willing revelation of one's all that Stepan embodies are constant themes in the world of the novel where the interior realm is in a perpetual state of bombardment and disintegration. Pyotr's remarkable, almost uncanny, knowledge of everyone's secrets (not only what Tolkachenko whispers in private, but even how Liputin pinched his wife under the sheets at midnight [10:418]), does not come from supernatural abilities. Rather he (like Liputin, the "spy" with "his maneuvers" to "worm out all your little secrets" [10:83]) capitalizes upon a general incapacity for secrecy that he perceives in the world around him, the "absolute powerlessness," observed by the narrator, of "these people to keep their desires within themselves" and the "uncontrollable urge to disclose them immediately, even in all their slovenliness, as soon as they arise" (10:140). While the author Karmazinov declares that there are things too "sacred" to be spoken aloud, yet he, of his own accord, proceeds to expose his deepest "*svyatynya*" ("sacred space") to a hostile and jeering crowd (10:365). Moreover, the "demonic" disorder and trickery that ascends in the town to new heights during this period, the "pranks" played by the younger generation, are invariably depictions of the violation of privacy, of space that has traditionally been considered inviolate.[23] Whether in the incursions into the intimate details of strangers' marriages (10:250), or the insertion of "vile photographs" into the bag of a Gospel-seller (10:251), or the absurd placement of a mouse in the smashed icon case in the church (10:253), or again, in a group of young people entering the cell of a recent suicide and eating the grapes from the table next to his corpse (10:255–56), the theme uniting these exploits is the invasion of inviolate space.

While Chernyshevsky celebrated the transparency of the Crystal Palace as a utopia of universal joy, Dostoevsky conceives of the loss of an interior, private realm within the self as directly related to the notion of demonic possession. Thus, Pyotr's revolutionary plans rest upon the premise that it is the absence of an "inner idea" within the personality (10:76) or the loss of the individual mind ("a mind of one's own'" [10:322]) that causes one to become "a plaything of the most diverse influences" (10:268) and to succumb to an "external [. . .] despotic will" (10:404).[24] Pyotr himself is described throughout as a kind of "half-person" (10:470), as the smaller part of a larger personality (10:408), and we discover that it is precisely because of his insubstantiality that he is able so effectively to take possession of others. In other words, the notion of interior emptiness characterizes both the possessed and the possessors, both demoniacs and demons. Though Kirillov, for instance, regards Pyotr with contempt, Dostoevsky depicts his subsequent possession by Pyotr, a process dramatized in the latter's act of dictation, that is, in Pyotr's near-literal annexation of Kirillov's executive will: "'I, Aleksei Kirillov,' firmly and commandingly dictated Pyotr Stepanovich, bending over Kirillov's shoulder and following every letter." Kirillov, we are told, falls under the other's command in a moment of weakness, as his "tormented spirit [. . .] plunged headlong" into an "exit" (10:472). In this scene, where the "half-person" latches onto the "paper person" (10:110, 111) and assumes control of his being, we are given a fully embodied depiction of demonic possession, that is, of two hollowed-out selves merging to form a collective personality.

Dostoevsky, in his exploration of the invasion of self into other, espouses a fully psychologized and strikingly literal conception of demonic possession.

In this context, the resolution to honor and preserve personal secrecy acquires a sacred connotation in the world of the novel. The private, inward realm becomes the site for the rebuilding of the self from its destruction and possession. The narrator, for his part, expresses a fervent wish to protect the secrets of his beloved Liza, even from his own inquiring mind: "Her secrets had suddenly become something sacred to me, and even if they were to start revealing them to me now, [. . .] I would have covered my ears" [109]); and Maria Timofeevna is distinguished from the others by her impassioned refusal to reveal her secrets, secrets, it could be argued, that the reader never ultimately discovers: "I won't say, I won't say, you can cut me, and I won't say [. . .] burn me, I won't say. And no matter what I endure, I won't say anything" (118). Most significantly, perhaps, we observe a distinctive change in Stepan Trofimovich. Just as the victims of the demonic pranks can only protect themselves by closing the blinds of their windows and opting out of the public space of the novel where all is known (10:250), so Stepan begins to fortify himself in his struggle against the "demons" by "locking himself in" and admitting no one (10:376), thus relying on "mysterious" sources for reinforcement (10:180), sources that lie outside of the realm of intersubjectivity. These closed doors, drawn curtains, and determined silences become, as we shall see, the sites of the defense in the novel against the demonic destruction, dispersal, and possession of the self.

THE "GREAT ETERNAL THOUGHT"

The pervasive sense of emptiness in these annexable personalities evokes the question of what, by contrast, would constitute a substantial self. The demanding feat of fleeing the dominion of others in pursuit of a realm of interiority is enacted by Stepan (the very person who helped to engender this condition in his pupils) in his journey of escape from Varvara's patronage. Stepan's quest, in this light, becomes more than the ironic depiction of a spoiled and financially dependent Russian gentleman's experiment with Western self-reliance. Rather, in Stepan's quest, for all its lack of success, we can observe the attempt to rebuild his personality, to recover the self from its scattered shreds, and thus to discover an antidote to the condition of demonic possession. In chapter 1, we traced Vasia Shumkov's harrowing struggle in "A Weak Heart" to disentangle his personality from that of his loving and domineering friend, Arkady. We observed that in the absence of his friend's surveillance, Vasia experiences an immediate descent into frenzy and self-destruction, a paradigm that repeats itself in Raskolnikov's hysterical and ultimately unsuccessful attempts at self-direction. Numerous textual resonances indicate that Dostoevsky held to the Vasia Shumkov paradigm when writing *Demons*, as distant and half-forgotten as the earlier story must have been a quarter of a century later. Reading *Demons* in light of that paradigm helps us to grasp the significance of Stepan's struggle and the religious dimension of his flight that extends, as we shall see, to the parallel journeys of Maria Timofeevna and Matryosha.

Early in the novel, in the face of the humiliations evoked by Varvara's growing tyranny, Stepan begins to turn inward and to search for interior sources of fortification (10:73).[25] Knowing him well, Varvara ridicules the notion that Stepan could exist apart from her sustenance, and the narrator seems to agree that Stepan lacks the resources that could free him from his profound dependency. "You're broken to pieces like an empty glass," he tells Stepan, emphasizing his friend's lack of inward substance. "Where will you go now without me? [. . .] You'll only perish" (10:376). As the narrator observes Stepan's newfound withdrawn solemnity, however, he marvels at the "extraordinary firmness" (10:376) of his friend's resolve. "From where did he get so much spirit?" he wonders (10:162), and surmises that Stepan, in attempting to wean himself from external sources, "fortified himself on some kind of final and extreme idea" (10:170). As Stepan launches his escape, he continually loses grasp, however, of his "mysterious resolve" and becomes disoriented amid an "enticing influx of ideas" (10:170).

In his new state of intense uncertainty, attempting to abide alone without his external sources of sustenance, Stepan is characterized both by a mysterious dignity and helpless paranoia—a combination of traits that evokes Vasia's condition in his parallel attempt to free himself from Arkady's control. In the earlier story, Vasia, awakening to a chaotic world in which he must bear responsibility for his actions, is overcome by nervous terror, and he imagines unlikely scenarios in which he will be sent, as punishment for his crimes, to military service, while Arkady, astonished at Vasia's growing insanity, attempts to assuage his friend's panic. These scenes are replayed in *Demons* as the narrator tries in vain to convince Stepan that his severe anxiety over the prospect of corporal punishment comes from a deluded and overanxious imagination: "it was obvious that he had become very confused. [. . .] He sobbed, sobbed for five minutes, convulsively [. . .] like a tiny, naughty boy waiting for a birching" (10:330–31). Stepan, in his state of awakening, is, like Vasia, both utterly unreachable and desperately dependent upon his interlocutor, "barely listening" to the latter while nevertheless "needing terribly for [him . . .] to speak incessantly" with calming reassurances: "I saw that he could not get by without me now and would not have let me go from him for anything" (10:331).[26] In both characters, the longing to accept responsibility comes from an explicit desire for greater personal

Chapter Five

wholeness. As Stepan explains, "I am a citizen and a person, and not a wood chip, [. . .] for twenty years I did not demand my rights, all my life I criminally forgot about them . . . but now I demand them" (10:334).[27]

The flight of the subdued self is much more intentionally crafted in *The Demons* than in the earlier story. Stepan, for instance, is conscious that, in leaving his twenty-two-year relationship with Varvara Petrovna, he has broken himself "into two halves," and is discarding entire facets of his personality (10:412).[28] In his flight, like Vasia who clutched at his burdensome head during his escape, Stepan does not possess a fully formed executive mind—his mind contains only "fragments of thoughts and impressions" (10:482), and he is vaguely aware of a "morbid weakness of mind" in himself (10:483) as he flitters in and out of consciousness, forgets where he is, and falls into oblivion in the middle of a conversation. Encountering him on his path, Liza sees him as a pitiful child (10:412), and the peasants notice that he is "mentally like a small child" (10:488). Unable ultimately to sustain himself emotionally, he binds himself almost immediately to yet another host, Sofia Matveevna, giving her all his money, and expressing the desire to transfer the burden of consciousness onto her: "take it, take it, I'm not able, [. . .] it seems to me that I want to sleep; something is spinning in my head" (11:491). The habitual pattern almost immediately reasserts itself, when, longing instinctively to "initiate" Sofia into his secrets, Stepan immediately proceeds to reveal "everything, everything" to his overwhelmed and disconcerted new companion (10:493–94), thus reducing her over the course of three ensuing sleepless nights to a shadow of her former self by means of his emotional voracity.

In Stepan's failed attempt to exist outside of a state of possession by others, he nevertheless, by means of his flight, discovers glimpses of an inwardly strengthening presence that lies both within and beyond the self. Initially, as we have mentioned above, the narrator notices that Stepan, in his detachment from Varvara, "fortified himself on some kind of final and extreme idea, which gave him calm" (10:170). The fortifying idea gradually acquires religious overtones over the course of Stepan's quest. At first taking the form of the ascetic ideal of "eternal Beauty" (10:266), the idea undergoes a subtle transformation during Stepan's flight into an inwardly beheld activity of divine energy that is both distinct from and intrinsic to the self.[29] On his deathbed, Stepan's "idea" appears as an indwelling activity, as "a fire of love for [God] that has flared up in [his] heart" that "fills the whole of [him] with boundless tenderness and glory" (10:505–6). He bemoans his friends' failure to realize the depths and riches of this newly discovered interiority: "they do not know that in them is contained the eternal Great Thought," the "crown of being," by virtue of which the personality is both "boundless" and "immortal" (10:506).[30]

Perhaps it is this discovery on Stepan's part that allows the two friends upon their reunion to see each other, however momentarily, not as the complementary and unequal agencies of a collective personality, but rather as separate selves. As Stepan expresses his love to Varvara (*"je vous aimais"*), she, for her part, admits, albeit idiosyncratically, to having been hurt by him. In her anger, she shakes him violently as if trying to awaken the atrophied interior agencies within her friend: "'Do you remember,' she jumped up from her place and having grabbed his pillow by both corners and shaking it together with his head, 'Do you remember, you empty, empty, ignominious, faint-hearted, eternally, eternally empty man!'" (10:502). Varvara, however, promptly gives up trying to wake him, and opts instead for the more habitual arrangement of their shared personality, forcefully sending him to sleep, and thus emphasizing the failure of Stepan's heroic quest for the reconstitution of the self: "If you don't fall asleep now, I'll . . . [. . .] sleep, sleep now, close your eyes" (10:502).

THE PRETEND SLEEPERS

As Stepan falls once again under Varvara's dominion and lies supine under her watchful gaze, the narrator adds the intriguing detail that Stepan, like Vasia under Arkady's watch, was "probably pretending" to sleep (10:502). A recurrent motif of the novel (as well as in Dostoevsky's works in general, as we have seen), this image of pretend sleep helps us to grasp the inherent religious dimension in the journey of escape from the other. We can recall briefly the appearance of this image in "A Weak Heart": In his dream, Arkady sits vigil over Vasia's bed, guarding his friend so as to ensure his rest and recuperation. Vasia it turns out, is only pretending to sleep, and begins to creep toward his writing desk, thus furtively pursuing an escape from his captivity. As Arkady moves to "grab" Vasia and "carry him to the bed," we are told that "Vasia screamed out in his arms" and became "a lifeless corpse" (2:43). In *Demons*, the image of pretend sleep is evoked not only in Stepan's subordination to Varvara, but equally in Stavrogin's subjugation of those selves he attempts to annex into himself. Experiencing the "tormenting sensation" of being unwillingly bound to Matryosha after his invasive embraces of her, Stavrogin observes the young girl through a screen, while she pretends to sleep (11:18). A similar scenario is established in the meeting of Stavrogin and Maria Lebiadkina. When he first sees her, he stands above her, "examining the sleeping woman" for almost a minute (10:214), although later she insists that she "was only pretending to sleep" (10:219).

If Vasia Shumkov was prompted to break away from Arkady's control by insisting upon his guilt before a higher power (the sublime authority of

Chapter Five

Yulian Mastakovich), the flight from the other in *Demons* is consistently presented as a religious quest. Lebiadkina's refusal to be ruled by Stavrogin, for example, replays Vasia's insistence on his own guilt before a divine authority. As Stavrogin (like Arkady) desperately attempts to calm her, Lebiadkina holds onto her secret fear and refuses to be comforted, insisting upon her "guilt" before a higher authority, a "bright falcon and a prince" whom Stavrogin, "a blind owl," has tried to replace: "I must be guilty before *him* [. . .] Always, all these five years, I was afraid day and night, that I was somehow guilty before him.[. . .] I would pray and think constantly about my great guilt before him. And so it turned out that it was true" (10:217). Like Vasia, she demands recourse not to another person, but to a divine judge, whom Stavrogin has attempted to supplant, but whom she continues to imagine as distant and inaccessible: "O Lord! I was happy all these five years in the knowledge alone that somewhere there beyond the mountains, my falcon lives and flies, peers at the sun" (10:219).[31] Stavrogin's decision to murder Lebiadkina brings Arkady's dream to life since her refusal to accept her subordinate role in a collective personality prompts him instead to force her into the gesture of a "lifeless corpse." In the parallel case of Matriosha, the young girl launches her rebellion by "suddenly leaping out from behind the screen" after pretending to sleep under Stavrogin's gaze for "a whole hour" (11:18). In Matryosha, however, we see an echo of the devastating power of Stepan's invasive lessons with his students. If Stepan and Lebyadkina fortified themselves, however unsteadily, through recourse to an eternal principle (encountered either inwardly or "somewhere there beyond the mountains"), Matriosha bemoans the impression that, in her embraces with Stavrogin, she has "killed God." In other words, the destruction of the personality begins with the invasion of the interior world of the child, an action that leaves only the possibility of an outward connection to the other, a form of utter imprisonment in relational space.[32]

In an environment determined by hungry, invasive intimacy, the image of forcibly closed eyes functions as a refuge against the violation and destruction of the self. The three pretend sleepers—Matryosha, Maria Timofeevna, and Stepan Trofimovich—are all fugitives from a larger collective self, and each, in closing his or her eyes, is attempting to nurture an inwardly sustaining realm that might free the self from its entrapment within the other. In Stepan's case, this final detail of pretend sleep under Varvara's watch suggests that the personality, though seemingly reclaimed and subdued by the other, nevertheless holds, at least potentially, to the newly discovered idea and therefore maintains the possibility of an inward anchoring. Among the dead bodies and destroyed selves that litter the novel's final pages, this subtle action, though by no means a triumph for the personality, lays the groundwork for the rebuilding of the personality that Dostoevsky will place at the center of his next novel, *The Adolescent*.

THE DEMONS, THE DEVILS, THE POSSESSED

The disparate renderings of the title of *Besy* in translation—*Demons, The Devils, The Possessed*—reflects a persistent sense of uncertainty among readers regarding Dostoevsky's concept of demonism and possession.[33] In the preface to his (and Larissa Volokhonsky's) illustrious translation, Richard Pevear argued that the demons indicated in the title are in fact the "ideas, the legion of isms that came to Russia from the West" which take possession of the novel's characters.[34] While there is no doubt that Dostoevsky conceived of certain kinds of ideas as demonic, that is, as capable of invading and taking possession of human beings, I would add that ideas are not the only, nor even the principal, demons of the novel. As I have argued in this chapter, the object of the novel was not simply to present a cast of characters possessed by demons in the traditional sense, but rather to conceive of the demon more viscerally as a diseased personality. In his study of the damaged and degraded personality, Dostoevsky, ever the idiosyncratic religious thinker, conceived of a remarkably original notion of the demon as that of a personality, which, having lost recourse to the indwelling "Eternal Thought," becomes reduced to a fragment of a self which both possesses other personalities and is possessed by them.

Dostoevsky's attempts in his correspondence to explain his use of the allegory of the Gadarene swine from the Gospel of Luke help to reinforce this notion that the novel's characters are simultaneously both the "demons" and the "possessed." As he explained to Maikov, the novel explores the idea that the events of Luke's narrative have come to pass in contemporary Russia: "the devils went out from the Russian person and entered into a herd of swine, that is, into the Nechaevs the Serno-Solov'eviches, and so on." In this sense, the revolutionaries, the Nechaevs—or Pyotr Verkhovensky and his comrades—are the *possessed*, the swine into which the demons enter. In the same letter, however, Dostoevsky conceives of the revolutionaries very differently as the "bastards entering the swine," "the bastards puked up" by Russia (29.1:145). In other words, these characters, in Dostoevsky's imagination, are *also* the demons that leave the demoniac and enter into the swine—both the masters, according to Shigalyov's system, who possess a form of agency, and the slaves who "must lose their personality and turn into something like a herd" (10:312). This dual activity of the demon—as both possessor and possessed—is most effectively crystallized in the quasi-comical figure of Stepan Trofimovich: the flimsy thoroughfare self, the "weak heart" that hungers to be possessed by an external mind, but longs meanwhile to fill others with its own unwanted mysteries.

The most pernicious disease, then, among the liberals of the 1840s, as Stepan realizes in his religious quest (his exorcism, as it were), is the loss of a substantive interior realm within the human psyche. Most vivid among the conceptions of selfhood embraced by the founding fathers of the Russian intelligentsia, the "Westernizers" of the 1840s, is Alexander Herzen's conception of the "new man" who has "executed" his past, who "boldly walks on," and who attempts to heal the divisions in the self through vigorous external action.[35] This notion of the self is reflected in Stepan's visceral desire for oblivion, in the paper-thinness of the outwardly directed human being who, as a result of his or her lack of interior substance, becomes susceptible to the control of any "half-person" willing to direct and sustain it. For his part, Pyotr experiments with the disappearance of interior depth in the personality by fabricating a mysterious political "center" as a substitute for a metaphysical center, providing his peers with "the warm belief" that "everyone depended on some kind of central, enormous, but mysterious place, which in its turn was connected organically with the European universal revolution" (10:303). In this way Pyotr encourages the absurd quasi-religious, quasi-mystical sensation reported by members of society that, though they could produce no evidence, they "felt with all their senses" that they "were under the influence of the Internationale" (10:355). By contrast, Stepan's semi-coherent religious awakening before his death dramatizes the discovery of this core activity not somewhere outside the self, but within.

In *Demons*, Dostoevsky, the ostensible enemy of bourgeois self-enclosedness, generates what seems to be at least a partial defense of the inviolate, private self, of personal interiority as grounded in the wellsprings of a divine interior source. Meanwhile, Dostoevsky continues to develop the notion of a positive (non-demonic) relationally constituted personality. Tikhon, for instance, does not advise Stavrogin to free himself from the bonds of dependency that issue forth from his personality, but rather to pursue yet another form of attachment, that is, to submit himself obediently to an external administrative mind:

> I know one elder [. . .] not far from here, a hermit and an ascetic, and of such profound Christian wisdom that you and I would not be able to understand [. . .]. Go and submit yourself in obedience to him, under his command for about five or seven years, for however many you will find necessary. (11:29)

By presenting the system of elders as a potential solution to the pathology of the extended, demonic self, Dostoevsky is preparing to think through the apparent paradox at the center of his anthropology: between merging with the other as demonic possession, on the one hand, and as a form of organic unity, on the other. As we shall see, it is this paradox that haunts Arkady Dolgoruky, the wounded protagonist of Dostoevsky's subsequent novel, who wants desperately to preserve his personality amid the nightmarish disorder of *bezlichnost'* by hiding the self away from those who are only too willing to take possession of it.

Chapter Six

The Hiding Places of the Self in *The Adolescent*

> Koshchei is difficult to overcome: his death is on the end of a needle, that needle is in an egg, that egg is in a duck, that duck is in a rabbit, that rabbit is in a chest, and the chest stands on a tall oak tree. Koshchei guards that tree like his own eye.
> —Afanasiev, "The Frog-Princess"

> For I am destitute and naked and an atom in the whirl of people . . .
> —Dostoevsky, *The Idiot*

THE EXTERNAL SOUL

In his memoirs, Carl Gustav Jung tells the story of how, as a child, he once placed a small figurine and a stone into a pencil case, which he then hid in the forbidden attic of his house. "All this was a great secret," Jung recalls. "In all difficult situations, whenever I had done something wrong or my feelings had been hurt, [. . .] I thought of my carefully bedded-down and wrapped-up manikin. [. . .] It was an inviolable secret, which must never be betrayed, for the safety of my life depended on it."[1] As Jung discovered later in life when studying the "soul-stones" of ancient peoples, his impulse to transfer his "soul" into a hiding place in the external world was in fact an unwitting recapitulation of an age-old religious practice. In *The Golden Bough*, Sir James Frazer presents an account of this article of folk belief, held in common by numerous ancient peoples and traditions. If the animating principle of the body, he explains, was thought to be "a little man or animal" concealed within, this meant that, under dangerous circumstances, a person might choose to take "his soul out of his body and deposit it for security in some snug spot." Upon discovering "some place of absolute security," Frazer adds, "he may be content to leave his soul there permanently," the advantage being that, "so long as the soul remains unharmed in the place where he has deposited it, the man himself is immortal."[2] While Jung in his youth eventually forgot about the contents of his hidden pencil case, he later reflected that they in fact constituted "the climax and conclusion of [his] childhood," his "first attempt, still unconscious and childish, to give shape," as he puts it, "to the secret."[3]

A similar notion lies at the heart of Dostoevsky's coming-of-age novel, *The Adolescent* (1875), in which the narrator and protagonist, Arkady Dolgoruky, attempts to hide his interior, essential self away in a series of locations (in objects, ideas, and people) in order to protect it from annihilation at the hands of others. Within the scope of Dostoevsky's larger project, Arkady's laborious efforts to preserve the principle of the self follow directly from the catastrophic denouement of *Demons* where the abdication of one's own personality to a collective will entailed the widespread devastation of the younger generation. The novel's plot follows the gradual loss and desolation of Arkady's hiding places, at first in response to the invasive activity of others, and finally as a voluntary act of self-renunciation on the part of the protagonist. In this sense, Dostoevsky's contribution to the modern European tradition of the novel of personal formation, or bildungsroman, is an unorthodox one. Rather than depict, in *The Adolescent*, the formation of a personality, the transition from unsteady youth to firm adulthood, Dostoevsky follows the gradual unraveling and stripping away of the trappings of the self.[4] In its portrayal of the ruin of the self at the hands of the world (albeit in a comic rather than tragic mode), *The Adolescent* prepares the way, as we shall see, for an articulation of the more genuine forms of interiority and selfhood that emerge in the wake of the destruction of the "external soul" and that will occupy the focus of his subsequent and final novel, *The Brothers Karamazov*. If the bildungsroman traditionally asks the question of how to integrate self into society, Dostoevsky enlists that genre to call into question the very validity of the self—as a private, indwelling phenomenon—by presenting his hero's journey as the search for a more robust theory of personhood that would allow for the survival of the individual principle amid the aggressive and faceless "whirlwind" of the collective.[5]

THE "MANY PLOTS"

In reading *The Adolescent* as an exploration of the problem of personhood, I hope to challenge the frequently expressed scholarly perception that the aesthetically unruly novel is incoherent in its plot structure. Related by its protagonist in the form of a first-person confession, the novel tells the story of Arkady's arrival in St. Petersburg to live with his family after having grown up in isolation from them. This family consists of his biological father, Andrei Versilov, a brilliant, fascinating, and charismatic, but impoverished and mentally unstable nobleman; Arkady's mother, Sofia Dolgorukaia, a wise and humble former peasant; and his sister, Liza. Both Arkady and Liza are Versilov's illegitimate children; their legal father, Makar Dolgoruky, after relinquishing his wife to Versilov, has spent the last two decades wandering Russia's far corners as a religious pilgrim. Arriving in Petersburg, Arkady has two secrets: the first is what he calls his "idea," that is, his plan "to become a Rothschild," to accumulate vast wealth through a combination of will power, isolation, and cunning. His other secret is that he possesses a compromising letter, stitched into his "side pocket," written by Katerina Akhmakova, the illustrious and beautiful widow of a general. The potentially compromising "document" (which testifies to Akhmakova's attempt to wrest control of her father's fortune) has immense value in the eyes both of its author and of her potential blackmailers, among whom is Versilov himself, who, though devoted to Arkady's mother, nevertheless conceals an all-consuming passion for the widow. While initially clinging to the hurt feelings of an abandoned son, Arkady gradually becomes enamored with his father and loses sight of his dreams of becoming a tycoon. In order to fund a newly discovered lifestyle of gambling and dissolution, Arkady borrows money continuously from his friend, the young Prince Seryozha Sokolsky, while oblivious of the fact that his sister, Liza, is secretly pregnant with Prince Seryozha's child, and that the Prince is only lending him money as a form of appeasement for Liza's "disgrace." Meanwhile, Arkady reencounters his old friend and tormentor from his boarding school days, Lambert, who has, in the intervening years, developed a blackmailing ring. Having plied Arkady with drink, Lambert unstitches the "document" from Arkady's vest while the latter is asleep and sews in a blank piece of paper in its stead. Toward the end of the novel, Arkady, ashamed of the ignominy of his first steps in the world, resolves, through the influence of his legal father, Makar, to enter upon a new quest for spiritual beauty, and he decides to return the letter nobly to Akhmakova, without realizing that it is in fact no longer in his possession. His friend, Prince Seryozha, having resolved to marry Liza and to suffer the legal consequences of some of his misdeeds, dies in a state of near insanity. Versilov, for his part, after a stormy effort to ruin and to possess Akhmakova, and after attempts of both murder and suicide, embraces a more steady existence of harmonious family life with Arkady's mother.

As even this truncated synopsis will suggest, the novel's plot appears to lack the cohesion and unity of Dostoevsky's other major novels, and has been said to consist of several ostensibly disconnected plots.[6] A pronounced compositional imbalance is often noted in the fading of Arkady's "Rothschild idea," the simultaneous intensification of Versilov's presence, and the extended descriptions of gambling and intrigue, it being unclear to many readers why, for example, Arkady would declare his intention of becoming a "Rothschild" at such length, only promptly to abandon it.[7] Critics, moreover, have almost unanimously derided Dostoevsky's use of the concealed "document" as the stale device of a "moth-eaten melodramatic plot."[8] Others have defended the impression of disorder in the novel by pointing out the crucial distinction between the narrator and author, the former a confused adolescent, and the latter an experimental genius at the height of his powers, in search of a novelistic form capable of adequately addressing—and even of enacting—the subject matter of a society coming apart at the seams.[9] While accepting this notion of a thematically necessitated formal disorder in the novel, I shall argue for what is nevertheless a striking cohesion among its various "plots" (from the "idea," to the "document," to the gambling episodes, to the mysterious all-importance of Versilov) when approached from the perspective of the hero's experiments with the deferral and defense of the self.

"I AM ALTOGETHER DIFFERENT, HIGHER AND DEEPER"

The first part of the novel focuses primarily on Arkady's attempts to imagine secure locations for the self as a form of defense against the external forces that threaten to destroy it or to deny its existence. In this sense, his sacred, much discussed "idea" is not really the pursuit of wealth, as it is phrased initially, nor can it be exhausted by the terms that clothe it throughout: "power," "solitude" (13:85, 264), "darkness" (13:264), or "mystery" (13:78). Each of these manifestations of the "idea" is an expression of Arkady's more general attempt to conceive of a nonmaterial indwelling identity, or soul. As he lets slip to Kraft, Arkady believes that he possesses a secure interior location for the self, a place of refuge from the world of others:

> "Wouldn't it be better to break from them utterly? Eh?"
> "And go where?" asked [Kraft . . .]
> "To yourself [*k sebe*], to yourself alone! That's what my whole idea consists of, Kraft!" I said triumphantly. [. . .]
> "And do you have such a place: 'to yourself'?"
> "I do." (13:60)

Arkady later admits that he might have been exaggerating his confidence on the matter of "having such a place" as a self: "I told Kraft that I have 'my own place' [. . .] I said this proudly" (13:64). Indeed, Arkady's notion of a stowed-away essence is still, at this early point in the novel, in its untested and experimental stages.

Because of the initial form of its expression ("My idea is to become a Rothschild" [13:66]), the hero's "idea" has often been interpreted as an attraction to forms of Western capitalist materialism.[10] As a result, critics have puzzled over Dostoevsky's intention, which he expressed in his notebooks, to focus his entire novel upon Arkady "as the bearer and inventor of *his idea*" (16:175), especially since the "Rothschild idea" fades from prominence in the narrative almost as soon as it has been formulated.[11] Arkady's "idea" of Rothschild, however, as we gradually discover, has little to do with actual material prosperity. "Was it really money that I needed?" he later asserts. "I swear I only needed the idea! I swear that not one chair, not one divan would I have ever upholstered in velvet" (13:388). In its Rothschild guise, the "idea" is presented rather as a perversion of European romantic notions of selfhood, something similar to what Marx had in mind in his identification of the "power of money" with the conception of the self in capitalist society. "That which is for me," Marx wrote in 1844, "through the medium of money—that for which I can pay (i.e., which money can buy)—that am I myself, the possessor of the money. [. . .] Money's properties are my—the possessor's—properties and essential powers."[12] Dostoevsky, in his notebook for 1880, described wealth in similar terms to Marx, as an "intensification of personality, a mechanical and spiritual embodiment" (27:49), and it is precisely in this sense, as an "intensification" of self, an "embodiment" of spirit, or in Marx's phrasing, an "essential power," that Arkady dreams of amassing a fortune.

The emphasis of Arkady's idea, then, is not upon money itself, but upon money's ability to defer identity; it represents the desire to locate the self elsewhere, away from the threatening gaze of others.[13] Inspired by accounts of beggars who sewed thousands of rubles into their tattered clothing (13:66), Arkady formulates his dream in imitation: "If I were a multimillionaire, I would find pleasure in walking in the oldest clothing so that they would take me for the most wretched person, who all but begs for alms" (13:36). In this sense, the "idea" of hidden riches acquires the vocabulary of soul, becoming for Arkady the "only source" of "life," "light," "dignity," and "consolation," a "treasure of power," an oasis beyond consciousness, a location of inviolability that continues to exist "regardless of how ridiculous and humiliated I seemed" (13:229). The "idea" also constitutes the location of identity and individuality since, as Arkady explains, "when I express my idea to someone, I'll suddenly have nothing left, so that I'll come to resemble everyone else, and maybe even discard my idea; and so I cherished and guarded it and trembled at the thought of blabbing" (13:48).

Such a fetishistic distortion of the romantic concept of inner depth is by no means original in the Russian literary tradition. Arkady draws here explicitly on Pushkin's *The Covetous Knight* (1830) in which the Baron's passion for hoarding wealth can be readily interpreted "in the context of the romantic concept of selfhood."[14] One also detects an implicit allusion to Gogol's Poprishchin of "Diary of a Madman" (1834) who defers his own identity into the "king of Spain" in order to escape his humiliating insignificance in the eyes of others.[15] Arkady's Rothschild, it could be argued, is an approximate equivalent of Poprishchin's Spanish monarch—an inviolable, distant, transcendental, majestic, interior second self, invisible to others. Indeed, Arkady's "idea" first shows up in Dostoevsky's notebooks as the "desire to become the king of an island known to no one, at the Pole, or in a lake in Central Africa" (16:93).[16] Both Pushkin's Baron and Gogol's clerk, moreover, were fodder for Arkady's precursor, Prokharchin, the titular protagonist of Dostoevsky's early short story ("Mr. Prokarchin," 1846), a humiliated, pathetic, Gogolian functionary who hides large amounts of wealth in his mattress and who, while lying silently upon his concealed riches, nurtures an alternate personality, an imperious "Napoleonic" self (1:257).

As he begins to test the effectiveness of his "idea" in his encounters with others, Arkady's concept of an inwardly deferred self falls immediately into a state of crisis. After all his work in conceiving a secure location for his identity, it takes Versilov only a moment to violate the carefully guarded space. Nothing, it turns out, has been successfully concealed:

"All your secrets are written on your honest face. He has 'his idea' [. . .]."

"Let's leave my honest face alone," I continued to burst, [. . .] "Yes, I do have 'my idea.' That you expressed it thus is of course a coincidence, but I am not afraid to admit: I have an 'idea' [. . .] In any case I will never reveal it to you." [. . .]

"You don't have to, my friend. I already know the essence of your idea; it's 'I will withdraw into the desert' [. . .] to become Rothschild or something of the sort and to withdraw into his greatness."

I trembled within myself. [. . .] He had guessed everything. (13:89–90)

Here we see that the "honest face," from which Arkady has sought to defer the principle of his identity, remains a compromising factor with which he must somehow contend in developing a more encompassing conception of selfhood. Similarly problematic, according to Arkady, is the enduring presence within him of "all [his] filth" which, as he expresses it, "hid itself as if under the idea" (13:79). In other words, the "idea" as the essential principle of the self fails to integrate these other aspects of the personality—the "face," for example, and the "filth" contained within (impulse, emotions, desires, bodily processes)—and thus constitutes only an experimental point of departure in conceiving of a defensible "place" for the self.

Arkady's "idea," we discover, is in fact only one part of a more comprehensive project of self-deferral that began in his embattled childhood. From his early boarding school days, Arkady describes how he would take refuge from beatings and humiliations at the hands of his teacher and classmates by covering himself with his blankets at night and fleeing into the realm of thought and fantasy. In one definitive episode from his childhood, Arkady tells of his discovery in his drawer of a handkerchief left behind by his mother, a piece of cloth that, as the child notes with interest, possesses a memory of its own: "I took it out and looked it over even with some curiosity; the end of the handkerchief still entirely retained the trace of its former knot and even was clearly stamped with the round form of a coin." Keeping the object hidden away in his drawer, Arkady takes it out only in the greatest secrecy, drawing upon the memory contained within it as a means of escape from his distressing external circumstances:

> I wrapped myself up to the head in my blanket and, from under my pillow, pulled out the little blue kerchief: [. . .] I instantly pressed it to my face and suddenly began to kiss it. "Mama, Mama," I whispered, remembering, and my whole chest became constricted as in a vise. I closed my eyes and saw her face [. . .]. [Lambert] runs up to me and begins to pull the blanket from me, but I hold ever so tightly onto the blanket in which I am wrapped up to my head, [. . .] he beats me, hitting me painfully with his fist in my back, in the side, more and more painfully. (13:273–74)

This description concisely establishes the rudiments of Arkady's developing approach to selfhood: he conceives of an impermeable self which, though besieged from without, fortifies itself inwardly by virtue of its recourse to a sacred, alternate dimension of being—a dimension which can be hidden and preserved, it turns out, within a seemingly ordinary object.

It is in this context of self-preservation and impermeability that Arkady's hidden "document" becomes central to the novel's philosophical substance. Indeed, Dostoevsky took great pains to weave the novel's plot directly into Arkady's experiment of self-deferral by distilling the hero's dream of being located "elsewhere" in the letter that he carries with him as the invisible manifestation of all his secret inward power.[17] Like Arkady's imagined wealth, the document is both unknown to all and stitched into the lining of his pocket: thus *interior* in the most literal sense. It becomes synonymous with Arkady's "idea" in that it allows him to remain remote, opaque, and "unfinalizable," to retain a secret, highly prized, locus of identity which affords him great power over others and infinite importance in their eyes.[18] Like the dream of wealth, the valuable "document" acts as an intensification of self by making Arkady powerful, desirable, unique, sought-after, and causing him to exist more fully in the eyes of others. Thus, arriving in Petersburg with his "idea" and his "document," Arkady no longer feels the need to wrap himself up in a blanket for protection. Instead he experiments with his newfound invulnerability by revealing even the most compromising personal details to strangers: introducing himself, for example, as "the illegitimate son of my former master," or responding to the mockery of his peers with "calm yourselves, I still haven't ever known a woman" (13:50). In other words, to risk revealing everything is to confirm to himself that there is something deeper that has been left unrevealed. As he says to Vasin, "I'm a trashy little boy and not worthy of you. I confess this precisely because in other minutes I am altogether different, higher and deeper" (13:152).

Both the Rothschild "idea" and the "document," however, ultimately become secondary proxies to Arkady's ideal location for the self, one which has remained with him as a form of protection and escape from his childhood—that is, his dream of identification with his father, Versilov. In his perpetual absence, Versilov, we are told, gradually becomes the central organizing principle of Arkady's imaginative interior life. "My every dream from my very childhood," Arkady explains, "was connected to [Versilov]; hovered around him, came down to him in the final result. [. . .] he filled all my future, all my plans for life" (13:16). Upon finally encountering his father in the flesh, Arkady, initially uncertain of Versilov's worthiness of such an exalted role in his imagination, resists Versilov's influence by relying on his "document" and his "idea" for interior fortification. When Versilov subsequently renounces an inheritance and thus demonstrates, through his noble action, that he indeed resembles his son's idealized image of him, Arkady discards his defenses and allows his father to "grasp and conquer [his] soul" (13:187): "'Now I have no need to fantasize and dream, now it is enough to have you! I'll follow you!' I said, giving myself over to him with my whole soul" (13:373). Having found an apparently robust, attractive, mysterious, and secure location into which he can displace his identity, Arkady attempts to blend himself into his father's personality as he continually insists on confusing the boundaries between them: he resolves to fight a duel on Versilov's behalf, borrows money in his name, falls passionately in love with the object of Versilov's desire, fastidiously protects Vesilov's reputation and image in the eyes of others, repeats the latter's thoughts as his own, and longs for his father to "invade his conscience" (13:373). Embracing Versilov as "a piece of [Arkady's] own living flesh" (13:111), and thus believing that he has a strong enough anchor to secure him and render him invulnerable, he now enters unrestrainedly into the "whirlwind" of social relations, which he has hitherto avoided out of fear for self-preservation.

"THE WHIRLWIND"

The canonical interpretive approach to Arkady's quest in the novel (as proposed, for example, by Konstantin Mochulsky) is to see it as an investigation of the possibility of organic collective unity, or *sobornost'*.[19] Such a reading draws on the inclination of spiritually minded interpreters in the prerevolutionary and early Soviet period to read Dostoevsky's novels as cosmic allegories.[20] In this context, Arkady's initial resistance to the "whirl" of collective selfhood appears in a decidedly negative light. If, according to Mochulsky, Versilov is the *"sobornyj* [. . .] *center of life,"* the organic unity to which everyone is drawn, then Arkady's experiments with positing a personal essence are a denial of *sobornost'*, a diseased form of individualism which opens up "a fetid underground [. . .] in the soul of the human being."[21] Instead of the "organic collectivity of souls" that is centered in the figure of Versilov, Arkady, according to Mochulsky, seeks "demonic separation and fragmentation" by means of "might" and "power."[22] Such a polarized reading of the novel, however, greatly reduces the complexity of Dostoevsky's notion of the individual personality by simply juxtaposing it with a grand conception of intersubjective harmony. What such readings tend to overlook is the destructive nature of the collective self that overwhelms and negates the inwardly ungrounded individual self.

A brief glance at the treatment of the image of the "whirlwind" in *The Gambler* (1866) can help to shed light on the corrupting and even demonic activity of the relational whirl upon the self in *The Adolescent*. Here Dostoevsky invokes the whirlwind (*vikhr', krugovorot*) to describe the powerlessness of becoming wholly immersed in the intensity of human relationships at the expense of any sense of personal agency, as the hero, "instead of thinking through [his] next step, live[s] under the influence of [. . .] the whirlwind" that "tears through" him, "grabs [him] with its wing" and disposes of him according to its own volition ("I'll spin, spin, spin!"), robbing him in the process of all the "dreams" and "memories" that formerly constituted his personality (5:281, 314).[23] The effect of the "whirl," in *The Gambler*, is most viscerally portrayed in the debilitating influence of the roulette wheel upon the self. When the Countess loses self-control at roulette, Dostoevsky describes her encounter with demons, "little Poles," who begin to climb over her, and even "through" her, overriding her will as they dispense with her wealth at random:

> [The little Poles] placed bets each from his own side, one [. . .] on red, the other on black. It ended with them completely encircling and confusing Grandmother, so that she, finally, almost in tears, addressed herself to the old croupier to [. . .] to drive them away. [. . .] But by the end of the day [. . .] as many as six little Poles stood behind her [. . .] Not only did they not listen to her, but they didn't even notice her, climbed directly through her to the table, grabbed the money themselves, dispensed of it on their own, staked it, argued, and cried out. (5:283)

If in the earlier novella, entering into the whirl means to open the self to foreign agencies, the demonic "little Poles" described here will become carefully woven into the plot of *The Adolescent* as fully fledged characters capable of possessing the self, annexing its agency, and feeding off of its energies.[24]

Having embraced his father and entered into the world of social relations, Arkady, in the second part of the novel, allows himself to relinquish his "idea" of indwelling depths and to become "drawn into the whirlpool" of other people's lives "like a sliver" (13:338), overcome as he is by the ecstasy of communion with others: "A boundless thirst for this life, for *their* life, he explains, "grasped my entire spirit [. . .]. My thoughts were spinning, but I allowed them to spin" (13:297). To be inside the "whirl," Arkady soon discovers, entails both the loss of personal identity ("I don't have any affairs of my own now" [13:242]) and the invasion of the self by others. "Since I consisted wholly of other people's thoughts," Arkady explains, "where was I to get my own?" [13:241]). In the context of his new, more robust moorings in Versilov, Arkady meditates on the uselessness of all the interior elements of his personality, those "gloominesses" (ideas, dreams, thoughts, memories) he had zealously protected and then so suddenly discarded:

> And what were all those former gloominesses for, [. . .] what for all these old sickly lacerations, my lonely and sullen childhood, my stupid dreams under the blanket, oaths, calculations and even the "idea"? All this I'd imagined and thought up, and it turns out it isn't at all like this in the world; it's so joyful and light. (13:164)

When Versilov, however, proves to be not an anchor for the self, but just another helpless figure "under the influence of a whirlwind of feelings" (13:445), Arkady, having relinquished the anchoring elements of his interior life, finds himself lost amid the endlessly "spinning [. . .] chaos" of the external world, his failing reason "a dark cloud of dry autumn leaves in the wake of a whirlwind" (13:398) within which his personality is powerless: "In my soul it was very troubled, and there was no wholeness [. . .]. Everything somehow flashed without connection and order, and, I remember, I myself did not want to stop on anything or to instill order" (13:140). In this "threshold space" to use Bakhtin's words, where "all *distance* between people is suspended" and "all things that were once self-enclosed, disunified, distanced from one another [. . .] are drawn into carnivalistic contacts and combinations,"[25] the self, as we shall see in the novel, becomes overwhelmed by the emptiness and randomness that lies at the center of the whirl. "As in a whirlwind," Arkady observes, "the figures of Liza, Anna Andreevna, Stebel'kov, the prince, Aferdov, of everyone, flashed tracelessly in my ailing mind. But the thoughts were becoming ever more formless and elusive" (13:263–64). Through these images of others spinning chaotically around nothing, Dostoevsky phrases his critique of relational selfhood. Rather than the "free unanimity" of *sobornost'* advanced by Khomiakov among the Slavophiles, or the "interaction of autonomous and internally unfinalized" and "unmerged" "consciousnesses" imagined by Bakhtin, the whirl is an invasive and impersonal system founded upon an expanding absence.[26]

In his depiction of the effect of the relational whirlwind upon the self in *The Adolescent*, Dostoevsky continues to develop his notion of the demon as an unfinished or inwardly collapsed, and thus hungrily dependent, self. The moneylender, Stebel'kov, is presented as the quintessence of *bezlichnost'* (impersonality or facelessness), first in that he quite literally lacks a distinctive face. His physical features, we are told, "not only did not help to personalize him [*ne sposobstvovali ego kharakternosti*], but precisely afforded him something general, like everyone else." Since Stebel'kov is characterized "precisely by [his] unfinishedness, scatteredness, and indefiniteness [*nezakonchennost', raskidchivost' i neopredelennost'*]," that is, by his lack of any determinate personality traits, it is impossible, Arkady discovers, to "say anything precise and definitive about him" (13:118). His speech, moreover, is marked by semi-coherent insinuation, a jumble of potential meanings designed to draw forth revealing and compromising reactions from his interlocutors. Driven by an immense social curiosity and an insatiable hunger for the secrets of others, Stebel'kov defines himself as a "second person," an inherently dependent self (13:182). Likewise, Lambert, who appears as if out of nowhere at the height of Arkady's enslavement to the whirlwind, is presented as an empty, eternally dependent self who, "lacking" his own "idea" (13:360), "depends on everyone" (13:349) and is "enslaved," as Arkady points out, "to the first person" he encounters (13:355).

Though Arkady recognizes Stebel'kov and Lambert clearly as demonic figures, he, nevertheless, in relinquishing his own will to the arbitrary pull of the whirlwind, finds himself inexorably drawn into an uncanny form of solidarity with them. Attaching himself to Prince Seryozha by taking his money and unwittingly driving him into a state of frenzied despair, Arkady in fact becomes yet another variation of Stebel'kov. He sees with "astonishment" that the Prince looks at him, Arkady, with "the same lost, pitiful and malicious look" with which he encounters Stebel'kov: "he was ashamed, it seemed, of us both and had equated me with Stebel'kov," a realization that causes Arkady to protest this affiliation by insisting on his parasitism with even greater aplomb. Relinquishing the ideal of the self and entering wholly into communal space, therefore, means not only to be "overtaken" (13:390) by others, but also to become reduced oneself to the status of a demon—an "unfinished," "scattered," "indeterminate," and dependent self. In despair, unable "with all [his] strength to pull [himself] away" from the "whirl" (13:297), Arkady comes to realize that, much like Lambert and Stebel'kov, he too has the "soul of a spider" (13:306), that is, of a being that catches others within its web and nourishes itself upon them.[27] Though fully aware of Lambert's insidious insubstantiality, Arkady finds himself inexplicably "yearning" to see him (13:327), so that Lambert ultimately rejoices at "finally possessing [*nakonets obladaia*]" him (13:418). For his part, Prince Seryozha, being "without character" (13:293) and thus lacking the resources to defend himself, ends up in a state of madness and ruin, becoming ultimately, like the Countess in the *Gambler*, consumed by the demons that come to possess, and act through, him. In his despair, before his death, the Prince dreams constantly in his sleep of "spiders," thus recognizing, albeit on an unconscious level, his entrapment within the relational world (13:335). For both Arkady and Seryozha, their captivity within the whirlwind is dramatized in their inexorable devotion to the roulette wheel, and especially in Arkady's insistence, recalling the Countess from *The Gambler*, to stake his wealth continually on "zero," as an image of the essential void at the heart of all order.

Like the protagonist of *The Gambler*, however, Arkady hopes that it is possible to preserve both dimensions of his being simultaneously, his private, inward self, on the one hand, and his status as a relational being, on the other. "Is it really impossible," he wonders, "to go to them, find out everything from them and suddenly to leave them forever, going harmlessly past the wonders and the monsters?" (13:338). "The 'idea,'" he insists to himself as he becomes ever further enmeshed in intrigue, "would be later, the 'idea' would wait" (13:164). At the height of his despair, having been betrayed by Versilov and humiliated in the gambling hall, where at the hands of the authorities, he is invasively searched "entirely down to the last fold" (13:267), Arkady seeks out the remaining shreds of his violated personality, attempting to return to those locations of identity he had prepared for himself, the "idea" and the "document": "'I have an "idea!' I thought suddenly, 'isn't that so? Didn't I learn it by heart? [. . .] but it is really possible now to crawl back into the former darkness. Ah, my God, I still hadn't burned the 'document!'" (13:264). The fate of the "document" in the novel is therefore directly connected to the survival of the self. Sensing "with horror [. . .] the absurdity and the loathsomeness of [his confessions] to Lambert, of [his] agreement with him," Arkady holds to the thought of his concealed letter as a guarantor of inviolability, without suspecting that Lambert will take this from him as well: "But thank God, the document still remained with me! Was still sewn into my side pocket; I felt it with my hand—it was there! This meant that I only had to get up and run away" (13:420).

Chapter Six

OPENING THE ENVELOPE

From out of the crisis of the unanchored self spinning powerlessly in the whirlwind, Dostoevsky depicts his protagonist's journey in the third and final part of the novel as the search for a more effective anchor for the self. This new idea, which Arkady discovers after his collapse, he terms *blagoobrazie* (roughly translatable as "seemliness" or, more literally, as "blessed form"), a notion which represents a radical reversal of Arkady's initial theory in that his emphasis has now shifted to an incarnational or revealed, rather than concealed, or deferred, self.[28] If we follow its unsteady and idiosyncratic usage in the text, "seemliness" comes to refer to the transformation of the body (or, more specifically, of the *face*) by "light," or by divine indwelling presence. Behind the idea of "seemliness," which Arkady grasps intuitively but struggles to understand and to implement, lies Dostoevsky's own conviction that "a human being's face is the image of his personality, his spirit, his human worth."[29] In his discussion of the Neoplatonic Russian Orthodox concept of the illumined countenance, Pavel Florensky explains that "high spiritual attainment transforms the face into a light-bearing countenance" as one comes "to incarnate the hidden inheritance of our sacred likeness to the image of God in the flesh of our personality."[30] According to the spiritual tradition into which Arkady has stumbled, the "substantive kernel," "core," or "essence" of the personality—which he has been so anxious to conceal—becomes inseparable from the revealed presence of the divine likeness within the human body, and particularly within the face as the expression both of the individual personality and of the divine life which illuminates it.[31]

In order to develop this somewhat obscure conception of a revealed self, Dostoevsky allows his characters several tangents on the topic of beauty as the illuminated countenance, all of which occur in the latter section of the novel while Arkady is trying to elucidate his newfound doctrine of "seemliness." Versilov, for example, explains to Arkady that photographs capture only the material features of the subject in a given moment. Since the "main thought of the face" is usually absent, the artist must endeavor to capture that "extremely rare" moment in which "we resemble ourselves." Versilov's rumination introduces the theme of the transfiguring effect of light on material features, since, in the daguerreotype of Sonya that he shows to Arkady, it is the light of the sun that "captured Sonya in her salient moment" (13:370). In yet another extended examination of the transformative power of light, Dostoevsky depicts a moment of joyful conversion in Arkady when his "corner," an image formerly associated with his attempts at self-concealment ("My idea is my corner" [13:48]), becomes flooded with sunlight. Under Makar's influence, Arkady shifts from being "infuriated to the point of malice" by the ray of the setting sun that lights up his room to rejoicing at it, "as if a new light had penetrated into my heart" (13:283, 291).[32]

According to Arkady's new manner of thinking, moreover, transfigurative light becomes synonymous with "mirth" or "cheerfulness" (*veselie*) since laughter, as a principle of illumination, is capable of bringing the whole of the person to the surface. Arkady considers it "one of the most serious conclusions of [his] life" that "character" or "the entire human being" or the "soul" reveals itself most fully in "cheerful" laughter. One can be "stumped," he explains, by the mystery of a personality, and through laughter "you suddenly see everything there is to know": "I'm [. . .] speaking about character, about the whole of a person. [. . .] If you want to discern a person and discover his soul, then don't look into how he keeps silent or how he talks, or how he weeps, or even how he worries himself with the noblest ideas, but it's better to look out for him when he laughs [. . .] Laughter is the most certain test of the soul" (13:285–86). To laugh in a truly "cheerful" way, as Arkady discovers through observing Makar, means to allow oneself to be flooded and overwhelmed by the sources which underlie and transfigure the self (13:290).

"Seemliness," however, like the version of en-souledness that Arkady had attempted to adopt, proves elusive in its applications. Throughout his attempts to posit an identity, either internally or externally, others continually remind Arkady that all of his deepest thoughts, desires, and emotions are already visible on his highly expressive face (13:89–90, 91, 111, 367, 371), and, terrified of such spiritual nakedness, he journeys, as we have seen, to great lengths to place the emphasis of his being anywhere else. Having adopted "seemliness" as his new doctrine, therefore, he becomes fascinated with how to exert control over his self-revelation so as to experience the reduction to incarnation as glory rather than humiliation and powerlessness; in other words, how to undergo the kenotic humiliation of Christ without a painful crucifixion. Thus, Arkady's notion of the revelation of the self acquires the idiosyncratic form of searching for the right way to reveal his concealed "document" without undergoing pain or mockery. In his anxious dreams, where people wait "outside the doors" for him to show himself, "seemliness" and self-revelation become conflated with the act of disclosing his "document," which he ultimately reveals, in one particularly vivid dream, to laughter and "unbearable mockery" (13:306). The revelation of the "document" accordingly takes on a mysterious religious significance, since Arkady comes to believe, in a rapturous moment of resolve, that to reveal it in a noble and self-sacrificial manner, "regardless of all temptation," will exert a redemptive effect not only upon himself, but also upon all the inhabitants of the whirlwind: "I wanted," Arkady explains, "to return the document to [Akhmakova], explaining everything once and for all [. . .] I wanted to justify myself once and for all. [. . .] I would take them to my place [. . .] reconcile the warring women there, resurrect the prince and . . . and . . . in short, make everyone happy, at least here in this group, today" (13:428). Arkady's intention, then, is to redeem the world not through his suffering, but through the destruction of the principle of selfhood—"to annihilate [the] I, to give it wholly to all and everyone, undividedly and selflessly" (20:172), as Dostoevsky expressed the ideal in his notebooks over a decade earlier.

Arkady's ultimate crucifixion falls instead into the comic mode. The document, it turns out, has been stolen by Lambert, and Arkady has been carrying a blank piece of paper within his vest. Arkady's loss of the power of speech, his reduction to a "pale," "powerless," almost "senseless" being underscores, even parodies, the utter loss of any form of interior "idea" or indwelling soul:

> We took out the letter; the old envelope was the very same, but from it protruded a blank piece of paper [. . .] But I was already standing there without language, pale . . . and suddenly in powerlessness I set myself down on the chair; it's true, I almost lost my senses. (13:439)

The scene that occurs so quietly in the novel lies at the heart of the hero's painful journey to chase the self out of its hiding places and to sacrifice it for the sake of others. In what was supposed to be the hour of his sacrificial glory, the inner principle has all but evaporated, and the body is revealed to be an empty envelope. When we finally see the "document" for the first time at the end of the novel, it is lying on Versilov's table, deflated of all value, as the discarded animating principle of Arkady's adolescence.

BEYOND THE EXTERNAL SOUL

Though Arkady's attempts to ground his personal identity in a series of "hiding places" verge, especially in the case of the "document," upon the ridiculous, the underlying impulse of his "idea" nevertheless survives intact in the hero at the end of the novel. As Arkady notes in his epilogue, a year after the events of the narrative, he still has not abandoned his "idea," which has now come to exist "in a completely different form, so that it is already impossible to recognize it" (13:451). Indeed, at its most foundational, Arkady's quest is to discover a spiritual core within the self that extends beyond the relational world. As Arkady's friend and mentor, Nikolai Semyonovich, points out in his critical remarks upon the hero's manuscript, Arkady's hero's "idea," even in its adolescent form, already exerts a protective power on its bearer and is valuable in that it has come from within, and has not been merely borrowed from others, as most ideas are: "young people of the current generation throw themselves for the most part on ideas that they didn't think up, but were given beforehand—narrow and often even dangerous ideas. Your idea for instance protected you at least for a while from the ideas of [Arkady's 'progressive' peers], which are, without a doubt, less original than yours" (13:452).

Arkady's efforts at self-deferral link him directly to the protagonists of Dostoevsky's earlier novels who, as we have seen, bind themselves to others as screens and substitutions for an interior life that they are not yet prepared to encounter or to acknowledge. Though to become stripped of the mannequin and the stone in the pencil case (to use Jung's example) means to be reduced to one's empirical self, it also entails the possibility of becoming initiated into previously unknown dimensions of interiority. As we shall see in Dostoevsky's final novel, the movement inward, for any given character, begins with the excruciating loss of one's external sources and anchors, a process presented in *The Adolescent* as the journey from youth into maturity. Indeed, in Dmitry Karamazov's insistence upon the essential significance of his "amulet" (a small bag containing money that he hides next to his heart), Dostoevsky returns directly to Arkady's notion of a placeholder soul, and in fact conceives of an image in Dmitry's case much more in keeping with Arkady's initial idea than Akhmakova's letter.[33] The exposure and destruction of Dmitry's "amulet," as we shall see, constitutes the end of his own belated adolescence, and the beginning of an inward journey in search of the transformative sources, glimpsed only fleetingly in *The Adolescent*, of all truly sincere and "mirthful" laughter.

Chapter Seven

The Apprenticeship of the Self in *The Brothers Karamazov*

> A mind is a good thing, but two minds are better. God gives one person one mind, and the other he gives two minds, and yet another he gives three . . . One mind with which your mother brought you into the world, another mind from learning, and a third from a good life. So you see, my brother, it is good for a person to have three minds. For that person not only living, but dying, is easier.
> —Chekhov, "The Steppe"

> Humility consists in knowing that in what we call "I" there is no source of energy by which we can rise. Everything without exception which is of value in me comes from somewhere other than myself, not as a gift but as a loan which must be ceaselessly renewed.
> —Weil, *Gravity and Grace*

THE INQUISITOR AND THE ELDER

The Brothers Karamazov (1880) is Dostoevsky's most comprehensive study of the collective self. The dissolution of the self into others and the need to subsist upon an external mind are pervasive phenomena in the novel, appearing in widely divergent forms that call attention to the extreme ambivalence of Dostoevsky's views with regard to collective personhood. In his plans for humanity, the Grand Inquisitor of Ivan's *poema* proposes a vision of the state as a vast all-embracing collective in which the weak are annexed and, thus, liberated from their suffering by the strong. The many, he predicts, will be grateful to the few for "bearing freedom" like "gods" on their behalf, and they will be only too eager to confess "all the most tormenting secrets of their consciences" as a means of deferring the attendant anxieties of freedom and responsibility to their masters (14:231, 236). This teaching—in which a fragile individual accepts the agency and administration of a master, and cleaves to the master's guidance as to an external conscience—appears simultaneously, though in a very different light, at the far opposite end of the novel's moral-philosophical spectrum, in Dostoevsky's presentation of the Russian Orthodox system of elders. Here the pupil, ostensibly much like the Inquisitor's future subjects, is compelled to "renounce [his] own will and to offer it in complete obedience" to his elder who wields "limitless and inconceivable power" over his pupil, and who takes the pupil's "soul [and] will into his own soul and will." In this case, however, the goal of such practice for the student, as expressed by the narrator, is not the purported bliss of moral and mental enslavement, but rather the very opposite: "absolute freedom," "self-mastery," and "moral rebirth" (13:26–27).[1]

These mutually evocative teachings of giving oneself up to the will of the other show us the outlines of Dostoevsky's larger examination of the collective self in his final novel, whose plot, I shall argue in this chapter, is constituted, in significant measure, by the very dramatic breach of a series of collective selves, a breach which in each case represents a critical moment for the formation of personality. As in the earlier works, where Dostoevsky's conception of the collective self was grounded in the inwardly debilitating effects of childhood trauma, the four brothers of his final novel are all conceived of as wounded and unstable personalities who fear introspection and who cling to another personality as a means of stabilization and nourishment. Alyosha has "welded" himself "in [his] soul" to his beloved elder; Dmitry longs for separation from his fiancée, his "god" and "conscience"; and Ivan is infuriated and bewildered by the uncanny executive power his "pupil," Smerdiakov, wields over him; while Smerdiakov, for his part, comes to imagine himself as a mere instrument of Ivan's will. The novel dramatizes the rupture of each of the relationships of extension that have hitherto provided protection from the terrors of the interior life: in Alyosha's hysteria and despair upon the death of Zosima; in Dmitry's frenzied and turbulent escape from his dependence on Katerina Ivanovna; and in Ivan's psychological collapse upon Smerdiakov's death. I shall examine three parallel crises that follow upon the sudden dissolution of the collective self—in Alyosha's dream of Cana of Galilee, Dmitry's dream of the freezing infant, and Ivan's dream of the devil—as constituting, when read together, a focused and panoptic exploration of the journey inward to "become a personality." The mutually illuminative synergy of these three parallel journeys sheds significant light, I shall argue, on Dostoevsky's unique synthesis of the individual and the collective self in his theological psychology.

Chapter Seven

"IF YOU ONLY KNEW HOW WELDED I AM IN MY SOUL WITH THIS PERSON!"

Critics have become increasingly attentive in recent years to the disturbed aspects of Alyosha's personality. James Rice, for one, has argued that Alyosha's fits, tears, "hallucinations," moments of "amnesia or obliviousness, [. . .] *mania grandiosa*," and sudden euphoria are all textbook symptoms of "hysteria in the clinical terms of the time, a major psychiatric disorder."[2] Though deliberately provocative in its attempt to wrest Alyosha from a perceived hagiographical critical tendency, Rice's assessment nevertheless calls attention to the palpable instability of Dostoevsky's charismatic, compassionate, but "very strange" protagonist (14:18).[3] It is noteworthy in this context that Alyosha's only vivid memory from childhood (a "bright spot in the darkness") is of a distinctly disturbing nature: that is, of his mother, "sobbing in hysterics, with screams and cries," and "grasping [Alyosha] in both arms [. . .] to the point of pain" (14:18).[4] Indeed, although rendered in affectionate terms by the narrator, Alyosha's characterization as a dependent who succeeds in "attaching" everyone to himself, who "never thought about whose means he was living on" (14:20), and who "attached himself" to Zosima "with all the fiery first love of his unquenchable heart" (14:306) vividly recalls such dependent personalities as Vasia Shumkov and Stepan Verkhovensky.[5]

For all his professed sympathy for Alyosha, the narrator invites us to consider Alyosha's connection to Zosima, though wholly in keeping with Russian Orthodox practice, as nevertheless informed by a potential pathology. As the "unquestionable ideal" to which "all [Alyosha's] youthful energies and striving" direct themselves "exclusively," Zosima, the narrator acknowledges, is "perhaps even incorrectly" (*mozhet byt' dazhe nepravil'no*) centralized in Alyosha's mind (14:306). Indeed, the pupil's impassioned reverence for his master, "to the point of such adoration, [. . .] even at times to the forgetting of 'everyone and all'" (14:306), presents us with a distinct echo of Netochka's fanatical worship of Katia that conveniently emptied her mind of everything but the object of her adoration. Alyosha's initial perception of Zosima, moreover, as the "ideal exit [*iskhod*] for his soul" (14:17) even bears some resemblance to Kirillov's submission to Pyotr's will in *Demons*, since Pyotr too offers Kirillov "some kind of exit [*iskhod*] into which his tormented spirit plunged headlong" (10:472). In both cases, the personality relinquishes itself to the will of the other as a form of "exit" from its own unbearable anguish. Alyosha's religious devotion at the beginning of the novel, in this sense, can be described as a quasi-idolatrous worship of an "extraordinary being," since Alyosha, we are told, is not "a mystic" but rather a "lover of human beings" (14:17), and since he himself suggests that "perhaps I don't even believe in God" (14:201).[6] His apprenticeship, then, is characterized by an uneasy duality between a loving bond, on the one hand, and an intense need, on the other, to be propped up and sustained by an all-powerful master. His attempts to explain the connection evoke both of these dimensions, that is, both love and an overwhelming sensation of dependence. "If you only knew," he exclaims to Lise, "how I am bound, how I am welded in my soul with this person!" (14:201).

The novel's opening pages depict the gradually mounting sense of panic in Alyosha as he anticipates with a "painfully contracting heart" not only the death of his beloved friend, but also the terrifying prospect of being torn from the sustenance of an external mind: "How would he remain without [his elder], how would he not see him, not hear him? And where will he go? [. . .] Alyosha had never felt such agony for a long time [. . .] he did not have the strength even to bear his thoughts so did they press down on him" (14:72). Alyosha's panic under the burden of "his thoughts" recalls the experiences of Vasia Shumkov and Stepan Verkhovensky in their failed attempts to carry the weight of consciousness within themselves when severed from their administrative counterparts. In each case, the loss of the external source of governance gives rise to an intense intellectual turmoil within the unformed mind of the dependent self. In the absence of his master's guidance, Alyosha feels "as though his mind were broken up and dispersed" to such an extent that he "felt afraid to connect the dispersed parts and to extract a general idea from all the tormenting contradictions" (14:132). When Ivan disturbs Alyosha's worldview with his rejection of the cosmic order, Alyosha, "frightened" from "something [. . .] to which he could give no answer" (14:241) and which "shook his soul" (14:307), flees to "the ruler of his heart and his mind" (14:305) and collapses at his feet hysterically, cleaving, in his confusion, to an external source of intellection, which would provide respite from the unbearable chaos of his interior life (14:258).[7] Zosima's death, therefore, incites a reckoning in Alyosha with these elements of the unconscious that have been rising up in him in such an oppressive manner—the "tormentingly," ominous but vague "something" (14:241, 258, 307) that keeps "growing in him, [but] to which he can give no answer" (14:241). As a guide and external mind, Zosima is, of course, utterly dissimilar from the earlier "masters" we have cited as parallels, in that his intention is not to bind his pupil but to prepare him to be released into the world. This process of being released, as we shall see, for Alyosha, begins in the harrowing confrontation with these interior forces.

FIRST DREAM: THE EXPANDING ROOM

Upon the loss of his external source of sustenance and stability, Alyosha undergoes a mystical or religious experience during which, we are told, he is transformed from a "weak youth" into "a steadfast warrior for his whole life" (14:328). Though this journey ultimately leads him inward, he begins by fleeing any encounter with the contents of his psyche. This flight is dramatized vividly through Alyosha's frantic reaction to his master's decaying corpse, a sight which brings the escalating sense of panic in the hero to its critical peak, inciting "a sort of breach and cataclysm in his soul" (14:297). Though the narrator admits that he cannot fully explain the effect of this phenomenon upon Alyosha (14:305), we are prompted to consider Alyosha's reaction to the corpse in the context of the lineage of this motif in Dostoevsky's writing. Indeed, Alyosha's flight from the dead body connects the protagonist to a long line of wounded characters for whom, as we have seen, the memory-image of a corpse acts as a prohibitive limit in the psyche. In the case of Netochka, the traumatic memory of her mother's dead body resulted in a state of amnesia which arrested the heroine's ability to reflect and propelled her into compulsive attempts to dissolve herself in others. Alyosha, for his part, does not mention or reflect upon his childhood (that is, apart from the memory of his mother's frenzied embraces before the icon). As with Myshkin who falls into convulsions when reminded of his childhood beatings, Alyosha is sent into a violent "hysterical fit" (14:127) at the description of his mother's suffering and hysteria. We are given no account of the effect of his mother's death upon him, but we are told, interestingly, that Alyosha initially returns to the town as the result of a sudden and seemingly inexplicable desire to find his mother's grave (14:21). The narrator remarks that Alyosha "himself probably did not know and could not answer the question of what precisely had risen up from his soul" but that it was the same force that "irresistibly pulled him" toward the monastery and to his elder (14:21). Thus, it is the "ris[ing] up from the soul" of painful memory and the search for the dead body from the past that "pulls" Alyosha toward his elder and ultimately to the initial dissolution of the self in the master.

The episode with Grushenka that takes place upon Alyosha's flight from his elder's corpse can be read in this light as an attempt on Alyosha's part to dissolve himself in yet another person as a means of evading the "something" that is "growing in him" but that he is desperate not to encounter (14:241, 258, 307). His intention in going to Grushenka's house, we are told, is "to perish" (14:321) and to be "swallowed up" by her (14:318), and, upon encountering Grushenka, he immediately succumbs to a new form of intimate embrace, with Grushenka "jumping onto his lap [. . .] and tenderly grasping his neck with her left arm" (14:315). What at first glance seems like a capricious plan on Grushenka's part for the sexual deflowering of a "righteous" young man is, upon closer inspection, the desire of a wounded individual to take control of another personality. Grushenka explains her plan to "consume" Alyosha in terms which directly evoke the notion of a collective self: sensing that Alyosha's "face" had taken up residence in her "heart," she was, in her words, "'taken over by such a feeling that [she] was surprised finally at [her]self'" and decided "'to swallow him up, swallow him up and laugh'" (14:320). Like Nastasia Filippovna with Myshkin, Grushenka refers to Alyosha as her "conscience," questions him about her own hidden feelings ("tell me: do I love him or not"), and defers her agency to him, asking him to decide her fate ("as you say, so it shall be" [14:322]). In the subsequent scene that Alyosha will later refer to as the moment of the "restoration of [his] soul," Grushenka, hearing of Zosima's death, relinquishes her embrace of Alyosha, a subtle gesture that nevertheless "shakes both of their souls" (14:318).

Alyosha's religious experience, in this sense, begins where Myshkin's journey ended, with the journey into the tomb to confront the decaying corpse.[8] In his resolve to return to the site of the dead body, he is strengthened, at least partially, by Grushenka's reflections on the nature of memory. Having been distracted from her own intention of "consuming" Alyosha by the reemergence of a painful memory from her own past—the sudden reappearance of her "offender"—Grushenka recounts the tale of the "onion," in which the peasant woman is lifted from the fiery lake of hell by means of her guardian angel's ability to remember the woman's one good deed (14:319).[9] Alyosha, shaken by this notion, returns to the site of Zosima's rotting corpse, before which he kneels and embarks, through meditative prayer, upon a journey inward.

Alyosha's prayer near the corpse recalls Zosima's characterization of prayer as a form of introspective "education." A "sincere" prayer, according to Zosima will bring "a new feeling [. . .] into view, and, in it, a new thought which you did not know hitherto and which will encourage you" (14:288–89). Having begun his prayer, Alyosha finds himself initially lost among chaotic and confusing "scraps of thoughts" that "flicker in his soul, catching fire, like little stars, and then going out, giving way to others." After wandering through the "scraps" in his mind, we are told that "he became aware within himself" of "something whole, firm, soothing" which "reigned in his soul" (14:325)—a description which evokes the "something" that had previously tormented him in the form of an insurgent force "growing" from within (14:241, 258, 307). The movement through the realm of thought into deeper, unconscious space, toward the "something" that is "whole" and "firm" within the psyche, is accompanied by the impression of expanding space. As he moves beyond the realm of thoughts and impressions into the farther realm of his dream, he asks himself "Why is the room expanding?" (14:327).

In our discussion of the "expanding room" as a motif of the journey into the unconscious mind in *The Insulted and Injured* (chapter 3), we saw that, for Vanya as a tortured amnesiac, the darkness of his room as it expanded evoked a visceral terror of "dead bodies," which led to the urgent desire to flee, "to tear [him]self out of [his] apartment, to go anywhere, even into the rain, into the mire" (3:207). Alyosha, having exhibited a similar unwillingness to inhabit this space and a parallel desire to escape, nevertheless persists in his inward turn to encounter the contents of the psyche. In his dream, presented as a movement through the inward into the innermost, Dostoevsky employs the image of the wedding feast as a depiction of the interior geography of the personality: a realm populated by many, all "rejoicing" and "drinking new wine, the wine of the new, great joy." In other words, the landscape of the unconscious mind is portrayed not as an isolated space, but as densely inhabited by people who have gathered to celebrate and to nourish themselves upon mysterious and miraculous sources.[10] From among the many assembled, three central figures compose the landscape: Alyosha, Zosima, and Christ. Zosima, now raised and restored from the dead, welcomes Alyosha and directs him toward the center of the feast, where Christ is performing the miracle of the transformation of the water into wine, which is then being given to all to drink. Though Alyosha is afraid and resists looking, Zosima counsels him to look past the "new wine," past those "carrying the jugs," to the source of the wine, at which point Alyosha finds himself overwhelmed by the "something" which "burned in [his] heart" and which "suddenly filled him to the point of pain," and wakes up from his dream (14:327).

If we think of Alyosha's dream as a depiction of the interior life of the psyche, we can discern the presence of three interlocutors: the self as the immediate experience of consciousness (Alyosha), the mind as the guide or director (Zosima), and the deeper terrain of the unconscious, or soul, which cannot be glimpsed directly since it opens up toward a deeper underlying mystical source (Christ). It is noteworthy that Alyosha, entering into a dream, is encountering these elements of the personality (mind, consciousness, and soul) as interior presences rather than as external addressees. And yet in this interior space the personality, according to this depiction, is not an enclosed realm, since both of Alyosha's interlocutors, Zosima and Christ, are not aspects of his own personality, but "visitors" from beyond the domain of the self. "Someone," according to Alyosha, "visited my soul in that hour" (14:328).[11] In other words, Zosima, for Alyosha, is not merely an introjection, but a presence extrinsic to the self. Christ, similarly, is not an aspect of the unconscious soul, but a nourishing presence which lies beyond the depths of the unconscious.[12] (We shall come back to this question of the "visitor" to the self after our discussion of Dmitry's and Ivan's experiences.) Having caught a glimpse of the divine source that extends beyond the self (which is linked directly to the "something" that had initially tormented and terrified him), Alyosha awakens and goes out to embrace the earth (which ostensibly reaches down toward the same inward sources as the psyche) and senses that "something firm and unshakable, like this heavenly vault, was descending into his soul," and that "something like an idea established its reign in his mind—and already for his whole life and forever and ever."[13] Alyosha's transformative journey can be described, in this sense, as the loss of an external source of sustenance which prompts an intensely difficult (and initially unwilling) turn toward introspection to discover an alternate indwelling source of nourishment and stabilization.

"I WILL BE HIS GOD TO WHOM HE WILL PRAY"

Dmitry begins the novel in a state of crisis which rivals that of Alyosha. His utter lack of capacity for self-governance is later testified to by Doctor Herzenstube at Dmitry's trial, and is described as the lack of "a head" (15:106).[14] Dmitry's headlessness, or rather, his "unbridled" nature (15:153) is not simply, however, the result of mental deficiency. Dmitry himself describes his condition best when he speaks of his desperate unwillingness to engage in any extensive activity of introspection as the result of an abiding sense of terror at what might lie within, at the presence of "unknown ideas" which he senses within himself but which he does not want to encounter: "unknown ideas were raging within me, and I got drunk, fought, raged about. In order to assuage them within me, I got into fights, in order to calm them, to suppress them" (15:31). The recurring dream Dmitry describes to his interrogators depicts his terror at the prospect of bringing the unconscious reaches of the personality to the scrutiny of the conscious mind: "Someone is chasing me, someone of whom I'm terribly afraid, chases me in the dark, at night, is searching for me, and I hide somewhere from him behind the door, or the dresser, I hide humiliatingly" (14:424). Dmitry's fear of his unexplored interior darkness and his incapacity for self-direction thus make him ideally suited to fall under Katerina Ivanovna's administrative guidance. As Alyosha points out, "such a character as Katerina Ivanovna needed to rule, but she could only rule over such a person as Dmitry, [. . .] For Mitia alone (let's say, at least over a long period of time) could submit himself to her" (14:170).

Katia, we gradually discover, is much more to Dmitry than a fiancée. Her plans for the administration of his personality resonate explicitly with those of the Grand Inquisitor for "the weak ones": "'All my life, all my life, I will follow him tirelessly [. . .] I'll insist that he will recognize me and will tell me everything, without being ashamed!' she exclaimed as if in a frenzy. 'I will be his god, to whom he will pray.'"[15] For Katia, the desire to supplant the place of God in Dmitry's mind is part of her rather bizarre intention to dissolve herself into Dmitry as a mere extension of his personality: "'I will turn myself simply into a means for his salvation . . . into an instrument, into a machine for his happiness, and that is for my whole life" (14:172). In her role as Dmitry's external conscience and "god," Katia atones on his behalf for sins which he has already forgotten committing, for example, his treatment of Snegiryov, which Katia, though not present at the event, "cannot remember without indignation" (14:176).[16] We discover from Dmitry's confession to Alyosha, moreover, that Katia has succeeded in acquiring a divine status in his imagination. In his obsession with Schiller's "Eleusinian Festival," Dmitry constantly replays in his mind the shame experienced by the debased human being when confronted with the majesty of the goddess Ceres, or Demeter, a sense of shame that he experiences perpetually as an "insect" in the face of Katia's "majestic [. . .] magnanimity" (14:105).[17] When Alyosha finally sees the two interact, he is astonished by the bizarre intensity of their intimacy: Katia "throws herself headlong" upon Dmitry, "squeezing" his hands "convulsively"; they stare into each other's eyes "silently, fixedly, as if chained to each other" for "about two minutes," and then continue to "babble speeches to each other that were meaningless and frenzied" (15:187–88). Katia, for her part, describes her attachment to Dmitry as more than love or friendship; rather, like the bond between Zosima and Alyosha, it extends into the very interior reaches of the self. "You," she explains to Dmitry, "will remain in my soul for my whole life as a wound, and I in yours" (15:187).

In Dmitry's attempt to flee from Katia's administrative tyranny and to exist independently from her, Dostoevsky depicts the frantic search for new, alternate sources of sustenance for the fragmented self. As a way of emancipating himself, in his desperate search for new sources of wealth, Dmitry devises (much like Arkady Dolgoruky with his concealed "letter" and his "idea") a makeshift soul, a secret, "interior" location of resources that he can draw upon for sustenance in his escape, though of course these concealed, inward "riches" are merely stolen from Katia herself. Here Dostoevsky expands on his critique (which he began, as we saw, in *The Adolescent*) of the Western conception of inviolate personhood, or ensouledness, as grounded ultimately in the idea of personal property. Dmitry in fact comes to associate the "amulet" or "talisman" (15:130) quite literally with his "heart" or "soul," though he realizes that this hastily conceived source is ultimately not sufficiently robust for his purposes.[18] Thus, Dmitry spends a significant portion of the novel searching for alternate sources of wealth that would not be ultimately derived from Katia. In this context, when Madame Khoklavova suggests that Dmitry journey to the "gold mines" in order to discover "infinitely more than three thousand" (14:348), she unwittingly touches upon the deeper significance of Dmitry's quest by evoking the canonical European romantic paradigm of the essential soul as the solution to his dilemma of sourcelessness.[19]

Dmitry's state of "terrible confusion" (14:328) that follows his abandonment of his fiancée resonates directly with that of Vasia Shumkov in his flight from his external mind. We are told that in the two days after breaking off the engagement, Dmitry was "literally tossing about in all directions" (14:329), that "the most fantastic whirlwind had risen up in his head" (14:332) and that he "was in such an unimaginable condition that he could really have fallen ill with an inflammation of the brain" (14:328). Dmitry's personality unravels even further into chaos when, through desperation, he tears apart the clothbag, and, existing now without any external "mind" or "soul," falls into a state of near insanity: "he was already unable to reason [. . .] everything was vague in his soul, vague to the point of suffering" (14:370). As he explains semi-coherently to Perkhotin, "there is no order in me, no higher order" (14:366). In this state, like "a little child" (14:372), Dmitry is easily taken over by the wills of others, becoming immediately subservient, for example, to Pyotr Ilyich's administrative commands; as the latter "ordered him to soap himself more and to scrub more, it was as if he took over command of Dmitry in that moment" (14:361).

Like Stepan Trofimovich who tore himself from his dependence upon Varvara Petrovna only to place himself soon afterward under the vigilant protection of another, Dmitry, in this state of agonizing incompleteness, is overwhelmed by a devastatingly intense longing for Grushenka as the "queen of [his] soul," as his "light," and his "shrine" (*svyatynya*) (14:418) or, in other words, as a new irreproachably divine external mind that will help him to stifle the confusion rising up within him. The unbearable sensations of inner turmoil rising in Dmitry are consistently accompanied by a desperate longing to fall under Grushenka's administration: "But it was vague, very vague in Dmitry's soul, and though there was much that tormented his soul, still in that moment his entire being irresistibly strained only towards her, to his queen" (14:369). Though at first glance this longing appears to be erotically driven, closer scrutiny shows that it stems in fact from Dmitry's urgent desire to stifle his inner chaos by dissolving his personality into a collective unity, a longing which is directly parallel to Alyosha's frantic need to fall at Zosima's feet amid the excruciating tumult in his thoughts:

> Never from Dmitry's breast had there ever arisen more love for this woman who was so fateful to his destiny, so much of a new feeling, never felt before, unexpected even for himself, a feeling that was tender to the point of prayer, to the point of his own disappearance before her. "And I will disappear!" he said suddenly in a fit of some kind of hysterical rapture. (14:370)

When Dmitry finally encounters Grushenka in this state (of passionate desire to "disappear before her") he is not an impassioned lover, but "a little dog" who can "only understand, shivering with his whole heart, that she was being affectionate to him" (14:378), a fragment of a self that longs to silence the unwanted dimensions that are awakening in the absence of an external source.

SECOND DREAM: THE HALF-BURNT VILLAGE

The events of his father's death force Dmitry to enter into the dreaded chaos of his interior life. As with his brother Alyosha upon the demise of Zosima, Dmitry's journey into the reaches of his unconscious mind begins with the dramatic rupture of the extended self: "He remembered later that several people tore him away from [Grushenka] by force, that they led her suddenly away, and that he only regained consciousness when he was already sitting on a chair" (412).[20] Whereas Alyosha, rent from Zosima, eventually enters voluntarily upon his inward journey through meditative prayer, for Dmitry the "journey of the soul through the torments" is forced upon him by the officials who insistently "bore" their way into the "privacy" and "depths" of his personality.[21] At first, Dmitry, unaccustomed to reflection, believes sanguinely that he can "open and pour out [his] entire soul [. . .] in a moment'" (14:419); he discovers, however, when the questioning begins, that the "opening" of the soul is in fact an excruciating and highly undesirable endeavor.

Dmitry's journey inward is presented as an excruciating "torment," undertaken unwillingly, but also, for Dmitry, painfully illuminative. "'In twenty years of life,'" he attests later, "'I didn't learn as much as I have discovered on this cursed night'" (14:438). Dmitry's recurring nightmare of being chased and of hiding fearfully is enacted now by the process of interrogation: "Now it's no longer a dream! [. . .] I'm the wolf, and you are the hunters" (14:424). In keeping with his nightmare, he continually attempts to hide elements of his life from inquiry, insisting that "these depths of the heart" (14:415) are part of "my private life, and I won't allow you to intrude into my private life" (14:422), but as the investigators "bore into him" (14:430), he is forced to relinquish all of his inviolate space until, having revealed his "great secret" (14:440), and being stripped even of his clothing, he feels as though there is nothing left in him to reveal.[22] It is significant that Dmitry blames the process of introspection for what he sees as the destruction and disgrace of his personality. "The fault is mine," he laments, "I shouldn't have poked into there" (*ne nado bylo sovat'sia* [14:448]).

As in Alyosha's experience, however, the turn inward leads Dmitry beyond the sphere of thought and feeling into a farther unconscious realm. Again, like Alyosha, Dmitry falls asleep quite suddenly while in the presence of others, and, as in Alyosha's dream, the landscape of Dmitry's unconscious is populated by a crowd of people. Instead of joyous revelers, however, Dmitry encounters a row of emaciated peasant women. Rather than an abundant, exuberant feast, he sees a burnt-down village plagued by drought and starvation, in which the peasants are "begging for their burnt-down place." The focal point of the dream is the freezing and starving infant who "is not being warmed up" (14:456) and who cannot be nourished at the "dried-up" breasts of his withered mother in which "there is not a drop of milk" (14:457). In his dream, Dmitry is particularly fixated upon the poverty of the scene, and asks, "why don't they embrace, why don't they sing joyful songs"—as they do in Alyosha's dream—"why have they turned so black from black poverty, why don't they feed the little child?" (14:457). Dmitry's lament is that there is no source of sustenance in this village—in other words, no infinite "source" of "new wine" that sustains the celebration. Instead, at the depth of the mind, there is a frozen and starving sourcelessness.

Dmitry's experience differs from Alyosha's then in that he does not encounter a nourishing source at the heart of the self; rather, he experiences the awakening of a hunger to discover these sources, a visceral awareness of the need to nourish the starved landscape of the psyche: "he feels that some kind of tender feeling he had never felt before is rising in his heart, that he wants to weep, that he wants to do something for everyone so that the infant would not cry anymore, so that the blackened and dried-out mother of the child would not cry either, so that there would be no more tears from this moment onward" (14:456–57). Having spent his days begging and searching for sources of sustenance in others (like the peasants in his dream, "begging for their burnt-down place"), Dmitry discovers the possibility in his dream of nonmaterial inward sources of nourishment.

In a subsequent series of illuminative, but highly confused, attempts to interpret his dream, Dmitry succeeds in bringing together at least two disparate paradigms of the self. His general approach is to understand the frozen infant as an image of the innermost self, the "soul" or "heart" at the deepest reaches of the psyche, "the potential person in him" (15:172). He views the appearance of the infant as a "prophecy," and explains it thus: "Why did I dream of the 'little infant' in that moment? [. . .] This was a prophecy to me! [. . .] One can find the human heart there in the mines, under the earth, [. . .] one can resuscitate and resurrect the deadened heart in this imprisoned person, one can look after him for years, and bring him out from the den into the light already as an elevated soul" (15:31). The parallel Dmitry establishes between the frozen infant and the underground prisoner becomes more coherent when we consider that Dmitry, in his elation, is conflating two symbolic paradigms of the unconscious. On the one hand, he is drawing from the imagery of his dream; on the other, he appears to be drawing on the paradigm of Demeter and the degraded human being which so tormented his every thought prior to his transformative experience.[23] If, previously, Dmitry's psyche was depicted always as tormented by an unbearable dualism (the majestic goddess confronting the debased human being; or the cruel "hunter" and the "humiliated [. . .] wolf"), the discovery of this "little infant" opens up a new third dimension, namely, the underground prisoner as the innermost self. We recall that, in Schiller's presentation of the myth, "debased man" encounters Demeter who is searching for her daughter, Persephone, an underground prisoner in Hades. By the end of the novel, Dmitry's personality has expanded from its embodied and humiliating hypostasis of a "debased man" to encompass all three archetypes in the myth: the goddess searching for the subterranean prisoner (15:31); the debased man ashamed of his embodied state; and the "prisoner," the "potential person" within (15:172) whom he wants so desperately to "resurrect" and not to lose (15:31); or in other words, mind, embodied self, and submerged soul (the gestures of watchman, redeemer, and prisoner that appeared so prominently in an externalized form in Dostoevsky's earlier novels).[24] Though Dmitry tends to understand his quest in literal terms, that is, that he must go to the mines in Siberia to redeem the underground prisoner and to find God (15:31), Alyosha insists that the paradigm can be grasped instead as a symbolic figuration of the inner work of the personality (15:185).

IVAN'S ARCHIVE

Ivan is initially introduced in the novel as an exception to the epidemic of dependency that characterizes so many of Dostoevsky's protagonists. Intellectually brilliant, punctilious, productive, prudent, and disdainful of the Karamazov lack of restraint, Ivan, in contrast to his brothers who cling to others for guidance, has learned not only to "support himself" from an early age, but also to keep his own counsel (14:20). His "rebellion," moreover, in which he returns his "ticket" to the celebration of universal harmony, is not merely a rejection of a world founded upon injustice, but also a passionate affirmation of his independence from that world.

As he becomes embroiled in the affairs of his family, however, Ivan displays a similar weakness to his brothers and one that is even more pronounced in him, namely, a fear of and utter incapacity for introspection, which emerges, in fact, as one of his defining characteristics. When we are given access to his thoughts, we see that he is continually attempting "not to think" (14:242), as he is sickened by what he senses as the vague underlying implications of his thoughts. His confused feelings about Dmitry's potential guilt are indicative of the general mood of his personality: "Why it was so, he didn't want to figure out; he even felt disgust at digging around in his feelings. He wanted as if to forget something as quickly as possible" (15:47).[25] Only too frequently, in fact, does he find himself hard-pressed to give any rational account of his behavior and feelings, either of why he abandoned his father on the eve of the murder or of whether he did in fact wish for his father's death (15:49, 54). Like such earlier precursors as Ordynov and Raskolnikov, Ivan longs to discard his memories, to "blow" on the "phantoms" from the past that "flicker in his mind" and to send them "flying away"; his relief at escaping to Chermashnia is a case in point: "Away all that is past, to finish with the past world forever, and let there be no news or mention of it; into the new world, into new places, and without looking back!" The discarding of memory, however, is not ultimately a liberating activity for Ivan, since subliminal and incomprehensible sensations of "gloom" and "sorrow" remain "howling in his heart" even in the absence of memory (14:255). The descriptions of Ivan's interior life are consistently presented as uncharted waters which suddenly and painfully "seethe" or "boil up" onto the shores of consciousness (e.g., "a terrible nightmare of thoughts and sensations seethed in his soul" [15:54]) only to be suppressed by means of an external distraction, in the sudden overwhelming need to search out an interlocutor.

Of all Dostoevsky's characters, Ivan most precisely corresponds to the Bakhtinian paradigm of the outwardly directed consciousness on the "threshold." Willfully directing his attention away from the "seething," "burning" sensations within his "soul," Ivan conceives of the self as fundamentally the carrier of an idea or as an activity of consciousness.[26] Therefore, for Ivan, the notions of personal "essence," "idea," and "thesis" are all synonymous. As he explains to Alyosha, "'the task is for me as quickly as possible to explain to you my essence, that is what kind of person I am, [. . .] I won't accept [the eternal harmony]. That is my essence [. . .], that is my thesis" (14:215).[27] In formulating a path for Ivan's spiritual regeneration, Alyosha confronts this peculiarity of his brother's character, when he declares that Ivan's passionate "love for life" means that "half [his] work is done," adding that the remaining task is for Ivan to awaken the other withered half of his personality: "'Now you must work on your second half, and you will be saved.' [. . .] 'And in what does it consist, [this] second half?' 'In that you must resurrect your dead, which perhaps never even died'" (14:210). In other words, according to Alyosha's idiosyncratic "profession of faith," to be "saved" means to bring together the outwardly directed activity of "love for life" with the inward work of fostering the elements of the psyche that have been discarded and left for dead.

As we have seen, Dostoevsky's amnesiacs (Ordynov, Netochka, Vanya, Raskolnikov, Myshkin) tend to bind themselves to a carrier of memory as a way of supplementing their own interior void. Ivan, as we first encounter him, represents a culmination of this theme in that he is a self-professed "collector" of other people's childhood experiences: "I have a great, great amount collected about Russian children" (14:220), he tells Alyosha. His archive, maintained in a series of notebooks, is distinguished by the vividness with which he imagines the experiences of these abused children. In his rendition, the newspaper accounts of child abuse take on the palpable, visceral quality of real memories. From the bare facts of a stranger's experiences, Ivan imagines "a little creature, who is not yet able to understand what's being done with her in a vile place, in the dark and in the cold, beating herself with her tiny little fist on her tormented breast, weeping her bloody, spiteless, meek little tears to 'God' that he would defend her" (14:220). In his agitated presentation of these experiences, we are prompted to consider the images he evokes as substitutes for his own forgotten childhood experiences, considering of course that he grew up in the midst of his mother's hysterical fits (herself a "young woman frightened from her very childhood" [14:13]) and his father's perverse and unrestrained cruelty.

As he walks away from his conversation with Alyosha in which he has evoked these distressing examples of abused children, Ivan wonders at his own "unbearable anguish" which "he could not at all define" (14:241), and he immediately externalizes the sensation, projecting it outwardly onto yet another abused and spurned orphan, in the person of Smerdiakov. The connection between Ivan and Smerdiakov is, therefore, initially established in the novel by means of the conflation between an unacknowledged interior anguish and an external "offending object" that catches his eye: "Ivan Fyodorovich tried 'not to think,' but was not able to ease [his anguish] this way. Most importantly what was annoying about it, this anguish, and what irritated him is that it had some kind accidental, completely external aspect; he felt this. Some kind of being or object stood and jutted out somewhere" (14:242).[28] Smerdiakov becomes the external object into which Ivan's stirred-up and unexamined anguish is displaced: "he figured out all at once what it was that was tormenting and bothering him.[. . .] Ivan Fyodorovich understood from the first glance at him that the lackey Smerdyakov was sitting in his soul too and that it was precisely this person that his soul could not bear" (14:242). Nonetheless, he does not merely stumble upon Smerdiakov by chance, for their relationship begins as an apprenticeship in which Ivan "trained Smerdiakov to speak with him" (14:243). Like Ordynov, drawn inexorably to Katerina (or Vanya to Nellie, and Myshkin to Nastasia Filippovna), Ivan is overwhelmed by a compulsion ("the strongest curiosity" [14:244]) to seek out Smerdiakov as the carrier of something suppressed in himself, though in this case Ivan finds himself bound not to a beautiful woman with mysterious memories, nor to an innocent and insulted orphan, but rather to a "trashy scoundrel" who disgusts him (14:242).[29]

We should note parenthetically that the "resemblance" between Ivan and his father, frequently mentioned in the novel, is founded precisely upon this quality of amnesia and displacement of interiority. Like Ivan with his past, Fyodor "waves his arms not only at the grave [of his dead wife], but at all his memories" (14:22).[30] The household functions only because the servant, Grigory, becomes the bearer of Fyodor's memory. Grigory, for instance, looks after the discarded children whom Fyodor has completely forgotten, rather than merely neglected, and it is also Grigory who builds a grave to Fyodor's dead wife. Grigory's duties extend beyond such menial tasks, and we are told that there were also "higher incidents" in which Fyodor experienced a "very subtle and complex" spiritual dependence upon his servant. When Fyodor "senses in himself, [. . .] a spiritual terror and moral commotion almost, that is to say, physically calling out in his soul [. . .] 'as if my soul is trembling in my throat,'" he needs the presence of Grigory to help him stifle these unwanted uprisings: "Precisely the main thing was that it would be necessarily an *other* person, [. . .] that one could call him in a morbid moment, only so that one could look him in the face, [. . .] It would happen . . . that Fyodor Pavlovich would go even at night into the wing to wake up Grigory, so that he would come to him for a minute, [then would . . .] let him go soon after, and himself, [. . .] would lie down and sleep now already the sleep of a righteous man" (14:86–87). Ivan resembles his father in the need to find an external projective screen as a way of stifling the rising up of an unwanted unconscious life, of quelling a "soul" that "cries out in one's throat" by finding "objects" in the external world as projective substitutions.

Smerdiakov is presented initially as "a weak mind" (14:428), a lower self that cleaves to Ivan as to a governmental agency, an ungainly echo of Alyosha cleaving to his elder, or of Vasia Shumkov to Arkady. Echoing in some way Grigory's service to Fyodor Pavlovich, Smerdiakov accepts Ivan as his master, and even, adopting a demeanor of obedience and awe, purports to view Ivan as "the Lord God,'" as his "defender" and "teacher" (15:44), insistently conceiving of himself as Ivan's "henchman," the instrument of Ivan's administrative will (15:59).

Ivan, however, as an unexamined personality intent on ridding himself of the contents of his unconscious life, becomes gradually subsumed into the will of his pupil, and perhaps even more inexorably than Dmitry or Alyosha to their administrative minds.[31] In Ivan's interactions with Smerdiakov, Dostoevsky continues to develop the notion of demonic possession as a psychological reality, as the relinquishment of one's personal will to the will of the other. Just as Myshkin, under the influence of his "demon," found himself compulsively obeying Rogozhin's expectations, abandoning his train in order to visit Nastasia Filippovna, so Ivan baffles himself by spontaneously fulfilling Smerdiakov's expectations: "'You see . . . I'm going to Chermashnia . . .'

somehow suddenly tore itself from Ivan Fyodorovich, [. . .] of its own accord and with some kind of nervous laughter" (14:254). Later Smerdiakov comments incredulously on how Ivan "went to Chermashnia without any reason, but simply according to my word" (15:53). Nor does this bizarre state of possession remain unnoticed by Ivan, who is both bewildered and infuriated by his own compulsion to obey Smerdiakov's expectations and forgo his own sense of agency:

> that he had so suddenly stopped and not passed by, as he had wanted to just a moment ago, enraged him to the point of trembling. [. . .] To his most extreme astonishment, something completely different flew off of his tongue [. . .] and suddenly, also completely unexpectedly, he sat down on the bench. For a moment it seemed to him almost frightening. (14:244)

In Ivan's compulsive subordination to Smerdiakov's will, Dostoevsky develops his notion of susceptibility to demonic possession as a state of mind that arises from the neglect, suppression, or erasure of the unconscious mind. Ivan, a stranger and enemy to the "nightmare of thoughts and sensations seething in his soul," becomes gradually invaded by the being to whom he is bound as to a substitute for this "seething" interior space.

THIRD DREAM: "HOW I WISH IT WERE *HE* AND NOT I"

Ivan's dream—the last of the three parallel journeys inward that compose the core of the novel—is induced by the sudden, dramatic rupture from the external mind, and, in fact, coincides with the moment of Smerdiakov's suicide.[32] Like his brothers' transformative experiences, the dream is preceded by a concerted effort to look inward. Terrified as he is of his interior dimensions and desperate not to acknowledge their existence, Ivan is considerably less capable than his brothers of undertaking an inward journey; thus his introspective turn is externalized as a series of three attempts to investigate his own motives and feelings ever more deeply through the questioning of Smerdiakov, a tripartite sequence that reflects the three "torments" of Dmitry's journey. Sensing vague and subdued feelings of guilt and shame arise within him, surfacing alongside "strange thoughts [which] torment him" concerning his feelings for his father (15:49), and "some peculiar indignation that suddenly boiled up in his soul" (15:56), Ivan, finding it impossible to reflect on any of these sensations, hurries instead to question Smerdiakov. In the ensuing investigations, Ivan (in a somewhat bizarre manner) interrogates his interlocutor on the nature of his own feelings: "'And did I really know about the murder then?' Ivan screamed finally" (15:51); Smerdiakov's answers therefore refer to his own imagining of Ivan's impulses and desires, rather than to the actual substance of Ivan's unconscious life: "you yourself wished then for the death of your parent" (15:51); "that someone else would kill him, this you did want" (15:52).

In this journey of (oxymoronic) projective introspection, Ivan seems to penetrate ever further into his own unconscious motives through his questioning of Smerdiakov until he, like the investigators with Dmitry, finally arrives at the core of his own "great secret" which, like Dmitry's, takes the form of a sum of money concealed secretly under one's clothing—a perverted image, as we have seen, of the notion of an individual soul (as an "interior" location of wealth which has in fact only been stolen from someone else).[33] As Smerdiakov sinks "his fingers deeply into [his] stocking" in search of this interior source, Ivan is characteristically terrified by what might lie within: "Ivan Fyodorovich looked at him and suddenly shivered in convulsive fright. 'Madman!' he screamed and [. . .] looked at Smerdyakov in mad horror" (15:60). Thus, like the Grand Inquisitor with his subjects, Smerdiakov, a rather unlikely candidate for the role in question, has, nonetheless, ostensibly carried Ivan's conscience (or his "soul" for him), allowing Ivan to live in a state of oblivion with regard to his "crime." Having now journeyed "inward" (though of course only into Smerdiakov's psyche and not into his own) and having taken on the burden of his "guilt" in his appropriation of the money, Ivan too senses "in himself some kind of infinite firmness" (15:68). This fortifying journey, however, into the self via Smerdiakov is subsequently exposed as a false and merely projective activity.[34] Ivan has in fact found out nothing about himself from Smerdiakov, and his "firmness" evaporates immediately as he enters into his own rooms and is forced, now in the absence of Smerdiakov as a projective addressee, to encounter his own interior space: "it was strange, almost all the joy, all the contentment with himself went away in an instant. As soon as he entered into his room, something icy suddenly touched his heart, as if a memory, or rather a reminder of something tormenting and disgusting, which was precisely in this room now, and which had been there before" (15:69).

The ensuing dream represents the moment in which Ivan, having lost recourse to a projective self, is finally compelled to peer into his own psyche—an activity for which he is altogether unprepared. If Alyosha's unconscious mind took on the aspect of an abundant wedding feast (expressing Alyosha's interior rootedness in a transcendent source), and Dmitry's dreamscape was a burnt-down village (reflecting the devastation of his personality and his need for new sources of sustenance), Ivan's dreamscape, appropriately, is simply his own living quarters, precisely the same rooms that furnish his conscious life. The room, unlike the space surrounding Alyosha, does not "expand." Instead, the shallowness of the dream reflects the fastidious contempt for interiority that characterizes Ivan; in other words, even his sleep is shallow, or, as he expresses it, "it is as if I am awake in my sleep" (15:88). Ivan's nightmare of the devil is thus the depiction of a psyche whose depths have been closed off and, as a result, do not extend beyond the self. Ivan wonders even how his "guest" could have gotten in, since all the doors and windows are closed (15:70). Unlike Zosima in Alyosha's dream, and the little child in Dmitry's dream, the phantasm generated by Ivan's imagination cannot acquire the status of a separate being. If Alyosha is aware that "someone" came to him in that hour (which signifies, among other things, that his dream is not a reflection of his own thoughts, but allows for a meeting with another person), Ivan continually insists to the "devil" that "it is I, I myself am speaking, and not you!" (15:72), though he wishes at the same time that his visitor were not simply an extension of himself: "I really wish it were *he* and not I" (15:87). The substance of Ivan's nightmare, then, is the terror of being trapped inside one's own personality which is only an activity of consciousness with no interior aperture extending beyond itself.[35] Indeed, if there were a "beyond" within, then the devil could in fact be more than an embodiment and projection of the self (and thus perhaps would no longer be the devil).

The central question posed by all three dreams, then, is the issue of an interior *source* that allows for the renewal of the self. Whereas Alyosha's wedding feast is animated by the "new wine" generated miraculously by indwelling sources which extend beyond the self, and Dmitry's burnt-down village is populated by beings who hungrily seek a new source of sustenance, Ivan encounters in his psyche only the endless recycling of the old: "everything that is stupid in my nature, outlived, milled over long ago in my mind, cast aside, like carrion, you are offering to me like some kind of news!" (15:82). While Zosima teaches that a sincere introspective turn will produce a "new feeling [. . .] and, in it, a new thought, which one did not know hitherto" (14:288–89), Ivan sees in his psyche only the interminable reverberations of things that have already been processed by consciousness: "You are *me*," he laments, "you are *me*, and nothing more! You are trash, you are my fantasy!" (15:77); the devil, a "sponger" or "dependent," cannot generate anything new since the sources of the new are those located more deeply beyond the closed doors of the unconscious.

What is remarkable in this context is Alyosha's insistence that both Smerdiakov and the devil are *not* aspects of Ivan's personality.[36] "Drop him," Alyosha declares, "and forget about him! Let him take away with himself everything that you now curse, and never come again!" (15:87). Similarly, Alyosha counsels Ivan to dissolve the connection of extension between himself and Smerdiakov and to cut himself away from the latter: "you are mis-

The Apprenticeship of the Self in *The Brothers Karamazov*

taken, you are not the murderer, do you hear me, not you! God has sent me to say this to you" (15:40). At the critical moment in Ivan's journey, Dostoevsky advocates, through Alyosha, the dissolution of the collective personality and the separation of the other from the self. Alyosha—who accepts Zosima's maxim that "all are guilty for everything and for all," and who thus sees the self as open-ended and overstepping the bounds of individualism—nevertheless asks Ivan to expel all the dependent "spongers" from his psyche, since this other, as we shall see, constitutes a prohibitive barrier in the mind, protecting the self from encountering what might lie in its depths.[37] The devil expresses the idea that in order to "destroy everything" one has only to "destroy in humanity the idea of God" (15:83). The dream itself, then, is a depiction of this process, since the devil for Ivan, like Smerdiakov, becomes the projective object that blocks the path in the mind toward a deeper and more expansive form of interiority.[38]

THE TERROR OF THE "LIVING GOD"

As we have seen, the world of *The Brothers Karamazov* is populated by characters intent on supplanting the role of "god" in the psyche of the other by becoming, through their energies and activities, the ultimate sources of sustenance for the dependent self. Significantly, Zosima, the one most fitted to this role, is also the most careful not to claim it for himself. In Alyosha's development, though Zosima too becomes a source of nourishment and guidance, the elder teaches the practice of inwardness as a way of gradually discerning the beyond within the self, for it is, as he asserts, in our own "thoughts and feelings" and in our "secret innermost sensation," that we find the "roots" of a "connection with [. . .] a celestial and higher world" (14:291). In Alyosha's interior wedding feast, as we have seen, Zosima directs his pupil's attention toward a third presence in the psyche, that of Christ performing the miracle at the banquet: "'And do you see our sun, do you see him?' 'I'm afraid . . . I don't dare to look . . .' whispered Alyosha. 'Don't be afraid of him'" (14:327). This moment in Alyosha's dream resonates with the parallel moment in Ivan's meeting with Smerdiakov in which Smerdiakov notes the existence of a third presence between them, but, unlike Zosima, discourages his pupil-master from looking: "'He is here now, this third, he is between the two of us.' 'Who's he? Who's here? Who's the third?' said Ivan Fyodorovich in fright, looking around and hurriedly searching for someone in all the corners [. . .]. 'This third, God, sir, Providence itself, sir, it is here now next to us, sir, only don't look for it, you won't find it'" (15:60). In Alyosha's and Ivan's distinct fear of this "third" presence, we come closest to perceiving the ultimate source of terror which propels Dostoevsky's characters into relational space: not merely the fear of a determinate, traumatic memory, but a more fundamental and overwhelming dread of an interior divine source beyond memory which threatens to destroy and overwhelm the self.

In order to protect the self from the terrifying presence of the "living God" that exists within, Dostoevsky's characters grasp onto other people as screens. Having become aware of this source within himself, Alyosha is pierced and tormented by its energies within him. His heroic moments of truth-telling are presented as excruciating experiences in which the self is ravaged by the sources for which it has become a conduit. When Dmitry asks whether or not Alyosha believes in his innocence, "Alyosha was as if all shaken, and in his heart it was as if something sharp had gone in [and the words] suddenly tore forth from his breast in a trembling voice" (15:36). A similar phenomenon occurs when Alyosha feels called upon to speak the truth to Ivan: the words "helplessly tear from him" while he "suffocates. [. . .] He spoke already as if beyond himself, as if not of his own will, as if obeying some indeterminate decree" (15:39–40). The agonizing experience of bearing witness to the truth—of becoming a conduit for the deeper forces that flow through the self—is something that requires a robust personality to withstand. Alyosha senses the rising up of this principle in Ivan's psyche, and observes Ivan's fearful attempts to close the doors of his mind from its approach, as "God in whom he did not believe and his truth were overwhelming his heart" (15:89).[39] Alyosha, therefore, comes to supplement this principle for Ivan, banging on the doors of his dream and tearing his brother from his encounter with the "devil," so as to help prepare Ivan for the encounter with his psyche, rather than simply to release the inexperienced seeker, unprepared, into the perils of the interior life and the "dread" of falling "into the hands of the living God" (14:281).

CONCLUSIONS

Dostoevsky's depictions of religious epiphany in his final novel appear at first glance to be in line with a traditional romantic expressivist view. Moments of spiritual discovery—ranging from Alyosha's mystical experience to Dmitry's restorative dream of the child—are arrived at by means of a solitary inward turn, in which the self reaches beyond the sphere of immediate consciousness to approach a transcendent source or a life-principle at the core of the self.[40] Dostoevsky, in this context, provides a practical response to Dmitry's frustrated question of how "to enter into union with nature" (short of "kissing the earth" or "cutting open her breast" or becoming a "peasant" or a "shepherd") (14:99): namely, to tear oneself away from one's external source of nourishment in the other and to embark upon a perilous journey inward—through one's terror at what lies both within and beyond the self—to discover a deeper, and more life-sustaining, divine source.

Two elements, however, of this inward journey, distinguish Dostoevsky's view of the self from other romantic conceptions and give shape to his own idiosyncratic view of the open-ended and plural personality. First, these experiences of becoming rooted in an inward source do not lead to the dissolution of the collective self, but rather to its reorientation. The more complete examination of this process is presented through Alyosha, who, following his dream, is perpetually taken in as a nourishing and guiding aspect of other people's personalities. Others continually "thirst" for his presence, and posit him as their conscience, a role that Katia, exiled from Dmitry's personality, envies (15:181). The entering into the other is most evident in Alyosha's care for Ivan, to whom he appears as a "pure cherub" (15:86) or, in other words, as a mediator between God and the unprepared seeker. Critics have pointed to the "collective personality" of the brothers as indicative of a Trinitarian understanding of the human being.[41] If this is the case, I would argue that it is not an allegory imposed upon the characters, but a reflection of the apprenticeship that the self offers to the other, becoming part of that self in order to prepare it, to develop it, until it can withstand its own annihilation and transformation by the divine energies to which it comes to give expression. The second element that distinguishes Dostoevsky's mystical psychology from other romantic models is the presence of "other people" within the psyche, the "visitors" from beyond the domain of the self that inform and shape the life of the mind. I shall explore this other, interior form of collective unity, which extends beyond the scope of *The Brothers Karamazov*, in the conclusion.

Conclusion

> My brother [. . .] died five years ago. Sometimes I see him in my dreams: he takes part in my affairs, we are very engaged in them, and at the same time I know full well that this is all a continuation of my dream, I know and remember that my brother is dead and buried. Why am I not surprised that although he is dead, he is nevertheless here next to me and busy with me? (25:108–9)

DOSTOEVSKY'S FICTIONAL WORLD is populated almost entirely by carriers of unnamed psychic wounds accrued in a distant, inaccessible narrative prehistory. Barred from the elements of the interior life, these characters find themselves trapped in the world of external relations, compelled to disperse themselves in the "whirlwind" of social connections and to constitute their inwardly collapsed personalities externally, through turning others into facets of their collapsed selves, and, in turn, becoming subsumed by the personalities of others. This book has argued that Dostoevsky, from his earliest works, portrays the unwillingness to look inward among his characters as the result of suppressed, discarded, or concealed elements from the past that haunt and oppress the psyche. In his major novels Dostoevsky retains the prototype of the wounded, outwardly constituted personality while gradually developing the notion of a deeper terror that underlies traumatic memory, a presentiment of indwelling and, ultimately for Dostoevsky, divine, sources which terrify the conscious mind and threaten the stability, and even the existence, of the self. Throughout his career, Dostoevsky continually reimagined the journey—which I have traced from its early (and markedly unheroic) expression in the sorrows of Vasia Shumkov—to overcome one's imprisonment in relational space and to expand the personality so as to encompass and integrate those elements of the interior life that have hitherto chased consciousness out to the "threshold."

As I have argued, Dostoevsky conceived of the journey inward not as an edifying intellectual exercise, but as an always perilous and often devastating endeavor: for, in encountering the landscape and inhabitants of the unconscious mind, one also approaches the radically destabilizing forces that underlie the interior life—those forces that would "annihilate the I," to use Dostoevsky's term from his theoretical writing. Dostoevsky, as we have seen, repeatedly depicts the disastrous inward journey of the unprepared seeker, of the individual who has persistently suppressed and avoided the upsurges of the "soul," and who has sought oblivion instead in compulsive intimacy. As these characters (whether Prince Myshkin or Stepan Verkhovensky) attempt to detach themselves from their external sources of intellection, guidance, and energy in pursuit of inward ones, they journey into the reaches of the mind only to be overwhelmed and destroyed by what they encounter there. To follow the evolution of Dostoevsky's writing is to observe the author's gradual conception of an education for the self, a training that might prepare consciousness for the dreaded and transformative encounter with what lies most deeply within, and beyond, the self. For this inward journey of fear and trembling, Dostoevsky imagines interior interlocutors who can either assist or undermine the formation of the personality. We have traced the development of this paradigmatic inward movement to its culmination in *The Brothers Karamazov*, where Dostoevsky presents at least three parallel versions of this quest, each providing a vivid representation of the inner life of the personality. At its most flourishing, in the case of Alyosha, the interior realm is a feast populated by many people, among them a trusted guide, preserved in memory, who directs consciousness farther inward toward its ever-renewable sources. In its state of greatest poverty and neglect, in the case of Ivan, the inner life is a closed room with a single interlocutor—a veiled projection of the I—who can only direct consciousness, along tortuous paths, ever back onto itself.

Over the course of his writing, Dostoevsky provides a variety of maps to help us envision the geography of the inner life. We observed his persistently recurring portrayal of protagonists who constitute themselves externally by compulsively attaching themselves to a "carrier of memory" as a substitute for their unconscious lives, and to an "external mind" as a source of guidance and direction. We identified the constituents of the volatile collective self as watchman, prisoner, and deliverer—archetypal agencies, which correspond roughly to interior faculties of mind, soul, and consciousness. The heroic journey of Dostoevsky's characters, in this sense, can be described as an attempt to free others from their projective confinement to one's extended personality by broadening the personality to encompass these dimensions from within. Dostoevsky's theory of evil, of demonism, we have argued, extends from this psychological paradigm according to which the self, barred from its indwelling sources by virtue of firmly placed taboos in the mind, comes to feast upon others as alternative sources, possessing them and annexing their agency, while being possessed and devoured by them in turn. The depiction of the journey into and beyond memory that constitutes, as we have argued, the continuous narrative preoccupation of Dostoevsky's late novels becomes the point of convergence for the psychological, philosophical, and theological strata of his meditation on the problem of selfhood.

"THE BLOODY WOUND OF THE HEART"

As a way of concluding and recapitulating the argument of this book, I would like to look more concretely into Dostoevsky's notion of the inner life—of the interlocutors within the self, of the wound in the psyche, and of the compatibility between interiority and collective personhood—through a brief reading of "Dream of a Ridiculous Man." This short "fantastical" story, written in 1877, four years before the author's death and shortly before he began work on *The Brothers Karamazov*, tells of an embittered "Russian progressive and vile Petersburger" (25:113) who, having decided to kill himself as a protest of sorts against the absurdity of existence, looks up at a star as he walks home one evening and decides that he will kill himself that very night. As he continues on his way, a pitiful eight-year-old girl accosts him and begs him in a feverish and hysterical state of despair to help her dying mother. The protagonist stamps his feet at her, scares her away, and mounts the stairs to his room, where, sitting in his chair, he unexpectedly falls asleep. In his sleep he dreams that he shoots himself in the heart, lies dead in a coffin, and then is guided by a mysterious figure through space to a distant star (the same star that had inspired him to kill himself earlier that night). The star, it turns out, is a planet, an exact replica of the earth, but populated by a race of loving, wise, humble prelapsarian human beings who become subsequently corrupted, ostensibly by the presence of the narrator himself in their midst. The hero watches with torment as these people, once perfectly good and innocent, advance through all the violent and distressing phases of human history, until he wakes up, pierced by love and anguish for them, and goes out to preach the "truth" of love for others.

The isolated and hyperconscious narrator is a return to a familiar figure in Dostoevsky's writing, and "Dream of a Ridiculous Man" can be viewed as the culminative sequel of several earlier first-person narratives, which feature a similarly isolated and unnamed protagonist: especially "White Nights" (1848) and *Notes from Underground* (1865).[1] Written at various stages in the author's career, these works, taken together, present the gradual embitterment and deepening despair of the prototypical Dostoevskian intellectual—from the lonely young romantic idealistic dreamer of "White Nights," to the proud, rebellious, resentful, and debilitatingly self-conscious recluse of

Notes from Underground, and finally, to the solipsistic nihilist of the "Dream of a Ridiculous Man," a character so worn out by the furious dialectic of self-consciousness that he resolves, ultimately, to opt out of existence. In this sense, Dostoevsky's late short story is an attempt to revisit the paradigmatic figure of the underground man in the light provided by over a decade of further artistic investigation into the riddle of selfhood that underlies the hero's dilemma.

The argument developed in this book helps to shed light on another significant dimension of these protagonists' predicament: beneath the agony of the "modern divided self" is a deeper void, a dread of what lies beyond consciousness, and, specifically, a fear of memory whose deeper contents are only gestured toward fleetingly in each of the earlier works that comprise the sequence leading up to "Dream of a Ridiculous Man." In "White Nights" the dreamer can only describe his memories by means of metaphor, by comparing himself to "an unhappy little kitten" who has been "rumpled, frightened, and offended in every possible way," and who finally "hid himself from them under the table, in the dark" so as to "bristle, snort and wash its offended snout with both paws" (2:20). The underground man, in recalling his "former adventures" (5:122), recoils from the farther rooms of unwanted memory which underlie his recollections: a "hateful childhood" which he wants to "cut away" (5:135), but which visits him in "the most hideous dreams" and "oppressive recollections" (5:139), prompting him to "break all ties, to curse the past and scatter it to dust" (5:140). While fastidiously avoiding these unwelcome memories, he remains oppressed by "something within, in the depth of [his] heart and conscience" which "refused to die and expressed itself with a burning anguish" (5:165).[2] We are invited, in this context, to look at Dostoevsky's archetypal "existential" hero—divided against himself and broken by self-consciousness—as also a fugitive from memory, whose inability to see others as others stems not only from hyperactive consciousness and pride, but also from the presence of a closed door in the mind that he is unable, or unwilling, to approach.

In the culmination of this character's journey in "Dream of a Ridiculous Man," the hero has initially succeeded, it seems, in blotting out these dreaded interior elements by projecting them into the world. The hero's stunning realization that *"there was nothing around me"* (*nichego pri mne ne bylo*; 25:105) appears at first glance to be a form of egocentric or philosophical solipsism, but it acquires a more nuanced and interesting form in his further reflection (prefiguring Ivan Karamazov's description of his night visitor) that "perhaps, this entire world and all these people—were just I myself" (25:108)—in other words, projective figurations of the psyche.[3] As with Myshkin who "attached his thoughts and memories to every external object" (8:189) as a means of relief from the oppression he experiences from within, the ridiculous man generates a shadowy projective world of the mind in the streets and people of St. Petersburg. Unable to escape the contents of his psyche entirely, he sees them outside of himself in the "menacing rain," the "vapor," and the "terribly dark" sky, where, between "the torn clouds," one could glimpse "bottomless dark spots" while longing for the "gaslights" to "go out" so that they would not "shed light on all this" (25:105). His squeamish contempt and disregard for the inhabitants of his building—the chaos that reigns behind the partition in his room, the abusive captain, and the sick, trembling children—is, in this context, an extension of the underground man's rigorous avoidance of the inward voices and memories that persist among the unexamined rooms of the mind.

There are, however, elements of this projective landscape that cry out more insistently to consciousness. The first of these is the "little star" that appears amid the "bottomless dark spots" in the sky, a phenomenon which stimulates the hero to kill himself "without fail that very night" (25:106).[4] Though the narrator can give no explanation of the star's significance or of why it should incite him so resolutely to suicide ("why the little star gave me this idea—I don't know" [25:106]), we nevertheless recall from Dostoevsky's subsequent novel, *The Brothers Karamazov*, the repeated image of childhood memory as the "one bright spot in the darkness" (14:18, 266).[5] Similarly, we recall Ordynov's expression in "The Landlady" that it "would be better" to die than to confront the impressions that insist on rising up from within the psyche (1:276). The appearance, moreover, of an inarticulately panic-stricken "little girl" who, "wet" and "shivering all over," grasps the protagonist by the elbow and refuses to let go, reminds us of Goliadkin's "forsaken little dog, all wet and shivering, [which] linked itself to Mr. Goliadkin and also ran around his side, hurriedly," provoking "a remembrance of some long ago occurring circumstance," and which "would not unlink itself from him" (1:142). In the girl's voice, we are told, "could be heard that sound which in very frightened children signifies despair" (25:106). The hero adds to this description a subtle confession, but one that resonates in a chilling manner in the context of his gallery of wounded characters: "I know that sound" (25:106). Though, like Goliadkin before him, the hero chases away this persistent being, the girl's entreaties nevertheless call something forth in him, a sense of "pity" that, in the confused words of the protagonist, leads "to the point even of some strange, and even completely improbable [. . .] pain" (25:107). He attests that it was this feeling—which we immediately recognize in the context of our argument as the stirring of a distant memory—that distracted him from his suicide by launching him instead unexpectedly upon a journey into the mind.

In the ridiculous man's dream-journey through the vast expanses of space toward a distant star, Dostoevsky depicts the hitherto suppressed landscape of the hero's psyche as a parallel universe of breadth and complexity that rivals, and perhaps surpasses, the external world. The voyage begins (like that of Ivan Karamazov's turn inward) as a shallow dream, wholly continuous with the hero's previous posture reclining in his chair at his table. The sudden expansion of the room ("my candle, table and wall suddenly began to move and sway") prompts him to shoot himself "right away" (25:109), as if out of fear of the possibilities entailed by such an expansion of space, and thus he achieves an even closer confinement as a dead body in a coffin. In this context, it is fitting that the subsequent movement from the closest possible confinement to an immeasurable cosmic expanse occurs as the result of a wound: "A profound indignation suddenly flared up in my heart, and suddenly I felt in it a physical pain: 'It's my wound,' I thought, 'it's the shot, the bullet's there . . . .'" The sensation of the wound calls forth an "appeal" rising up from the hero's "entire being to the master of all that had occurred with [him]" (25:110), and causes him to exit his grave to fly out into "dark and unknown spaces" toward the "little star," the most remote realm of the unconscious mind, which, as we might expect, evokes a growing "fear [. . .] in [his] heart" and "a terrible anguish" as he approaches it (25:111). The psychic wound—"the bloody wound of [the] heart" (25:115)—exerts a dual effect upon the self, inciting, on the one hand, the desperate desire to avoid the deeper reaches of the psyche while, on the other hand, also providing a point of access to them.

As he journeys through the seemingly infinite expanses of the unconscious mind, the hero moves beyond the realm of personal memory into the very cradle of human history, and thus comes to walk the full length of the collective memory of humankind reaching up to the present moment.[6] According to the hero, this deeper, revelatory form of memory had existed in him before his dream and had been "calling out to him" even in his conscious state in "presentiments" rising up from the unconscious and in "an anguish which sometimes reached the point of an unbearable sorrow" (25:114). After his dream, having encountered these people and having felt the full force of the tragedy of their devastation, the hero describes his own transformation into a conduit for the love and ecstasy that emanates constantly from "there" through him into the world, as he is compelled to tell others about the "feeling of love" that he has witnessed. "The feeling of love from those innocent and beautiful people," he explains, "stayed in me for all time, and I feel that their love pours out onto me from there even now" (25:112–13).[7]

It is important to note that, for Dostoevsky, this decisive journey into the collective unconscious of humankind (or what might be the world soul for Solovyov) does not lead to a harmonious communal life with others in society; in the case of the ridiculous man, it in fact only incurs further, and even greater, social alienation.[8] Dostoevsky's ideal of communal unity, as I have argued in this book, was not primarily of an external nature, and I have outlined two very different notions of collectivism that emerge from Dostoevsky's meditation on the self. On the one hand, Dostoevsky's notion of *external unity* is that of a pathologically intimate and destructive collectivism, one which we have observed in various memorable forms: a group of wounded individuals who, recognizing themselves in each other, merge to form a compound personality and thus gradually elicit their own mutual, collective destruction (*The Idiot*); a band of murderers howling and clutching onto each other as they fall under the administrative control of a single mind (*Demons*); or a whirlwind of faceless beings who have given up their own identities to circle aggressively around an expanding emptiness (*The Adolescent*). On the other hand, Dostoevsky's more positive notion of intersubjective unity consists in the transformative effect upon the self of the journey through the personal unconscious to discover the collectively shared indwelling sources of the psyche—the *"living image"* within the psyche which "fills [the] soul for all time" (25:118) and which constitutes an intrinsic connection to all other consciousnesses that share this memory, though perhaps without yet having accessed it in themselves. In the final, unequivocally sanguine, note of the story, when the hero informs us that he "found that little girl" (25:119), we observe that the ridiculous man has achieved something that eluded Prince Myshkin in his quest to save Nastasia Filippovna—that is, to disentangle the other from projective confinement to one's own psyche by means, first, of encountering and embracing the dreaded inward sources of the self, and then, of searching out and finding the other in the external world.

"THE INTERIOR LIFE OF THE PERSONALITY"

It is worthwhile to recall that Dostoevsky's ideas concerning the inner life were of a highly marginal and peculiar nature in late imperial Russia, where the overwhelming emphasis of mainstream culture was upon the transformation of external social forms.[9] It was almost two decades after Dostoevsky's death that the question of the "interior life of the personality" emerged at the forefront of Russian political controversy with the publication of *Vekhi* (*Landmarks*, 1909) by a group which included such thinkers as Mikhail Gershenzon, Nikolai Berdiaev, and Sergei Bulgakov.[10] This volume of essays, which generated thunderous debate from all quarters of the Russian cultural establishment, pursued the thesis (with frequent reference to Dostoevsky) that Russia's critical social and political problems could only be alleviated through an introspective turn on the part of the Russian intelligentsia.[11] Educated Russians, the authors claimed, were preoccupied with the hysterical pathos of political activism as a means of diverting attention away from a much more insidious problem: namely, the utter lack of any "doctrine of the personality" in society, and the diseased, imbalanced, atrophied, and dangerously neglected interior space within each modern Russian individual.[12]

Though rhetorically powerful, the warnings of these authors for Russian educated society to "turn inward" and to "root [. . .] intellectual life organically in the personality" (*Vekhi*, 66) *or else*, were invariably difficult to translate into practical advice. While agreeing with their basic premise, Lev Tolstoy noted, rather acidly, the irony that the *Vekhi* authors displayed the same confusion about the inner life as the culture they criticized. "Nothing shows better the powerlessness of these people," he remarked in his review of the book, "than that they are unable to say anything about what exactly this internal life of the soul is supposed to comprise, and if they do speak about it, they speak the most pathetic and empty nonsense."[13] Tolstoy's dismissive attitude did not alleviate, however, his own tormenting struggle with this problem during this late period in his life.[14] Indeed, the argument has often been made (and both Dostoevsky and Tolstoy would have most certainly agreed) that the "catastrophe of the self" felt so pervasively in the late nineteenth century was partly the result of an already excessively inward orientation among educated Russians, in their egoistic navel-gazing and decadent bourgeois absorption in the "cult of one's own psychic 'I.'"[15] It was certainly not this kind of interiority that Dostoevsky had in mind when he delivered his triumphant speech at the Pushkin memorial in 1880. In celebrating the great poet who, in his view, had discovered the whole of Russia within himself, Dostoevsky identified the interior life of the human being as the region of all genuine discovery and political progress: "Truth is not outside of you, but within you; find yourself within yourself, [. . .] take possession of yourself—and you will see truth" (26:139).

What does it mean, then, in terms of Dostoevsky's extended meditation on the nature of the personality, to "find yourself within yourself"? In this book, I have sought to answer this question through an examination of the arduous, dangerous, and revelatory inward journeys of his characters. In many cases, when Dostoevsky's protagonists have unraveled and projected themselves into the external world and have stifled the oppressive upsurges of the psyche, the interior life appears only in brief glimpses in the form of nightmares—a landlady being clobbered mercilessly on the stairs below, or an old man torturing a child with horrific, whispered tales. In the later novels, we see Dostoevsky's characters insistently attempting to move more intrepidly into this inner space, to encounter the inhabitants of the mind and to become rooted in, and transformed by, what lies beyond its farthest reaches. Having lost so many of his beloved friends and family members over the course of his life, Dostoevsky, an author whose own imagination teemed with living beings, conceived of the interior life as populated by a wealth of interlocutors who survive not merely as memories but who continue to live independent lives within the life of the psyche itself. Zosima is resurrected in Alyosha's dream and becomes a force of direction and guidance within that landscape, just as Alyosha's mother, screaming and trembling, continually holds him up, in his memory, toward the icon. In guiding the self toward its inward sources, the departed other takes up residence in the self and thus is able to bear a portion of the agony of this journey.

Dostoevsky ends his final novel with the image of a dead child returning to life through the act of remembering, that is, in Alyosha's entreaty to the boys that they keep the image of the "dead boy" alive in their minds as a unifying and nourishing principle and, in fact, as "the best education of all" (15:195) for the developing personality. The "Dream of a Ridiculous Man" asks us to expand the inhabitants of the psyche's memory to include those who precede our existence as well, those whom we encounter in our dreams and presentiments and whose "love"—if we are capable of making the journey to meet them—"pours out onto us" from that region that also evokes within us the greatest terror.

Notes

INTRODUCTION

1. All passages from Dostoevsky are taken from F. M. Dostoevskii, *Polnoe sobranie sochinenii i pisem v tridtsati tomakh*, 30 vols. (Leningrad: Nauka, 1972–84), 11:96. Hereafter citations of this work will appear in parentheses with volume and page number. All translations are mine.

2. By Dostoevsky's theoretical writings on the self, I mean three pieces, all written within the space of just over one year: (1) the "*Masha lezhit na stole*" ("Masha is lying on the table") journal entry (1864), written the day after his first wife's death, in which Dostoevsky speculates that the process of human development in overcoming the "law of personality" as self-love points to the probability of "a future heavenly life" and of some form of personal immortality (20:172–74); (2) an extended passage from the journalistic essay *Winter Notes on Summer Impressions*, which appeared in *Time* (*Vremia*) in 1863, in which Dostoevsky presents his critique of the European bourgeois practice of selfhood in contradistinction to the self-sacrificing Christian ideal (5:78–82); and (3) an unfinished essay in his notebooks for 1864–65 on the fundamental differences between "Socialism and Christianity" with regard to understanding the human being (20:191–94).

3. Albert Camus, *The Myth of Sisyphus and Other Essays*, trans. Justin O'Brien (New York: Vintage, 1983), 110.

4. Major works of this period include Charles Taylor's *Sources of the Self: The Making of Modern Identity* (Cambridge, Mass.: Harvard University Press, 1989) and Jerold Seigel's *The Idea of the Self: Thought and Experience in Western Europe since the Seventeenth Century* (Cambridge: Cambridge University Press, 2005). For descriptions of the crisis surrounding the question of the self in contemporary culture, see Raymond Martin and John Barresi, who trace the history of the notion of the self from the "unity" and "changelessness" of the soul in Plato and Aristotle to the "disunity" and discarding of the self in the contemporary world: Martin and Barresi, *The Rise and Fall of Soul and Self: An Intellectual History of Personal Identity* (New York: Columbia University Press,

2006), 4–5. See also Paul C. Vitz for an overview of postmodern challenges to the notion of a self: Vitz, "Introduction: From the Modern and Postmodern Selves to the Transmodern Self," in *The Self: Beyond the Postmodern Crisis*, ed. Paul C. Vitz and Susan M. Felch (Wilmington, Del.: ISI Books, 2006), xi–xxii.

5. Derek Offord's representative reading takes Dostoevsky's views as expressed in *Winter Notes on Summer Impressions*—on the voluntary and complete sacrifice of oneself for the good of society as the highest expression of human development—to be the central and most explicit statement of Dostoevsky's concept of personality: Offord, "*Lichnost'*: Notions of Individual Identity," in *Constructing Russian Culture in the Age of Revolution: 1881–1940*, ed. Catriona Kelly and David Shepherd (Oxford: Oxford University Press, 1998), 13–25, esp. 22–25.

6. Steven Cassedy has established the "fatal paradox" (136) of Dostoevsky's belief in and repudiation of collectivism in the context of his characterization of Dostoevsky as anything but a stable dogmatic Christian thinker: as someone possessing a "tortured and ambivalent [. . .] attitude toward religion" (27) and who was always prepared to succumb to the temptation of holding conflicting views, especially when it came to religion" (113): Cassedy, *Dostoevsky's Religion* (Stanford, Calif.: Stanford University Press, 2005), see esp. 114–48. Readers have often remarked on the mysterious ambivalence in Dostoevsky's characters who are "both separate from other personalities and incomprehensibly connected with them all": L. A. Zander, *Dostoevsky*, trans. Natalie Duddington (London: SCM, 1948), 84. Nikolai Berdiaev observed that Dostoevsky was unable to reconcile philosophically his "fanatical" belief in the "personal principle" with his simultaneous attraction to the "temptation" of "collectivism, which paralyzes the principle of [. . .] personal spiritual discipline": Nikolai Berdiaev, *Mirosozertsanie Dostoevskogo* (Prague: YMCA, 1923), 232–33.

7. Mikhail Bakhtin argued that Dostoevsky was not in fact attempting to depict "real" people in his novels, but rather was experimenting with "voices" encountering each other under highly liberating, "non-Euclidian" space-time conditions. "The hero interests Dostoevsky not as some manifestation of reality that possesses fixed and specific socially typical or individually characteristic traits, nor as a specific profile assembled out of unambiguous and objective features which, taken together, answer the question 'Who is he?'": Bakhtin, *Problems of Dostoevsky's Poetics*, ed. and trans. Caryl Emerson (Minneapolis: University of Minnesota Press, 1984), 47. Lydia Ginzburg observes that "in creating his novel of ideas, Dostoevskii departed from classical nineteenth-century psychologism, the basic principle of which was explanation, whether explicit or concealed": Ginzburg, *On Psychological Prose* (Princeton, N.J.: Princeton University Press, 1991), 259. Lev Zander argued that "as soon as good or evil reach the highest degree of intensity in the human heart" Dostoevsky no longer operates within the realm of realism and psychology. [. . .] When this happens, the limits of person-

ality cease, for him, to be clear and definite: man, as it were, is no longer merely himself, but is merged into something else, attaining a different kind of being": Zander, *Dostoevsky*, 13. This attitude is, of course, not confined to classical Russian and Soviet scholarship. Joseph Frank, for example, also approached Dostoevsky's greatest works as those in which "psychology" becomes "strictly subordinate to ideology," in which "every feature of the text serves to bring out the consequences in personal behavior of certain ideas; and the world that Dostoevsky creates is entirely conceived as a *function* of this purpose": Joseph Frank, *Dostoevsky: The Stir of Liberation, 1860–1865* (Princeton, N.J.: Princeton University Press, 1986), 346.

8. Berdiaev, *Mirosozertsanie Dostoevskogo*, 17. Berdiaev's description of Dostoevsky's "whirlwind anthropology" is emblematic of some of the most influential early investigations of personality in Dostoevsky (by such interpreters as Viacheslav Ivanov, Dmitri Chizhevsky, Konstantin Mochulsky, Lev Zander, Sergei Bulgakov, and Vasilii Rozanov). According to Berdiaev, in Dostoevsky's writing, "some kind of center, a central human personality takes shape and everything turns around this axis." Berdiaev, *Mirosozertsanie Dostoevskogo*, 39. Dmitrii Chizhevskii describes this phenomenon as an illustration of the *mikrokosmichnost'* ("microcosmic nature") of the Dostoevskian personality: the human being is a center of the universe that incorporates all other personalities into itself: Chizhevskii, "Dostoevskij—psikholog," in *O Dostoevskom: Sbornik statej* 1 (Prague, 1929): 51–72, 55. In Vasily Rozanov's words, "It is not finished characters, each with his own inner center, that move before us in his works, but a series of shadows of some single thing: as if they are various transformations, twists of one [. . .] spiritual being": Rozanov, *Legenda Velikogo Inkvizitora* (Munich: Wilhelm Fink Verlag, 1970), 48. For a related view, see also Konstantin Mochulsky, *Dostoevsky: His Life and Work*, trans. Michael A. Minihan (Princeton, N.J.: Princeton University Press, 1967), 298–99. It should be noted that Bakhtin disagreed implicitly with this notion of the many as one. "Each novel," he argued, "presents an opposition, which is never canceled out dialectically, of many consciousnesses": Bakhtin, *Problems of Dostoevsky's Poetics*, 26.

9. See, for example, Louis Breger, who describes Dostoevsky's development of the novel as a protracted attempt at psychoanalysis, an attempt to discover balance between the "characters who embody different sides of his conflicts—who represent his different inner selves": Breger, *Dostoevsky: The Author as Psychoanalyst* (New York: New York University Press, 1991), 9–11. Related approaches can be found in A. L. Bem's *Psikhoanaliticheskie etiudy* (Prague: Petropolis, 1938), or in Elizabeth Dalton's *Unconscious Structure in "The Idiot"* (Princeton, N.J.: Princeton University Press, 1979). In the words of I. I. Evlampiev, Dostoevsky's "artistic method is [. . .] *anti-psychological* (at least in the sense that his protagonists are very far from being real people [. . .]. Dostoevskii is not interested in the psychological nuances of a person's inner [*dushevnaia*]

life that ground his behavior [. . .] though his protagonists, at first glance, in no way differ from ordinary 'empirical' people. [. . .] Most important is a metaphysical dimension in which [. . .] the empirical protagonists are connected in some kind of unity, which expresses an integral energy [. . .] *in the form of a metaphysical Personality, of a single metaphysical Protagonist*": Evlampiev, "Lichnost' kak absoliut: Metafizika F. Dostoevskogo," in *Istoriia russkoi metafiziki v XIX–XX vekakh: Russkaia filosofiia v poiskakh absoliuta, Chast' 1* (St. Petersburg: Izdatel'stvo "Aleteiia," 2000), 103, 119–20.

10. See Marina Kostalevsky, *Dostoevsky and Soloviev* (New Haven, Conn.: Yale University Press, 1997), 148. See also Mochulsky's reading of *Crime and Punishment* in *Dostoevsky: His Life and Work*, esp. 298–300.

11. In this light, the religious experiences of these characters—Myshkin's epileptic vision of "divine harmony," Alyosha's tremulous agony that leads to his life-altering dream—are reinterpreted not as mystical epiphanies but rather as morbid descriptions of pathology. For an example of this approach, see James Rice's description of Alyosha Karamazov's pathology in James L. Rice, "The Covert Design of 'The Brothers Karamazov': Alesha's Pathology and Dialectic," *Slavic Review* 68, no. 2 (Summer 2009): 355–75. For Dostoevsky's characters as "carriers" of an "idea," see Bakhtin, *Problems of Dostoevsky's Poetics*, esp. 85–90.

12. René Girard's reading of self and other in Dostoevsky serves as an important counterpoint to the argument presented in this book. Girard, particularly with reference to *The Demons*, examined the confusion of self and other in Dostoevsky as a crisis of misplaced desire, or as a symptom of a worldview in which, as a result of human pride, divine mediation has been excised. In the absence of a divine principle according to which value and desire are articulated, "the need for transcendency is 'satisfied' by" the mediation of the other, and "imitation of Christ becomes the imitation of one's neighbor" (59): Girard, *Deceit, Desire, and the Novel: Self and Other in Literary Structure*, trans. Yvonne Freccero (Baltimore: Johns Hopkins University Press, 1965). Girard's emphasis upon imitative and infectious desire, which became central to his own theoretical system, differs from the emphasis of the present study: the manner in which the self merges with other selves as the result of collapsed and unexamined interior space.

13. The distinction was established most categorically, and influentially, by Berdiaev, *Mirosozertsanie Dostoevskogo*, 23.

14. The connections between theology and psychology have taken prominence in Western scholarship in the last two decades. In calling for theologians "not to construct but to reclaim [. . .] Christian psychology," Ellen Charry notes that "Christian theology, quite apart from modern secular psychology, is and always has been a psychological enterprise" (576). In presenting Saint Augustine as the founding father of experimental psychology, Charry emphasizes Augustine's view that "there is no psychological problem that is not also a spiritual

problem" (579): Charry, "Augustine of Hippo: Father of Christian Psychology," *Anglican Theological Review* 88 (2006): 575–89. In setting up the parameters of the "dialogue between theology and psychology," Peter J. Hampson and Johannes Hoff state that "psychology can be suitably oriented by theology as a secular, rational tradition whose project clearly requires complementation" (565). Augustine's "account of the person," the authors maintain, can "challenge some of the core assumptions" of clinical psychology, particularly by advancing the notion that "the human self is determined in and through its *dependence on God*, in whom we live and move as *philosophizing* beings" (551): Hampson and Hoff, "Whose Self? Which Unification? Augustine's Anthropology and the Psychology-Theology Debate," *New Blackfriars* 91, no. 1035 (September 2010): 546–66. Numerous volumes fostering the dialogue between theology and psychology have appeared in the last decade, including Léon Turner's *Theology, Psychology and the Plural Self* (Farnham, Eng.: Ashgate, 2008). None of these works, to my knowledge, makes reference to Dostoevsky's immense contribution to this dialogue.

15. For an examination of Dostoevsky's nonliterary thought, see James P. Scanlan, *Dostoevsky the Thinker* (Ithaca, N.Y.: Cornell University Press, 2002). In treating Dostoevsky as a highly idiosyncratic Christian thinker, I tend to agree with Malcolm Jones's notion of Dostoevsky as a practitioner of "minimal religion," a nondogmatic form of religious thought that "brings to the surface only those beliefs that the honest believer actually knows, understands and treasures from his or her own personal experience": Jones, *Dostoyevsky and the Dynamics of Religious Experience* (London: Anthem, 2005), xi.

16. According to an important tradition of Dostoevsky scholarship, questions of personality, for Dostoevsky, are inseparable from questions of aesthetic form. As Robert Louis Jackson observed in the first of his monumental studies, "form and humanity for Dostoevsky are interchangeable concepts. Man finds in art the symbol and embodiment of his own completion, ideal form, humanity": Jackson, *Dostoevsky's Quest for Form: A Study of His Philosophy of Art* (New Haven, Conn.: Yale University Press, 1966), 125. Gary Saul Morson espoused the notion of Dostoevsky as a formal experimenter who studied the question of the self through the innovation of novelistic technique. According to Morson, Dostoevsky's resolve in addressing the chaos and disorder of "the underground" required "a poetics of the underground" (9) and the invention of new approaches to literary form that would allow him to portray the new kinds of "psychological disfigurement" (11) and inharmoniousness of character that he saw around him: Morson, *The Boundaries of Genre: Dostoevsky's "Diary of a Writer" and the Traditions of Literary Utopia* (Austin: University of Texas Press, 1981), esp. 8–14. By taking up image and characterization (rather than genre and form) as central to Dostoevsky's meditation on the self, I intend my own study as complementary to such approaches.

17. For an illuminating overview of the historical tensions in literary theory and criticism between "formalist and referential positions" with regard to characterization, and an account of the growing trend in literary studies to be "troubled by the excision of the human from narratology," see Alex Woloch, *One vs. the Many: Minor Characters and the Space of the Protagonist in the Novel* (Princeton, N.J.: Princeton University Press, 2003), esp. 12–21. See also James Wood's engaging attempt to navigate the space between "those who believe too much in [the reality of fictional characters]" and "those who believe too little" (101): Wood, *How Fiction Works* (New York: Farrar, Straus and Giroux, 2008), esp. 95–137. My argument does not touch upon the more abstract question, acquiring greater prominence in literary studies and philosophy today, of the "metaphysics" and "ontology" of fictional characters. For philosophical examinations of the kind of existence enjoyed by the implied people and things that populate fictional texts, see, for example, Stuart Brock and Anthony Everett, eds., *Fictional Objects* (New York: Oxford University Press, 2015) and R. M. Sainsbury, *Fiction and Fictionalism* (New York: Routledge, 2010).

18. My discussion of forgotten extra-textual memory draws implicitly on Gary Saul Morson's discussion of the "disease" of the "isolated present" as it expresses itself in Dostoevsky's work, whose characters, at their most desperate, live "without memories in a temporality contracted virtually to a moment or to an archipelago of isolated moments" (203). Morson elucidates Dostoevsky's preoccupation with the "morally dangerous" temporality of the all-consuming "intensified moment" (202), a phenomenon that he links to such phenomena (in Dostoevsky's writing and life) as gambling addiction and epileptic ecstasy. I build on Morson's diagnosis of the "'diseases' of presentness" by addressing Dostoevsky's fascination with the challenges of the inward turn toward unacknowledged memory (and to what lies beyond it) as a way of escaping one's imprisonment in the intensity of the present moment. See Gary Saul Morson, *Narrative and Freedom: The Shadows of Time* (New Haven, Conn.: Yale University Press, 1994), esp. 201–14.

19. For an important discussion that places the "psychology" and "metaphysics" of the "underground"—the pride that makes the inner dislocation between subject and object, ideal and real, self and other, so unbearable, urgent, and generative—at the epicenter of Dostoevsky philosophical, psychological, and artistic journey, see René Girard, *Resurrection from the Underground: Feodor Dostoevsky*, ed. and trans. James. G. Williams (East Lansing: Michigan State University Press, 2012). See also Tsvetan Todorov's discussion of the centrality of *Notes from Underground* not only in articulating the philosophical and psychological themes that dominate Dostoevsky's work (the dialectic of self-consciousness, the role of reason in the human being, the problem of freedom and determinism, and of master and slave) but in developing a poetics according to which the self and the ideas it expresses, and even the text it inhabits, are destabilized, subjec-

tivized, and rendered fragile by their dependence for existence upon the other. Tsvetan Todorov, "Notes from the Underground," in *Genres in Discourse* (Cambridge: Cambridge University Press, 1990), 72–92.

20. As Derek Offord notes, "once the concept of *lichnost'* did firmly establish itself in Russia its formulation was inevitably affected by the lateness of its arrival, by the largely unfavorable conditions for the development of the creative personality, and by the intellectual climate" (15). For an overview of the emergence and development of the concept of the personality in Russian culture from the Petrine reforms into the nineteenth century, see Offord, *"Lichnost'*: Notions of Individual Identity," 13–25. In his illuminating discussion of the emergence of the concept of *lichnost'* in Russia, Nikolai Plotnikov points out that, whereas the notion of the self in Western thought was understood in terms of three intersecting dimensions (autonomy, identity, and individuality), in Russia, the overwhelming emphasis was upon individuality, and thus, when contrasted with communality, *lichnost'* was accompanied by the persistent negative connotation of self-enclosedness: Plotnikov, "Ot 'individual'nosti' k 'identichnosti' (istoriia poniatii personal'nosti v russkoi kul'ture)," *Novoe Literaturnoe Obozrenie* 91 (2008): 64–83.

21. For a discussion of the distinction between *lichnost'* and *samost'* in Dostoevsky, see T. A. Kasatkina, "O lichnosti i samosti," in *Kharakterologiia Dostoevskogo: Tipologiia emotsional'no-tsennostnykh orientatsii* (Moscow: Nasledie, 1996), 179–82.

22. As Vladimir Solovyov describes it, "the I, as simply an act of self-consciousness, is devoid in and of itself of any content, and is only a bright spot amid the dim currents of psychic states": V. S. Soloviev, *Sobranie sochinenii Vladimira Sergeevicha Solov'eva*, 10 vols. (St. Petersburg: Izdatel'stvo tovarishestvo "Prosveshchenie," 1912), 3:124. Semyon Frank, echoing Solovyov, describes consciousness as "that center or nucleus of our psychic life which also serves as the guiding and ruling principle, and which we call our 'I'": Semyon Frank, *Man's Soul: An Introduction in Philosophical Psychology*, trans. Boris Jakim (Athens: Ohio University Press, 1993), 69.

23. One difficulty that attends the use of the word "soul" is the general scholarly dislike of the term. As philosopher Anthony Quinton put it in 1962, the term "has uncomfortably ecclesiastical associations, and [. . .] seems to be bound up with a number of discredited or at any rate generally disregarded theories": Quinton, "The Soul," in *Personal Identity*, ed. John Perry (Berkeley: University of California Press, 2008), 53–72, 53. A renewed interest in the intellectual history of "soul" has grown in the last thirty years along with the more pronounced and widespread fascination with the problem of the self. See, for example, Steward Goetz and Charles Taliafero, *A Brief History of the Soul* (Oxford: Wiley-Blackwell, 2011), which attempts to situate the possibilities for "soul's" integration into contemporary philosophical and scientific culture. See also the attempt

to reclaim the concept of "soul" in contemporary theological attractions to psychology. Ellen Charry notes that "for modern secular psychology the self is not a translation of psyche but an alternative to the soul." She argues that "in its rigorously atheistic form, secular psychology's abandonment of the soul and embrace of the self cut us off from the transcendent and the possibility of finding it": Charry, "Augustine of Hippo," 580. A more pressing difficulty in employing the term "soul" arises from the many possible definitions it carries. Semyon Frank, who, like Dostoevsky, has been characterized as an "expressivist," describes the soul (the "unknown element with which we are intimately familiar and which is always present in us") as the unconscious depth and the foundation of the personality, which opens up in its innermost inscrutable reaches to a universal principle that transcends the individual: Semyon Frank, *Man's Soul*, 46. See Philip J. Swoboda, "Semen Frank's Expressivist Humanism," in *A History of Russian Philosophy 1830–1930: Faith, Reason, and the Defense of Human Dignity*, ed. G. M. Hamburg and Randall A. Poole (Cambridge: Cambridge University Press, 2010), 205–26, 212. In terms of the Russian Orthodox tradition, we have in mind *psyche* (soul) as distinct from *nous* (mind, spirit), although the two have traditionally been viewed as inextricably integrated agencies of the soul. See Vladimir Lossky, "Image and Likeness," in *The Mystical Theology of the Eastern Church* (Crestwood, N.Y.: St. Vladimir's Seminary Press, 1976), 127. In the Russian Orthodox tradition, the concept of the soul bears a direct relation to that of the "heart" as the "seat of the soul." In Russian Orthodox thought, the heart is conceived of as the physical "seat of all cognitive activities of the soul" and the "concentrated center of the moral life of the human being": P. D. Iurkevich, "Serdtse i ego znachenie v dukhovnoj zhizni cheloveka, po ucheniiu slova Bozhiia," in *Filosofskie proizvedeniia* (Moscow: Pravda, 1990), 69–103, 70–72. A. M. Bulanov explored Dostoevsky's inheritance of the conception of the "heart" from ancient Greek, Eastern Christian, and European philosophical sources, placing emphasis on Pascal and Tikhon of Zadonsk as two of Dostoevsky's beloved precursors. Among the definitions of the "heart" that Bulanov discusses, prominent is "the teaching of the Church Fathers on the 'heart' as of the innermost [*sokrovennyj*] center of the personality" (8) and "the root of [its] energetic capacities, of intellect and will" (13): Bulanov, *Tvorchestvo Dostoevskogo-romanista: Problematika i poetika (Khudozhestvennaia fenomenologiia "serdechnoi zhizni"): Monografiia* (Volgograd: Peremena, 2004).

24. My reference throughout is to Bakhtin's early thought, since this was the period of his most intense engagement with Dostoevsky. For a more comprehensive discussion of Bakhtin's contribution to the philosophy of the self, see Caryl Emerson, "Building a Responsive Self in a Post-Relativistic World: The Contribution of Mikhail Bakhtin," in *The Self: Beyond the Postmodern Crisis*, ed. Paul C. Vitz and Susan M. Felch (Wilmington, Del.: ISI Books, 2006), 25–41.

25. Bakhtin phrases his criticism of the essentialist view of soul this way:

"The soul as an empirical reality that is neutral toward [the forms generated by intersubjective aesthetic activity] represents an abstract construction produced by the thought of psychology": Mikhail Bakhtin, "Author and Hero in Aesthetic Activity," trans. Vadim Liapunov, in *Art and Answerability: Early Philosophical Essays by M. M. Bakhtin*, ed. Michael Holquist and Vadim Liapunov (Austin: University of Texas Press, 1990), 4–256, 103. For a discussion of Bakhtin as a "non-mystic and anti-essentialist," see Caryl Emerson, "Russian Orthodoxy and the Early Bakhtin," in *Religion and Literature* 22, no. 2/3 (Summer-Autumn, 1990): 109–31, 119. Michael Holquist describes Bakhtin's adaptation of Hermann Cohen's principle that "the world exists as the subject of thought, and the subject of thought, no matter how material it might appear, is still always a subject that is *thought*": Holquist, *Dialogism: Bakhtin and His World*, 2nd ed. (New York: Routledge, 2002), xiv. Bakhtin was hostile to the notion of the unconscious life as an example of a force which lies "outside consciousness, externally (mechanically)" defining it: "Consciousness under the influence of these forces loses its authentic freedom, and personality is destroyed. There, among these forces, must one also consign the unconscious (the 'id')": Bakhtin, *Problems of Dostoevsky's Poetics*, 297. See Gerald Pirog for a discussion of Bakhtin's "life-long antipathy to psychologism and the psychoanalytic concepts of impersonal instinctual forces and the unconscious": Pirog, "Bakhtin and Freud on the Ego," in *Russian Literature and Psychoanalysis*, ed. Daniel Rancour-Laferriere (Amsterdam: John Benjamins, 1988), 401–15, 405.

26. See Caryl Emerson's description of this process in *The First Hundred Years of Mikhail Bakhtin* (Princeton, N.J.: Princeton University Press, 1997), 214. In Gerald Pirog's words: "It is in this sense that we can speak of our absolute aesthetic need for the other, who alone can create my completed personality. This personality would not exist if the other did not create it [. . .]. We are [. . .] in a constant state of complementarity with others, who must also seek in us their own completed selves": Pirog, "Bakhtin and Freud on the Ego," 407–8.

27. The concept of trauma, pioneered originally by Sigmund Freud and Pierre Janet, among others, refers to the tendency, in Freud's words, "to repeat [. . .] repressed material as a contemporary experience instead of, as the physician would prefer to see, remembering it as something belonging to the past": Freud, "Beyond the Pleasure Principle," in *The Freud Reader*, ed. Peter Gay (New York: Norton, 1989), 594–627, 602. The concept became enshrined in modern-day psychiatry as post-traumatic stress disorder by its inclusion, since 1980, in the *Diagnostic and Statistical Manual of Mental Disorders*. Cathy Caruth, who in the 1990s shaped the foundations of what is now often referred to as "classical trauma theory," characterizes the disorder as "a response, sometimes delayed, to an overwhelming event or events, which takes the form of repeated, intrusive hallucinations, dreams, thoughts, or behaviors stemming from the event, along with numbing that may have begun during or after the experi-

ence, and possibly also increased arousal to (and avoidance of) stimuli recalling the event": Caruth, *Trauma: Explorations in Memory* (Baltimore: Johns Hopkins University Press, 1995), 4. Trauma theory, it has been observed more recently, "is perhaps less a field or a methodology than a coming together of concerns and disciplines": Gert Buelens, Sam Durrant, and Robert Eaglestone, "Introduction," in *The Future of Trauma Theory: Contemporary Literary and Cultural Criticism* (New York: Routledge, 2014), 1–8, 3.

28. For the view that trauma had a premodern existence, see, for example, Judith Herman, *Trauma and Recovery* (New York: Basic Books, 1997). For a brief survey of commentary arguing for a "pre-history" of trauma (Pepys, Shakespeare, and indeed Gilgamesh), see Allan Young, *The Harmony of Illusions: Inventing Post-Traumatic Stress Disorder* (Princeton, N.J.: Princeton University Press, 199), 73–74. On the concept of "terror" in eighteenth- and early nineteenth-century French culture as a precursor to "trauma," see Erika Naginski, "Canova's Penitent Magdalene: On Trauma's Prehistory," in *Trauma and Visuality in Modernity*, ed. Lisa Saltzman and Eric Rozenberg (Hanover, N.H.: Dartmouth College Press, 2006), 51–81. See also, for example, Jonathan Shay's discussions of Homer's depictions of post-traumatic stress disorder in *Odysseus in America: Combat Trauma and the Trials of Overcoming* (New York: Scribner, 2002).

29. Young, *Harmony of Illusions*, 4. For the view that the idea of trauma was an entirely new phenomenon in European history in the late nineteenth century, see especially Roger Luckhurst, who argues that trauma "is a concept that can only emerge within modernity [. . .] as an effect of the rise, in the nineteenth century, of the technological and statistical society that can generate, multiply and quantify the 'shocks' of modern life": Luckhurst, *The Trauma Question* (London: Routledge, 2008), 19. See also Ian Hacking who claims, among other things, that before the late nineteenth century, concepts of psychic trauma may have existed, but that no notion existed of a *"forgotten* trauma": Hacking, "Memory Sciences, Memory Politics," in *Tense Past: Cultural Essays in Trauma and Memory*, ed. Paul Antze and Michael Lambek (New York: Routledge, 1996), 67–87, 82. See also Mark Micale and Paul Lerner, *Traumatic Pasts: History, Psychiatry, and Trauma in the Modern Age, 1870–1930*, ed. Mark Micale and Paul Lerner (Cambridge: Cambridge University Press, 2001), 10, 26. Furthest of all goes Allan Young, in *The Harmony of Illusions*, in his assertion that not only did no notion of post-traumatic stress exist in the late nineteenth century, but that it would even have been impossible to *experience* trauma—as we understand it today—before that moment in history.

30. Young, *Harmony of Illusions*, 39.

31. Belinsky, letter to V. P. Botkin, April 16–21, 1840, in V. G. Belinskii, *Polnoe sobranie sochinenii* (Moscow: Izdatel'stvo akademii nauk, 1956), 11:512.

32. I. Volgin, *Rodit'sia v Rossii: Dostoevskii i sovremenniki: Zhizn' v dokumentakh* (Moscow: Kniga, 1991), 184.

33. Ibid.

34. A. S. Dolinin, ed., *F. M. Dostoevskii: Stat'i i materialy*, vol. 2 (Leningrad-Moscow: Mysl', 1924), 393. Dostoevsky's daughter, Liubov', moreover, identified the onset of her father's epileptic attacks in an upsetting quarrel that occurred between Dostoevsky's parents during his childhood. In his documentary biography of early Dostoevsky, Thomas G. Marullo dismisses such an idea as ungrounded. See Marullo, *Fyodor Dostoevsky: Portrait of the Artist as a Young Man (1821–1845): A Life in Letters, Memoirs, and Criticism* (DeKalb: Northern Illinois University Press, forthcoming). For the foundational examination of Dostoevsky's psychopathology and medical history in his early life, a consideration of the "chronic childhood nervous condition that prefigured his epilepsy" (52), and of the possibility, as suggested by Dostoevsky's physician, Yanovsky, of a "'tragic event' in the novelist's childhood as the triggering cause of epilepsy" (46–49), see James Rice, *Dostoevsky and the Healing Art: An Essay in Literary and Medical History* (Ann Arbor, Mich.: Ardis, 1985), esp. 43–65.

CHAPTER ONE

The chapter epigraphs are from 1 Samuel 18:1–4, *The David Story: A Translation with Commentary of 1 and 2 Samuel*, trans. Robert Alter (New York: W.W. Norton, 1999), 112–13; from Andrei Platonov, *Soul: And Other Stories*, trans. Robert and Elizabeth Chandler with Katia Grigoruk, Angela Livingstone, Olga Meerson, and Eric Naiman (New York: New York Review Books, 2008), 130; and from Dostoevsky's *Crime and Punishment* (6:155).

1. By "expressivist," I mean the view that the human personality expresses the sources of the universe which lie in its depths. For Charles Taylor's espousal of the term "expressivism, see "The Expressivist Turn," in *Sources of the Self*, 368–92. On Dostoevsky and expressivism, see Malcolm V. Jones, *Dostoyevsky after Bakhtin* (Cambridge: Cambridge University Press, 1990), 3.

2. Vladimir Soloviev, *Sobranie sochinenii Vladimira Sergeevicha Solov'eva* (St. Petersburg: Izdatel'stvo tovarishestvo "Prosveshchenie," 1912), 3:185.

3. Chizhevskii, "Dostoevskij—psikholog," 55.

4. In the words of Isaiah Berlin, "if everything in nature is living, and if we ourselves are simply its most self-conscious representatives, the function of the artist is to delve within himself, and above all to delve within the dark and unconscious forces which move within him, and to bring these to consciousness by the most agonizing and violent internal struggle. This is Schelling's doctrine": Berlin, *The Roots of Romanticism* (Princeton, N.J.: Princeton University Press, 1999), 98. For an account of Augustine's sources (from Plotinus to the Stoics to Heraclitus) on the positing of divinity as an inwardly discovered source, see Richard Sorabji, *Self: Ancient and Modern Insights about Individuality, Life, and Death* (Chicago: University of Chicago Press, 2006), esp. 50–53.

5. Edith Clowes expresses some of this ambivalence when, after having compared Dostoevsky to Nietzsche as a proponent of the romantic emphasis on integrating the subliminal natural forces that undergird consciousness, she nevertheless points out that "Dostoevsky's moral consciousness is much more socially oriented than Nietzsche's"; Dostoevsky is less interested in "penetrating the complex interactions of subliminal forces in the *intra*personal sphere" and more focused on "resolution of conflicts between demands of personal integrity and social conformity in the *inter*personal sphere." This tantalizing observation, however, does not occupy the focus of Clowes's study: Clowes, "Self-Laceration and Resentment: The Terms of Moral Psychology in Dostoevsky and Nietzsche," in *Freedom and Responsibility in Russian Literature: Essays in Honor of Robert Louis Jackson* (Evanston, Ill.: Northwestern University Press, 1995), 119–33, 133.

6. Todorov, *Genres in Discourse*, 89. Echoing Bakhtin, Todorov asserts that Dostoevsky locates "the essence of being in the other" (87).

7. Malcolm Jones accepts "expressivism" as an important aspect of Dostoevsky's philosophical outlook, and argues, interestingly, that the "fantastic realism" of a Bakhtinian Dostoevsky is "not to be located in the process of spiritual evolution described by Dostoyevsky [. . .] but in the 'deviations,' 'false developments,' the 'departures from normal reality,' the result of external pressures, the destabilizing effects of what Bakhtin calls heteroglossia in urban life where man is torn from his roots": Jones, *Dostoyevsky after Bakhtin*, 6–7.

8. Bakhtin, *Problems of Dostoevsky's Poetics*, 108. See Irina Sandomirskaia's forceful critique of Bakhtin's concept of the self: "a body without a name, without a personality and without borders—such is the subject in the inhuman political economy that goes by the name of dialogue": Sandomirskaia, "Golaia zhizn', zloi Bakhtin i vezhlivyi Vaginov: Tragediia bez khora i avtora," in *Telling Forms: 30 Essays in Honour of Peter Alberg Jensen,* ed. Karin Grelz and Susanna Witt (Stockholm: Almqvist & Wiksell, 2004).

9. Bakhtin, *Problems of Dostoevsky's Poetics*, 61. See Michael Holquist's discussion of Bakhtin's move against "untrammeled subjectivity," the "old conviction that the Individual subject is the seat of certainty, whether the subject so conceived was God, the soul, the author, or my self" (19). For Bakhtin, Holquist argues, the self is "a cognitive necessity, not a mystified privilege" (23): Holquist, *Dialogism*, esp. 14–27. For an example of Bakhtin's resonance in the fields of psychology and cultural theory as a thinker who "challenges the idea of a core, essential self," see Hubert J. M. Hermans, "The Dialogical Self: Toward a Theory of Personal and Cultural Positioning," *Culture and Psychology* 7, no. 3 (2001): 243–81. For a reading of Bakhtin's Dostoevsky as a dramatization of the "crumbling away of the representational system" ("Dostoevsky's writings 'represent' nothing: no characters, no reality, no author outside the stuff in which they come to life" [114]), see Julia Kristeva, "The Ruin of a Poetics," in *Russian Formalism:*

A Collection of Articles and Texts in Translation, ed. Stephen Bann and John E. Bowlt (Harper and Row, 1973), 102–21.

10. Victor Terras, *The Young Dostoevsky (1846–1849): A Critical Study* (The Hague: Mouton, 1969), 39.

11. For example, W. J. Leatherbarrow describes Vasia's demise as "the total absorption and destruction of the lowly individual by an impersonal and rigidly stratified social reality—as one of the injustices which socialism purports to erase." The "overblown and sentimental friendship" reflects the agonized conflict between public and private lives, between "the anonymous social machine" and the "meaning and freedom afforded his private existence by his friendship with Arkadii Nefedevich and his love for Liza Artem'yeva" (534): Leatherbarrow, "Idealism and Utopian Socialism in Dostoyevsky's *Gospodin Prokharchin* and *Slaboye serdtse*," *Slavonic and East European Review* 58, no. 4 (October 1980): 524–40. For a similar view, see Joseph Frank, *Dostoevsky: The Seeds of Revolt, 1821–1849* (Princeton, N.J.: Princeton University Press, 1979), 318–22. Donald Fanger avoids the political context, characterizing Vasia as a prototype for "the generous dreamer" who "cannot stand the anomalous burden of happiness in an imperfect world": Fanger, *Dostoevsky and Romantic Realism: A Study of Dostoevsky in Relation to Balzac, Dickens, and Gogol* (Evanston, Ill.: Northwestern University Press, 1965, repr. 1998), 168.

12. See N. A. Dobroliubov, "Zabitye liudi," in *Literaturno-kriticheskie stat'i* (Moscow: Khudozhestvennaia literatura, 1937), 480–81.

13. Identical handwriting was a feature of the doppelganger in German romanticism; see Ralph Tymms, *Doubles in Literary Psychology* (Cambridge: Bowes and Bowes, 1949), 68.

14. Katherine Strelsky has suggested "feminine identification resulting in homosexual panic" as the real reason for Vasia's demise: Strelsky, "Dostoevsky's Early Tale, 'A Faint Heart,'" *Russian Review* 30, no. 2 (April 1971): 146–53, 148.

15. Arkady's imitative passion for Liza could be said to evoke René Girard's notion of mimetic desire. In fact, Girard called attention to this moment in the story in his first book without analyzing it in light of his yet-to-be-espoused notion of the imitative self. See Girard, *Resurrection from the Underground*, 6.

16. Rene Girard observed (mistakenly in my view) that "the story is that of *The Double* but viewed from the outside by an observer who does not share in the hallucinations of the hero." His reading overlooks how intimately Arkady participates in Vasia's crisis. Girard, *Resurrection from the Underground*, 6.

17. This relationship recalls Jean Paul's influential description of doubling as passionate, intersubjective friendship. For more on this kind of doubling in Jean Paul, see Leonard Kent: "Bound together by a single soul, two bodies function independently, yet both are mutually complementary"; "[Jean Paul] developed the concept of separate (sometimes contradictory, but nevertheless interdependent and inextricably enmeshed) parts of a single personality, described a per-

sonality which had somehow managed to shake itself free of its host body, confront it, threaten its own concept of self [. . .] And we note the implication that there is a part of man which is repressed, a part of personality that cannot forever be confined and stilled": Kent, *The Subconscious in Gogol' and Dostoevskij and Its Antecedents* (The Hague: Mouton, 1969), 44–45.

18. Bakhtin reads the vision as a "carnivalized sense of Petersburg" (180fn), a way of placing the city itself "on the threshold" so that it too, like Dostoevsky's personalities, is "devoid of any internal grounds for justifiable stabilization": Bakhtin, *Problems of Dostoevsky's Poetics*, 167. Fyodor Stepun reads Arkadii's vision of the city as the epiphanic moment for Dostoevsky which announces his own flight into the beyond, a "new birth" for the author that "began on that frosty day at the Neva with the extinguishing of earthly reality and with the exaltation above it of another spiritual reality": Stepun, *Vstrechi* (Munich: Tovarishchestvo zarubezhnykh pisatelei, 1962), 15. Donald Fanger characterizes it as a "mystical" "vision" too great for Arkadii to digest, a "discovery [for Dostoevsky] that life is more terribly strange than fiction": Fanger, *Dostoevsky's Romantic Realism*, 168. Arkadii's vision is repeated almost verbatim, now from the first person, in Dostoevsky's 1861 journalistic feuilleton, "Petersburg Dreaming in Verse and Prose" ("Peterburgskoe snovidenie v stikhakh i proze," 19:67–85).

19. Bakhtin, "Author and Hero in Aesthetic Activity," 101. Caryl Emerson notes that the "Bakhtinian self acknowledges no equivalent of a Freudian 'Id' with its inner (but presumably universal) drives. It also appears to know no firm or punitive 'Superego.' It can be stabilized only in categories that originate in a concrete consciousness external to it": Emerson, "Bakhtin, Lotman, Vygotsky, and Lydia Ginzburg on Types of Selves: A Tribute," in *Self and Story in Russian History*, ed. Laura Engelstein and Stephanie Sandler (Ithaca, N.Y.: Cornell University Press, 2002), 20–45, 31.

20. Bakhtin, "Author and Hero in Aesthetic Activity," 101.

21. Bakhtin, *Problems of Dostoevsky's Poetics*, 26. On "unmerged" and "sovereign" consciousnesses in Bakhtin's thought see Alina Wyman, "Bakhtin and Scheler: Toward a Theory of Active Understanding," *Slavic and East European Review* 86, no. 1 (January 2008): 58–89. "Remarkably," observes Caryl Emerson, "Bakhtin assumes that the other's finalizing efforts are always benign—or at least a given self is presumed resilient enough to incorporate, or counter, any definition the other might thrust upon it": Emerson, "Russian Orthodoxy and the Early Bakhtin," in *Religion & Literature* 22, no. 2/3 (Summer-Autumn, 1990): 109–31, 116. Sasha Spektor points out that dialogue in Dostoevsky is "the site of an intense struggle for authorial power," a struggle fueled by characters' "metaphysical anxiety" concerning the absence of a divine author: Spektor, "From Violence to Silence: Vicissitudes of Reading (in) *The Idiot*," *Slavic Review* 72, no. 3 (Fall 2013): 552–72, 557. For an extensive examination of the difference between

the ideal of harmonious intersubjectivity and the "abyss [. . .] where polyphony threatens to become cacophony" (xiv), see Malcolm V. Jones's *Dostoevsky after Bakhtin*. For an authoritative look at some of the most persuasive challenges mounted against Bakhtin's theory of polyphony and dialogue with regard to Dostoevsky, see Emerson, *The First Hundred Years of Mikhail Bakhtin*, esp. 130–49.

22. Joseph Frank, *Dostoevsky: The Miraculous Years, 1865–1871* (Princeton, N.J.: Princeton University Press, 1995), 98–99.

23. Richard Peace presents the foundational reading in his description of Raskolnikov as "the living example of the folly of basing human actions on reason and reason alone. [. . .] Raskolnikov is, above all else, a man whose actions are based on cool and calculating reason": Peace, *Dostoevsky: An Examination of the Major Novels* (Cambridge: Cambridge University Press, 1971), 19.

24. Joseph Frank notes the similarity between Arkady and Razumkhin in *Dostoevsky: The Miraculous Years*, 99.

25. Frank suggests that his surname ("Razum-Reason") "indicates Dostoevsky's desire to link the employment of this faculty not only with the cold calculations of utilitarianism but also with spontaneous human warmth and generosity": Frank, *Dostoevsky: The Miraculous Years*, 99. Malcolm Jones argues that he is a depiction of "ways in which the Dionysian elements in life may be harnessed and directed toward positive ends": Jones, *Dostoyevsky: The Novel of Discord* (London: Paul Elek, 1976), 23. Marina Kostalevsky describes Razumikhin as "the positive personification of rational good": Kostalevsky, *Dostoevsky and Soloviev*, 154.

26. Thomas G. Marullo explores "morbid codependency" in Dostoevsky's early work in *Heroine Abuse: The Poetics of Codependency in "Netochka Nezvanova"* (DeKalb: Northern Illinois University Press, 2015). For a description of "projective identification," see the second chapter of this book, as well as Richard J. Rosenthal, "Dostoevsky's Experiment with Projective Mechanisms and the Theft of Identity in *The Double*," in *Russian Literature and Psychoanalysis*, ed. Daniel Rancour-Laferriere (Amsterdam: John Benjamins, 1989), 59–88.

27. Olga Meerson has illuminated the importance of the "taboo" in Dostoevsky, the way in which the author turned "the sore spot into a literary motif" (13). Arguing that "Dostoevsky taboos what matters in his books" (20), Meerson encourages us to look for what is not mentioned. Meerson's emphasis differs from mine in that she focuses on the importance of "tabooed cultural motifs" in uncovering Dostoevsky's value system: Meerson, *Dostoevsky's Taboos* (Dresden: Dresden University Press, 1998).

28. Of course, Dostoevsky likely has in mind an echo of Max Stirner's atheistic radical egoism in his mentioning of anthropophagy: "Where the world comes in my way—and it comes in my way everywhere—I consume it to quiet the hunger of my egoism. For me you are nothing but—my food, even as I too am fed

Notes to Pages 30–32

upon and turned to use by you": Max Stirner, *The Ego and Its Own*, ed. David Leopold (Cambridge: Cambridge University Press, 2005), 263.

CHAPTER TWO

The chapter epigraphs are from Pyotr Chaadaev, "Philosophical Letters: I," in *Major Works of Peter Chaadaev*, trans. Raymond T. McNally (Notre Dame, Ind.: University of Notre Dame Press, 1969), 32; from Friedrich Schiller, "Letters on the Aesthetic Education of Man," in *Essays*, ed. Walter Hinderer and Daniel Dahlstrom (New York: Continuum, 2005), 98; and Dostoevsky's *The Idiot* (8:189).

1. In Bakhtin's words, "[In Dostoevskii's art] all is simultaneous, everything coexists. That which [. . .] is valid only as past, or as future [. . .] is for him nonessential and is not incorporated into his world." That is why his characters "remember nothing, they have no biography in the sense of something past and fully experienced. They remember from their own past only that which has not ceased to be present for them, that which is still experienced by them as the present, an unexpiated sin, a crime, an unforgiven insult." Bakhtin observes, moreover, that Dostoevsky "leaps over" "biographical time," placing his characters always in the "living present," on the "threshold"; in his novels, "there is no interior of drawing rooms, dining rooms, halls, studios, bedrooms where biographical life unfolds and where events take place in the novels of writers such as Turgenev, Tolstoy, and Goncharov": Bakhtin, *Problems of Dostoevsky's Poetics*, 29, 170.

2. Bakhtin, *Problems of Dostoevsky's Poetics*, 297.

3. On the phenomenon of shame in Dostoevsky, see Deborah Martinsen, who locates shame "on the boundary between self and other and [. . .] thus intimately linked to the question of identity" (xiv): Martinsen, *Surprised by Shame: Dostoevsky's Liars and Narrative Exposure* (Columbus: Ohio State University Press, 2003), esp. 1–17.

4. In terms of Dostoevsky's approach, I prefer the term "suppressed" over "repressed," since, in each case, the characters seem actively, albeit only semiconsciously, to pursue the erasure of memory, rather than engaging in automatic, unconscious "repression." On the distinction between the two terms, see, for example, Eric Rassin, *Thought Suppression* (London: Elsevier, 2005), 31–36.

5. Ralph Tymms described the double in romantic literature, especially in the works of E. T. A. Hoffmann, as a "secondary, non-conscious self," a "part of the mind inaccessible to the conscious personality," which, "freed from its hiding-place," becomes "projected into the outside world in the visible form of a physical double": Tymms, *Doubles in Literary Psychology*, 119. Many of Dostoevsky's readers apply this theory of doubling, including Mochulsky, *Dostoevsky: Life and Works*, 50; Joseph Frank, *Dostoevsky: The Seeds of Revolt*, 304; and Kent, *The Subconscious in Gogol' and Dostoevskij*: "[Goliadkin's] double is a

manifestation of the repressed unconscious" (90). Tymms's reading of Dostoevsky reduces his work to an intensification of this theme; the doppelganger does not "lose this romantic character when it reappears in Dostoevsky's works [. . .] for his use of the theme only corroborates Hoffmann's half-intuitive understanding of the obscurest processes of the mind" (*Doubles in Literary Psychology*, 121). See also Charles E. Passage for a reading of Goliadkin as a reformulation of Hoffmann's Medardus: Passage, *Dostoevski the Adapter: A Study of Dostoevski's Use of the Tales of Hoffmann* (Chapel Hill: University of North Carolina Press, 1954), 14–37.

6. On Dostoevsky and Neoplatonism, Carus, and Mesmer, see Chizhevskii, "Dostoevskij—psikholog." For an appraisal of Dostoevsky's reading of Carus during his exile, and the many similarities between their respective treatments of the unconscious, see George Gibbian, "C. G. Carus' *Psyche* and Dostoevsky," *American Slavic and East European Review* 14, no. 3 (October 1955): 371–82. For an account of German literature's development of the unconscious in the context of Russian literature, see Leonard J. Kent, "Towards the Literary 'Discovery' of the Subconscious," in *The Subconscious in Gogol' and Dostoevskij*, 15–52. This tradition of the double encompasses both metaphysical conceptions of interiority (the dissonance between the conscious rational self and a deeper underlying essential identity—e.g., Sonia is Raskolnikov's soul) and psychoanalytic conceptions of unconscious agencies in the mind (e.g., Rogozhin is Myshkin's id). On Sonia as Raskolnikov's soul, see, for example, Zander, who argues that "the fate of the 'Sonias,' of Maria Lebydakina, symbolizes the life of a feminine soul and even of the world-soul": Zander, *Dostoevsky*, 100. On Rogozhin as Myshkin's id, see Dalton, *Unconscious Structure in "The Idiot,"* 83.

7. The field was pioneered in the 1940s by Melanie Klein, who influentially described the "projective identification" exhibited by "schizoid personalities" who externalize the self, a normal process in childhood development, but which underlies deeper mental illness when "a weakened ego feels incapable of taking back into itself the parts which it projected into the external world" (12): Klein, "Notes on Some Schizoid Mechanisms," in *Envy and Gratitude and Other Works 1946–1963* (New York: Free, 1975), 1–24. On projective mechanisms and *The Double*, see Rosenthal, "Dostoevsky's Experiment with Projective Mechanisms," 59–88. See also Louis Breger, *Dostoevsky: The Author as Psychoanalyst*, 123.

8. In this sense, the doubles are an expression of conflicting orientations within consciousness (the distinction between I-for-myself and I-for-others that informs twentieth-century phenomenological models of selfhood, with their foundations in German idealism). Kathryn Szczepanska's examination of Dostoevsky's doubles tends toward this avenue, especially in her emphasis on the significance of Hegel's dialectic of self-consciousness as an explanatory paradigm: "characters become the physical representation of thesis and antithesis; the pro-

tagonist himself represents at the same time the conflicts and its possible synthesis" (22): Szczepanska, "The Double and Double Consciousness in Dostoevsky" (Ph.D. diss., Stanford University, 1978). This aspect of the doppelgänger tradition is the focus of Dmitris Vardoulakis's recent book *The Doppelgänger: Literature's Philosophy* (New York: Fordham University Press, 2010) in his contention that the "doppelgänger makes possible an ontology of the subject" without entailing "a lapse into metaphysics" (1).

9. Malcolm Jones describes this gaze as "the disconfirming glance of the other," which "constantly throws [Goliadkin] into a state of inarticulate panic": Jones, *Dostoyevsky after Bakhtin*, 42.

10. A third voice, Bakhtin says, is the voice of the narrator, yet another aspect of Goliadkin's self-consciousness: Bakhtin, *Problems of Dostoevsky's Poetics*, 217.

11. Bakhtin, *Problems of Dostoevsky's Poetics*, 217. Alex Woloch proposes a similar reading of Goliadkin's double as a "hypostatized version of [his] lingering sense of his own exteriority": Woloch, *The One vs. the Many*, 240. Compare Bakhtin's (and Woloch's) approach with the widely held contrasting view, for example, in Leonard J. Kent's analysis: "the subconscious is the single most important factor governing Goljadkin's life, controlling him not only from within, but flowing over to infect the total context of his life": Kent, *The Subconscious in Gogol' and Dostoevskij*, 94. Others have read Goliadkin's dualism as a comic parody of the romantic tradition. See, for example, Viktor Shklovsky, *Za i protiv: Zametki o Dostoevskom* (Moscow: Sovetskij pisatel', 1957), 57; and Victor Terras, who sees in Goldyadkin's division "a struggle not between Heaven and Hell for a man's soul, but between two ridiculous underlings—for a snug little job [. . .] These grotesque antics can well be viewed as a travesty of the frenzied sciamachies of Hoffmanesque Doppelgangers": Terras, *The Young Dostoevsky*, 14.

12. Goethe apparently approved of the reading of *Faust* in which Mephisto is interpreted as a projected aspect of Faust's personality. See Tymms, *Doubles in Literary Psychology*, 34–35.

13. For more than 150 years now, "The Landlady" has been panned by critics. Belinsky set the tone for the story's reception shortly after its appearance, describing it as "far-fetched, exaggerated, stilted, spurious and false." For more on this, see Joseph Frank, *Dostoevsky: The Seeds of Revolt*, 342.

14. For a foundational reading of Ordynov as a romantic dreamer who projects fairy tale qualities onto his interlocutors, see W. J. Leatherbarrow, "Dostoevsky's Treatment of the Theme of Romantic Dreaming in 'Khozyayka' and 'Belyye nochi,'" *Modern Language Review* 69, no. 3 (July 1974): 584–95.

15. Reactions have been divided over whether Ordynov's experience is real, a subjective fantasy, or whether the entire story should be read allegorically. A. L. Bem argued that Ordynov's experiences are entirely imaginary. Ordynov, in his feverish state, projects fairy tale qualities onto the normal lives of Katerina and

Notes to Page 36

Murin: Bem, "Dramatizatsiia breda (Khoziaika Dostoevskogo)," in *Dostoevsky: Psikhoanaliticheskie etiudy* (Prague: Petropolis, 1938), 77–141, a conclusion that W. J. Leatherbarrow supports in "Dostoevsky's Treatment of the Theme of Romantic Dreaming," 584–85; and in "The Sorcerer's Apprentice: Authorship and the Devil in Dostoevsky's *Poor Folk* and 'The Landlady,'" *Slavic and East European Review* 83, no. 4 (October 2005): 599–616, where Leatherbarrow emphasizes the tyranny of Orydnov's imagination as it imposes narratives on his interlocutors. Terras describes two plots, "objective" and "subjective," suggesting that the story calls attention to the dissonance between reality and the fantastic subjectivity of the romantic dreamer: Leatherbarrow, *The Young Dostoevsky (1846–1849)* (The Hague: Mouton, 1969), 195–96; and Dina Khapaeva examines the story as part of Dostoevsky's career-long investigation into the temporality of nightmares. Khapaeva, *Nightmare: From Literary Experiments to Cultural Projects*, trans. Rosie Tweddle (Leiden: Brill, 2013), 151-55. Another tendency in criticism puts the emphasis upon the relationship that Ordynov observes, not upon Ordynov himself. Joseph Frank, for example, dismissed Bem's reading as unlikely: "the story itself does not center thematically on this type ['the dreamer'] at all. As the title indicates, the focus is on Katerina and her relation both to Murin and Ordynov; the psychology of the latter is sketched in briefly but not really developed": Joseph Frank, *Dostoevsky: The Seeds of Revolt*, 342. Other readings of the relationship among the three characters have been symbolic and allegorical. For example, in Rudolf Neuhauser's argument: "the landlady is meant to represent the Russian people"; "we can define [Murin] as the personification of [. . .] national traditions reaching back to pre-Petrine times," while Ordynov is the newfangled idealist/utopian socialist who wants to rescue the Russian soul from repressive autocracy: Neuhauser, "'The Landlady': A New Interpretation," *Canadian Slavonic Papers / Revue Canadienne des Slavistes* 10, no. 1 (Spring 1968): 42–67.

16. Rudolf Neuhauser presents an allegorical psychoanalytic reading, associating Ordynov with the life of the spirit which tries to gain mastery over the soul: "the main characters of the tale form one composite figure: man, particularly adolescent man, on his uncertain path to maturity. The prince symbolizes human spirituality, the intellectual component of man; the princess or bewitched beauty embodies the principle of the soul, the emotional component of man; the wizard represents evil drives, the psychological substratum in man, which rises against him in adolescence and has to be overcome before the intellect can be united to the soul, that is, gain power over the emotional, animalistic self. Only then has adolescent man, the composite hero of the tale, reached maturity": Neuhauser, "'The Landlady': A New Interpretation," 45.

17. In this sense, critics are justified in evaluating the story as derivative of romantic literature, and echoes of Murin's tyranny can readily be found in Hoffmann's Alban ("The Magnetizer"), or in Nikolai Gogol's Antichrist ("A Terrible Vengeance"), both of whom present themselves as tyrants who have cap-

tivated and subdued the feminine soul. Many readings of "The Landlady" have emphasized its derivative qualities. See, for example, Charles E. Passage, "The Landlady," in *Dostoevski the Adapter: A Study of Dostoevski's Use of the Tales of Hoffmann* (Chapel Hill: University of North Carolina Press, 1954), 40–62. See Terras's overview of "The Landlady" and romantic antecedents in *The Young Dostoevsky*, 27–30.

18. The image of the tears on the face is repeated between them on three occasions (1:277, 278, 292).

19. In the interactions of Arkady and Vasia, we see a preponderance of the verb *vzdrognut'*, "to shudder" or "to give a start" (Arkadii, 2:36, 44, 48; Vasia, 2:36, 43)

20. The mechanism that binds the three protagonists evokes elements of object-relations theory in twentieth-century psychoanalysis, especially Melanie Klein's concept of "projective identification" in narcissistic personalities: "a person treats others as though they were part of oneself" and then attempts "to control the parts of the self that have [. . .] been lodged into the other person": David E. Scharff, *Object Relations Theory and Practice: An Introduction* (Northvale, N.J.: Jason Aronson, 1996), 137. As Richard J. Rosenthal observes, this process can become successfully externalized as the schizoid personality "induce[s] complementary or identical states of mind in the recipient" through "subtle, usually unconscious, affective or cognitive communications and behaviors": Rosenthal, "Dostoevsky's Experiment with Projective Mechanisms," 63.

21. Mochulsky sees this as a compositional defect in the work: "Netochka is too pale a figure, too much the narrator and not the heroine. With discreet modesty she invariably yields the foreground to other individuals and is incapable of focusing the novel's events on her own personality": Mochulsky, *Dostoevsky: His Life and Work*, 108.

22. References are to the 1860 revised text.

23. The section with Laria was removed from the unfinished novel in Dostoevsky's later revision. See Terras, *The Young Dostoevsky*, 145–47.

24. Joseph Frank describes Laria as a "'reflector' for Netochka [who] helps her, even at this early stage, to understand the significance of her own twisted psychic history": Joseph Frank, *Dostoevsky: The Seeds of Revolt*, 357.

25. Thomas G. Marullo examines the relationships of the novel's characters from the perspective of "morbid codependency," a state in which the boundaries between self and other are obscured and dissolved: "Initially, in morbid codependency with others, the child Netochka enjoys untold happiness. To her the advantages are obvious. She can take from others what she believes she lacks [. . .]. Fearing loneliness, abandonment, and eviction, she latches onto her host with gritted teeth and white-knuckled hands" (32–33). Marullo stresses the infectious nature of "morbid codependency" in *Netochka Nezvanova*: "morbid code-

pendents bend their hosts into their own image and likeness; or, they transmute to doubles, mirroring with stunning veracity the (often bizarre and unstable) thoughts, actions, and emotions of their partners": Marullo, *Heroine Abuse*, 5.

26. See, for example, Konstantin Mochulsky, who argues that "Raskolnikov is [. . .] the spiritual center of the novel [. . .]. The tragedy springs up in his soul and the external action only serves to reveal his moral conflicts"; "The battle between good and evil that is waged within the murderer's soul, is substantialized in the opposition between these two personalities, Sonia and Svidrigailov": Mochulsky, *Dostoevsky: His Life and Works*, 298–99; as well as Richard Peace's foundational examination of the parallels between Raskolnikov's dual personality and the polarized characters around him: Peace, *Dostoevsky: An Examination of the Major Novels* (Cambridge: Cambridge University Press, 1971), 34–58. In the words of Fyodor Stepun, the "connection of Dostoevsky's heroes with each other" makes us "agree [. . .] that they are not psychologically profound types of Russian life, but the embodiment of the religious-philosophical ideas of the author": Stepun, *Vstrechi*, 19. Or, to quote Richard Peace, "We are dealing here not so much with the realistic portrayal of character as with its symbolic meaning": Peace, *Dostoevsky: An Examination of the Major Novels*, 38. For more on the good/evil dualism as externalized in Sonya and Svidrigailov, see R. L. Busch, "The Myshkin-Ippolit-Rogozhin Triad," *Canadian-American Slavic Studies* 3 (1983): 372–83, 372–73.

27. According to the *Diagnostic and Statistical Manual of Mental Disorders*, 5th ed. (Washington, D.C.: American Psychiatric Publishing, 2013), "intrusion symptoms" include "dissociative reactions [. . .] in which the individual feels or acts as if the traumatic event(s) were recurring" (271).

28. For the importance of this peasant-horse-child dream in *Crime and Punishment*, and to Dostoevsky himself, see Breger, *Dostoevsky: The Author as Psychoanalyst*, 1–3, 56–67; Raskolnikov, Breger points out, is "peasant, young boy, and old nag" (3).

29. Later on, when Raskolnikov's mother and sister are on their way to visit Raskolnikov, they notice "that the landlady's door was open by a small crack and that two quick black eyes watched them both from the darkness" before "the door suddenly slammed shut" (6:170), an image which could be said to reflect the flicker of intimacy in their ensuing meeting with Raskolnikov.

30. Interestingly in this context, while Raskolnikov never sees his landlady in the novel, Razumikhin (also, as we have seen in chapter 1, an aspect of Raskolnikov's extended personality) spends a great deal of time with her, even engages romantically with her as he attempts to reconcile her with her lodger, behaving as their mediator. Among the numerous models of the externalized tripartite self presented in the novel (Raskolnikov-Alyona-Lizaveta; Raskolnikov-Svidrigailov-Sonia), the subtly delineated relationship connecting Razumikhin, Raskolnikov, and his landlady seems to be the least intentional on Dostoevsky's part, though it

is highly evocative as a tripartite image of the self: the administrative mind (Razumikhin), the silent, unseen soul (Praskovia), and the conscious I (Raskolnikov), a fragmented agency that fears and avoids its unconscious life while also longing to escape its vigilant self-conscious awareness.

31. Eric Naiman reads the scene as enacting a form of "discursive coitus," a violation or "rape" of the mind: Naiman, "Gospel Rape," paper delivered at Association for Slavic, East European, and Eurasian Studies Convention, November 2014. For a close analysis of Sonya's "interpretive reading of the Lazarus passage" (264), see Elizabeth Blake, who argues that the scene allows us "to read [Sonya] not as a religious fanatic but as a woman struggling to reconcile her belief in God with acute personal suffering": Blake, "Sonya, Silent No More: A Response to the Woman Question," *Slavic and East European Journal* 50, no. 2 (2006): 252–71, 263–64.

CHAPTER THREE

The chapter epigraphs are from Jean-Jacques Rousseau, *Julie, or the New Heloise*, trans. P. Stewart and J. Vaché (Hanover, N.H.: University Press of New England, 1997), 349; and from Fyodor Dostoevsky, *Notes from Underground* (5:122).

1. N. G. Chernyshevskii, *Polnoe sobranie sochinenii N. G. Chernyshevskago v desiati tomakh* (Saint Petersburg: Tipografiia M. M. Stasiulevicha, 1906), vol. 10.2, 230–240

2. Dostoevsky's innovative concept of self-consciousness, it has been argued, renders broad gestures of self-exposition (those, for example, of the underground man, of Ippolit Terentiev, of Nikolai Stavrogin, and of Mitya Karamazov) always dubious and incomplete. "Because of the nature of consciousness," writes J. M. Coetzee of Dostoevsky, "the self cannot tell the truth of itself to itself and come to rest without the possibility of self-deception"; in the "sterile monologue of the self [. . .] behind each true, final position lurks another position truer and more final, [and] the truth [is deferred] endlessly, coming to no end." Such, Coetzee argues, is Dostoevsky's implicit critique of Rousseau's doctrine of transparency and self-revelation. Yet, he also argues that here, in the first of his six major novels, Dostoevsky had not yet discovered the complex, self-conscious personality that would be so central to his later work. Coetzee reads Valkovsky's confession, for example, as a "mere expository device," "a way of allowing a character to expose himself," though he admits that "an element of gratuitousness" does creep in. What is missing, I would argue, from Coetzee's analysis of the confession is a notion of the effect of the wound upon consciousness in Dostoevsky's writing, both as a prohibitive limit within the psyche (obviating the possibility of self-exposition) and as an aperture in the self toward a deeper form of interiority and thus toward the possibility of a meaningful confession. Coetzee, "Confession

and Double Thoughts: Tolstoy, Rousseau, Dostoevsky," *Comparative Literature* 37, no. 3 (Summer 1985): 193–232, 230–32, 215.

3. Robin Feuer Miller illuminates two kinds of confessions in Dostoevsky's world in general: on the one hand the "literary-bookish-written confession" à la Rousseau, which "most often tends to lie, to seek self-justification, or to aim at shocking the audience"; and, on the other hand, "the successful confession," which "retains a sacrament, a sacred communication" and which "always serves to reunite man with other men and with the whole universe": Miller, "Dostoevsky and Rousseau: The Morality of Confession Reconsidered," in *Dostoevsky: New Perspectives*, ed. Robert L. Jackson (Englewood Cliffs, N.J.: Prentice-Hall, 1984), 82–98, 98.

4. "Emile is worse at disguising his feelings than any man in the world": Jean-Jacques Rousseau, *Emile, or On Education*, trans. Allan Bloom (New York: Basic Books, 1979), 415. For the foundational discussion of Rousseau's plea for a "restoration of transparency," see Jean Starobinski, *Jean-Jacques Rousseau: Transparency and Obstruction*, trans. Arthur Goldhammer (Chicago: University of Chicago Press, 1988), 13.

5. For the more traditional critique of Alyosha's character, see Konstantin Mochulsky, who sees Alyosha as Dostoevsky's way of attacking the "idealist-utopians in the spirit of Petrashevsky," the worshipers of "all the 'noble and beautiful'" among whom Dostoevsky had once counted himself. Dostoevsky, according to Mochulsky, "executes his 'innocent' beautiful-soul of the forties" in the person of Alyosha. "After the experience of penal servitude it appeared to him as unmitigated light-headedness": Mochulsky, *Dostoevsky: His Life and Work*, 212.

6. My focus upon the notion of the transparent self differs from the general critical emphasis on Stirner's influence on Dostoevsky as a representative of "Western egoism, individualism, and capitalism": Joseph Frank, *Dostoevsky: The Stir of Liberation*, 124. For an authoritative account of Stirner's influence upon Dostoevsky, especially for the manner in which the arguments "of the hero from the underground base themselves on the Stirnerian philosophy of extreme individualism and nihilism," see Sergei Kibal'nik, *Problemy intertekstual'noi poetiki Dostoevskogo* (St. Petersburg: Petropolis, 2013), 219–32. For an account of Stirner's resounding popularity in Russian society, the discussions of his work by such figures as Belinsky, Herzen, and Khomiakov, see N. Otverzhennyj, *Shtirner i Dostoevskii* (Moscow: Golos truda, 1925). Otverzhennyj speculates that Dostoevsky's presentation to the Petrashevsky circle in the late 1840s, titled "On the Personality and On Egoism," probably engaged to some extent with Stirner's thought (*Shtirner i Dostoevskii*, 27).

7. Joseph Frank argues that Dostoevsky is engaging here directly not only with Stirner but also with Chernyshevsky who was influenced by the former, and thus Dostoevsky is already formulating his critique of Chernyshevsky's rational egoism, namely that "to base morality on egoism was to risk unleashing forces in

the human personality over which Utilitarian reason had little control": Joseph Frank, *Dostoevsky: The Stir of Liberation*, 122–25.

8. For an account of Stirner as a forerunner of existentialism (and an influence on Dostoevsky) in his "endeavor to displace the authority of essences and stress the primacy of the *I*," see John Carroll, *Break-Out from the Crystal Palace: The Anarcho-Psychological Critique: Stirner, Nietzsche, Dostoevsky* (London: Routledge and Kegan Paul, 1974), 39–48.

9. Stirner, *The Ego and Its Own*, 283–84.

10. Ibid., 148.

11. See Robin Feuer Miller's account of Dostoevsky's "life-long argument with Rousseau" and of Valkovsky's "metaphor of confession as indecent exposure": Miller, "Dostoevsky and Rousseau," 82–98, 82, 84. Mochulsky reads this image of the madman in the coat allegorically as part of Dostoevsky's attack upon secular humanism; the ideology once exposed, is ultimately shallow, a "symbol of humanistic goodness: nakedness under an ostentatious cloak": Mochulsky, *Dostoevsky: Life and Work*, 217.

12. For the connections between Valkovsky's confession and Rousseau's *Confessions* and Laclos's *Les Liasons Dangereuses*, as well as to the Marquis de Sade, Max Stirner, and Chernyshevsky, see Joseph Frank, *Dostoevsky: The Stir of Liberation*, 122–25. For a fuller discussion of de Sade's influence on Dostoevsky, and of "Valkovsky's philosophy" as "Sadean to the letter," see Robert L. Jackson's "Dostoevsky and the Marquis de Sade," in *Dialogues with Dostoevsky: The Overwhelming Questions* (Stanford, Calif.: Stanford University Press, 1996), 144–61.

13. Susanne Fusso illuminates the sexual subtext of Valkovsky's confessional exhibitionism in this scene as part of Dostoevsky's struggle with the "moral problem" of "presenting sexual material in his artistic works" (3): Fusso, *Discovering Sexuality in Dostoevsky* (Evanston, Ill., Northwestern University Press, 2006), 3–16, esp. 8–12.

14. According to Joseph Frank, Alyosha's "most striking attribute [. . .], and one that most clearly stamps him as Myshkin's predecessor, is his capacity—or weakness, depending on the point of view—for living so totally in each moment of time, or in each experience and encounter, that he lacks any sense of continuity or consequence": Joseph Frank, *Dostoevsky: The Stir of Liberation*, 129. Here we encounter another (albeit morally compromised) echo of Rousseau, who prided himself on his ability to exist fully in the intensity of the present moment. As he declares in his *Confessions*, "solely occupied with the present, my heart fills up all its capacity, all its space with it; and, aside from past pleasures, which from now on cause my only enjoyment, there is not an empty corner left in it for what no longer exists": Rousseau, *The Confessions and Correspondence*, trans. Christopher Kelly, ed. Christopher Kelly, Roger Masters, and Peter Stillman (Hanover, N.H.: University Press of New England, 1995), 109.

15. Dostoevsky, according to Bakhtin, displayed a "stubborn urge to see everything as coexisting, [. . .] to perceive and show all things side by side and simultaneous, as if they existed in space and not in time. [. . .] That which has meaning only as 'earlier' and 'later,' which is sufficient only unto its own moment, which is valid only as past, or as future [. . .] is for him nonessential and is not incorporated into his world": Bakhtin, *Problems of Dostoevsky's Poetics*, 28–29.

16. In James P. Scanlan's discussion of Dostoevsky's moral philosophy, he identifies the "lowest level" of moral decrepitude not as the unrepentant sinner, but the sinner who does not recognize that any crime has taken place at all: "On the [. . .] lowest level, both remorse and the sense of guilt are absent: conscience is no longer evident at all." Scanlan uses Dostoevsky's phrase, "the naked depravity of egoism," to describe this state of the death of conscience: Scanlan, *Dostoevsky the Thinker*, 93.

17. The nature of pathogenic secrecy was investigated by the Viennese physician Moritz Benedikt between the years 1864 and 1895. For an account of how the concept of "the pathogenic effect of a heavily disturbing secret upon the bearer [. . .] known from time immemorial" gradually informed the field of psychiatry, see Henri F. Ellenberger, "The Pathogenic Secret and Its Therapeutics," in *Beyond the Unconscious: Essays of Henri F. Ellenberger in the History of Psychiatry*, ed. Mark S. Michale (Princeton, N.J.: Princeton University Press, 1993), 341. Allan Young distinguishes between two kinds of concealment of memory: "In one, the owner wants to hide the contents of his recollection from other people. In addition, he wants to forget the memory himself or, failing this, he wants to push it to the edges of awareness. This kind of secret memory has a long history in the West. In Latin and Orthodox Christianity, it is the hiding place of sins and transgressions, and it is the object of rituals of confession. [. . .] The second kind of concealment involves a memory that the owner is hiding from himself. He knows that he has a secret memory, because he senses its existence, but he is unable to retrieve it; or, what is more common, he does not remember that he has forgotten and has to learn about his memory from someone else, typically a therapist. [. . .] Ordinary memories fade [. . .]. The pathogenic secret is different. Years after its creation, it remains unassimilated, a self-renewing presence, perpetually reliving the moment of its origin": Allan Young, *Harmony of Illusions*, 29.

18. Henri F. Ellenberger, *The Discovery of the Unconscious: The History and Evolution of Dynamic Psychiatry* (New York: Basic Books, 1970), 46.

19. James P. Scanlan describes him as a "saint," a "moral antipode" to Valkovsky: "As the prince's chief antagonist in the narrative, Ivan is his polar opposite with respect to both egoism and goodness": Scanlan, "Introduction: Exploring Egoism," in *The Insulted and the Injured*, by Fyodor Dostoevsky (Grand Rapids, Mich.: William B. Eerdmans, 2011), vii–xxiii: xiv–xv. Susan McReynolds notes that Vanya is the novel's manifestation of "Christian caritas" and is thus

"linked to later characters like Myshkin and Alyosha Karamazov: he is so free of self-interest and loves others so deeply that he simply doesn't perceive any insult to himself": McReynolds, *Redemption and the Merchant God: Dostoevsky's Economy of Salvation and Antisemitism* (Evanston, Ill.: Northwestern University Press, 2008), 84.

20. Frank calls attention to Vanya's "ineffectuality" as a character "when openly challenged by Prince Valkovsky," allowing us to see "Ivan Petrovich from a more objective and critical point of view": Joseph Frank, *Dostoevsky: The Stir of Liberation*, 122. Edward Wasiolek observes that Vanya's "idealism [. . .] is pitted against Valkovsky's voracious self-interest" but without any of the metaphysical significance such an opposition will acquire once Dostoevsky begins to see the real threat of the "rational organization of human happiness" that underlies Vanya's worldview: Wasiolek, *Dostoevsky: The Major Fiction* (Cambridge, Mass.: MIT Press, 1964), 36.

21. See, for example, Joseph Frank who sees Prince Valkovsky as "so stagey and melodramatic an aristocratic villain that it is difficult for us now to take him at all seriously." Joseph Frank, *Dostoevsky: The Stir of Liberation*, 116–17. The Enlightenment model of transparency (= good) vs. concealment (= evil) had reached its apogee roughly a century prior in the philosophical psychology of Jean-Jacques Rousseau. Jean Starobinski describes how, even in Rousseau's time, "the deceiver, the 'vile flatterer,' the scoundrel in disguise were the common currency of comedy and tragedy. Every well-wrought plot required the unmasking of a deceiver [. . .]. The antithesis between appearance and reality belonged to common parlance: the idea had become a cliché. Yet [with Rousseau] the cliché came back to life: it blazed up and glowed white hot": Starobinski, *Jean-Jacques Rousseau: Transparency and Obstruction*, 3–4.

22. Mochulsky describes him as "a passive intermediary" in the employ of the others: Mochulsky, *Dostoevsky: His Life and Work*, 206–7.

23. Natasha expresses astonishment at Vanya's capacity for self-effacement: "not one word about yourself! I left you first, and you have forgiven everything, you're only thinking about my happiness" (3:197). Valkovsky expresses similar astonishment at his "readiness to play the role of a secondary person": "Of course, one of your writers even, I recall, said somewhere: that perhaps the greatest feat of a person is if he is able to limit himself in life to the role of a secondary person" (3:358).

24. Some have suggested that this transparent quality is a convenient novelistic device, a way of granting the narrator access to the interior lives of other characters. See, for example, N. A. Dobrolyubov, "Zabitye liudi," in *Literaturno-kriticheskie stat'i* (Moscow: Khudozhestvennaia literatura, 1937), 503.

25. Smith's "meaninglessly intent gaze" recalls Murin's from the earlier story, evoking "extremely unpleasant, even unbearable" feelings of self-consciousness in those upon whom it falls (3:173).

26. Joseph Frank's explanation that Vanya as "a young observer of life" is "intrigued by the eccentric appearance and behavior of the old man" only rings true if we ignore all of these lengthy descriptions of mysterious compulsion: Joseph Frank, *Dostoevsky: The Stir of Liberation*, 112. Most readers explain the strangeness of Vanya's compulsion as dictated by Hoffmanesque romantic convention. See, for example, Wasiolek, *Dostoevsky: The Major Fiction*, 33.

27. In the commentary on this "Gothic" scene, I have not found any analysis that places emphasis on the hero's attempts to forget. Frank argues that the description foreshadows "Dostoevsky's great theme of the impotence of reason to contend with the dark mysteries of human existence—with all those mysteries symbolized by the fear of the unknown": Joseph Frank, *Dostoevsky: The Stir of Liberation*, 122.

28. For a different interpretation of this encounter and of the relationship between Vanya and Nellie in general, see Susanne Fusso's argument for the "strong erotic undercurrent" that exists between the two from their first encounter and which "goes largely unacknowledged" by Vanya (20): Fusso, *Discovering Sexuality in Dostoevsky*, 18–22.

29. Vanya and Nellie, in their relationship, exhibit the full array of the imagistic vocabulary of the shared self that we observed in the previous chapters: like Arkady and Vasya, Vanya and Nellie share a room; like Arkady, Vanya locks his friend into the apartment when he leaves ("I locked her in because I didn't trust her. It seemed to me that she would suddenly take it into her head to leave me," 3:284), and pursues her through the city as she escapes her imprisonment in the apartment and attempts to emancipate herself from his kindness and administration. Like those other subdued selves, Nellie, literally a "weak heart" (3:371), "pretends to sleep," as he sits in vigil over her (3:280, 298). Like Razumikhin with Raskolnikov, Vanya buys her clothes (for a reasonable price) and is able to accurately guess her size (3:284). And like Raskolnikov in his attempt to outrun his external conscience, Nellie calls out for Vanya's help despite her attempts to conceal and escape: "though [she] gave the impression that she didn't want to speak with me, these quite frequent calls, this need to turn to me with all her perplexities, showed the opposite" (3:280). The delirious sense of intimacy between Katerina and Ordynov is replayed (though without the sexual overtones) as Nellie cares for Vanya during his delirious illness: he feels "as if in a fog, and the lovely image of the poor little girl flickered before me amid my oblivion, like a vision [. . .] Once I remember her quiet kiss on my face" (3:294). Like Ordynov with Katerina, Vanya draws Nellie's concealed memories out, in the midst of "torments and convulsive sobbing" (3:299). Vanya can hear the "thump of her heart" from "two, three feet away" (3:255), as though their body were extended through space. Like Netochka and Laria, in being initiated to Nellie's memories, Vanya conquers her "weak heart," assimilates her into his personality: "now I knew that [. . .] this

proud and loving little heart [. . .] was devoted to me forever" (3:297). Finally, as with all of the extended personalities we have seen so far, the connection begins as a mysterious, irrational, overpowering force of attraction. In his fascination with her, Vanya puzzles at the "insurmountable" and mysterious force ("I myself do not know what drew me to her" [3:255]), "the influence of a heavy and strange impression" (3:257).

30. Also John 11:21, 32.

31. Joseph Frank, *Dostoevsky: The Stir of Liberation*, 113. Susan McReynolds's analysis of the scene represents an exception to the general embarrassed scholarly attitude. McReynolds devotes a chapter of her recent book to the episode, arguing that in it Dostoevsky "contrasts the failure of art to the success of child sacrifice." "Because a Dostoevsky figure [Vanya] and his art fail to deliver the promises made for literature in essays like 'Mr.–bov,' a different vehicle of redemption becomes necessary, a child sacrifice": McReynolds, "'God Sent Her to Us as a Reward for Our Sufferings': The Origins of Dostoevsky's Preoccupation with Child Sacrifice in the Dialogue between *Time* and *The Insulted and Injured*," in *Redemption and the Merchant God*, 78–89, 79.

32. Joseph Frank argues that Vanya's impending death serves to lend "an additional element of pathos," as well as launching an implicit criticism of an ideal "whose world and life are shattered because his convictions prove inadequate to cope with the deeper forces of human passion and egoism that overwhelm his well-meaning innocence": Joseph Frank, *Dostoevsky: The Stir of Liberation*, 113, 118. On "presentness" and its pitfalls in Dostoevsky, see Morson, *Narrative and Freedom*, 201–6.

CHAPTER FOUR

The chapter epigraphs are from Charles Dickens, *A Christmas Carol* (New Haven, Conn.: Yale University Press, 1993), 28; and from Walt Whitman, "Pioneers! O Pioneers!" in *The Complete Poems*, ed. Francis Murphy (New York: Penguin Books, 2004), 257–61, 260.

1. In Mochulsky's words, "Myshkin eludes us. By no direct characteristic can we grasp his *essence*. One has only to tear him away from the world in which he lives, to consider him *separately*, and at once his image becomes obscure. In effect, alone, separately, he does not even exist. He lives not in space, but in the souls of the people surrounding him, as their love, dream, ideal, or as their hatred, envy, malice": Mochulsky, *Dostoevsky: His Life and Work*, 352–53.

2. To my knowledge two scholarly works have been dedicated centrally to the topic of Myshkin as a psychologically wounded individual in *The Idiot*. Elizabeth Dalton's groundbreaking *Unconscious Structure in "The Idiot"* proposes a Freudian reading of the interactions among Myshkin, Rogozhin, and Nastasia Filippovna by emphasizing the pervasive presence of the "sadistic concep-

tion of the primal scene" in the novel. Nastasia Filippovna, in Myshkin's sexually repressed psyche, comes to represent "the mother, the forbidden incestuous object whom the son unconsciously desires and wishes to rescue from the father [Rogozhin]": Dalton, *Unconscious Structure in "The Idiot,"* 101, 106. Alexander Burry traces Dostoevsky's interest in trauma in *The Idiot* in the context of the author's own "continued obsession with unresolved trauma from his averted execution" (269); in his discussions of Myshkin, Rogozhin, Nastasia Filippovna, and Ippolit as engaged variously in processes of recovery, Burry calls attention to these characters' more immediate traumatic experiences: Myshkin's witnessing of the execution abroad, Rogozhin's "recent traumatic family ruptures" (265), Ippolit's experience of looking at the Holbein painting ("the painting traumatizes [Ippolit] by confronting him with the meaninglessness of life" [267]): Burry, "Execution, Trauma, and Recovery in Dostoevsky's *The Idiot*," *Slavic and East European Journal* 54, no. 2 (Summer 2010): 255–71. By contrast with Burry's more immediate concept of trauma in the novel, my focus is upon a submerged and obliterated memory system, whose source is lost though the reverberations are still keenly felt.

3. Viacheslav Ivanov argues that Myshkin's memories are of the eternal forms: "The primitive memory is so strong in him that until his twenty-fourth year he cannot adjust himself to this world of ours. [. . .] He is entirely made up of memory of all that he has seen, he has a sunshine-clear, divinely illumined eye for all that is visible": Ivanov, "The Stranger," in *Freedom and the Tragic Life: A Study in Dostoevsky*, trans. Norman Cameron, ed. S. Konvalov (New York: Noonday, 1952), 90–96. Mochulsky sees Myshkin's "terrible transparency and elusiveness" as a facet of his otherworldliness, of his "different destiny" and his belonging to "another aeon—before the Fall": Mochulsky, *Dostoevsky: His Life and Work*, 375.

4. For a balanced discussion of Myshkin's epilepsy which allows for both possibilities of medical pathology and saintliness, see Hariet Murav, "'The Idiot' and the Problem of Recognition," in *Holy Foolishness: Dostoevsky's Novels and the Poetics of Cultural Critique* (Stanford, Calif.: Stanford University Press, 1992), esp. 73–81. For analyses of Myshkin's epileptic medical condition, see Brian Johnson, "Diagnosing Prince Myshkin," *Slavic and East European Journal* 56, no. 3 (Fall 2012): 377–93. For a discussion of Dostoevsky's own accounts of memory loss in connection with his epilepsy, see Rice, *Dostoevsky and the Healing Art*, 78–9.

5. Albert Camus saw Myshkin's illness as placing him in the "perpetual present," a "blissful state" that resembles "eternal life": Camus, *Myth of Sisyphus*, 111.

6. Mochulsky emphasizes Myshkin's desire, unique among the "dreamers" from whose number he is drawn, to be healed. The "new element" here is that "the prince not only analyzes his infirmity, but yearns for a cure. He returns to

Russia in order to discover the soil, to reunite himself with the people, to return to the sources of living life": Mochulsky, *Dostoevsky: His Life and Work*, 367–68.

7. For an influential interpretation of this moment of recognition as a dramatization of Platonic anamnesis and as part of a larger allegorical mystical journey to awaken and free the "Eternal Feminine," symbolically embodied in the figure of Nastasia Filippovna, see Ivanov, "The Stranger," 96–97. For a related view, see Tatiana Kasatkina, *O tvoriashchei prirode slova: Ontologichnost' slova v tvorchestve F. M. Dostoevskogo kak osnova "realisma v vysshem mysle"* (Moscow: IMLI RAN, 2004), 253.

8. One of the benefits of reading Myshkin as oppressed by memory is that it is one of the few ways in which we are not forced to agree begrudgingly with Radomsky's socially conscious assessment of Myshkin's actions as an attempt to reenact Christ's redemption of the harlot (8:482). For the sense of uneasiness the reader feels with Radomsky's interpretation as "accurate" but "also misleading," see Sasha Spektor, "From Violence to Silence: Vicissitudes of Reading (in) *The Idiot*," 553.

9. Our reading presents itself in opposition to those who read Myshkin as an ideal interlocutor. Sarah Young, for example, sees Myshkin as having perceived Nastasia's "real self" in her portrait (40): "By identifying the heroine's subjective sense of selfhood in the photograph, [. . .] the hero becomes an ethically ideal reader of Nastas'ia Filippovna. [. . .] Unlike the other characters [. . .] Myshkin reacts to the photograph, and therefore to the person depicted in it, with empathy and compassion, rather than objectifying and finalizing her": Sarah Young, *Dostoevsky's "The Idiot" and the Ethical Foundations of Narrative: Reading, Narrating, Scripting* (London: Anthem, 2004), 37. For a similar reading of the Prince as open to the realities and souls of others, see Kasatkina, *O tvoriashchei prirode slova*, 252–53. Leslie Johnson picks up on the projective aspect of Myshkin's recognition in her very apt suggestion—presented almost as an aside—that Myshkin's recognition of Nastasia stems "perhaps, at the deepest and dimmest remove, from the projected image of himself as a child, orphaned and abused like Nastasia [. . .], almost out of his mind, trapped in the incommunicating chaos of a traumatized, autistic face" (876–77). The observation occurs, however, within the context of her argument that the Prince alone, of all the characters in the novel, maintains the ethical practice of regarding and honoring the face of the other in Nastasia Filippovna as "a locus of subjectivity so literally transcendent as to configure the idea of infinity" (870): Leslie Johnson, "The Face of the Other in *The Idiot*," *Slavic Review* 50, no. 4 (Winter 1991): 867–78. Val Vinokurov, who observes Myshkin's tendency to impose an image upon Nastasia Filippovna's face, interprets this practice (mistakenly, in my view) as an aspect of Myshkin's Christian aesthetic vision: "Myshkin is someone who only truly loves persons as manifestations of an iconic meta-face and not as concrete individuated faces" (25); "Myshkin's love of the beautiful pre-

vents him from seeing the face in its vulnerable nakedness" (26). By interpreting Myshkin's attitude to Nastasia Filippovna as doctrinally motivated, Vinokurov misses the pathological implications of the face Myshkin imposes upon the other, and the fact that Nastasia Filippovna, in this sense, is one of the exceptions rather than the rule to Myshkin's behavior. Vinokurov, "The End of Consciousness and the Ends of Consciousness: A Reading of Dostoevsky's *The Idiot* and *Demons* after Levinas," *Russian Review* 59, no. 1 (January 2000): 21–37. Michael C. Finke, by contrast, sees Myshkin's authoring activity as part of his attempt "to shape a Petersburg story on the model of the Switzerland story" (81), that is, to place Nastasia Filippovna in the mold of the redeemed Marie from his Swiss experiences: Finke, *Metapoesis: The Russian Tradition from Pushkin to Chekhov* (Durham, N.C.: Duke University Press, 1995), 77–85. Building on Finke's insight, William Leatherbarrow argues that Myshkin "tends to reduce live models to generic types of his own making, turning them from individuals into mere characters in his own authored 'fiction' and stripping them of their 'otherness' in the process," a tendency most evident," Leatherbarrow observes, "in his dealing with Nastasia Filippovna": Leatherbarrow, *A Devil's Vaudeville: The Demonic in Dostoevsky's Major Fiction* (Evanston, Ill.: Northwestern University Press, 2005), 109. Both Finke and Leatherbarrow see this "authoring" activity in terms of genre confusion on the part of the Prince. For a different view, according to which Myshkin becomes compromised by the coercive, authorial nature of discourse in the novel that stems from "metaphysical anxiety" over the loss of a divine author, see Spektor, "From Violence to Silence," 552–72. See also Caryl Emerson, who argues that Myshkin "monologizes his fellow characters." When Myshkin protests to Nastasia Filippovna that she is not the way she pretends to be, Emerson points out that "he is wrong." Myshkin's interlocutors "*are* that sort of people (along, of course, with much else at the same time), and as such contradictory wholes, they deserve to be taken seriously": Emerson, "Word and Image in Dostoevsky's Worlds: Robert Louis Jackson on Readings That Bakhtin Could Not Do," in *Freedom and Responsibility in Russian Literature: Essays in Honor of Robert Louis Jackson*, ed. Elizabeth Cheresh Allen and Gary Saul Morson (Evanston, Ill.: Northwestern University Press, 1995), 246–306, 256.

10. For the notion of money as an image of the inviolate indwelling soul in Dostoevsky, see chapter 6. For a very different reading of the scene, see Boris Christa, who argues that by placing the money into the fire, Nastasia demonstrates that "her days as a powerless victim of money-based, sexual conquest are behind her" and that "she is now fully in control of her independent status. By burning the money she signals that [Rogozhin] has not bought her, but that she has chosen to enter the relationship on her own terms": Christa, "Dostoevsky and Money," in *The Cambridge Companion to Dostoevsky*, ed. William J. Leatherbarrow (Cambridge: Cambridge University Press, 2002), 93–110, 103.

11. Robin Feuer Miller presents a foundational perspective on this phe-

nomenon in the novel in her analysis of the specific narrative voice that "deliberately keeps [Myshkin] a mystery to the reader" and who enters "the hero's mind merely to report on the confusion reigning there," thus satisfying "the reader's impatience to know what his hero is thinking without really telling him anything." According to Miller, the narrator embraces this technique in order "to limit disclosure to the reader and entice the reader's interest through an air of mystery. [. . .] The reader cannot tell if the narrator is withholding information, if he himself is puzzled, or if he is making his own language match Myshkin's": Miller, *Dostoevsky and "The Idiot": Author, Narrator, and Reader* (Cambridge, Mass.: Harvard University Press, 1981), 103–4.

12. For an opposing view, see Diana Burgin, who argues that Myshkin "falls in love with Nastasia Filippovna" and becomes a passionate lover in the sense of the ardent Platonic lover, "aroused by beauty" and "touched with [the] madness" of "divine possession" that beauty instills in the lover: Burgin, "Prince Myskin, the True Lover and 'Impossible Bridegroom': A Problem in Dostoevskian Narrative," *Slavic and East European Journal* 27, no. 2 (Summer 1983): 158–75, 165.

13. Michael Finke observes that Myshkin's recognition of something "'eternal' in Nastasia Filippovna is but a repetition of the sufferings and desire for redemption of Marie. Myshkin's dim recollections are meant to refer back to the Swiss girl": Finke, *Metapoetics*, 84. I would add that Marie herself is caught within a repetitive compulsive paradigm generated unconsciously by the protagonist.

14. On Nastasia Filippovna's trauma, see Burry, "Execution, Trauma, and Recovery," 263–65. Linda Ivanits notices that the names of the estates in which Myshkin and Nastasia Filippovna were reared by their benefactors are parallel: both Otradnoe (Delight) and Zlatoverkhovo (Golden Summit) evoke "the motif of the Garden of Eden" and its ruination: Ivanits, *Dostoevsky and the Russian People* (Cambridge: Cambridge University Press, 2008), 82–83.

15. Jostein Bortnes points out a connection between Stavrogin and Myshkin, a sense of emptiness that allows others to "project their ideologies onto [Stavrogin], seeing in him, this empty figure, an incarnation of all their dreams": Bortnes, "Dostoevskij's *Idiot* or the Poetics of Emptiness," *Scando-Slavica* 40 (1994): 5–14.

16. For a very different explanation of Myshkin's destructive effect upon Nastasia Filippovna, see Murray Krieger's influential essay in which he argues that Myshkin gives others "a greater moral burden than in their human weakness they can carry. They break under it and become worse than without Myshkin they would be": Krieger, "Dostoevsky's 'Idiot': The Curse of Saintliness," in *Dostoevsky: A Collection of Critical Essays*, ed. Rene Wellek (Englewood Cliffs, N.J.: Prentice-Hall, 1962), 32–52, 48. From among the more negative assessments of Myshkin's activity and personality in the novel that seek to explain his destructive impact, see Elena Mestergazi who emphasizes his ostensible mate-

rialism, his lack of faith, and the "deep defectiveness" of his "spiritual nature": Mestergazi, "Vera i kniaz' Myshkin: Opyt 'naivnogo' chteniia romana 'Idiot,'" in *Roman F. M. Dostoevskogo "Idiot": Sovremennoe sostoianie izucheniia*, ed. T. Kasatkina (Moscow: Nasledie, 2001), 291–318.

17. This projective recognition is similar in some respects to Sarah Young's concept of "scripting" in the novel (and to Michael Finke's concept of "authoring"), though, unlike the literary urge to narrate that Young discovers in many of the novel's characters, Prince Myshkin does not project a chosen narrative onto Nastasia Filippovna; the recognition, I would argue, is much more impulsive, unconscious and non-discursive: Sarah Young, *Dostoevsky's "The Idiot" and the Ethical Foundations of Narrative*, 17; Finke, *Metapoesis*, 82.

18. David K. Danow observes that Nastasia Filippovna "rarely appears—and then more like a phantom or apparition than as flesh and blood; more often, it seems, in Myshkin's dreams than in his reality": Danow, *The Dialogic Sign: Essays on the Major Novels of Dostoevsky* (New York: Peter Lang, 1991), 58.

19. For a reading of the troubled backgrounds of these three characters, see Elizabeth Dalton, who perceives a "cluster of facts and fantasies concerning the fathers and substitute fathers of the Myshkin-Nastasya-Rogozhin triad [. . .] that reflect] the principal elements of the sadomasochistic primal scene and the son's response to it": Dalton, *Unconscious Structure in "The Idiot,"* 117–23.

20. Sarah Young argues that "this lacuna has to be of central importance, as it comprises the most significant period of interaction among the three protagonists [Myshkin, Rogozhin and Nastasia Filippovna]"; the narrator suppresses "any meaningful reference to the traumatic experience in Moscow, which has evidently had a profound effect on all three characters": Sarah Young, "Holbein's *Christ in the Tomb* in the Structure of *The Idiot*," *Russian Studies in Literature* 44, no. 1 (Winter 2007–2008): 90–102, 92, 100.

21. Sarah Young, "Holbein's *Christ in the Tomb* and the Structure of *The Idiot*," 96. Myshkin, Young argues, has fallen "from grace," has lost his "purity of intentions," and "has been compromised by his relations with other people" (98). Elizabeth Dalton interprets Rogozhin as Myshkin's id: "the lust and aggression forced out of Myshkin's character [. . .] erupt in the character of Myshkin's polar opposite, Rogozhin": Dalton, *Unconscious Structure in "The Idiot,"* 83. As has been noted, however, Rogozhin appears after the trip to Moscow not as a raging sexual maniac, but rather as a disembodied set of eyes. Dalton's interpretation of the ubiquity of Rogozhin's eyes is the least satisfactory aspect of her argument: "Rogozhin's eyes represent at once the visual aspect of the child's sexual wishes and the threat of discovery and punishment for those wishes, which is castration": Dalton, *Unconscious Structure in "The Idiot,"* 114.

22. According to Elizabeth Dalton, Rogozhin, unlike the novel's other characters, "seems to stand on another plane of reality" and "is not fully fleshed out with [the . . .] detail that makes for the illusion of reality." She notes that while "in

the first section, his appearance and dress are described, giving him a physical body, and he is treated as a real person [. . .] after the end of the first part, Rogozhin becomes strikingly unreal." She concludes that "one could not subject Rogozhin to the kind of psychological analysis that can be done with Myshkin because he does not have the internal psychological complexity that would make it possible to discuss him almost as if he were a real person": Dalton, *Unconscious Structure in "The Idiot,"* 83–85.

23. As Richard Peace observes, there is something other than romantic passion at play here: "Nor in his dealings with Nastasya Filippovna is Rogozhin motivated by sensual passion; his behavior, however, does reveal fanaticism with strong religious overtones. [. . .] The love of Rogozhin for Nastasya Filippovna is not a sensual love: it is a fanatical love; and like all fanaticism it distorts and kills a great ideal": Peace, *Dostoevsky: An Examination of the Major Novels*, 85–86.

24. For a more positive (and not incompatible) view of intersubjective unity in the novel, see Donna Orwin's description of how the "world soul" is broken up into "a myriad of separate personalities" in *The Idiot*. Orwin observes that Dostoevsky begins to express his belief in the "primary existence of one universal soul, of which we are all part" in the novel: "This unified soul becomes the metaphysical source of the inherent pull we feel toward community and of our compassion for each other. For Dostoevsky it is not only different voices that are important, but the common vision, that comes to different characters and which bears witness to the truth that is common to all." Among the examples of this underlying unity in the novel, Orwin cites the sense of recognition that unites Myshkin and Nastasia as well as the reaction that Myshkin, Nastasia, and Ippolit all share toward the Holbein painting: Orwin, "'Idiot' i problema liubvi k drugim i sebialiubiia v tvorchestve F. M. Dostoevskogo," in *Roman F. M. Dostoevskogo "Idiot": Sovremennoe sostoianie izucheniia*, 405–24, 415.

25. Like Murin's, Rogozhin's eyes watch them, both Myshkin and Nastasia Filippovna, "even when they aren't there" (8:380).

26. For a reading of Nastasia as a "resistant hero," that is, as a character who attempts to withstand or escape the authorial power of others upon her, see Finke, *Metapoesis*, 82. Sarah Young's concept of the "disappearing heroine" also emphasizes Nastasya Filippovna's "struggle against objectification and attempt to assert a different script from the one to which she has been assigned" (41): Sarah Young, *Dostoevsky's "The Idiot" and the Ethical Foundations of Narrative*, 28–74. For a reading of Nastasia Filippovna that sees her by contrast as powerful and self-directing—as the "author" not only of her own life but even of the novel itself, see Diana Lewis Burgin, "The Reprieve of Nastasja: A Reading of a Dreamer's Authored Life," *Slavic and East European Journal* 29, no. 3 (Autumn 1985): 258–68.

27. As an aside, we can observe that the figure of Ippolit emphasizes and

reinforces the conception in the novel of the wounded personality, which constitutes itself outwardly through the projective annexation of others. Much of the notion we have, in fact, of Rogozhin and Myshkin as "great symbols" of flesh and spirit, respectively, or body and soul (see Ivanits, *Dostoevsky and the Russian People*, 103) comes from Ippolit's projective appropriation of these two personalities as aspects of himself. Ippolit continually associates Rogozhin with his own body, with his own sense of mortal entrapment within the phenomenal world, and Myshkin with the higher characteristics of soul as the animating principle of the body. Finding himself drawn mysteriously to visit Rogozhin while contemplating his suicidal revolt against the "implacable and dumb beast" of nature, Ippolit begins to identify this dumb beast, the "strange, offensive forms" of nature, with Rogozhin's ever "silent" and "mocking" presence (8:341). Wasting away from his sickness, he dreams of Rogozhin suffocating him with a wet rag (8:465), an ostensible image of his own illness, or of his body which is gradually destroying him with its disease. (On the problematic connection between Rogozhin and Myshkin in the novel, see Sarah Young, "Holbein's *Christ in the Tomb*," 99.) Ippolit's projection of "soul" onto Prince Myshkin is even more pronounced. He irrationally blames all of his emotional outpourings, his "faintheartedness," on the Prince (8:249), and, before attempting suicide, externalizes his connection to life through his "strange grasping at the Prince's hand, as if frightened of letting it go," "embracing the Prince" as somehow representative of the human form itself: "I want to look into your eyes . . . [. . .] I will say farewell to Man" (8: 348). Ippolit's intense hatred for the Prince ("Long ago I understood you and hated you, when I first heard of you, I hated you with all the hatred of my soul") is unmistakably of course a flimsily disguised projection of disgust for his own "treacly little soul" (8:249). Like with Myshkin and Nastasia, moreover, Ippolit seems to have somehow appropriated Myshkin's memories as his own, as we discover in Myshkin's astonishment at Ippolit's ability to draw a whole section of his manuscript directly from the Prince's own secret thoughts (8:352). Ippolit's compulsive need to scatter the aspects of his personality into others is tied to an unwillingness to encounter the images that dwell within him—the corpse of the frozen infant, for example, that he wants to bury under the earth in his dreams (8:338), or the "endless torments, [. . .] wounds, tortures, and beatings" that he imagines with so much fury in his intensely personal reaction to the "horrible, swollen and bloody bruises" (8:339) of Holbein's *Dead Christ*.

28. The notion of the Prince's sexuality has been the source of some controversy in commentary. Echoing Viacheslav Ivanov, Mochulsky sees the hero's "asexuality" as stemming from "the fact of [Myshkin's] not being fully incarnated": Mochulsky, *Dostoevsky: His Life and Work*, 375–76. Diana Burgin disagrees and argues that "Myshkin is neither a holy fool who shuns the flesh, nor an 'incomplete' man. He is what he says he is: a man who, for good reasons beyond

his control, is a virgin. Therefore he seems and acts sexually young for his age": Burgin, "Prince Myskin, the True Lover and 'Impossible Bridegroom,'" 163.

29. Drawing upon Levinas, Leslie Johnson powerfully expresses the spiritual nature of the face of the other in *The Idiot*. With reference to Myshkin's observations about the infant smiling at its mother as the "essence of religious feeling," she explains that the moment in which the other becomes differentiated from the self is "a protoreligious event": "to smile is to greet the other rather than to grab the object, to make room for the other as a separate being. The face of the other is thus the most irrefutable token we have of the holy—that which transcends us and calls us into account. [. . .] Religious feeling inheres in an experience of transcendence as commonplace—and every bit as challenging—as their present stance, face-to-face, on the landing": Leslie Johnson, "The Face of the Other in *The Idiot*," 873.

30. Aglaya expresses her discomfort at being turned into a disembodied principle of beauty, or into an aperture through which the ideal can be glimpsed. "Why do you look at me like this, Prince?" Aglaya asks him, protesting against his fixed and longing gaze: "I'm afraid of you." (8:287).

31. Here she misinterprets Myshkin's devotion to Nastasia Filippovna, imagining that Nastasia, and not she herself, is the "ideal" to which the Prince is devoted.

32. Ksana Blank points out that the obsessive devotion to the "mystical vision" of pure beauty was presented as a negative form of seduction in Pushkin's original version of "The Poor Knight"; thus a possible negative dimension to the knightly quest figures in Dostoevsky's novel: Blank, *Dostoevsky's Dialectics and the Problem of Sin* (Evanston, Ill.: Northwestern University Press, 2010), 74–75.

33. For a different reading of this scene, see Liza Knapp, who argues that Myshkin encounters Aglaya and Nastasia as potential symbolic embodiments of what their names suggest: "light" on the one hand, and "resurrection" on the other. "With Nastasya's 'resurrection' seeming more and more of an impossible task, Dostoevsky introduces another source of energy and life" and gives Myshkin "a second chance": Knapp, *The Annihilation of Inertia: Dostoevsky and Metaphysics* (Evanston, Ill.: Northwestern University Press, 1996), 83. Tatiana Kasatkina argues that the problem depicted in this scene lies in Myshkin's attempt to love in a perfect and selfless way while still wanting to be part of this world. He loves both women, but the "central law of earthly family love, that is, the law of exclusivity" is alien to his character: Kasatkina, "'I utail ot detei . . .': Prichiny nepronitsatel'nosti kniazia L'va Myshkina," in *Kharakterologiia Dostoevskogo: Tipologiia emotsional'no-tsennostnykh orientatsii* (Moscow: Nasledie, 1996), 202–8, 208. Richard Peace, for his part, reads Myshkin's choice between the two women as an allegorical one between Nastasia Filippovna as "a Russian religious ideal tainted alas by schism and fanaticism" and Aglaya as "a secu-

lar 'ideal of civilized Europe'": Peace, *Dostoevsky: An Examination of the Major Novels*, 94–96.

34. In her analysis of this episode, Robin Feuer Miller illuminates the Gothic genre markers that inform the "deliberately mysterious" language that the narrator uses "to create an overbearing, all-encompassing mystery." The episode, she argues, is in keeping with the Gothic tradition of terror (as opposed to horror) which holds that "fears merely intimated provoke a greater effect than ones that are fully described." I would argue, however, that the reader is shielded from the nature of Myshkin's fear (which would create suspense), but that Myshkin himself is unwilling to consider the nature or provenance of these fears (which generates some suspense but more confusion and frustration for the reader). See Miller, *Dostoevsky and "The Idiot,"* esp. 116–20. Liza Knapp explains the darkness of the scene as signifying Myshkin's sensation of "his own death sentence" under Rogozhin's murderous gaze: Knapp, *The Annihilation of Inertia*, 80–81.

35. For a different reading, see Olga Meerson, who argues that Myshkin is struggling with a "localized narrative taboo" regarding the theme of "death," which Rogozhin embodies: Meerson, *Dostoevsky's Taboos*, 101–8.

36. Robin Feuer Miller connects this element with the "cliché of the Gothic novel [. . .] to link a character's mood to the current state of the natural world." She argues that, in line with this Gothic tradition, "Myshkin's sense of foreboding and his oncoming fit parallel the approach and breaking of a thunderstorm": Miller, *Dostoevsky and "The Idiot,"* 117. I would argue that Dostoevsky pushes farther than the generic in the scene by explicitly depicting Myshkin's active projection of his unwanted "impressions" into the external world.

37. Leatherbarrow describes both scenes as instances of "demonic possession": Leatherbarrow, *A Devil's Vaudeville*, 108.

38. Denys Turner refers to the "common agreement among [the Christian] 'Neoplatonists,' from Augustine to John of the Cross, in the description of that *itinerarium mentis* as [. . .] a journey of 'inwardness'; it was commonly agreed, moreover that the journey of 'inwardness' could also be described as an 'ascent,' whether of a ladder or of a mountain. And it was commonly agreed that as the soul ascended to God it would approach a source of light which, being too bright for its powers of reception, would cause in it profound darkness": Denys Turner, *The Darkness of God: Negativity in Christian Mysticism* (Cambridge: Cambridge University Press, 1995), 3.

39. In Augustine's words addressed to God, "I will pass beyond memory to find you—where? Where my sure and loving stay, shall I find you? If I find you beyond memory, is that not to forget—would I be finding by forgetting you?": Saint Augustine, *Confessions*, trans. Garry Willis (New York: Penguin Books, 2006), 228. For the connections between Saint Augustine and Dostoevsky, par-

ticularly the striking similarities in their notions of theodicy, see V. K. Kantor, "Ispoved' i teoditseia v tvorchestve Dostoevskogo (retseptsiia Avreliia Avgustina)," *Voprosy filosofii* 4 (2011): 96–103. Kantor speculates that "Dostoevsky probably knew Augustine, since St. Augustine recognized Orthodoxy, and was cited by Orthodox writers," adding that "one can speak of a close acquaintance with" Augustine's philosophy through Soloyvov's influence. For a discussion of the problems with drawing "upon the Latin, Western Augustine to illuminate the theological meanings of Dostoevsky when so many theologically minded commentators locate the novelist within his own Russian Orthodox tradition," see Paul Contino, "'Descend That You May Ascend': Augustine, Dostoevsky, and the Confessions of Ivan Karamazov," in *Augustine and Literature*, ed. Robert P. Kennedy, Kim Paffenroth, and John Doody (New York: Lexington Books, 2006), 179–214, 180.

40. Harriet Murav reads Myshkin's doubts as to the divine nature of his experience as a method of forestalling "a possibly monologizing response from a reader, that is, a reader who would categorize Myshkin's experience from a purely medical perspective": Murav, *Holy Foolishness*, 82.

41. For a very different view of this episode, see Linda Ivanits, who emphasizes the inward "direction of Myshkin's vision" as part of what makes it "problematic": "it moves not outward, toward the other, but inward. Myshkin's experience does not transcend his Self." Ivanits juxtaposes this *"inner* light" with his descriptions of the "peasants' experiences" which do "move beyond the Self." Ivanits indicates that this vision is part of a larger characterization of Myshkin as lacking "the enfleshment necessary to truly enter into the suffering and joy of the novel's unhappy people and instill in them something of his elevation": Ivanits, *Dostoevsky and the Russian People*, 98–100. Since the outer world, however, I argue has been compromised by what has been forgotten but which still persists, Dostoevsky, anticipating the central insight of psychoanalysis, depicts the movement inward as the attempt to redeem the compromised world of others and free them from their confinement to one's psyche. For a more positive reading of Myshkin's experience as illustrative of the "momentary experience of unitive consciousness in its fullest presentation" in the context of Platonic and Orthodox Christian mysticism, see Lonny Harrison, "The Numinous Experience of Ego Transcendence in Dostoevsky," *Slavic and East European Journal* 57, no. 3 (2013): 388–402, 397–99.

42. William Comer associates Rogozhin with Dostoevsky's conception of a "real Russian type," as he "exhibits all the turmoil and restlessness of a soul deeply rooted in Russia, and he is equally at risk of committing the extreme actions that mark the 'real Russian types,' Russia's Stenka Razins and Daniil Filippoviches": Comer, "Rogozhin and the 'Castrates': Russian Religious Traditions in Dostoevsky's *The Idiot*," *Slavic and East European Journal* 40, no. 1 (Spring 1996): 85–99, 89.

43. Carol Apollonio points out that "the painting in Rogozhin's house is not an icon; it is a print. [. . .] The real question it poses in Dostoevsky's novel," Apollonio argues, is *"who would allow something so trivial to shake his faith?"*: Apollonio, *Dostoevsky's Secrets: Reading Against the Grain* (Evanston, Ill.: Northwestern University Press, 2009), 95.

44. Comer, "Rogozhin and the 'Castrates,'" 85–99. Tatiana Kasatkina illuminates the deep roots of Rogozhin's house in Russian history when she argues that the description of the house draws upon a fifteenth-century Moscow cathedral of the Dormition of the Virgin Mary, which was used as a burial place for high church officials. Kasatkina, *O tvoriashchei prirode slova*, 383–88.

45. Sarah Young notes the connection between the Holbein painting and the painting of Nastasia Filippovna in "Holbein's *Christ in the Tomb*," 96.

46. In his massively influential "First Philosophical Letter," written in the late 1820s, Pyotr Chaadaev diagnosed the catastrophic rootlessness and unhappiness of the modern educated Russian person as stemming from a profound absence of memory and a disconnection from the life-sustaining sources of universal history. The modern Russian person, Chaadaev argued, possessed no recourse to the "vivid recollections," the "myths," and "all the strongest and most fertile ideas" that lie in the cultural memory of European civilization: "No charming memories and no gracious images live in our memory, no forceful lessons in our national tradition. Glance over all the centuries through which we have lived, all the land which we cover, you will find not one endearing object of remembrance [. . .]. We live only in the most narrow kind of present without a past and without a future in the midst of a shallow calm": Chaadaev, "Philosophical Letters: I," in *Major Works of Peter Chaadaev*, 29, 24, 30.

47. In this context, Tatiana Kasatkina's argument (which goes against the mainstream interpretation of the painting as an expression of spiritual despair) that the painting (when viewed straight on and not from below) depicts the first stirrings of the dead Christ toward resurrection, if correct, would suggest that the fear of the corpse and the refusal to look directly at it are what cause it to remain a terrifying presence in the collective psyche. See Kasatkina, "Posle znakomstva s podlinnikom: Kartina Gansa Gol'beina Mladshego 'Khristos v mogile' v structure romana F. M. Dostoevskogo 'Idiot,'" *Novyi Mir* 2 (2006): 154–68, http://magazines.russ.ru/novyi_mi/2006/2/kasa10.html.

48. For a very different view, see Tatiana Kasatkina, who argues that Nastasia Filippovna has been resurrected in the final scene: Kasatkina, *O tvoriashchei prirode slova*, 387–88, 264–65.

49. Tatiana Kasatkina reads the painting as a "mirror" ("enclosing the world within its own boundaries") as opposed to the "window" or "exit" provided by religious iconography. This distinction is helpful in thinking about the painting as a limit in the self instead of an aperture: Kasatkina, *O tvoriashchei prirode slova*, 250.

50. As Linda Ivanits observes, "there is no mention of the Holbein painting" in the final scene at Rogozhin's, "for the masterful 'picture' of Myshkin and Rogozhin holding vigil over Nastasia Filipovna's mutilated body has usurped its role": Ivanits, *Dostoevsky and the Russian People*, 102.

51. Mochulsky, *Dostoevsky: His Life and Work*, 298. Konstantin Barsht describes Dostoevsky's "unusual 'medieval' anthropology" which posits "polar oppositions between good and evil" in the human being and an "open conflict in his works between the 'corporeal' and the 'spiritual'": Barsht, "Defining the Face: Observations on Dostoevskii's Creative Process," in *Russian Literature, Modernism and the Vistual Arts*, ed. Catriona Kelly and Stephen Lovell (Cambridge: Cambridge University Press, 2000), 23–57, 32. On this topic, see especially Marina Kostalevsky's argument that, unlike Solovyov, who, like Augustine and Schelling, "regards evil as a falling away from the good," Dostoevsky's "correlation of the categories of good and evil have [. . .] an air of Manichaeism; [. . . they] are declared to be two absolutely independent primordial elements": Kostalevsky, *Dostoevsky and Soloviev*, 148.

52. See, for example, R. L. Busch's depiction of Ippolit as a central figure, torn between "holy and satanic forces" (372) represented respectively by Myshkin and Rogozhin: Busch, "The Myshkin-Ippolit-Rogozhin Triad," *Canadian American Slavic Studies* 17, no. 3 (Fall 1983): 372–83. Marina Kostalevsky reads Myshkin and Rogozhin as the respective symbolic embodiments of good and evil in *The Idiot* (with Nastasia Filippovna as the embodiment of "beauty," the third corner of the "tragic triangle"): Kostalevsky, *Dostoevsky and Soloviev*, 155–61.

53. The "contrastive doubling" between Myshkin and Rogozhin has been read in a variety of ways, often or simply enacting a Manichaean dualism of good and evil in the fight for Nastasia Filippovna's soul. A widespread approach has been to interpret the friends as one personality broken into two, with Rogozhin as a "grisly [. . .] id [. . .] that corresponds exactly to the elements denied and repressed in Myshkin": Dalton, *Unconscious Structure in "The Idiot,"* 83. In Ulrich Schmid's words, the "innerly divided character initially intended as the protagonist is now split between two characters: into the light Prince Myshkin and the dark Rogozhin": Schmid, "Split Consciousness and Characterization in *The Brothers Karamazov*," trans. Katherine Bowers and Susan McReynolds, reprinted in *The Brothers Karamazov*, by Fyodor Dostoevsky, 2nd ed. (New York: Norton, 2011), 779. I. R. Akhundova describes them as recalling the Zoroastrian eternal battle between Ormuzd and Ahriman: Akhundova, "Voploshchenie khaosa i nebytiia (Parfen Rogozhin—demon smerti ili personifikatsiia sud'by)," in *Roman F. M. Dostoevskogo "Idiot": Sovremennoe sostoianie izucheniia*, 364–89, 369.

54. Akhundova, "'Voploshchenie khaosa i nebytiia,'" 364–89.

55. See especially Sarah Young, who argues that "the polarity inherent in Nastas'ia Filippovna's character and its reflection in the relationship of Mysh-

Notes to Pages 84–87

kin and Rogozhin to the heroine [. . .] informs the structure of the novel as a whole": *Dostoevsky's "The Idiot" and the Ethical Foundations of Narrative*, 44–46.

56. Linda Ivanits observes that in *The Idiot*, "the use of light imagery does not quite adhere to the precept that light signifies good and darkness evil." She points out that "darkness is the dominant motif in Nastasia Filippovna's depiction: her portrait presents a dark-haired, dark-eyed woman dressed in black," and that Myshkin "treats this portrait with religious awe," while Aglaya, associated with all that is light, meets "one of the worst fates that can befall anyone in Dostoevsky's fiction" in her "marriage and conversion to Catholicism": Ivanits, *Dostoevsky and the Russian People*, 86.

57. For a psychologically acute discussion of evil in Dostoevsky, see Donna Orwin, who argues, among other things, that "intentional and otherwise pointless evil seems to be the consequence of the incompleteness of the self and the neediness that results" (158–59): Orwin, *Consequences of Consciousness* (Stanford, Calif.: Stanford University Press, 2007), 158–79.

58. For a more traditional view of the demonic in *The Idiot*, see Akhundova, "'Voploshchenie khaosa i nebytiia,'" esp. 367–75.

59. Camus, *Myth of Sisyphus*, 111.

CHAPTER FIVE

The chapter epigraphs are from A. I. Herzen, *S togo berega*, in *Sobranie sochinenii v tridtsati tomakh* (Moscow: Akademiia nauk SSSR, 1954–56), 6:44–46; and from Soren Kierkegaard, *The Sickness Unto Death: A Christian Psychological Exposition for Upbuilding and Awakening*, ed. and trans. Howard V. Hong and Edna H. Hong (Princeton, N.J.: Princeton University Press, 1980), 42.

1. W. J. Leatherbarrow, for example, describes how Dostoevsky "sacrifices verisimilitude to mythography" and "transmutes" the events of his contemporary Russia "into mythical landscapes onto which metaphysical [. . .] struggles are projected": Leatherbarrow, "*The Devils* in the Context of Dostoevsky's Life and Works," in *Dostoevsky's "The Devils": A Critical Companion*, ed. Leatherbarrow (Evanston, Ill.: Northwestern University Press, 1999), 3–59, 36.

2. S. N. Bulgakov, "Russkaia tragediia," in *Sochineniia v dvukh tomakh*, vol. 2 (Moscow: Nauka, 1993), 499–526, 501. Stavrogin's personality, it has been argued, encompasses the novel as a whole, with all its "people, [. . .] conspiracies, revolts, fires, murders, and suicides" being but "vibrations" emanating from "the depths of the hero's consciousness": Mochulsky, *Dostoevsky: His Life and Work*, 434–36. For similar views, see Wasiolek, *Dostoevsky: The Major Fiction*, 119; Peace, *Dostoevsky: An Examination of the Major Novels*, 179–217; and Berdiaev, *Mirosozertsanie Dostoevskogo*, 39. For an account of the striking level of agreement among Russian religious philosophers (Berdiaev, Stepun, Ivanov,

Losskii, S. Bulgakov, Gessen) in their "joint effort [to] create a uniform and coherent, though relatively open, religious ontological interpretation of the character of Stavrogin," see Slawomir Mazurek, "The Individual and Nothingness (Stavrogin: A Russian Interpretation)," *Studies in East European Thought* 62 (2010): 41–54, 42.

3. Berdiaev's categorical statement that Dostoevsky "is not a psychologist; he is a pneumatologist and a metaphysician symbolist" is founded to a great extent upon his reading of *Besy*: Berdiaev, Mirosozertsanie Dostoevskogo, 22.

4. The most unequivocal proponent of this reading is Edward Wasiolek: "There is the political pamphlet and the metaphysical drama, and they have only the weakest of structural ties. [. . .] Most of the characters belong to one or the other": Wasiolek, *Dostoevsky: The Major Fiction*, 111. See also Richard Peace's description of the novel's "double warp" which he argues is characteristic of Dostoevsky's writing in general: "on one hand polemics against the nihilists; on the other the exploration of religious and philosophical problems": Peace, *Dostoevsky: An Examination of the Major Novels*, 141. See also R. M. Davison, "*The Devils*: The Role of Stavrogin," in *New Essays on Dostoevsky*, ed. Malcolm V. Jones and Garth M. Terry (Cambridge: Cambridge University Press, 1983), 95–114: 95.

5. Dostoevsky's own expressed intention was to portray the "kindredness and continuity of thought, developing from fathers to children" (29.1:260). Charles A. Moser identifies Stepan as the spokesman for the generation of Westernizing liberalism of the 1840s "which brought the radicals of the 1860s into being": Moser, "Stepan Trofimovic Verkhovenskij and the Esthetics of His Time," *Slavic and East European Journal* 29, no. 2 (1985): 157–63, 157. For an account of the formation of Stepan Trofimovich from such figures as Timofei Granovsky and Alexander Herzen, as well as for an account of Herzen's ostensible culpability for the radical materialism of the new nihilism of the 1860s, see Joseph Frank, *Dostoevsky: The Miraculous Years*, esp. 454–61. Fyodor Stepun describes "the ringleaders of the revolutionary movement" as Stepan's "spiritual children, thrown into the camp of godless-amoral socialism": Stepun, "'Besy' i bol'shevistskaia revoliutsiia," in *Vstrechi*, 40. René Girard describes Stepan as "the father of all the possessed. He is Pyotr Verkhovensky's father; he is the spiritual father of Shatov, of Daria Pavlovna, of Lizaveta Nikolaevna, and especially of Stavrogin, since he taught them all": Girard, *Deceit, Desire, and the Novel*, 254.

6. Joseph Frank, *Dostoevsky: The Miraculous Years*, 467. Marina Kostalevsky reads Stavrogin's "magnetic charm, under which practically all those around him fall," but for which Dostoevsky "never once offers a satisfactory explanation" as an allegorical reversal of the passion narrative, with the man-god rather than the God-man at the center: Kostalevsky, *Dostoevsky and Soloviev*, 93–96.

7. Readers have proposed several ways to see "two novels" as more thor-

oughly integrated, by emphasizing similarities and complementary attributes in Stepan Verkhovensky and Stavrogin. Richard Peace observes that Stepan often appears as a "substitute" for Stavrogin—as Varvara Petrovna's "son," as Dasha's suitor, as carrying "on the search for truth [. . .] after the collapse of Stavrogin" and mirroring Stavrogin's quest in the night with his own quest in the day: Peace, *Dostoevsky: An Examination of the Major Novels*, 155, 201. Gordon Livermore describes the movement of characters between "the political pamphlet" and the "metaphysical drama" as reflective of a more pervasive dialectic between the material world, which Pyotr represents, and the ideal world in which Stepan dwells: Livermore, "Stepan Verkhovensky and the Shaping Dialectic of Dostoevsky's *Devils*," in *Dostoevsky: New Perspectives*, ed. R. L. Jackson (Englewood Cliffs, N.J.: Prentice-Hall, 1984), 176–92. Robin Feuer Miller explores the connection that both tutor and student are, in different ways, drawn from the figure of Jean-Jacques Rousseau, a connection which shows the structure of the novel to be "finer and more subtle": Miller, *Dostoevsky's Unfinished Journey* (New Haven, Conn.: Yale University Press, 2007), esp. 92–104, 103. R. M. Davison argues that Verkhovensky serves as the "moral ballast for goodness" in the novel. Stavrogin, Davison argues, is a "nebulous central character who is represented on the good side by Stepan Trofimovich and on the bad side by Peter Stepanovich" (124): Davison, "Dostoevsky's *The Devils*: The Role of Stepan Trofimovich Verkhovensky," in *Dostoevsky's "The Devils": A Critical Companion*, ed. W. J. Leatherbarrow (Evanston, Ill.: Northwestern University Press, 1999), 119–34, 132. Craig Cravens points out that, as opposed to all the characters who hover around Stavrogin and live in the "atemporal void" of "eternity," Stepan Trofimovich lives in "the mutable, terrestrial world" and in this sense is "the only biographically developed *and* developing character": Cravens, "The Strange Relationship of Stavrogin and Stepan Trofimovich as Told by Anton Lavrent'evich G-v," *Slavic Review* 59, no. 4 (Winter 2000): 782–801, 798.

8. As scholars have pointed out, Stepan's status as the "breeding ground" for "all these fruits" (10:345) is highly problematic on a practical level. In Carol Apollonio's words, "if what he taught his pupils was the beauty of art (Pushkin), the classic values of idealism and honor, poetry and platonic love, then of what is he truly guilty? Yet the root of the evil—or at least the guilt—in the novel rests on Stepan Trofimovich." She argues that "Stepan Trofimovich's guilt is not simply a matter of choosing the wrong theory; it stems from a more profound inadequacy," one that yields such symptoms as "impotence" and "irresponsible fatherhood": Apollonio, *Dostoevsky's Secrets*, 113, 104–5. Charles Moser points out that though Stepan "shares with [the radicals] a devotion to ideas, [. . .] he believes strongly in the importance of the idea of the infinite and the eternal for human life, and he has an inborn sense of the beautiful which the younger generation no longer possesses. [. . .] If intellectually Stepan belongs with Granovskij and the great generation of the 1840s, as a poet he fits in with Russian Roman-

ticism of the 1830s": Moser, "Stepan Trofimovic Verkhovenskij and the Esthetics of His Time," 158, 162–63. Steven Cassedy argues that it is Stepan's atheism that is passed to the younger generation: Cassedy, *Dostoevsky's Religion*, 30, 44.

9. Deborah A. Martinsen portrays the friends as engaged in "collusion" in order to "sustain [Stepan's] self-deception": Martinsen, *Surprised by Shame*, 105. Mochulsky describes the connection as a "twenty-year-long platonic feeling for Varvara Petrovna, composed of habit, vanity, egoism, and the most lofty sincere attachment": Mochulsky, *Dostoevsky: His Life and Works*, 441. Connor Doak describes Stepan as a "textbook case" of Max Nordau's "portrait of the degenerate" man and examines the relationship between Stepan and Varvara "as representing anxieties that are specific to the *fin-de-siècle* moment with its overturning of" gender norms: Doak, "Masculine Degeneration in Dostoevskii's *Demons*," in *Russian Writers at the Fin de Siècle: The Twilight of Realism*, ed. Katherine Bowers and Ani Kokobobo (Cambridge: Cambridge University Press, 2015), 105–25, 110–11. In her reading of the relationship, Carol Apollonio calls attention to Stepan Trofimovich's doubtful "ontological grounding," pointing to evidence that he does not exist in the full sense. She refers to those passages which describe Varvara Petrovna as "alone," although Stepan Trofimovich was there: "Varvara Petrovna is alone, but Stepan Trofimovich is with her nevertheless." For Apollonio, this "reinforces the literariness and artificiality—the created nature—of his identity." He "fades in and out of life in a way impossible for a man of flesh and blood": Apollonio, *Dostoevsky's Secrets*, 105–6.

10. Richard Pope and Judy Turner describe Varvara Petrovna as a "narcissistic mother, for whom her children are not independent entities but primarily figures in her dream—projected aspects of herself": Pope and Turner, "Toward Understanding Stavrogin," *Slavic Review* 49, no. 4 (Winter 1990): 543–53, 548.

11. Deborah Martinsen diagnoses Stepan's central flaw as weakness of will, and she notes that "his nocturnal crying sessions with the young Stavrogin, his hysterical one-sided correspondence with Varvara Stavrogina, his constant demands on his confidant, and his drinking all demonstrate this weakness": Martinsen, *Surprised by Shame*, 106.

12. A fragment of a person herself, Varvara Petrovna's motherhood consists of little more than a disembodied gaze: "She spoke with [her son] little, rarely hindered him very much in anything, but he always morbidly felt her fixed gaze upon him, following him everywhere" (10:35). For a psychoanalytic study of Stavrogin's development in light of "inadequate parenting—particularly by his mother," see Pope and Turner, "Toward Understanding Stavrogin," esp. 546–49, 547.

13. As Robin Feuer Miller observes, "the overtones or undertones of these passages seem particularly dark in today's cultural milieu where it is not masturbation that is feared but child abuse. The ramifications for Stavrogin of Stepan's middle-of-the-night encounters and tearful embraces of the child are dreadful to

contemplate": Miller, *Dostoevsky's Unfinished Journey*, 211 n15. Susanne Fusso suggests that Stepan is initiating Stavrogin into the practice of masturbation during these nocturnal encounters: Fusso, *Discovering Sexuality in Dostoevsky*, 172–73 n30. For a reading of these sessions as "homosexual seduction" on the part of Stepan, see John S. Williams, "Stavrogin's Motivation: Love and Suicide," *Psychoanalytic Review* 69, no. 2 (1982): 249–65, 259.

14. Connor Doak offers a balanced discussion of the "harmful effects" of Stepan's relationship with Stavrogin upon the formation of his character, and of Stepan's possible "homosexual paedophilia." Doak observes that "unlike the early chapters that treat Stepan Trofimovich's performances of his own effeminacy and masochism rather comically, Stavrogin describes his own sexuality in much darker, more violent terms": Doak, "Masculine Degeneration in Dostoevskii's *Demons*," 111–13.

15. And, by extension, of Hoffmann's "Der Magnetiseur." On Hoffmann's influence, see Passage, *Dostoevski the Adapter*, 46–54.

16. Leatherbarrow notes the "strange and general irritability distributed among many of the characters" as "suggestive of possession of some kind": Leatherbarrow, *A Devil's Vaudeville*, 121.

17. Marina Kostalevsky argues that Stepan's "influence on his son [is] not formative" (due to the short period of their acquaintance) but rather "genetic;" the connection between father and son emphasizes "nihilism's hidden, 'genetic' link to liberalism and rationalistic humanism": Kostalevsky, *Dostoevsky and Soloviev*, 162.

18. Sergei Bulgakov describes him as "absent, terribly, ominously, hellishly absent [. . .] for the spirit of nonbeing holds sway over him [. . .] In him only a psychological skeleton remains [. . .] and in him lives 'legion'": Bulgakov, "Russkaia tragediia," 503–4. René Girard describes him as "the incarnation of that zero point, the pure nothingness of absolute pride": Girard, *Deceit, Desire and the Novel*, 255. In Jostein Bortnes's words, "Stavrogin's figure is a symbol of emptiness": "the final manifestation [. . .] the dead body of the citizen of Uri, hanging from the rope in the ceiling, represents nothing but nothingness": Bortnes, "The Last Delusion in an Infinite Series of Delusions: Stavrogin and the Symbolic Structure of *The Devils*," *Dostoevsky Studies* 4 (1983): 53–67, 67. In Carol Apollonio's words, "the creature who emerges at the end of this exhaustive process [of trying to determine Stavrogin's character in the notebooks] is drained of human content. He is not to be read indicatively": Apollonio, *Dostoevsky's Secrets*, 125.

19. That is, if we accept the visit to Tikhon as part of the novel. See Malcolm Jones, for example, who accepts the confession as "an integral part of Stavrogin's characterization": Jones, *Dostoyevsky after Bakhtin*, 157. For an opposing view, see A. L. Bem's argument that Stavrogin's confession plays "only a subsidiary role, as a footprint in the development of [Stavrogin's] image" (157). Bem argues that, after the forced exclusion of the chapter, Dostoevsky's view

of Stavrogin evolved, became darker, no longer admitting of redemption: Bem, "Evoliutsiia obraza Stavrogina," in *Issledovaniia: Pis'ma o literature*, ed. S. G. Bocharov (Moscow: Iazyki slavianskoi kul'tury, 2001), 111–57.

20. As Carol Apollonio points out, "this language simply doesn't make sense. Was it a dream or not? What is a 'real vision' if not a 'vision'? If something is a hallucination, then by definition it is not a reality": Apollonio, *Dostoevsky's Secrets*, 141.

21. The pattern intriguingly suggests a depiction of post-traumatic behavior: the repeated (willing or unwilling) rehashing of the same wound in the attempt to process some suppressed painful experience. For the compulsion to repeat abuse in the novel, see Williams, "Stavrogin's Motivation: Love and Suicide," 249–65.

22. Susanne Fusso reads the encounter between Stavrogin and Matryosha as a recasting of the relationship between Vanya and Nellie in *The Insulted and Injured*. Her argument sees the parallel not in terms of the extension of the self into the other, but as a concentration of the "quasi-erotic gestures [. . .] scattered innocuously throughout" the earlier novel into "a powerfully distilled narrative of sexual abuse" in *Demons*: Fusso, *Discovering Sexuality in Dostoevsky*, 36.

23. Leatherbarrow's analysis of these events as demonic emphasizes the notion that "in Russian folklore the devil traditionally plays the role of prankster": Leatherbarrow, *A Devil's Vaudeville*, 125. Indeed, the inability to keep the private secret could be read as a generic element of the carnival. See, for example, Harriet Murav's discussion of the Bakhtinian notion of the clown and the fool as "making public and externalizing what is hidden and private": Murav, *Holy Foolishness*, 9.

24. Rima Iakubova explains this puppetlike quality with reference to the Russian *balagan* tradition in "Roman Dostoevskogo *Besy* i russkii balagan," in *Tvorchestvo F. M. Dostoevskogo i khudozhestvenaya kul'tura* (Ufa: "Gilem," 2003), 151–64; initially accessed through Carol Apollonio, *The New Russian Dostoevsky: Readings for the Twenty-First Century* (Columbus, Ohio: Slavica, 2010). For the importance of the Russian puppet theater tradition for the notion of the demonic in the novel, see also Leatherbarrow, *A Devil's Vaudeville*, esp. 126–28.

25. Thus, Stepan's "pilgrimage to find the real Russia" is undergirded by a more immediate quest to discover independent sources in the self. For the journey as national pilgrimage, see Leatherbarrow, "*The Devils* in the Context of Dostoevsky's Life and Works," 34–35.

26. Numerous textual echoes can be found in these depictions. For example, "tears pour" (*slyozy tak i khlynuli* [10:331]) from Stepan as they did from Vasia (*Slyozy gradom khlynuli iz glaz Vasi* [2:37]).

27. As Craig Cravens points out, Stepan Trofimovich is the only character

capable of development in the novel, "the one truly biographically motivated character who evolves throughout the novel": Cravens, "The Strange Relationship," 797. Deborah Martinsen examines how on his deathbed, Stepan Trofimovich is able to "renounce his self-defining roles": Martinsen, *Surpised by Shame*, 107.

28. Robin Feuer Miller presents Rousseau's flight from Mme d'Epinay as a potential source for Stepan's escape from Varvara Petrovna. See Miller, *Dostoevsky's Unfinished Journey*, 97–98.

29. See Charles Taylor's description of interiority in Augustine: "God is behind the eye, as well as the One whose Ideas the eye strives to discern clearly before it. He is found in the intimacy of my self-presence. Indeed he is closer to me than I am myself, while being infinitely above me": Taylor, *Sources of the Self*, 135–36. For Stepan's "chivalrous loyalty to the idea of eternal beauty," see Mochulsky, *Dostoevsky: His Life and Work*, 442.

30. The notion that the "great Eternal thought" is separate from the "I" is important as a refutation of Feuerbach's rejection "of the belief in God as a being with an objective essence outside human consciousness," an idea that was so influential to the Westernizers of Granovsky's and Herzen's generation. See Derek Offord, "Alexander Herzen," in *A History of Russian Philosophy 1830–1930: Faith, Reason, and the Defense of Human Dignity*, ed. G. M. Hamburg and Randall A. Poole (Cambridge: Cambridge University Press, 2010), 52–68, 53. According to Joseph Frank, it was Granovsky's refusal to accept the Feuerbachian rejection of personal immorality that drew Dostoevsky to this figure as a prototype for Stepan. See Joseph Frank, *Dostoevsky: The Miraculous Years*, 454. For a dissenting view on Stepan's "transformation," see Steven Cassedy, who argues that Stepan's beliefs do not in fact change and that the "profession of faith" at the end of the novel is simply the expression of someone "who has taken Feuerbach and a philosophy of egoism, put them into a tall glass, stirred them, and drunk them down in one draught": Cassedy, *Dostoevsky and Religion*, 43.

31. Ludmilla Saraskina offers a very different explanation for Lebiadkina's rejection of Stavrogin. She argues that Lebiadkina worships Stavrogin as "prince-Lucifer" and that she anathematizes him for his weakness, "because he wanted to subdue his pride, wanted to take people into consideration, bore the slap in the face and did not kill his offender." See Saraskina's "Iskazhenie ideala (Khromonozhka v 'Besakh')" in *"Besy": Roman preduprezheniia* (Moscow: Sovetskii pisatel', 1990), 130–58, 152.

32. Nancy Anderson emphasizes this idea—the replacement of a transcendent ideal with a counterfeit one, "when a genuine ideal is stripped of its transcendent nature and reduced to the purely earthly"–as the main theme of the novel: Anderson, *The Perverted Ideal in Dostoevsky's "The Devils"* (New York: Peter Lang, 1997). We could rephrase this conclusion slightly as the inner con-

nection to the divine which is replaced by an external relationship. Or, in a different formulation, offered by René Girard with regard to *Demons*, "Dostoevsky's consciousness [. . .] renounces the divine mediator only to fall back on the human mediator": Girard, *Deceit, Desire and the Novel*, 58.

33. As Leatherbarrow puts it, "the range of titles [*The Possessed, The Devils, Demons*] is suggestive of conceptual uncertainty on the part of Dostoevsky's translators"; he adds that "Dostoevsky's Russian title—*Besy*—is neutral to the degree that it creates uncertainty even among interpreters drawing on the same cultural tradition and discourse": Leatherbarrow, *A Devil's Vaudeville*, 117.

34. Richard Pevear, "Foreword," in Fyodor Dostoevsky, *Demons*, trans. Richard Pevear and Larissa Volokhonsky (New York: Vintage, 1994), xvii. In Pevear's view (one very much in keeping traditional Orthodox spirituality), while the title *The Possessed* "made it possible to speak of Dostoevsky's characters as demoniacs in some unexamined sense, which lend them a certain glamour and even exonerates them to a certain extent," the reversal of the title as *Demons* risks our applying the term "'demons' to the same set of characters in the same unexamined way." Pevear reasons that Stepan and Varvara could "hardly" be the titular demons, that neither can Stavrogin who has "no odor of brimstone about" him, and that the ranks of Stavrogin's "disciples" could not be understood as demons either since "the contagion of evil does not originate with any of them." Pevear concludes that Dostoevsky chose the title *Demons* "precisely because the demons in it *do not appear*, and the reader might otherwise overlook them. [. . .] The demons, then, are ideas, that legion of isms that came to Russia from the West": Pevear, "Foreword," xiii–xviii. For the notion of demons as *logismoi* or "thoughts" in the patristic theology that informs the Russian Orthodox view, see David Brakke's discussion of Evagrius's demonology in *Demons and the Making of the Monk: Spiritual Combat in Early Christianity* (Cambridge, Mass.: Harvard University Press, 2006), 48–77.

35. Herzen, *Sobranie sochinenii*, 6:45

CHAPTER SIX

The chapter epigraphs are from "Tsarevna-lyagushka," in *Narodnye russkie skazki A. N. Afanas'eva*, 3 vols. (Moscow: Nauka, 1985), 2:267; and from Dostoevsky's *The Idiot*, (8:168).

1. C. G. Jung, *Memories, Dreams, Reflections*, recorded and edited by Aniela Jaffé, trans. Richard Winston and Clara Winston (New York: Vintage Books, 1989), 21–22.

2. James George Frazer, *The Golden Bough: A Study in Magic and Religion*, ed. Robert Fraser (Oxford: Oxford University Press, 2009), 153, 756–57. See Frazer also for a discussion of the ubiquity of the theme in ancient folkloric traditions (757–84). For a popular illustration of this motif in contemporary fiction,

see J. K. Rowling, *Harry Potter and the Half-Blood Prince* (New York: Scholastic, 2005), 492–512.

3. Jung, *Memories, Dreams, Reflections*, 21–22.

4. *The Adolescent* both entices and frustrates an inclination among scholars to read it as a bildungsroman. In her examination of the bildungsroman, Elena Krasnoshchekova perceives the transition in Arkady from "early adolescence into young adulthood" ("*iz rannei iunosti—v molodost'*") (440), emphasizing the harmony he achieves with his family as a "reward for the difficulties of the 'school of life" (461): Krasnoshchekova, *Roman vospitaniia—Bildungsroman—na russkoi pochve: Karamzin, Pushkin, Goncharov, Tolstoi* (St. Petersburg: Pushkinskii fond, 2008), esp. 435–67. See also E. I. Semenov, who sees Arkady's *Bildung* as the discovery of the "path of the return of the personality to society": Semenov, *Roman Dostoevskogo "Podrostok" (Problematika i zhanr)* (Leningrad: Nauka, 1979), 70. The timeline, however, of Arkady's *Bildung*, as Krasnoshchekova points out, is highly accelerated; the whole novel takes place over the space of several months, and is narrated less than a year afterward by a slightly older Arkady whose *Bildung* appears to be still very much in progress. If we submit its protagonist to the three-part "list of initiatory tests that every inwardly developing *Bildungsheld* must at least try to pass," offered by Thomas L. Jeffers (namely, 1. "the sexual test [. . .] in which [the hero finds . . .] an appropriate partner outside the family to love"; 2. "the vocational test, in which" the hero finds a way to "do work that will contribute to the commonwealth"; and 3. the test of specific rumination "about the *connections* between art, ethics, and metaphysics"), the novel fails on the grounds of its inattention to the first two points: Thomas L. Jeffers, *Apprenticeships: The Bildungsroman from Goethe to Santayana* (New York: Palgrave Macmillan, 2005), 52–53. Arkady does not come close to forming a reciprocal romantic love attachment; nor is it at all clear that he has become a stable adult by the end of the novel. He has not "attained certainty of his purpose in the world," as Wilhelm Dilthey required of the *Bildungsheld* (*Poetry and Experience*, ed. Rudolf A. Makkreel and Firthjof Rodi [Princeton, N.J.: Princeton University Press, 1985], 335). Arkady's coming to terms with his family and his newfound willingness to study at the university suggest a newfound maturity, but do not, in themselves, substantiate Lina Steiner's conclusion (in her otherwise illuminating study of the bildungsroman in Russian culture) that Arkady "has completely abandoned his 'underground' self-hatred as well as hatred of others and has emerged as a person with his own identity [. . . who] can now become a true man of action": Steiner, *For Humanity's Sake: The Bildungsroman in Russian Culture* (Toronto: University of Toronto Press, 2011), 172. Critics have dealt with the absence of a clear personal denouement for Arkady—a satisfying synthesis between self and world—by examining Arkady's growth along allegorical or figurative paths. Kate Holland argues that the novel "is a particular kind of bildungsroman, one that focuses on the hero's, author's, and reader's narrato-

logical educations": Holland, *The Novel in the Age of Disintegration: Dostoevsky and the Problem of Genre in the 1870s* (Evanston, Ill.: Northwestern University Press, 2013), 106. Lina Steiner sees Arkady's journey as an allegorical depiction of national identity formation: Steiner, *For Humanity's Sake*, 135–73. Perhaps the novel corresponds more closely to the form of an *Entwicklungsroman* (novel of development), which is sometimes described as a subgenre of the bildungsroman, sometimes as its distinct "near relation." See Martin Swales, *The German Bildungsroman from Wieland to Hesse* (Princeton, N.J.: Princeton University Press, 1978), 14.

5. On the bildungsroman as staging the encounter between, and potential synthesis of, self and society, see Franco Moretti, who influentially envisions the genre as a response to Europe's sudden "plunge into modernity, but without [yet] possessing a culture of modernity," without, that is, knowing in practical terms how to contain the energies of its youthful dynamism within a stable social structure. Thus the bildungsroman addresses the "dilemma conterminous with modern bourgeois civilization: the conflict between the ideal of *self-determination* and the equally imperious demands of *socialization*. [. . .] How can the tendency toward *individuality*, which is the necessary fruit of a culture of self-determination, be made to coexist with the opposing tendency to *normality*, the offspring, equally inevitable, of the mechanism of socialization?": Moretti, *The Way of the World: The Bildungsroman in European Culture*, trans. Albert Sbragia (London: Verso, 2000), 15–16.

6. Susanne Fusso summarizes the "many plots" of what she sees as a "maddeningly chaotic and unreadable novel" in the following manner: (1) the "psychological mystery novel, in which Arkadii seeks to solve the riddle of [Versilov,] his complex and enigmatic biological father"; (2) the "bildungsroman, in which the young man tries out several designs for living, including miserly accumulation of capital, the dissipated gambling life of a young aristocrat, and the holy quest for 'blagoobrazie' ('blessed form')"; and (3) the "penny-dreadful tale of intrigue" involving the concealed "document" that Arkady wields, with the blackmail plot that it entails: Fusso, *Discovering Sexuality in Dostoevsky*, 42–68, 44, 231.

7. As Nicholas Rzhevsky points out, "a major part of the critics' case for the novel's compositional weakness has been the lack of connection between Rothschild and Versilov and the apparent disposition of the book into split thematic lines": Rzhevsky, "*The Adolescent*: Structure and Ideology," *Slavic and East European Journal* 26, no. 1 (Spring 1982): 27–42, 33. Konstantin Mochulsky accounts for the novel's deficiencies by arguing that Dostoevsky tried "to consign [Versilov] to a second plane" but failed as Versilov grew in stature, thus pushing the protagonist, Arkady, into the more "modest role" of "timid disciple" and "witness": Mochulsky, *Dostoevsky: His Life and Work*, 491. By contrast, Tatiana Kasatkina emphasizes that Arkady's personality, rather than Versilov's, is

the focal point of the novel: "against the background of the *external story* which moves the plot, the inner life of the protagonist, *the story of his personality* is what develops and truly organizes the novel and its composition": Kasatkina, *O tvoriashchei prirode slova*, 415.

8. Joseph Frank, *Dostoevsky: The Mantle of the Prophet, 1871–1881* (Princeton, N.J.: Princeton University Press, 2002), 171. Apart from a reading by Tatiana Kasatkina (see note 17 below) and a brief discussion by E. I. Semenov (*Roman Dostoevskogo "Podrostok,"* 80–81), interpretations of the novel tend to dismiss the "document" as a mere plot device. According to Mochulsky, in resorting to "a commonplace device of the crime novel [. . .] Dostoevsky [shows that] he is not afraid sometimes to sacrifice artistry for the sake of sustaining 'interest'": Mochulsky, *Dostoevsky: His Life and Work*, 509. Nathan Rosen comments that "neither the letter nor the crude melodrama is believable, but Dostoevsky had to resort to them in order to overcome Dolgoruky's powerlessness as a hero": Rosen, "Breaking Out of the Underground: The 'Failure' of 'A Raw Youth,'" *Modern Fiction Studies* 4, no. 3 (Fall 1958): 225–39, 234. See also Cox, *Tyrant and Victim in Dostoevsky*, 19.

9. Dostoevsky's initial impetus in writing *The Adolescent*, as indicated in his notebooks, was to explore the overwhelming sense of "disintegration" and "disorder" that he perceived in contemporary Russian society (16:16–17). In arguing for the coherence of the general unifying theme of the search for the self in the novel, I do not mean to argue that *The Adolescent* is aesthetically harmonious. As Kate Holland has argued, this novel "constitutes Dostoevsky's most significant attempt to represent in novelistic form the embryonic, transitional forms of the postreform period [. . .], the uncertainties and tensions of Russia's transition to modernity" (129): Holland, *The Novel in the Age of Disintegration*, 101–30. On the connection between the aesthetic form of the novel and the "moral" reality of the "current disorder" that is Dostoevsky's theme, see also Jackson, *Dostoevsky's Quest for Form*, 112–18; and Nathan Rosen, who argues that "Dostoevsky's decision to write a poem about youth inevitably made for a chaotic structure": Rosen, "Breaking Out of the Underground," 234.

10. See, for example, Nicholas Rzhevsky's representative reading in which he emphasizes the materialism of Arkady's idea: Rzhevsky, "*The Adolescent*: Structure and Ideology," 27–42, 33. Susanne Fusso describes Dostoevsky's intention as the depiction of "a world in which the disintegrative force of capitalism has shaken all firm foundations and disrupted all traditional relationships" (230). Arkady, she argues, has taken on the capitalist idea without having understood the "cost in human suffering" associated with material acquisition (234): Fusso, "The Weight of Human Tears: *The Covetous Knight* and *A Raw Youth*," in *Alexander Pushkin's Little Tragedies: The Poetics of Brevity*, ed. Svetlana Evdokimova (Madison: University of Wisconsin Press, 2003), 229–42.

11. Konstantin Mochulsky argues that Dostoevsky fails in his plan to make

the "idea" central to the novel: "the novel's significance does not lie in [the hero's 'idea'], and the raw youth with his idea of Rothschild does not determine it": Mochulsky, *Dostoevsky: His Life and Work*, 491. Tatiana Kasatkina emphasizes "the lack of clarity in the hero's 'idea' and [. . .] the enigmatic nature of [its] evolution." She interprets the hero's idea as the desire to place himself at the center of the web of relations, as a substitute for Christ and as the wellspring of life: Kasatkina, *O tvoriashchei prirode slova*, 419. For a similar view, see Ingunn Lunde, "'Ia gorazdo umnee napisannogo': On Apophatic Strategies and Verbal Experiments in Dostoevskii's 'A Raw Youth,'" *Slavonic and East European Review* 79, no. 2 (April 2001): 264–89, 288.

12. Karl Marx, "Economic and Philosophic Manuscripts of 1844," in *Collected Works*, vol. 3 (New York: International Publishers, 1975), 228–346, 324. E. I. Semenov comments on this aspect of Arkady's idea and connects it to Marx's notion of deferred "essence": Semenov, *Roman Dostoevskogo "Podrostok,"* 63–64. An argument similar to Marx's also surfaced in the Slavophile rhetoric of the 1850s. In his critique of Western individualism, Ivan Kireevsky pointed out that, in contrast to the West where "a person was defined in terms of landed property [. . .], [traditional] society [in Russia] was made up not of private property to which persons were attached, but of individuals to whom property was attached": Kireevsky, "On the Nature of European Culture and on Its Relation to Russian Culture," in *A Slavophile Reader*, ed. and trans. Robert Bird and Boris Jakim (Hudson, N.Y.: Lindisfarne Books, 1998), 187–232, 221. A recent study places the development of the self from the mid-eighteenth century onward with the rise of the concept of money, money and selfhood mutually reinforcing each other's apparent validity and overcoming each other's limitations. See Fritz Breithaupt, *Der Ich-Effekt des Geldes: Zur Geschichte einer Legitimationsfigur* (Frankfurt am Main: Fischer Taschenbuch Verlag, 2008). For a general discussion of the importance of the theme of money in Dostoevsky's life and work, see Boris Christa, "Dostoevsky and Money," 93–110.

13. Horst-Jürgen Gerigk touches on this aspect of Arkady's "idea," describing it as a "stratagem of the soul," a "back door" that offers escape from any potentially humiliating situation: Gerigk, *Versuch über Dostojewski's "Jüngling," ein Beitrag zur Theorie des Romans* (Munich: Wilhelm Fink, 1965), 140.

14. Svetlana Evdokimova draws on Percy Shelley's observation that "money is the visible incarnation" of "the principle of Self" (114) to read the Baron's hoarding of money as a twisted spiritual or religious quest. See Evdokimova, "The Anatomy of the Modern Self in *The Little Tragedies*," in *Alexander Pushkin's Little Tragedies*, 106–43. For more on Arkady's engagement with Pushkin, see Semenov, *Roman Dostoevskogo "Podrostok,"* 65–66.

15. For a reading of Poprishchin's "displacement" of self as a strategy of contending with his outward insignificance, see Robert Maguire, *Exploring Gogol* (Stanford, Calif.: Stanford University Press, 1994), 49–66.

16. Rothschild, in Dostoevsky's time, was arguably more powerful than most kings, whether Spanish or African, not to mention also the proprietor of just such an island in the Antarctic. See Niall Ferguson, *The House of Rothschild: Money's Prophets (1748–1848)* (New York: Viking, 1998), 2.

17. Tatiana Kasatkina observes the parallel between the "idea" and the "document," though for somewhat different reasons. "The 'document' is the absolute equivalent of the 'Rothschild idea,'" she argues, in that "the freedom of the human being, achieved through money [as through the power afforded by the document], is realized negatively—as the inevitable, almost automatic enslavement of others": Kasatkina, *O tvoriashchei prirode slova*, 418.

18. On Arkady's insistence on his "unfinalizability," see Brian Egdorf, "Fyodor Dostoevsky's *The Adolescent* and the Architectonics of Author and Hero," in *The Dostoevsky Journal: An Independent Review* 12–13 (2011–12): 15–36, esp. 23–25.

19. Caryl Emerson's description of *sobornost'* in Russian Orthodox spirituality is useful in this context: "Every face is different, every personality is distinct, but each needs the other (or many others) in order to realize the contours of its own self. It is significant that the Russian language has no native word for privacy, and also that Russian culture did not develop the metaphysical image so productive in Western Christendom, that of the soul imprisoned in the body. The body (and especially the face) was not a prison but a vehicle, a responsive mirror, the 'soul made flesh.' Light moved through the body and sanctified it": Emerson, *The Cambridge Introduction to Russian Literature* (Cambridge: Cambridge University Press, 2008), 31.

20. Nikolai Berdiaev, for example, describes Dostoevsky's use of a "Dionysian whirlwind" as an experimental device that pulls characters into philosophically meaningful patterns of intersection. Dostoevsky's "whirlwind anthropology," Berdiaev argues, allows us to observe in Dostoevsky's novels a universal human consciousness contending with all the scattered fragments of its expansive being (e.g., Stavrogin and all the characters who cling to him in *The Devils*; Versilov and his extended family in *The Adolescent*). Mochulsky presents a similar argument: "At the center of all Dostoevsky's novels there stands a person who is striving to resolve the enigma of his personality. [. . .] On the surface this process is psychological, but beneath this exterior plan the questions disclose themselves as having fundamental ontological import. [. . .] Dostoevsky's heroes are spiritual, are pure consciousness [. . .] They struggle and contend against one another while at the same time remain open to a communal synthesis": Mochulsky, *Dostoevsky: His Life and Work*, 299–300.

21. Ibid., 506, 514.

22. Ibid., 511.

23. On the loss of humanity in *The Gambler* and the imprisonment of the hero within an eternal present, see Morson, *Narrative and Freedom*, 203. In his

discussion of the evil of gambling for Dostoevsky, R. L. Jackson observes that "the very act of gambling becomes a conscious or unconscious affirmation of the meaninglessness of the universe, the emptiness of all human choice. [. . .] The risk itself is by its very nature a dangerous inquiry into the sources of power and an arrogant form of self-assertion": Jackson, *The Art of Dostoevsky: Deliriums and Nocturnes* (Princeton, N.J.: Princeton University Press, 1981), 210.

24. On gambling and demonic possession in *The Gambler*, see Leatherbarrow, "*The Devils* in the Context of Dostoevsky's Life and Works," 29–30.

25. Bakhtin, *Problems of Dostoevsky's Poetics*, 252.

26. Aleksei Khomiakov, "Letter to the Editor of *L'Union Chretienne*, on the Occasions of a Discourse by Father Gagarin, a Jesuit," in *On Spiritual Unity: A Slavophile Reader*, ed. and trans. Robert Bird and Boris Jakim, (Hudson, N.Y.: Lindisfarne Books, 1998), 139.

27. My account of Arkady's encounter with others ignores the sexual aspect of his journey as that of a virgin among potential "sexual predators." For an account of this dimension, see Susanne Fusso, *Discovering Sexuality in Dostoevsky*, 69–72.

28. For a reading of Makar's teachings as a refutation of Arkady's "idea" in an even more direct sense, see Liza Knapp, *The Annihilation of Inertia*, 159–60.

29. For an in-depth examination of Dostoevsky's "quest to uncover the meaning and the moral profile of a specific *human face*," see Barsht, "Defining the Face: Observations on Dostoevskii's Creative Process," esp. 23–37.

30. Pavel Florensky, *Iconostasis*, trans. Donald Sheehan and Olga Andrejev (Crestwood, N.Y.: St. Vladimir's Seminary Press, 1996), 52–56. On the hesychastic belief that the human being becomes divinized by "receiving the radiance of uncreated light," see Georgios Mantzaridis, *The Deification of Man: St. Gregory Palamas and the Orthodox Tradition*, trans. Liadain Sherrard (Crestwood, N.Y.: St. Vladimir's Seminary Press, 1984), esp. 96–104. See also Liza Knapp's reading of Palamas in the context of the light imagery in *The Adolescent*: Knapp, *The Annihilation of Inertia*, 164–65.

31. Florensky, *Iconostasis*, 54–55.

32. Arkady's legal father, Makar, comes to embody the virtue of "seemliness" for Arkady. He is characterized, as opposed to Versilov, by his "extreme candor" (13:308), by his lack of concealment in communicating "something childlike and impossibly attractive in his fleeting laughter" (13:285), and, finally, by his "extremely rare" ability to "respect himself without doubt and precisely in his position, whatever it might be" (13:109). "His soul," Arkady observes, "was quite well organized, even to the point that I haven't yet met among people anything better in this sense" (13:308).

33. Nathan Rosen observes that "in Dolgoruky's impetuosity, his broad Russian nature, and his thirst for life we have the prototype of Dmitri Karamazov": Rosen, "Breaking Out of the Underground," 238.

CHAPTER SEVEN

The chapter epigraphs are from A. P. Chekhov, "Step'," in *Polnoe sobranie sochinenii i pisem v tridtsati tomakh* (Moscow: Nauka, 1974), 7:50 and from Simone Weil, *Gravity and Grace*, trans. Emma Crawford and Mario von der Ruhr (London: Routledge Classics, 2002), 31.

1. P. I. Fokin addresses this parallel in examining Zosima as a prototype for the Grand Inquisitor in Ivan's imagination. See P. I. Fokin, "Poema Ivana Karamazova 'Velikii inkvizitor,'" in *Roman F. M. Dostoevskogo "Brat'ia Karamazovy": Sovremennoe sostoianie izucheniia*, ed. T. A. Kasatkina (Moscow: Nauka, 2007), 115–36, esp. 124–25.

2. Rice, "The Covert Design of 'The Brothers Karamazov,'" 365–70, 357.

3. Among more positive interpretations of Alyosha's epiphany, for example, are Julian W. Connolly, "Dostoevskij's Guide to Spiritual Epiphany in 'The Brothers Karamazov,'" *Studies in East European Thought* 59, no. 1/2 (June 2007): 39–54; and Mark G. Pomar, "Alesa Karamazov's Epiphany: A Reading of 'Cana of Galilee,'" *Slavic and East European Journal* 27, no. 1 (Spring 1983): 47–56. For explicitly hagiographical readings of Alyosha, see Jostein Bortnes, "The Function of Hagiography in Dostoevskij's Novels," in *Critical Essays on Dostoevsky*, ed. Robin Feuer Miller (Boston: G. K. Hall, 1986), 188–93; and Valentina A. Vetlovskaia, "Alyosha Karamazov and the Hagiographic Hero," in *Dostoevsky: New Perspectives*, ed. Robert Louis Jackson (Englewood Cliffs, N.J.: Prentice-Hall, 1984), 206–26.

4. As Carol Apollonio observes, "the evidence suggests not a vision of spiritual grace and comfort, but a *traumatic memory*": Apollonio, *Dostoevsky's Secrets*, 154 (emphasis in the original). See also Michael R. Katz, "The Theme of Maternity in Alesa Karamazov's Four-Year-Old Memory," *Slavic and East European Journal* 34, no. 4 (1990): 506–10, 509.

5. Here we see a potential weakness in Vladimir Kantor's argument that the "lackey" or "hanger-on" is the "embodiment of Russia's evil." Kantor argues that "a line can be drawn through the novel connecting a whole series of characters most unpleasant to the author, and all of them falling under the rubric of 'lackey'—beginning with Fyodor Pavlovich and ending with the devil." Alyosha, however, begins the novel also as just such a dependent. See Vladimir Kantor, "Pavel Smerdyakov and Ivan Karamazov: The Problem of Temptation," in *Dostoevsky and the Christian Tradition*, ed. George Pattison and Diane Oenning Thompson (Cambridge: Cambridge University Press, 2001), 189–225, 200.

6. For a critique of Alyosha's faith in the beginning of the novel as reminiscent of the social revolutionaries of Dostoevsky's time, see Gary Saul Morson, "The God of Onions: *The Brothers Karamazov* and the Mythic Prosaic," in *A New Word on "The Brothers Karamazov,"* ed. Robert L. Jackson (Evanston, Ill.: Northwestern University Press, 2004), 107–24, 109–11.

7. For a different view of the relationship between Zosima and Alyosha as evocative of brotherhood and thus as antonymous to the "paternal despotism" embodied in the Grand Inquisitor, see Anna Berman, "Siblings in *The Brothers Karamazov*," *Russian Review* 68 (April 2009): 263–82, 264, 271–72.

8. Robin Feuer Miller points out the impossibility of locating the moment of the regenerative turn in Alyosha's crisis: "Was [Grushenka's fable] the crucial moment when he began to reconsolidate his faith? Or did that moment occur before the telling of the fable when a light seemed to dawn in his face and he said in a firm, loud voice that she had raised up his soul?": Miller, *"The Brothers Karamazov": Worlds of the Novel* (New Haven, Conn.: Yale University Press, 1992), 88.

9. For a very different, but not incompatible, account of Grushenka's transformative effect upon Alyosha, which emphasizes the prosaic and quotidian nature of the miraculous, see Morson, "The God of Onions," 113–15. Tatiana Kasatkina underscores the central significance of Grushenka's fable for the novel's engagement with the notion of "apocatastasis," or "restoration" of all things to their originary state. In the onion, Dostoevsky conceives of the notion that only that which we give away becomes part of our being since it serves to forge a "connection linking personalities in unity." As Kasatkina notes, if the old woman in the fable were to hold out her hands to the others instead of kicking at them, then hell itself would be transformed into heaven; as she puts it, "hell exists only because its inhabitants make it into hell" (306–7). I would add to this analysis that the onion is not only representative of a good deed, but appears as the result of the ability to *remember* a good deed. This aspect acquires significance in the context of Zosima's and Alyosha's notions of a good memory as constituting the ground for the salvation of the personality: Tatiana Kasatkina, "'Brat'ia Karamazovy': Opyt mikroanaliza teksta," in *Roman F. M. Dostoevskogo "Brat'ia Karamazovy": Sovremennoe sostoianie izucheniia*, ed. Kasatkina (Moscow: Nauka, 2007), 283–319, 305–8.

10. For a meditation on Alyosha's "epiphanic vision" that emphasizes the wedding feast itself and the notion of marriage as key to Dostoevsky's "vision of a spiritual ideal," see Connolly, "Dostoevskij's Guide to Spiritual Epiphany," 42–44.

11. Gary Saul Morson points out that by "someone" Alyosha "presumably means the Holy Spirit, for such inspiring visions and moments are traditionally the gifts of the Spirit": Morson, "The God of Onions," 118. See Lonny Harrison's analysis of Alyosha's discovery of an "authentic self that replaces the lower category of [the illusory] self" in this passage. Harrison argues that the possibility of a unified self is "explicitly postulated" in this scene: Harrison, "The Numinous Experience of Ego Transcendence," 399–400.

12. This paradigm bears much in common with the Neoplatonic Augustinian mystical notion of the journey inward to encounter the transcendent sources

of the self. Denys Turner describes Augustine's conception of interiority thus: "That place where the self and interiority intersect opens out to the God, the eternal light of Truth, who is *above*. The *itinerarium intus* [journey inward] is also an *acsensio superius* [ascension upward]. The two metaphors of inwardness and ascent themselves intersect at the point where God and the self intersect, so that which is most interior to me is also that which is above and beyond me; so that the God who is within me is also the God I am in": Denys Turner, *The Darkness of God*, 99.

13. The culmination of Alyosha's symptomatology, according to Rice, is his epiphanic vision in "Cana of Galilee" and his passionate pact with the earth, which Rice sees as a "textbook hysteric seizure" examined with "clinical precision. [. . .] Only pathology," Rice contends, "can explain this sequence of events, and the author meticulously designates his hero's symptoms, from which readers routinely avert their eyes." Rice explains the cessation of hysterical symptoms after Alyosha's mystical experience as a strategy of deferral on the part of the author: "From this point to the end of the novel, Alesha reverts to his quiescent, obliging type, without symptoms of hysteria." In this, Rice completely ignores the hysterical nature of Alyosha's truth-telling to his brothers later in the novel (e.g., "It was not you!" [15:40]) and generally refuses in his argument to consider the connection in Dostoevsky's writing between spirituality and pathology. Consequently, he dismisses the "option" which explains Alyosha's experience as "the emergence of a spiritual paragon from Alesha's shaky, hysterical debut" on extremely insubstantial grounds: "I prefer to dismiss *that* option because Dostoevskii had tried it with Prince Myshkin, and it did not work": Rice, "The Covert Design of 'The Brothers Karamazov,'" 369–73.

14. "As the Russian saying goes [. . .] one head is good, but two are much better. But to him the second mind didn't come, and he let his own go [. . .] for a walk" (15:106).

15. As Robert L. Jackson observes, Dmitry from one perspective corresponds directly to the human being as "foolish" "little children" who need an external authority imposed upon them. On the other hand, as Jackson argues, Dmitry "is man in transition, [. . .] groping for a new ethic. It is impossible to understand, or accept, Dmitrij other than as a symbolic figure—a representation of raw, historical man at the fringe of moral evolution, man at the point at which moral self has crystallized in perfect form, but still remains embedded in a more ancient protean consciousness. [. . .] What Dostoevsky attempts [. . .] is to realize in this figure of Dmitrij this awakening from sensuous slumber, to realize at the very least the transition from naïve, and therefore tragic, Schilleresque humanism (as we find it in Dmitrij) to a condition of mature self-consciousness": Jackson, "Dmitrij Karamazov and the 'Legend,'" *Slavic and East European Journal* 9, no. 3 (Autumn 1965): 257–67, 262–63.

16. Nathan Rosen sees this creation of an external conscience in Katerina as

a positive, salvific action for Dmitry: Rosen, "Why Dmitrii Karamazov Did Not Kill His Father," *Canadian-American Slavic Studies* 6, no. 2 (Summer 1972): 209–24, 223–24.

17. As Nathan Rosen suggests, Dmitry's way of speaking about Katia "suggests that we are dealing with an icon rather than a human being [. . .]. Mitia accepts Katya consciously as a god, as his conscience, and his need to pay off his debt to her becomes his deepest obsession, his greatest disgrace": Rosen, "Why Dmitrii Karamazov Did Not Kill His Father," 222.

18. Having ripped the amulet in half, he describes the contents of his "soul" using the same imagery: "Have mercy, gentlemen, I have torn my soul into two halves before you, and you made use of it and are digging around in the torn place on both sides" (14:446). Critics have often pointed out this conflation of amulet and soul, though mistakenly (in my view) attributing the symbolism to Dostoevsky the author rather than to Dmitry the character. See, for example, Richard Peace, *An Examination of the Major Novels*, 234. For an altogether different view of the "amulet" within the context of Dostoevsky's narrative strategies, see Kate Holland, "The Legend of the *Ladonka* and the Trial of the Novel," in *A New Word on "The Brothers Karamazov,"* 192–99.

19. Theodore Ziolkowski argues that "the mine in the German Romantic view is not simply a cold dark hole in the ground; it is a vital, pulsing place into which man descends as into his own soul in order to encounter broader, shared dimensions of human experience: history, religion, and sexuality": Ziolkowski, *German Romanticism and Its Institutions* (Princeton, N.J.: Princeton University Press, 1990), 18–63, esp. 33.

20. The parallels between Dmitry's and Alyosha's dream-epiphanies, emphasized in Dostoevsky's notebooks for the novel, have been often discussed (though, to my knowledge, not as contrastive depictions of the topography of the unconscious, and not in the broader context of yet another, third, dream—that is, Ivan's nightmare). As Carol Apollonio points out, "both are dreams; both are laden with religious elements; both are infused with poetic language that communicates a message of divine revelation; both are 'miracles.'" Apollonio adds that the festivity at Mokroe directly reflects the wedding feast of Cana from Alyosha's dream and "reinforces the link": Apollonio, "The Passion of Dmitrii Karamazov," *Slavic Review* 58, no. 3 (Fall 1999): 584–99, 596. See also Julian Connolly's examination of the of parallels between the two experiences in "Dostoevsky's Guide to Spiritual Epiphany," esp. 46–50.

21. Woven into the image of the clothbag as a principle of interiority is the Orthodox legend of "the torments of the soul" related by Saint Theodora in a dream to Gregory in the tenth century. According to the account, after her death, Theodora's soul encounters a series of demonic tormentors who legalistically and systematically weigh all of her past misdeeds upon her. Angels escort her through these torments, attempting to argue in her favor and pointing to her

past virtues and good deeds. However, as Theodora explains, she was allowed to pass through each torment because of the interference of Saint Basil who came to her and "took out from inside his shirt a small bag of gold" (*on vynul iz-za pazukhi kak by nekij meshochek s zolotom*), which represents "the treasure of [Basil's] prayers to the Lord for Theodora's soul." As she encounters the twenty torments, the angels redeem her past transgressions by paying the demons from the little bag: "The Journey beyond Death," in *Eternal Mysteries beyond the Grave: Orthodox Teachings on the Existence of God, the Immortality of the Soul, and Life beyond the Grave*, ed. Archimandrite Panteleimon (Jordanville, N.Y.: Holy Trinity Monastery, 1968), 69–87. One wonders whether Theodora's bag of gold was a source for Dmitry's amulet.

22. According to Richard Peace, "the Dmitri who stands before them naked, embarrassed by his own feet, ashamed and yet enraged, seems to invite the epithets which open 'Das Eleusische Fest': 'Shy, naked, and wild'—the description of man, the savage, unredeemed by eternal union with the earth": Peace, *An Examination of the Major Novels*, 224.

23. Ksana Blank points out the connection between Dmitry's dream and Schiller's poema, and argues that Dmitry's subsequent concept of descending "into the mines" is connected to Persephone's imprisonment in Hades: Blank, *Dostoevsky's Dialectic and the Problem of Sin*, 46–48.

24. According to Edith Clowes, "Dmitri goes farthest [of the brothers] in his spiritual quest. While he spends most of the novel in a condition of torment, of earnest confrontation with all the ugliness in his nature, in Mokroe he reaches a resolution in the dream about the dying child. Here he discovers in himself a new sensitivity and tenderness, a profound acceptance of human nature and, in particular, his *own* nature. The impending years of Siberian incarceration become less daunting because he has punctured his contempt for human suffering, whether of others or his own, and embraced the shared humanity that links him with other people": Clowes, "Self-Laceration and Resentment," 132.

25. Edith Clowes identifies this disgust as a symptom of the "self-lacerating" consciousness of the underground man, "a passionate rejection of the earth, of everything ugly and base in human nature," and the attraction to a "high ideal that promises to purify and deliver one from oneself and one's baser nature," a syndrome shared among Dostoevsky's fastidious idealists and dreamers: Clowes, "Self-Laceration and Resentment," 130. As Mochulsky originally formulated it, Ivan's fastidious contempt for the "disorderly, accursed and, perhaps, diabolic chaos" of the world of phenomena is a completion of the "age-old development of the *philosophy of reason* from Plato to Kant": Mochulsky, *Dostoevsky: His Life and Work*, 614–15. For a general discussion of Ivan's penchant toward forgetting, see Diane O. Thompson, *The Brothers Karamazov and the Poetics of Memory* (Cambridge: Cambridge University Press, 1991), esp. 179–86.

26. Bakhtin, *Problems of Dostoevky's Poetics*, 85–90.

27. Vladimir Kantor points out that Ivan's journey is to "understand that his potential is not exhausted with his idea." While "Smerdyakov tries to persuade Ivan that he exists wholly and essentially in his theory," Alyosha's role is to convince him that he is not his idea. As Kantor reasons, if Ivan's theory (of "all is permitted") "really expresses the essence of Ivan, then he is the real murderer of his father": Kantor, "Pavel Smerdyakov and Ivan Karamazov: The Problem of Temptation," 213.

28. Smerdiakov has been widely described as Ivan's double: they are half-brothers, approximately the same age, alike in their squeamish intellectualism and attraction to abstract thought, and bound to each other by a mysterious unspoken agreement. The connection is summarized succinctly by Carol Apollonio: "Ivan and Smerdiakov are 'twins,' born approximately at the same time to mothers who themselves were doubles through their connection to Fedor Pavlovich: a pagan earth spirit (moist mother Russia earth) and a gentle but troubled woman, a Christian wife possessed by a demon": Apollonio, *Dostoevsky's Secrets*, 162.

29. Deborah Martinsen argues that both Fyodor Pavlovich and the devil are conflated in Ivan's mind as a source of unbearable shame connected with himself. The two figures are "figurative and literal embodiments of Ivan's shame," and thus confronting them signifies a confrontation with the hated and discarded aspects of the self [. . . and] provides an opportunity for greater self-knowledge." Martinsen, "Shame's Rhetoric, or Ivan's Devil, Karamazov Soul," in *A New Word on "The Brothers Karamazov,"* 53–67, 54–55.

30. Robert L. Belknap contrasts "Alyosha, the rememberer" with "his father, the forgetter" in his analysis of the theme of memory in the novel. See Belknap, *The Genesis of "The Brothers Karamazov": The Aesthetics, Ideology, and Psychology of Making a Text* (Evanston, Ill.: Northwestern University Press, 1990), 79–87. For an account of Ivan's rebellion against his genetic information as embodied in his father, see F. F. Seeley, "Ivan Karamazov," in *New Essays on Dostoevsky*, ed. Malcolm V. Jones and Garth M. Terry (Cambridge: Cambridge University Press, 1983), 115–36, esp. 121–26.

31. Smerdiakov has sometimes been interpreted as Ivan's apprentice and instrument and at others as his tempter, an incarnation of the devil who has a hold on Ivan's soul, like Ivan's devil. Bakhtin argues that Smerdiakov "co-opts" the inner voice that Ivan hides from himself. Smerdiakov, according to Bakhtin, heard this "second voice" and understood it to be not part of a larger interior dialogue, but a "distinctly expressed desire": Bakhtin, *Problems of Dostoevsky's Poetics*, 258–60. Caryl Emerson elucidates this insight further in her assertion that "evil doubles, who succeed in gaining control of their more benevolent 'originals' because those originals refuse to attend consciously to ugly voices that are also part of their indwelling selves. What is Bakhtin cautioning us against? Ignore your own inner dialogue, he warns, and the most dangerous side of your personality will become so hungry for interlocutors that it will court attention

from anywhere—and clamor to control the whole to the extent that its point of view has been slighted": Emerson, "Translator's Afterword" to Vladimir Kantor's "Pavel Smerdyakov and Ivan Karamazov: The Problem of Temptation," 221.

32. According to Vladimir Kantor, the devil is "Smerdyakov's new hypostasis." He points out that "it is no accident that as soon as Smerdyakov departs from the pages of the novel, the devil appears—who, as it were, plays the double to the 'lackey' who has committed suicide": Kantor, "Pavel Smerdyakov and Ivan Karamazov: The Problem of Temptation," 216, 211. For an account of the connection between Smerdiakov and the devil, see Marina Kanevskaya, "Smerdiakov and Ivan: Dostoevsky's *The Brothers Karamazov*," *Russian Review* 61, no. 3 (July 2002): 358–76, esp. 371–75.

33. Mochulsky includes the "'long white stocking,' which conceals the packet of rainbow-colored notes" among the "artistic symbols" which "can be shown, but not explained": Mochulsky, *Dostoevsky: His Life and Work*, 625.

34. According to Vladimir Kantor, Smerdiakov "is one dimensional. He judges Ivan by his own measurement. [. . .] Smerdyakov cannot hear Ivan's inner voice. [He repeats . . .] not some secret, hidden voice of Ivan's but that which had been turned outwards, to the surface": Kantor, "Pavel Smerdyakov and Ivan Karamazov: The Problem of Temptation," 212–13.

35. For a different kind of reading of this scene, see Carol Apollonio, who argues that "in Dostoevsky the devil takes many forms. In Ivan's case, he comes to the one who *doubts* (that is, who does not give himself over to Christian belief). Smerdiakov lurks at the gate for Ivan, whose religious doubt gives rise to the deadly sins of pride, greed, and envy. He is the spirit of revenge": Apollonio, *Dostoevsky's Secrets*, 161. See also Maria Kanevskaya who argues that "Ivan is the most distant from God and therefore the most vulnerable to the devil's temptation": Kanevskaya, "Ivan and Smerdiakov," 368.

36. Deborah Martinsen argues that "by exposing Ivan to himself, the devil expresses and embodies Ivan's self-consciousness. Ivan desires to rid himself of the devil, thereby cutting himself off from the painful aspects of himself": Martinsen, "Shame's Rhetoric," 54.

37. Vladimir Kantor argues that Alyosha "tries to convince Ivan" that the inward and outward are not "self-congruent" in his attempts "to dis-identify [Ivan] from Smerdyakov, from his double" while "Smerdyakov [. . .] on the contrary, attempts to persuade Ivan that they, the two of them, are identical": Kantor, "Pavel Smerdyakov and Ivan Karamazov: The Problem of Temptation," 214–15. Robin Feuer Miller emphasizes the philosophical significance of Smerdiakov's attribution of guilt to Ivan. Smerdyakov, she argues, "is the first to raise the philosophical question that each of the brothers must eventually face: Where is the ethical boundary between thought and deed? At what point does thought become deed?": Miller, *"The Brothers Karamazov": Worlds of the Novel*, 45. In this context, Alyosha insists that a thought is not a deed.

38. In his argument that the devil reflects a Neoplatonic view of matter-evil, Kevin Corrigan emphasizes that the devil is both dependent on Ivan and yet independent—"although he is dependent on Ivan (i.e. he is 'a lie, an illness a phantasm' [. . .] who enters through Ivan's sickness and repeats his thoughts), he is also independent, for he is a problem which cannot be resolved by Ivan himself or by anyone else": Corrigan, "Ivan's Devil in *The Brothers Karamazov* in the Light of a Traditional Platonic View of Evil," *Forum for Modern Language Studies* 22, no. 1 (January 1986): 1–9, 4.

39. Paul Contino argues that Ivan "can be understood as suffering less from 'a breakdown' than from the experience of being broken down by God." In being exorcised of his pride, Contino notes, Ivan "is visited—brutally, healingly" by Christ: Contino, "'Descend That You May Ascend,'" 198.

40. Edith Clowes provides an eloquent description of the romantic dimension of interiority in the novel in her argument that Dostoevsky affirms "the *daimon* within human nature, which [he] calls sensuality [. . .]. This subliminal realm of dark, violent impulses both gives a person the energy and desire to live and dictates to the ego [. . .] how it should proceed. [. . .] In its naked form [Karamazov sensuality] is a brutish display of violence, lust, and power [and . . .] yet is also the source of life energy": Clowes, "Self-Laceration and Resentment," 129.

41. See, for example, David S. Cunningham's reading of the Karamazov brothers as illustrative of the intersecting and interpenetrating life of one more complete personality, and ultimately as an icon of the divine trinity: Cunningham, "'The Brothers Karamazov' as Trinitarian Theology," in *Dostoevsky and the Christian Tradition*, 144–50. According to Mochulsky, the brothers represent "an organically collective personality in its triple structure: the principle of reason is embodied in Ivan [. . .] the principle of feeling is represented in Dmitry [. . .] the principle of will, realizing itself in active love as an ideal, is presented in Alyosha," while "Smerdyakov [. . .] is their embodied temptation and personified sin": Mochulsky, *Dostoevsky: His Life and Work*, 597–98. Or in Richard Peace's words: "It is as though the central figure so typical of Dostoyevsky's previous writing is ultimately unable to withstand its own dichotomous inner tensions and has here broken apart into separate and distinct facets; in Alesha we have the soul; in Dmitri the emotions; in Ivan the intellect: but behind them all lurks Smerdyakov—the devious, unlit recesses of man's psyche": Peace, *Dostoevsky: An Examination of the Major Novels*, 229.

CONCLUSION

1. Robert Belknap conceives of these three works and "The Gentle Creature" as a "four-part novel that does not exist, but that almost exists": Belknap, "'The Gentle Creature' as the Climax of a Work of Art That Almost Exists," *Dostoevsky Studies*, new series 4 (2000): 35–42. For the connection between *Notes*

from Underground and "Dream of a Ridiculous Man" (which begins "almost [as] a continuation" of the former and "takes things to an extreme not reached in the earlier text"), see Robin Aizlewood, "'The Dream of a Ridiculous Man': Both Knowing and Not Knowing, and Questions of Philosophy" in *Aspects of Dostoevsky: Art, Ethics and Faith*, ed. Robert Reid and Joe Andrew (Amsterdam: Rodopi, 2012), 167–86, 167–70.

2. On the traces of traumatic experience in the protagonist of *Notes from Underground*, see Shoshana Felman and Dori Laub, *Testimony: Crises of Witnessing in Literature, Psychoanalysis, and History* (London: Routledge, 1992), 9–12.

3. For an account of the ridiculous man as a megalomaniac and solipsist (both before, during, and after his dream), see Holquist, *Dostoevsky and the Novel* (Princeton, N.J.: Princeton University Press, 1977), 155–64. In Gary Saul Morson's words, "this school of interpretation usually argues the story's narrator converts not from solipsistic atheism to true faith, but rather from nihilistic egoism to monomaniacal egoism. The solipsist, it is contended, is recognizable in his religious rebirth, especially in the conviction that he alone knows the Truth": Morson, *The Boundaries of Genre*, 180.

4. In light of Dostoevsky's entry on suicides among the youth in *Diary of a Writer*, Robert L. Jackson identifies the star as evoking suicidal despair by reminding the protagonist of his deepest longings for the "sublime goals of life": Jackson, *The Art of Dostoevsky*, 275.

5. In Zosima's words, "One only needs a small seed, a tiny one: throw it into the soul of a commoner and it will not die, it will live in his soul for his whole life, will be concealed in him amid the darkness, amid the stench of his sins like a light spot, like a great memory" (14:266). Alyosha's most sacred childhood memory is presented using the same terms: "Such recollections can stay in one's memory (everyone knows this) even from an earlier age, even from the age of two, but only appearing for one's whole life as bright spots from the darkness, like a torn corner from an enormous painting, which is entirely faded and vanished, except for this one corner" (14:18).

6. In Robin Feuer Miller's illumination of the textual parallel between Dickens's "A Christmas Carol" and Dostoevsky's "Dream of a Ridiculous Man," she notes that "although the ridiculous man does not journey to his own past, he too is led to what he already somehow knows—the past of all humanity—yet does not know": Miller, *Dostoevsky's Unfinished Journey*, 121.

7. This interpretation of the dream as a form of collective memory in my view avoids the pitfalls of either taking "the story as an unambiguous utopia" or looking at the vision as a mere function of psychology. For a balanced assessment of both strategies within the ambiguous generic context of Dostoevsky's *Diary*, see Morson, *Boundaries of Genre*, 180–82.

8. Michael Holquist points to the fact that "*before, in,* and *after* the dream—

the narrator is isolated from others [and] misunderstood" as evidence of the solipsistic and non-revelatory quality of the dream: Holquist, *Dostoevsky and the Novel*, 161. Robin Feuer Miller points out one of the problems with such a reading, namely "the ridiculous man's conscious effort to dissociate himself from solipsism," in stressing that he "beheld" truth and did not "invent it" with his "own mind": Miller, *Dostoevsky's Unfinished Journey*, 117.

9. As Vasily Rozanov observes, Tolstoy and Dostoevsky wrote with a voice that "resonated in contradiction to everything that society desired and to everything that it was thinking. [. . .] At the very height of the fascination with external reforms, in the moment of the unconditional negation of everything interior, religious, mystical in life in the human being, they rejected everything external as absolutely insignificant—and turned their attention to the internal and the religious": Rozanov, *Legenda o velikom inkvizitore*, 59–60.

10. Sergei Horujiy points out that *Vekhi* was just one of "a multitude of such collections that appeared in those legendary years," and that it remained in the cultural mindset because it was the "rarest act of extremely honest self-examination of the Russian consciousness, a gesture of unique authenticity and depth. And this purity of gesture, of a radical, remorseless, thorough gesture, does not get old": Horujiy, "Dve-tri Rossii spustya," *Literaturnaya Gazeta* 14, no. 6217 (April 1, 2009), www.lgz.ru/article/8298/.

11. On *Vekhi* as an "exploding bomb," see A. Stolypin, "Intelligenty ob intelligentakh," in *Vekhi: Pro et Contra*, ed. V. V. Sapov (Moscow: Izdatel'stvo Russkogo Khristianskogo gumanitarnogo instituta, 1998), 84–85, 85. Commentary on *Vekhi* came from readers as diverse as Andrei Bely, V. I. Lenin, and the Archbishop Antonii, to name three of many.

12. Sergei Bulgakov, "Heroism and Asceticism," in *Vekhi (Landmarks): A Collection of Articles about the Russian Intelligentsia*, trans. Marshall S. Shatz and Judith E. Zimmerman (New York: M. E. Sharpe, 1994), 17–49, 34.

13. Lev Tolstoi, "O Vekhakh," in *Polnoe sobranie sochinenii*, ed. Chertkov, vol. 38 (Moscow, 1936), 285–90, 289.

14. For an account of Tolstoy's attempts to conceive of the self in his personal diaries during this period, see Irina Paperno,"'I Felt a Completely New Liberation from Personality': Tolstoy's Late Diaries," in *"Who, What Am I?": Tolstoy Struggles to Narrate the Self* (Ithaca, N.Y.: Cornell University Press, 2014), 128–58.

15. Mark Steinberg, *Petersburg Fin de Siècle* (New Haven, Conn.: Yale University Press, 2011), 160–65, 168. See also Olga Matich, *Erotic Utopia: The Decadent Imagination in Russia's Fin de Siecle* (Madison: University of Wisconsin Press, 2007), 15.

Bibliography

Afanas'ev, A. N. *Narodnye russkie skazki A. N. Afanas'eva*. 3 vols. Moscow: Nauka, 1985.
Aizlewood, Robin. "'The Dream of a Ridiculous Man': Both Knowing and Not Knowing, and Questions of Philosophy." In *Aspects of Dostoevsky: Art, Ethics and Faith*, edited by Robert Reid and Joe Andrew, 167–86. Amsterdam: Rodopi, 2012.
Akhundova, I. R. "Voploshchenie khaosa i nebytiia (Parfen Rogozhin—demon smerti ili personifikatsiia sud'by)." In *Roman F. M. Dostoevskogo "Idiot": Sovremennoe sostoianie izucheniia*, edited by T. Kasatkina, 364–89. Moscow: Nasledie, 2001.
Alter, Robert, trans. *The David Story: A Translation with Commentary of 1 and 2 Samuel*. New York: W. W. Norton, 1999.
Anderson, Nancy. *The Perverted Ideal in Dostoevsky's "The Devils."* New York: Peter Lang, 1997.
Apollonio, Carol. *Dostoevsky's Secrets: Reading Against the Grain*. Evanston, Ill.: Northwestern University Press, 2009.
———, ed. and trans. *The New Russian Dostoevsky: Readings for the Twenty-First Century*. Columbus, Ohio: Slavica, 2010.
———. "The Passion of Dmitrii Karamazov." *Slavic Review* 58, no. 3 (Fall 1999): 584–99.
Augustine, Saint. *Confessions*. Translated by Garry Willis. New York: Penguin Books, 2006.
Bakhtin, Mikhail. "Author and Hero in Aesthetic Activity." Translated by Vadim Liapunov. In *Art and Answerability: Early Philosophical Essays by M. M. Bakhtin*, edited by Michael Holquist and Vadim Liapunov, 4–256. Austin: University of Texas Press, 1990.
———. *Problems of Dostoevsky's Poetics*. Edited and translated by Caryl Emerson. Minneapolis: University of Minnesota Press, 1984.
Barsht, Konstantin. "Defining the Face: Observations on Dostoevskii's Creative Process." In *Russian Literature, Modernism and the Vistual Arts*, edited by

Catriona Kelly and Stephen Lovell, 23–57. Cambridge: Cambridge University Press, 2000.
Belinskii, V. G. *Polnoe sobranie sochinenii*. 13 vols. Moscow: Izdatel'stvo akademii nauk, 1953–59.
Belknap, Robert L. *The Genesis of "The Brothers Karamazov": The Aesthetics, Ideology, and Psychology of Making a Text*. Evanston, Ill.: Northwestern University Press, 1990.
———. "'The Gentle Creature' as the Climax of a Work of Art That Almost Exists." In *Dostoevsky Studies*, new series 4 (2000): 35–42.
Bem, A. L. "Dramatizatsiia breda ('Khoziaika' Dostoevskogo)." In *Dostoevskii: Psikhoanaliticheskie etiudy*, 77–141. Prague: Petropolis, 1938.
———. "Evoliutsiia obraza Stavrogina." In *Issledovaniia: Pis'ma o literature*, edited by S. G. Bocharov, 111–57. Moscow: Iazyki slavianskoi kul'tury, 2001.
Berdiaev, Nikolai. *Mirosozertsanie Dostoevskogo*. Prague: YMCA, 1923.
Berlin, Isaiah. *The Roots of Romanticism*. Princeton, N.J.: Princeton University Press, 1999.
Berman, Anna. "Siblings in *The Brothers Karamazov*." *Russian Review* 68 (April 2009): 263–82.
Blake, Elizabeth. "Sonya, Silent No More: A Response to the Woman Question." *Slavic and East European Journal* 50, no. 2 (2006): 252–71.
Blank, Ksana. *Dostoevsky's Dialectics and the Problem of Sin*. Evanston, Ill.: Northwestern University Press, 2010.
Bortnes, Jostein. "Dostoevskij's *Idiot* or the Poetics of Emptiness." *Scando-Slavica* 40 (1994): 5–14.
———. "The Function of Hagiography in Dostoevskij's Novels." In *Critical Essays on Dostoevsky*, edited by Robin Feuer Miller, 188–93. Boston: G. K. Hall, 1986.
———. "The Last Delusion in an Infinite Series of Delusions: Stavrogin and the Symbolic Structure of *The Devils*." *Dostoevsky Studies* 4 (1983): 53–67.
Brakke, David. *Demons and the Making of the Monk: Spiritual Combat in Early Christianity*. Cambridge, Mass.: Harvard University Press, 2006.
Breger, Louis. *Dostoevsky: The Author as Psychoanalyst*. New York: New York University Press, 1990.
Breithaupt, Fritz. *Der Ich-Effekt des Geldes: Zur Geschichte einer Legitimationsfigur*. Frankfurt am Main: Fischer Taschenbuch Verlag, 2008.
Buelens, Gert, Sam Durrant, and Robert Eaglestone, eds. *The Future of Trauma Theory: Contemporary Literary and Cultural Criticism*. New York: Routledge, 2014.
———. "Introduction." In *The Future of Trauma Theory: Contemporary Literary and Cultural Criticism*, edited by Gert Beulens, Sam Durrant, and Robert Eaglestone, 1–8. New York: Routledge, 2014.
Bulanov, A. M. *Tvorchestvo Dostoevskogo-romanista: Problematika i poetika*

(Khudozhestvennaia fenomenologiia "serdechnoi zhizni"): Monografiia. Volgograd: Peremena, 2004.

Bulgakov, Sergei. "Heroism and Asceticism." In *Vekhi (Landmarks): A Collection of Articles about the Russian Intelligentsia*, trans. Marshall S. Shatz and Judith E. Zimmerman, 17–49. New York: M. E. Sharpe, 1994.

———. "Russkaia tragediia." *Sochineniia v dvukh tomakh.* Vol. 2:499–526. Moscow: Nauka, 1993.

Burgin, Diana. "Prince Myskin, the True Lover and 'Impossible Brideground': A Problem in Dostoevskian Narrative." *Slavic and East European Journal* 27, no. 2 (Summer 1983): 158–75.

———. "The Reprieve of Nastasja: A Reading of a Dreamer's Authored Life." *Slavic and East European Journal* 29, no. 3 (Autumn 1985): 258–68.

Burry, Alexander. "Execution, Trauma, and Recovery in Dostoevsky's *The Idiot*." *Slavic and East European Journal* 54, no. 2 (Summer 2010): 255–71.

Busch, R. L. "The Myshkin-Ippolit-Rogozhin Triad." *Canadian American Slavic Studies* 17, no. 3 (Fall 1983): 372–83.

Camus, Albert. *The Myth of Sisyphus and Other Essays.* Translated by Justin O'Brien. New York: Vintage, 1983.

Carroll, John. *Break-Out from the Crystal Palace: The Anarcho-Psychological Critique: Stirner, Nietzsche, Dostoevsky.* London: Routledge and Kegan Paul, 1974.

Caruth, Cathy. *Trauma: Explorations in Memory.* Baltimore: Johns Hopkins University Press, 1995.

———. *Unclaimed Experience: Trauma, Narrative, and History.* Baltimore: Johns Hopkins University Press, 1996.

Cassedy, Steven. *Dostoevsky's Religion.* Stanford, Calif.: Stanford University Press, 2005.

Chaadaev, Peter. *The Major Works of Peter Chaadaev.* Translated by Raymond T. McNally. Notre Dame, Ind.: University of Notre Dame Press, 1969.

Charry, Ellen. "Augustine of Hippo: Father of Christian Psychology." *Anglican Theological Review* 88 (2006): 575–89.

Chekhov, A. P. *Polnoe sobranie sochinenii i pisem v tridtsati tomakh.* 30 vols. Moscow: Nauka, 1974.

Chernyshevskii, N. G. *Polnoe sobranie sochinenii N. G. Chernyshevskogo v desiati tomakh.* 10 vols. Saint Petersburg: Tipografiia M.M. Stasiulevicha, 1906.10.2, 230–240.

Chizhevksii, Dmitrii. "Dostoevskij—psikholog." In *O Dostoevskom: Sbornik statej*, edited by A. L. Bem, 51–72. Prague, 1929.

Christa, Boris. "Dostoevsky and Money." In *The Cambridge Companion to Dostoevsky*, edited by W. J. Leatherbarrow, 93–110. Cambridge: Cambridge University Press, 2002.

Clowes, Edith W. "Self-Laceration and Resentment: The Terms of Moral Psychology in Dostoevsky and Nietzsche." In *Freedom and Responsibility in Russian Literature: Essays in Honor of Robert Louis Jackson*, edited by Elizabeth Cheresh Allen and Gary Saul Morson, 119–33. Evanston, Ill.: Northwestern University Press, 1995.

Coetzee J. M. "Confession and Double Thoughts: Tolstoy, Rousseau, Dostoevsky." *Comparative Literature* 37, no. 3 (Summer 1985): 193–232.

Comer, William. "Rogozhin and the 'Castrates': Russian Religious Traditions in Dostoevsky's 'The Idiot.'" *Slavic and East European Journal* 40, no. 1 (Spring 1996): 85–99.

Connolly, Julian W. "Dostoevskij's Guide to Spiritual Epiphany in 'The Brothers Karamazov.'" *Studies in East European Thought* 59, no. 1/2 (June 2007): 39–54.

Contino, Paul. "'Descend That You May Ascend': Augustine, Dostoevsky, and the Confessions of Ivan Karamazov." In *Augustine and Literature*, edited by Robert P. Kennedy, Kim Paffenroth, and John Doody, 179–214. New York: Lexington Books, 2006.

Corrigan, Kevin. "Ivan's Devil in *The Brothers Karamazov* in the Light of a Traditional Platonic View of Evil." *Forum for Modern Language Studies* 22, no. 1 (January 1986): 1–9.

Cox, Gary. *Tyrant and Victim in Dostoevsky*. Columbus, Ohio: Slavica, 1983.

Cravens, Craig. "The Strange Relationship of Stavrogin and Stepan Trofimovich as Told by Anton Lavrent'evich G-v." *Slavic Review* 59, no. 4 (Winter 2000): 782–801.

Cunningham, David S. "'The Brothers Karamazov' as Trinitarian Theology." In *Dostoevsky and the Christian Tradition*, edited by George Pattison and Diane O. Thompson, 134–55. Cambridge: Cambridge University Press, 2001.

Dalton, Elizabeth. *Unconscious Structure in "The Idiot."* Princeton, N.J.: Princeton University Press, 1979.

Davison, R. M. "*The Devils*: The Role of Stavrogin." In *New Essays on Dostoevsky*, edited by Malcolm V. Jones and Garth M. Terry, 95–114. Cambridge: Cambridge University Press, 1983.

———. "Dostoevsky's *The Devils*: The Role of Stepan Trofimovich Verkhovensky." In *Dostoevsky's "The Devils": A Critical Companion*, edited by W. J. Leatherbarrow, 119–34. Evanston, Ill.: Northwestern University Press, 1999.

Danow, David K. *The Dialogic Sign: Essays on the Major Novels of Dostoevsky*. New York: Peter Lang, 1991.

Diagnostic and Statistical Manual of Mental Disorders. 5th edition. Washington, D.C.: American Psychiatric Publishing, 2013.

Dickens, Charles. *A Christmas Carol*. New Haven, Conn.: Yale University Press, 1993.

Dilthey, Wilhelm. *Poetry and Experience*. Edited by Rudolf A. Makkreel and Firthjof Rodi. Princeton, N.J.: Princeton University Press, 1985

Bibliography

Doak, Connor. "Masculine Degeneration in Dostoevskii's *Demons*." In *Russian Writers at the Fin de Siècle: The Twilight of Realism*, edited by Katherine Bowers and Ani Kokobobo, 105–25. Cambridge: Cambridge University Press, 2015.

Dobroliubov, N. A. "Zabitye liudi." In *Literaturno-kriticheskie stat'i*. Moscow: Khudozhestvennaia literatura, 1937.

Dolinin, A. S., ed. *F. M. Dostoevskii: Stat'i i materialy*, vol. 2. Leningrad-Moscow: Mysl', 1924.

Dostoevskii, F. M. *Polnoe sobranie sochinenii i pisem v tridtsati tomakh*. 30 vols. Leningrad: Nauka, 1972–84.

Egdorf, Brian. "Fyodor Dostoevsky's *The Adolescent* and the Architectonics of Author and Hero." *The Dostoevsky Journal: An Independent Review* 12–13 (2011–12): 15–36.

Ellenberger, Henri F. *The Discovery of the Unconscious: The History and Evolution of Dynamic Psychiatry*. New York: Basic Books, 1970.

———. "The Pathogenic Secret and Its Therapeutics." In *Beyond the Unconscious: Essays of Henri F. Ellenberger in the History of Psychiatry*, edited by Mark S. Michale. Princeton, N.J.: Princeton University Press, 1993.

Emerson, Caryl. "Bakhtin, Lotman, Vygotsky, and Lydia Ginzburg on Types of Selves: A Tribute." In *Self and Story in Russian History*, edited by Laura Engelstein and Stephanie Sandler, 20–45. Ithaca, N.Y.: Cornell University Press, 2002.

———. "Building a Responsive Self in a Post-Relativistic World: The Contribution of Mikhail Bakhtin." In *The Self: Beyond the Postmodern Crisis*, edited by Paul C. Vitz and Susan M. Felch, 25–41. Wilmington, Del.: ISI Books, 2006.

———. *The Cambridge Introduction to Russian Literature*. Cambridge: Cambridge University Press, 2008.

———. *The First Hundred Years of Mikhail Bakhtin*. Princeton, N.J.: Princeton University Press, 1997.

———. "Russian Orthodoxy and the Early Bakhtin." *Religion and Literature* 22, no. 2/3 (Summer-Autumn 1990): 109–31.

———. "Word and Image in Dostoevsky's Worlds: Robert Louis Jackson on Readings That Bakhtin Could Not Do." In *Freedom and Responsibility in Russian Literature: Essays in Honor of Robert Louis Jackson*, edited by Elizabeth Cheresh Allen and Gary Saul Morson, 246–306. Evanston, Ill.: Northwestern University Press, 1995.

Evdokimova, Svetlana. "The Anatomy of the Modern Self in *The Little Tragedies*." In *Alexander Pushkin's Little Tragedies: The Poetics of Brevity*, edited by Svetlana Evdokimova, 106–43. Madison: University of Wisconsin Press, 2003.

Evlampiev, I. I. "Lichnost' kak absoliut: metafizika F. Dostoevskogo." In *Istoriia*

Bibliography

russkoi metafiziki v XIX–XX vekakh: Russkaia filosofiia v poiskakh absoliuta, Chast' 1. St. Petersburg: Izdatel'stvo "Aleteiia," 2000.

Fanger, Donald. *Dostoevsky and Romantic Realism: A Study of Dostoevsky in Relation to Balzac, Dickens, and Gogol*. Evanston, Ill.: Northwestern University Press, 1965, reprinted 1998.

Ferguson, Niall. *The House of Rothschild: Money's Prophets (1748–1848)*. New York: Viking, 1998.

Felman, Shoshana, and Dori Laub. *Testimony: Crises of Witnessing in Literature, Psychoanalysis, and History*. London: Routledge, 1992.

Finke, Michael C. *Metapoesis: The Russian Tradition from Pushkin to Chekhov*. Durham, N.C: Duke University Press, 1995.

Florensky, Pavel. *Iconostasis*. Translated by Donald Sheehan and Olga Andrejev. Crestwood, N.Y.: St. Vladimir's Seminary Press, 1996.

Fokin, P. I. "Poema Ivana Karamazova 'Velikii inkvizitor.'" In *Roman F. M. Dostoevskogo "Brat'ia Karamazovy": Sovremennoe sostoianie izucheniia*, edited by T. A. Kasatkina, 115–36. Moscow: Nauka, 2007.

Frank, Joseph. *Dostoevsky: The Mantle of the Prophet, 1871–1881*. Princeton, N.J.: Princeton University Press, 2002.

———. *Dostoevsky: The Miraculous Years, 1865–1871*. Princeton, N.J.: Princeton University Press, 1995.

———. *Dostoevsky: The Seeds of Revolt, 1821–1849*. Princeton, N.J.: Princeton University Press, 1979.

———. *Dostoevsky: The Stir of Liberation, 1860–1865*. Princeton, N.J.: Princeton University Press, 1986.

Frank, Semyon. *Man's Soul: An Introduction in Philosophical Psychology*. Translated by Boris Jakim. Athens: Ohio University Press, 1993.

Frazer, James George. *The Golden Bough: A Study in Magic and Religion*. Edited by Robert Fraser. Oxford: Oxford University Press, 2009.

Freud, Sigmund. "Beyond the Pleasure Principle." In *The Freud Reader*, edited by Peter Gay, 594–627. New York: Norton, 1989.

Fusso, Susanne. *Discovering Sexuality in Dostoevsky*. Evanston, Ill.: Northwestern University Press, 2006.

———. "The Weight of Human Tears: *The Covetous Knight* and *A Raw Youth*." In *Alexander Pushkin's Little Tragedies: The Poetics of Brevity*, edited by Svetlana Evdokimova, 229–42. Madison: University of Wisconsin Press, 2003.

Gerigk, Horst-Jürgen. *Versuch über Dostojewski's "Jüngling," ein Beitrag zur Theorie des Romans*. Munich: Wilhelm Fink, 1965

Gibbian, George. "C. G. Carus' Psyche and Dostoevsky." *American Slavic and East European Review* 14, no. 3 (October 1955): 371–82.

Ginzburg, Lydia. *On Psychological Prose*. Translated and edited by Judson Rosengrant. Princeton, N.J.: Princeton University Press, 1991.

Girard, René. *Deceit, Desire, and the Novel: Self and Other in Literary Struc-*

ture. Translated by Yvonne Freccero. Baltimore: Johns Hopkins University Press, 1976.

———. *Resurrection from the Underground: Feodor Dostoevsky*. Edited and translated by James G. Williams. East Lansing: Michigan State University Press, 1996.

Goetz, Steward, and Charles Taliafero. *A Brief History of the Soul*. Oxford: Wiley-Blackwell, 2011.

Guerrard, Albert J. "On the Composition of Dostoevsky's *The Idiot*." *Mosaic* 8 (1974/1975), 201–15.

Hacking, Ian. "Memory Sciences, Memory Politics." In *Tense Past: Cultural Essays in Trauma and Memory*, edited by Paul Antze and Michael Lambek, 67–87. New York: Routledge, 1996.

———. *Rewriting the Soul: Multiple Personality and the Sciences of Memory*. Princeton, N.J.: Princeton University Press, 1995.

Hampson, Peter J., and Johannes Hoff. "Whose Self? Which Unification? Augustine's Anthropology and the Psychology-Theology Debate." *New Blackfriars* 91, no. 1035 (September 2010): 546–66.

Harrison, Lonny. "The Numinous Experience of Ego Transcendence in Dostoevsky." *Slavic and East European Journal* 57, no. 3 (2013): 388–402.

Herman, Judith. *Trauma and Recovery*. New York: Basic Books, 1997.

Hermans, Hubert J. M. "The Dialogical Self: Toward a Theory of Personal and Cultural Positioning." *Culture and Psychology* 7, no. 3 (2001): 243–81.

Herzen, A. I. *Sobranie sochinenii v tridtsati tomakh*. 30 vols. Moscow: Akademiia nauk SSSR, 1954–56.

Holland, Kate. "The Legend of the Ladonka and the Trial of the Novel." In *A New Word on "The Brothers Karamazov,"* edited by Robert L. Jackson, 192–99. Evanston, Ill.: Northwestern University Press, 2004.

———. *The Novel in the Age of Disintegration: Dostoevsky and the Problem of Genre in the 1870s*. Evanston, Ill.: Northwestern University Press, 2013.

Holquist, Michael. *Dialogism: Bakhtin and His World*. 2nd edition. New York: Routledge, 2002.

———. *Dostoevsky and the Novel*. Princeton, N.J.: Princeton University Press, 1977.

Horujiy, Sergei. "Dve-tri Rossii spustya." *Literaturnaya Gazeta* 14, no. 6217 (April 1, 2009). www.lgz.ru/article/8298/

Howe, Susanne. *Wilhelm Meister and His English Kinsmen: Apprentices to Life*. New York: Columbia University Press, 1930.

Iakubova, Rima. *Tvorchestvo F. M. Dostoevskogo i khudozhestvenaya kul'tura*. Ufa: "Gilem," 2003.

Iurkevich, P. D. *Filosofskie proizvedeniia*. Moscow: Pravda, 1990

Ivanits, Linda J. "Dostoevskij's Mar'ja Lebjadkina." *Slavic and East European Journal* 22, no. 2 (Summer 1978): 127–40.

———. *Dostoevsky and the Russian People*. Cambridge: Cambridge University Press, 2008

Ivanov, Viacheslav. *Freedom and the Tragic Life: A Study in Dostoevsky*. Translated by Norman Cameron, edited by S. Konovalov. New York: Noonday, 1952.

Jackson, Robert Louis. *The Art of Dostoevsky: Deliriums and Nocturnes*. Princeton, N.J.: Princeton University Press, 1981.

———. *Dialogues with Dostoevsky: The Overwhelming Questions*. Stanford, Calif.: Stanford University Press, 1996.

———. "Dmitrij Karamazov and the 'Legend.'" *Slavic and East European Journal* 9, no. 3 (Autumn 1965): 257–67.

———. *Dostoevsky's Quest for Form: A Study of His Philosophy of Art*. New Haven, Conn.: Yale University Press, 1966.

Jeffers, Thomas L. *Apprenticeships: The Bildungsroman from Goethe to Santayana*. New York: Palgrave Macmillan, 2005.

Johnson, Brian. "Diagnosing Prince Myshkin." *Slavic and East European Journal* 56, no. 3 (Fall 2012): 377–93.

Johnson, Leslie. "The Face of the Other in *The Idiot*." *Slavic Review* 50, no. 4 (Winter 1991): 867–78.

Jones, Malcolm V. *Dostoyevsky after Bakhtin*. Cambridge: Cambridge University Press, 1990.

———. *Dostoyevsky and the Dynamics of Religious Experience*. London: Anthem, 2005.

———. *Dostoyevsky: The Novel of Discord*. New York: Harper and Row, 1976.

Jung, C. G. *Aion: Researches into the Phenomenology of the Self*. 2nd edition. Translated by R. F. C. Hull. Princeton, N.J.: Princeton University Press, 1978.

———. *Memories, Dreams, Reflections*. Recorded and edited by Aniela Jaffé, translated by Richard Winston and Clara Winston. New York: Vintage Books, 1989.

Kanevskaya, Marina. "Smerdiakov and Ivan: Dostoevsky's *The Brothers Karamazov*." *Russian Review* 61, no. 3 (July 2002): 358–76.

Kantor, V. K. "Ispoved' i teoditseia v tvorchestve Dostoevskogo (retseptsiia Avreliia Avgustina)." *Voprosy filosofii* 4 (2011): 96–103.

———. "Pavel Smerdyakov and Ivan Karamazov: The Problem of Temptation." In *Dostoevsky and the Christian Tradition*, edited by George Pattison and Diane Oenning Thompson, 189–225. Cambridge: Cambridge University Press, 2001.

Kasatkina, Tatiana. "'Brat'ia Karamazovy': Opyt mikroanaliza teksta." In *Roman F. M. Dostoevskogo "Brat'ia Karamazovy": Sovremennoe sostoianie izucheniia*, edited by T. Kasatkina, 283–319. Moscow: Nauka, 2007.

———. *Kharakterologiia Dostoevskogo: Tipologiia emotsional'no-tsennostnykh orientatsii*. Moscow: Nasledie, 1996.

———. *O tvoriashchei prirode slova: Ontologichnost' slova v tvorchestve F. M. Dostoevskogo kak osnova "realisma v vysshem smysle."* Moscow: IMLI RAN, 2004.

———. "Posle znakomstva s podlinnikom: Kartina Gansa Gol'beina Mladshego 'Khristos v mogile' v structure romana F. M. Dostoevskogo 'Idiot.'" *Novyi Mir* 2 (2006): 154–68.

Katz, Michael R. "The Theme of Maternity in Alesa Karamazov's Four-Year-Old Memory." *Slavic and East European Journal* 34, no. 4 (1990): 506–10.

Kent, Leonard J. *The Subconscious in Gogol' and Dostoevskij and Its Antecedents.* The Hague: Mouton, 1969.

Khapaeva, Dina. *Nightmare: From Literary Experiments to Cultural Projects,* translated by Rosie Tweddle. Leiden: Brill, 2013.

Khomiakov, Aleksei. "Letter to the Editor of *L'Union Chretienne,* on the Occasions of a Discourse by Father Gagarin, a Jesuit." In *On Spiritual Unity: A Slavophile Reader,* edited and translated by Robert Bird and Boris Jakim, 135–40. Hudson, N.Y.: Lindisfarne Books, 1998.

Kibal'nik, Sergei. *Problemy intertekstual'noi poetiki Dostoevskogo.* St. Petersburg: Petropolis, 2013.

Kierkegaard, Soren. *The Sickness Unto Death: A Christian Psychological Exposition for Upbuilding and Awakening,* edited and translated by Howard V. Hong and Edna H. Hong. Princeton, N.J.: Princeton University Press, 1980.

Kireevsky, Ivan. "On the Nature of European Culture and on Its Relation to Russian Culture." In *A Slavophile Reader,* edited and translated by Robert Bird and Boris Jakim, 187–232. Hudson, N.Y.: Lindisfarne Books, 1998.

Klein, Melanie. *Envy and Gratitude and Other Works, 1946–1963.* New York: Free, 1975.

Knapp, Liza. *The Annihilation of Inertia: Dostoevsky and Metaphysics.* Evanston, Ill.: Northwestern University Press, 1996.

Kostalevsky, Marina. *Dostoevsky and Soloviev: The Art of Integral Vision.* New Haven, Conn.: Yale University Press, 1997.

Krasnoshchekova, Elena. *Roman vospitaniia—Bildungsroman—na russkoi pochve: Karamzin, Pushkin, Goncharov, Tolstoi.* St. Petersburg: Pushkinskii fond, 2008.

Krieger, Murray. "Dostoevsky's 'Idiot': The Curse of Saintliness." In *Dostoevsky: A Collection of Critical Essays,* edited by Rene Wellek, 32–52. Englewood Cliffs, N.J.: Prentice-Hall, 1962.

Kristeva, Julia "The Ruin of a Poetics." In *Russian Formalism: A Collection of Articles and Texts in Translation,* edited by Stephen Bann and John E. Bowlt, 102–21. New York: Harper and Row Publishers, 1973.

Leatherbarrow, William J. "*The Devils* in the Context of Dostoevsky's Life and Works." In *Dostoevsky's "The Devils": A Critical Companion,* edited by W. J. Leatherbarrow, 3–59. Evanston, Ill.: Northwestern University Press, 1999.

———. *A Devil's Vaudeville: The Demonic in Dostoevsky's Major Fiction*. Evanston, Ill.: Northwestern University Press, 2005.

———. "Dostoevsky's Treatment of the Theme of Romantic Dreaming in 'Khozyayka' and 'Belyye nochi.'" *Modern Language Review* 69, no. 3 (July 1974): 584–95.

———. "Idealism and Utopian Socialism in Dostoyevsky's Gospodin Prokharchin and Slaboye serdtse." *Slavonic and East European Review* 58, no. 4 (October 1980): 524–40.

———. "The Sorcerer's Apprentice: Authorship and the Devil in Dostoevsky's *Poor Folk* and 'The Landlady.'" *Slavonic and East European Review* 83, no. 4 (October 2005): 599–616.

Livermore, Gordon. "Stepan Verkhovensky and the Shaping Dialectic of Dostoevsky's *Devils*." In *Dostoevsky: New Perspectives*, edited by Robert L. Jackson, 176–92. Englewood Cliffs, N.J.: Prentice-Hall, 1984.

Lossky, Vladimir. *The Mystical Theology of the Eastern Church*. Crestwood, N.Y.: St. Vladimir's Seminary Press, 1976.

Luckhurst, Roger. *The Trauma Question*. London: Routledge, 2008.

Lunde, Ingunn. "'Ia gorazdo umnee napisannogo': On Apophatic Strategies and Verbal Experiments in Dostoevskii's 'A Raw Youth.'" *Slavonic and East European Review* 79, no. 2 (April 2001): 264–89.

Maguire, Robert. *Exploring Gogol*. Stanford, Calif.: Stanford University Press, 1994.

Mantzaridis, Georgios. *The Deification of Man: St. Gregory Palamas and the Orthodox Tradition*. Translated by Liadain Sherrard. Crestwood, N.Y.: St. Vladimir's Seminary Press, 1984.

Martin, Raymond, and John Barresi. *The Rise and Fall of Soul and Self: An Intellectual History of Personal Identity*. New York: Columbia University Press, 2006.

Martinsen, Deborah A. "Shame's Rhetoric, or Ivan's Devil, Karamazov Soul." In *A New Word on "The Brothers Karamazov,"* edited by Robert L. Jackson, 53–67. Evanston, IL: Northwestern University Press, 2004.

———. *Surprised by Shame: Dostoevsky's Liars and Narrative Exposure*. Columbus: Ohio State University Press, 2003.

Marullo, Thomas G. *Fyodor Dostoevsky: Portrait of the Artist as a Young Man (1821–1845): A Life in Letters, Memoirs, and Criticism*. DeKalb, Ill.: Northern Illinois University Press, forthcoming.

———. *Heroine Abuse: The Poetics of Codependency in "Netochka Nezvanova."* DeKalb: Northern Illinois University Press, 2015.

Marx, Karl. "Economic and Philosophic Manuscripts of 1844." In *Collected Works*, vol. 3, 228–346. New York: International Publishers, 1975.

Matich, Olga. *Erotic Utopia: The Decadent Imagination in Russia's Fin de Siecle*. Madison: University of Wisconsin Press, 2007.

Mazurek, Slawomir. "The Individual and Nothingness (Stavrogin: A Russian Interpretation)." *Studies in East European Thought* 62 (2010): 41–54.

McReynolds, Susan. *Redemption and the Merchant God: Dostoevsky's Economy of Salvation and Antisemitism*. Evanston, Ill.: Northwestern University Press, 2008.

Meerson, Olga. *Dostoevsky's Taboos*. Dresden: Dresden University Press, 1998.

Mestergazi, Elena. "Vera i kniaz' Myshkin: Opyt 'naivnogo' chteniia romana 'Idiot.'" In *Roman F. M. Dostoevskogo "Idiot": Sovremennoe sostoianie izucheniia*, edited by T. Kasatkina, 291–318. Moscow: Nasledie, 2001.

Micale, Mark, and Paul Lerner, eds. *Traumatic Pasts: History, Psychiatry, and Trauma in the Modern Age, 1870–1930*. Cambridge: Cambridge University Press, 2001.

Miller, Robin Feuer. *"The Brothers Karamazov": Worlds of the Novel*. New Haven, Conn.: Yale University Press, 1992.

———. "Dostoevsky and Rousseau: The Morality of Confession Reconsidered." In *Dostoevsky: New Perspectives*, edited by Robert L. Jackson, 82–98. Englewood Cliffs, N.J.: Prentice-Hall, 1984.

———. *Dostoevsky and "The Idiot": Author, Narrator, and Reader*. Cambridge, Mass.: Harvard University Press, 1981.

———. *Dostoevsky's Unfinished Journey*. New Haven, Conn.: Yale University Press, 2007.

Mochulsky, Konstantin. *Dostoevsky: His Life and Work*. Translated by Michael A. Minihan. Princeton, N.J.: Princeton University Press, 1967.

Moretti, Franco. *The Way of the World: The Bildungsroman in European Culture*. Translated by Albert Sbragia. London: Verso, 2000.

Morson, Gary Saul. *The Boundaries of Genre: Dostoevsky's "Diary of a Writer" and the Traditions of Literary Utopia*. Austin: University of Texas Press, 1981.

———. "The God of Onions: *The Brothers Karamazov* and the Mythic Prosaic." In *A New Word on "The Brothers Karamazov,"* edited by Robert L. Jackson, 107–24. Evanston, Ill.: Northwestern University Press, 2004.

———. *Narrative and Freedom: The Shadows of Time*. New Haven, Conn.: Yale University Press, 1994.

Morson, Gary Saul, and Caryl Emerson, eds. *Rethinking Bakhtin: Challenges and Extensions*. Evanston, Ill.: Northwestern University Press, 1989.

Moser, Charles A. "Stepan Trofimovic Verkhovenskij and the Esthetics of His Time." *Slavic and East European Journal* 29, no. 2 (1985): 157–63.

Murav, Harriet. *Holy Foolishness: Dostoevsky's Novels and the Poetics of Cultural Critique*. Stanford, Calif.: Stanford University Press, 1990.

Naginski, Erika. "Canova's Penitent Magdalene: On Trauma's Prehistory." In *Trauma and Visuality in Modernity*, edited by Lisa Saltzman and Eric Rozenberg, 51–81. Hanover, N.H.: Dartmouth College Press, 2006.

Naiman, Eric. "Gospel Rape." Conference paper delivered at Association for Slavic, East European, and Eurasian Studies Convention. November 2014.

Neuhauser, Rudolf. "'The Landlady': A New Interpretation." *Canadian Slavonic Papers / Revue Canadienne des Slavistes* 10 (Spring 1968): 42–67.

Offord, Derek. "Alexander Herzen." In *A History of Russian Philosophy 1830–1930: Faith, Reason, and the Defense of Human Dignity*, edited by G. M. Hamburg and Randall A. Poole, 52–68. Cambridge: Cambridge University Press, 2010.

———. "'Lichnost': Notions of Individual Identity." In *Constructing Russian Culture in the Age of Revolution: 1881–1940*, edited by Catriona Kelly and David Shepherd, 13–25. Oxford: Oxford University Press, 1998.

Orwin, Donna Tussing. *Consequences of Consciousness: Turgenev, Dostoevsky, and Tolstoy*. Stanford, Calif.: Stanford University Press, 2007.

———. "'Idiot' i problema liubvi k drugim I sebialiubiia v tvorchestve F. M. Dostoevskogo." In *Roman F. M. Dostoevskogo "Idiot": Sovremennoe sostoianie izucheniia*, 405–24. Moscow: Nasledie, 2001.

Otverzhennyj, N. *Shtirner i Dostoevskii*. Moscow: Golos truda, 1925.

Panteleimon, Archimandrite, ed. *Eternal Mysteries beyond the Grave: Orthodox Teachings on the Existence of God, the Immortality of the Soul, and Life beyond the Grave*. Jordanville, N.Y.: Holy Trinity Monastery, 1968.

Paperno, Irina. *"Who, What Am I?": Tolstoy Struggles to Narrate the Self*. Ithaca, N.Y.: Cornell University Press, 2014.

Passage, Charles E. *Dostoevski the Adapter: A Study of Dostoevski's Use of the Tales of Hoffmann*. Chapel Hill, N.C.: University of North Carolina Press, 1954.

Peace, Richard. *Dostoevsky: An Examination of the Major Novels*. Cambridge: Cambridge University Press, 1971.

Pevear, Richard. "Foreword." In Fyodor Dostoevsky, *Demons*, translated by Richard Pevear and Larissa Volokhonsky, vii–xxiii. New York: Vintage, 1994.

Pirog, Gerald. "Bakhtin and Freud on the Ego." In *Russian Literature and Psychoanalysis*, edited by Daniel Rancour-Laferriere, 401–15. Amsterdam: John Benjamins, 1988.

Platonov, Andrei. *Soul: And Other Stories*. Translated by Robert and Elizabeth Chandler with Katia Grigoruk, Angela Livingstone, Olga Meerson, and Eric Naiman. New York: New York Review Books, 2008.

Plotnikov, Nikolai. "Ot 'individual'nosti' k 'identichnosti' (istoriia poniatii personal'nosti v russkoi kul'ture)." *Novoe Literaturnoe Obozrenie* 91 (2008): 64–83.

Pomar, Mark G. "Alesa Karamazov's Epiphany: A Reading of 'Cana of Galilee." *Slavic and East European Journal* 27, no. 1 (Spring 1983): 47–56.

Pope, Richard, and Judy Turner. "Toward Understanding Stavrogin." *Slavic Review* 49, no. 4 (Winter 1990): 543–53.

Quinton, Anthony. "The Soul." In *Personal Identity*, edited by John Perry, 53–72. Berkeley: University of California Press, 2008.

Rassin, Eric. *Thought Suppression*. London: Elsevier, 2005.

Rice, James. "The Covert Design of 'The Brothers Karamazov': Alesha's Pathology and Dialectic." *Slavic Review* 68, no. 2 (Summer 2009): 355–75.

———. *Dostoevsky and the Healing Art: An Essay in Literary and Medical History*. Ann Arbor, Mich.: Ardis, 1985.

Rosen, Nathan. "Breaking Out the Underground: The 'Failure' of 'A Raw Youth.'" *Modern Fiction Studies* 4, no. 3 (Fall 1958): 225–39.

———. "Why Dmitrii Karamazov Did Not Kill His Father." *Canadian-American Slavic Studies* 6, no. 2 (Summer 1972): 209–24.

Rosenthal, Richard J. "Dostoevsky's Experiment with Projective Mechanisms and the Theft of Identity in *The Double*." In *Russian Literature and Psychoanalysis*, edited by Daniel Rancour-Laferriere, 59–88. Amsterdam: John Benjamins, 1989.

Rousseau, Jean-Jacques. *The Confessions and Correspondence*. Translated by Christopher Kelly, edited by Christopher Kelly, Roger D. Masters, and Peter G. Stillman. Hanover, N.H.: University Press of New England, 1995.

———. *Emile, or On Education*. Translated by Allan Bloom. New York: Basic Books, 1979.

———. *Julie, or the New Heloise*. Translated by Philip Stewart and Jean Vaché. Hanover, N.H.: University Press of New England, 1997.

Rowling, J. K. *Harry Potter and the Half-Blood Prince*. New York: Scholastic, 2005.

Rozanov, V. V. *Legenda velikogo inkvizitora*. Munich: Wilhelm Fink Verlag, 1970.

Rzhevsky, Nicholas. "*The Adolescent*: Structure and Ideology." *Slavic and East European Journal* 26, no.1 (Spring 1982): 27–42.

Sainsbury, R. M. *Fiction and Fictionalism*. New York: Routledge, 2010.

Saltykov-Shchedrin, M. E. *Sobranie sochinenii*. 20 vols. Moscow: Khudozhestvennaia literatura, 1965–77.

Sandomirskaia, Irina. "Golaia zhizn', zloi Bakhtin i vezhlivyi Vaginov: Tragediia bez khora i avtora." In *Telling Forms: 30 Essays in Honour of Peter Alberg Jensen*, edited by Karin Grelz and Susanna Witt, 337–55. Stockholm: Almqvist & Wiksell, 2004.

Saraskina, Liudmila. "*Besy*": *Roman-preduprezhdenie*. Moscow: Sovetskii pisatel', 1990.

Scanlan, James P. *Dostoevsky the Thinker*. Ithaca, N.Y.: Cornell University Press, 2002.

———. "Introduction: Exploring Egoism." In *The Insulted and the Injured*, by Fyodor Dostoevsky, vii–xxiii. Grand Rapids, Mich.: William B. Eerdmans, 2011.

Scharff, David E. *Object Relations Theory and Practice: An Introduction*. Northvale, N.J.: Jason Aronson, 1996.

Schiller, Friedrich. "Letters on the Aesthetic Education of Man." In *Essays*, edited by Walter Hinderer and Daniel Dahlstrom. New York: Continuum, 2005.

Schmid, Ulrich. "Split Consciousness and Characterization in *The Brothers Karamazov*." Translated by Katherine Bowers and Susan McReynolds. In Fyodor Dostoevsky, *The Brothers Karamazov*, edited by Susan McReynolds, 776–85. 2nd edition. New York: Norton, 2011.

Seeley, F. F. "Ivan Karamazov." In *New Essays on Dostoevsky*, edited by Malcolm V. Jones and Garth M. Terry, 115–36. Cambridge: Cambridge University Press, 1983.

Seigel, Jerold. *The Idea of the Self: Thought and Experience in Western Europe since the Seventeenth Century*. Cambridge: Cambridge University Press, 2005.

Semenov, E. I. *Roman Dostoevskogo "Podrostok" (Problematika i zhanr)*. Leningrad: Nauka, 1979.

Shay, Jonathan. *Odysseus in America: Combat Trauma and the Trials of Overcoming*. New York: Scribner, 2002.

Shklovsky, Viktor. *Za i protiv: Zametki o Dostoevskom*. Moscow: Sovetskij pisatel', 1957.

Soloviev, Vladimir. *Sobranie sochinenii Vladimira Sergeevicha Solov'eva*. 10 vols. St. Petersburg: Izdatel'stvo tovarishestvo "Prosveshchenie," 1912.

Sorabji, Richard. *Self: Ancient and Modern Insights about Individuality, Life, and Death*. Chicago: University of Chicago Press, 2006.

Spektor, Sasha. "From Violence to Silence: Vicissitudes of Reading (in) *The Idiot*." *Slavic Review* 72, no. 3 (Fall 2013): 552–72.

Starobinski, Jean. *Jean-Jacques Rousseau: Transparency and Obstruction*. Translated by Arthur Goldhammer. Chicago: University of Chicago Press, 1988.

Steinberg, Mark. *Petersburg Fin de Siècle*. New Haven, Conn.: Yale University Press, 2011

Steiner, Lina. *For Humanity's Sake: The Bildungsroman in Russian Culture*. Toronto: University of Toronto Press, 2011.

Stepun, Fyodor. *Vstrechi*. Munich: Tovarishchestvo zarubezhnykh pisatelei, 1962.

Stolypin, A. "Intelligenty ob intelligentakh." In *Vekhi: Pro et Contra*, edited by V. V. Sapov, 84–85. Moscow: Izdatel'stvo Russkogo Khristianskogo gumanitarnogo instituta, 1998.

Stirner, Max. *The Ego and Its Own*. Edited by David Leopold. Cambridge: Cambridge University Press, 2005.

Straus, Nina Pelikan. *Dostoevsky and the Woman Question: Rereadings at the End of the Century*. New York: St. Martin's, 1994.

Strelsky, Katherine. "Dostoevsky's Early Tale, 'A Faint Heart.'" *Russian Review* 30, no. 2 (1971): 146–53.
Swales, Martin. *The German Bildungsroman from Wieland to Hesse*. Princeton, N.J.: Princeton University Press, 1978.
Swoboda, Philip J. "Semen Frank's Expressivist Humanism." In *A History of Russian Philosophy 1830–1930: Faith, Reason, and the Defense of Human Dignity*, edited by G. M. Hamburg and Randall A. Poole, 205–26. Cambridge: Cambridge University Press, 2010.
Szczepanska, Kathryn. "The Double and Double Consciousness in Dostoevsky." Ph.D. dissertation, Stanford University, 1978.
Taylor, Charles. *The Sources of the Self: The Making of Modern Identity*. Cambridge, Mass.: Harvard University Press, 1989.
Terras, Victor. "Dostoevsky's Detractors." *Dostoevsky Studies* 6 (1985): 165–72.
———. *The Young Dostoevsky (1846–1849): A Critical Study*. The Hague: Mouton, 1969.
Thompson, Diane O. *"The Brothers Karamazov" and the Poetics of Memory*. Cambridge: Cambridge University Press, 1991.
Todorov, Tzvetan. *Genres in Discourse*. Cambridge: Cambridge University Press, 1990.
Tolstoi, L. N. *Polnoe sobranie sochinenii v 90 tomakh*. 90 vols. Moscow-Leningrad, 1928–58.
Turner, Denys. *The Darkness of God: Negativity in Christian Mysticism*. Cambridge: Cambridge University Press, 1995.
Turner, Léon. *Theology, Psychology and the Plural Self*. Farnham, Eng.: Ashgate, 2008.
Tymms, Ralph. *Doubles in Literary Psychology*. Cambridge: Bowes and Bowes, 1949.
Vardoulakis, Dmitris. *The Doppelgänger: Literature's Philosophy*. New York: Fordham University Press, 2010.
Vetlovskaia, Valentina A. "Alyosha Karamazov and the Hagiographic Hero." In *Dostoevsky: New Perspectives*, edited by Robert Louis Jackson, 206–26. Englewood Cliffs, N.J.: Prentice-Hall, 1984.
Vinokurov, Val. "The End of Consciousness and the Ends of Consciousness: A Reading of Dostoevsky's *The Idiot* and *Demons* after Levinas." *Russian Review* 59, no. 1 (January 2000): 21–37.
Vitz, Paul C. "Introduction: From the Modern and Postmodern Selves to the Transmodern Self." In *The Self: Beyond the Postmodern Crisis*, edited by Paul C. Vitz and Susan M. Felch, xi–xxii. Wilmington, Del.: ISI Books, 2006.
Volgin, I. *Rodit'sya v Rossii: Dostoevskii i sovremenniki: Zhizn' v dokumentakh*. Moscow: Kniga, 1991.
Wasiolek, Edward. *Dostoevsky: The Major Fiction*. Cambridge, Mass.: MIT Press, 1964.

Weil, Simone. *Gravity and Grace*, translated by Emma Crawford and Mario von der Ruhr. London: Routledge Classics, 2002.
Whitman, Walt. *The Complete Poems*. Edited by Francis Murphy. New York: Penguin Books, 2004.
Williams, John S. "Stavrogin's Motivation: Love and Suicide." *Psychoanalytic Review* 69, no. 2 (1982): 249–65.
Woloch, Alex. *One vs. the Many: Minor Characters and the Space of the Protagonist in the Novel*. Princeton, N.J.: Princeton University Press, 2003.
Wood, James. *How Fiction Works*. New York: Farrar, Straus and Giroux, 2008.
Wyman, Alina. "Bakhtin and Scheler: Toward a Theory of Active Understanding." *Slavonic and East European Review* 86, no. 1 (January 2008): 58–89.
Young, Allan. *The Harmony of Illusions: Inventing Post-Traumatic Stress Disorder*. Princeton, N.J.: Princeton University Press, 1997.
Young, Sarah. *Dostoevsky's "The Idiot" and the Ethical Foundations of Narrative: Reading, Narrating, Scripting*. London: Anthem, 2004.
———. "Holbein's *Christ in the Tomb* in the Structure of *The Idiot*." *Russian Studies in Literature* 44, no. 1 (Winter 2007–2008): 90–102.
Zander, L. A. *Dostoevsky*. Translated by Natalie Duddington. London: SCM, 1948.
Ziolkowski, Theodore. *German Romanticism and Its Institutions*. Princeton, N.J.: Princeton University Press, 1990.

Index

administrative mind. *See* external mind
Afanasiev, Alexander, 104
agency, 22–23, 26–27; self-government, 25. *See also* freedom
Aizlewood, Robin, 213n1
Akhundova, I. R., 190nn53–54, 191n58
allegory, 5–7, 36, 46, 86–87, 153n9
amnesia, 6, 20, 30–31, 36–40, 40–50, 53, 60–63, 69–71, 73–75, 77, 88, 122, 133–36; moral amnesia, 57–58
Anderson, Nancy, 197n32
anima, 8, 73, 74
Antonii, Archbishop, 214n11
apartment edifice (as map of self), 47–49, 62–63, 75, 80–83, 125–26, 137–38
Apollonio, Carol, 189n43, 193n8, 194n9, 195n18, 196n20, 196n24, 205n4, 208n20, 210n28, 211n35
apprenticeship. *See* education
archetype. *See* symbolic vocabulary of selfhood; tripartite self
Aristotle, 151n4
ascetic ideal. *See* transcendent ideal
atheism, 158n23, 165n28, 194n8, 213n3
Augustine, Saint, 17, 79–80, 154n14, 161n4, 187n38, 187n39, 190n51, 197n29, 207n12

Bakhtin, Mikhail, 4, 7–8, 12–13, 17, 18, 24, 30–31, 32, 33, 49, 57, 152n7, 153n8, 154n11, 158n24, 158n25, 159n26, 161n1, 162nn6–9, 164nn18–21, 166nn1–2, 168nn9–11, 175n15, 196n23, 204n25, 209n26, 210n31
Barresi, John, 151n4
Barsht, Konstantin, 190n51, 204n29
Basil, Saint, 209n21

Belinsky, Vissarion 13–14, 160n31, 168n13, 173n6
Belknap, Robert L., 210n30, 212n1
Bely, Andrei, 214n11
Bem, A. L., 168n15, 195n19
Benedikt, Moritz, 175n17
Berdiaev, Nikolai, 5, 148, 152n6, 153n8, 154n13, 191n2, 192n3, 203n20,
Berlin, Isaiah, 161n4
Berman, Anna, 206n7
bezlichnost' (impersonality), 9, 12, 93–99, 102–3
bildungsroman, 105, 199n4, 200n5
Blake, Elizabeth, 172n31
Blank, Ksana, 186n32, 209n23
body. *See* external body; selfhood, as embodied
Body of the Dead Christ in the Tomb (Holbein), 75, 81–82
Bortnes, Jostein, 182n15, 195n18, 205n3
Brakke, David, 198n34
Breger, Louis, 153n9, 167n7, 171n28
Breithaupt, Fritz, 202n12
Buelens, Gert, 160n27
Bulanov, A. M., 158n23
Bulgakov, Sergei, 148, 153n8, 191n2, 195n18, 214n12
Burgin, Diana, 182n12, 184n26, 185n28
Burry, Alexander, 179n2, 182n14
Busch, R. L., 171n26, 190n52

Camus, Albert, 4, 151n3, 179n5, 191n59
Carroll, John, 174n8
Carus, Carl Gustav, 32, 167n6
Caruth, Cathy, 159n27
Cassedy, Steven, 152n6, 194n8, 197n30
Chaadaev, Pyotr, 30, 82, 189n46

Index

characterization, 7–8, 156n17
Charry, Ellen, 154n14, 158n23
Chekhov, Anton, 120
Chernyshevsky, Nikolai, 52, 66, 95, 172n1, 173n7, 174n12
child abuse, 90–94, 194n13
Chizhevsky, Dmitri, 153n8, 161n3, 167n6
Christ, 56, 64, 65, 66, 81–83, 88, 117, 126; as indwelling presence, 81–83, 126, 139; and renunciation of selfhood, 3–4, 12, 60. See also *Body of the Dead Christ in the Tomb* (Holbein); Christianity; divine humanity
Christa, Boris, 181n10, 202n12
Christianity, 3, 4, 5, 12, 59, 60, 64–66, 79–80, 81, 154–55n14
Clowes, Edith, 162n5, 209nn24–25, 212n40
codependency, 6, 28
Coetzee, J. M., 172n2
Cohen, Hermann, 159n25
collective selfhood, 6, 9, 18–29, 31, 39–40, 42–43, 45, 47–48, 50, 69–70, 73–76, 87, 88–90, 92–93, 102–3, 111–15, 120–21, 124–25, 139, 141, 147–48, 203n20. See also "paradox" of selfhood (as collective and individual); "whirlwind" (as symbol of collective self); *sobornost'*
collective superego. See external mind
collective unconscious, 8, 147–48
Comer, William, 188n42, 189n44
confession, 53–55, 172n2, 173n3
Connolly, Julian W., 205n3, 206n10, 208n20
conscience, 19, 111, 121, 125, 128, 137, 141, 207n16. See also external mind
consciousness: as site of awareness, 12, 14, 22, 29, 33, 40, 47, 48, 57–58, 63, 66, 108, 114, 133, 138, 142, 143, 146; as burden, 10, 98, 123; disembodied, 23–24, 25. See also tripartite self
Contino, Paul, 188n39, 212n39
corpse, 22–23, 41, 66–67, 81–83, 124–25. See also *Body of the Dead Christ in the Tomb* (Holbein)
Corrigan, Kevin, 212n38
Cox, Gary, 201n8
Cravens, Craig, 193n7, 196n27
Crime and Punishment, 9, 10, 16, 25–29, 45–50, 64, 66, 83

crucifixion, 64–65, 117–18
Cunningham, David S., 212n41

Dalton, Elizabeth, 153n9, 167n6, 178n2, 183n19, 183nn21–22, 190n53
Danow, David K., 183n18
Davison, R. M., 192n4, 193n7
dead body. See corpse; *Body of the Dead Christ in the Tomb* (Holbein)
demonism, 83–85, 87–88, 94–96, 101–3, 114–15, 135–36, 143–44, 198n34. See also devil; evil; possession
determinism, 31, 47, 52, 65, 156n19. See also freedom
devil, 34, 73, 83, 86, 121, 138–39, 140, 196n23, 205n5, 210n29, 211n32, 211nn35–36, 212n38. See also demonism; Mephistopheles
Dickens, Charles, 68, 213n6
Dilthey, Wilhelm, 199n4
divine humanity, 192n6, 204n30
Doak, Connor, 194n9, 195n14
Dobroliubov, N. A., 163n12, 176n24
dog (as motif of collective self), 33–35, 49, 61–62, 146
Doppelgänger, 20, 31–33, 163n13, 166n5. See also doubling
doubling, 9, 31–35, 163n17, 166n5, 167n6, 167n8, 168n11
Dostoevskaia, Anna Grigorievna, 14–15
Dostoevskaia, Liubov', 161n34
Dostoevsky, Andrei, 14
Dostoevsky, Fyodor: *The Adolescent*, 9, 10, 56, 101, 103, 104–19, 148; *The Brothers Karamazov*, 8, 9, 10, 20, 23, 32, 83, 84, 120–141, 143, 144, 145, 147, 150; campaign against radical materialism, 52; *Crime and Punishment*, 9, 10, 16, 25–29, 45–50, 64, 66, 83, 84; *Demons* (*The Devils, The Possessed*), 7, 9, 10, 23, 86–103, 122, 123, 129, 148; *Diary of a Writer*, 3–4, 51–52; *The Double*, 8, 20–21, 32, 33–34, 35, 44, 61, 146; "Dream of a Ridiculous Man," 10, 144–48, 150; and Europe, 3–4; and experience of trauma, 14–15; *The Gambler*, 112; "The Grand Inquisitor," 120–21, 127, 137, 205n1; *The Idiot*, 9, 10, 39, 45, 63, 67, 68–85, 125, 133, 148; *The Insulted and Injured*, 9, 34–

232

Index

35, 51–67, 74, 81, 125–26, 133; "The Landlady," 8, 11, 25, 35–40, 41, 42, 43, 46, 47, 48, 61, 63, 70, 71, 73, 81, 92, 133; "Masha lezhit na stole" journal entry, 3–4, 151n2; and medical condition, 179n4; "Mr. Prokharchin," 109; *Netochka Nezvanova*, 8, 40–45, 46, 61, 63, 72, 73, 74, 122, 133; *Notes from ground*, 10, 25, 51, 144–145, 156n19; Siberian imprisonment and exile of, 6–7, 11, 52; "Socialism and Christianity," 151n2; and theoretical writings on selfhood, 3–4, 151n2; "A Weak Heart," 8, 11, 18–29, 38, 45, 96–100, 122, 123, 135, 142; "White Nights," 25, 31, 144; *Winter Notes on Summer Impressions*, 3–4, 151n2
dreamer (*mechtatel'*), 35–38, 179–80n6
dreams, 22–23, 37–38, 123–27, 130–32, 136–39
dualism, 9, 10, 29, 132; conscious-unconscious, 32–33; good-evil (light-dark), 5–6, 83–85; mind-heart, 36, 43; subject-object (mind-body), 10, 32–33
Durrant, Sam, 160n27

Eaglestone, Robert, 160n27
education, 9, 87–88, 90–94, 125, 141, 143
Egdorf, Brian, 203n18
ego (the "I"), 3, 56, 149, 157n22, 174n8; "annihilation" of, 4, 12, 105, 118, 140, 142–43, 152n5; "law of personality," 151n2
egoism, 56–58, 59, 60, 165n28
elders, system of, 102–3, 120–21, 123–24
Ellenberger, Henri F., 175nn17–18
embraces, 3, 5–6, 19–20, 28, 38–39, 44–45, 90–94, 124–25, 128, 177n29
Emerson, Caryl, 158n24, 159nn25–26, 164n19, 164n21, 181n9, 203n19, 210n31
emptiness. *See bezlichnost'*; interiority, as atrophied, collapsed
eros. *See* sexuality
essence. *See* selfhood, as essentialist
Evagrius of Pontus, 198n34
Evdokimova, Svetlana, 202n14
evil, 46, 83–85, 93, 143–44, 169n16, 171n26, 190nn51–53, 191n57, 198n34, 212n38. *See also* demonism; devil

Evlampiev, I. I., 153n9
existentialism, 56, 174n8
expressivism, 17, 140–41, 158n23, 161n1, 161n4, 162n7
external body, 19–20, 22, 23. *See also* collective selfhood
external conscience. *See* external mind
external mind, 19–29, 39–40, 43, 88–90, 92–93, 102–3, 120–23, 127–30, 135–36. *See also* collective selfhood
external soul, 9, 22–25, 38–40, 48, 70–73, 76, 104–5, 107–11, 128–29, 133–36. *See also* collective selfhood; memory, carrier of

face (as transfigured countenance, *lik*), 116–17, 204n20, 204n29. *See also* seemliness (*blagoobrazie*)
facelessness. *See bezlichnost'*
Fanger, Donald, 163n11, 164n18
fantastic realism, 23, 164n18
Faust (Goethe), 34, 88
Felman, Shoshana, 213n2
Ferguson, Niall, 203n16
Feuerbach, Ludwig, 197n30
Finke, Michael C., 181n9, 182n12, 183n17, 184n26
Fokin, P. I., 205n1
Florensky, Pavel, 116, 204nn30–31
Frank, Joseph, 153n7, 163n11, 165n22, 165n24, 165n25, 166n5, 168n13, 169n15, 170n24, 173n6, 173n7, 174n12, 174n14, 176nn20–21, 177nn26–27, 178nn31–32, 192nn5–6, 197n30, 201n8
Frank, Semyon, 157n22, 158n23
Frankenstein (Shelley), 36
Frazer, Sir James, 104–5, 198n2
freedom, 10, 30, 47, 49, 120–21, 159n6, 203n17. *See also* determinism
Freud, Sigmund, 4, 8, 32, 159n27, 164n19, 178n2
friendship. *See* intimacy
Fusso, Susanne, 174n13, 177n28, 195n13, 196n22, 200n6, 201n10, 204n27

Gadarene swine, parable of, 101–2
Gerigk, Horst-Jurgen, 202n13
Gershenzon, Mikhail, 148
Gibbian, George, 167n6

Index

Ginzburg, Lydia, 152n7
Girard, René, 4, 154n12, 156n19, 163nn15–16, 192n5, 195n18, 198n32
God, 17, 22, 98–100, 116–17, 139–40. *See also* Christ; indwelling divinity; source (indwelling)
God-man. *See* Christ; divine humanity
Goethe, J. W. von, 34, 168n12
Gogol, Nikolai, 36, 169n17; "Diary of a Madman," 108–9
Goncharov, Ivan, 166n1
Gothic, 92, 177n27, 187n34, 187n36
Granovsky, Timofei, 192n5, 193n8, 197n30

Hacking, Ian, 160n29
Hampson, Peter J., 155n14
Harrison, Lonny, 188n41, 206n11
heart (as seat of "soul"), 43, 158n23
Hegel, G. W. F., 167n8
Herman, Judith, 160n28
Hermans, Hubert J. M., 162n9
Herzen, Alexander, 86, 102, 173n6, 192n5, 197n30, 198n35
hesychasm, 204n30
Hoff, Johannes, 155n14
Hoffmann, E. T. A., 32, 36, 166n5, 168n11, 169n17, 177n26, 195n15
Holbein, Hans, 75, 81–82
Holland, Kate, 199n4, 201n9, 208n18
Holquist, Michael, 159n25, 162n9, 213n3, 213n8
homosexuality, 28, 163n14, 195nn13–14
Horujiy, Sergei, 214n10
human being. *See* selfhood

Iakubova, Rima, 196n24
idealism, 25
Ikhmeneva, Natasha, 53–54, 58
immanence. *See* indwelling divinity; interiority
impersonality. *See bezlichnost'*
individualism, 3–4, 11, 96, 112, 139, 173n6, 202n12. *See also* "paradox" of selfhood (as collective and individual)
indwelling divinity, 6, 17, 79–80, 83, 97–100, 102, 116–17, 138–40, 142, 161n4. *See also* source (indwelling)
interiority: as atrophied, collapsed, 6, 8, 19, 24–25, 28–29, 36, 61–63, 84, 86–103, 114–15, 132–36, 140 (see also *bezlichnost'*); concealment of, 22, 27–28, 56–57, 95–96, emergence of, 22, 28–29, 96–101; fear of, 25–29, 31, 121, 127, 132–33, 139–40; as inviolate, sacred, 21, 48–50, 71, 95–96, 107–11; as political controversy, 10, 102, 148–49; as transcendent, 66–67. *See also* journey inward; introspection; maps of the self; memory, as leading beyond itself; unconscious
intimacy, 3, 5, 6, 18–29, 38–39, 42–45, 72–73, 88–96, 122–23, 127–28, 147–48, 163n17, 177n29. *See also* embraces; invasion (annexation) of other
introspection, 28–29, 33, 66, 121, 125–26, 127, 130–31, 148–50
invasion (annexation) of other, 18–29, 44–45, 90–96, 99–100, 105, 113–15
Iurkevich, P. D., 158n23
Ivanits, Linda, 182n14, 185n27, 188n41, 190n50, 191n56
Ivanov, Viacheslav, 153n8, 179n3, 180n7, 185n28, 191n2

Jackson, Robert Louis, 155n16, 174n12, 201n9, 204n23, 207n15, 213n4
Janet, Pierre, 159n27
Jeffers, Thomas L., 199n4
Johnson, Brian, 179n4
Johnson, Leslie, 180n9, 186n29
Jones, Malcom V., 155n15, 161n1, 162n7, 165n21, 165n25, 168n9, 192n4, 195n19, 210n30
journey inward, 79–83, 96–99, 123–27, 130–32, 136–41, 142–50, 187n38, 206n12. *See also* indwelling divinity; interiority; introspection
Jung, Carl Gustav, 8, 104–105, 119, 198n1, 199n3

Kanevskaya, Maria, 211n32, 211n35
Kant, Immanuel, 32
Kantor, V. K., 188n39, 205n5, 210n27, 211n32, 211n34, 211n37
Kasatkina, T. A., 157n21, 180n7, 180n9, 186n33, 189n44, 189nn47–49, 200n7, 201n8, 202n11, 203n17, 205n1, 206n9
Katz, Michael R., 205n4

Index

kenosis, 117
Kent, Leonard, 163n17, 166n5, 167n6, 168n11
Khapaeva, Dina, 169n15
Khomiakov, Alexei, 114, 173n6, 204n26
Kibal'nik, Sergei, 173n6
Kierkegaard, Soren, 86
Kireevsky, Ivan, 202n12
Kirillov, Alexei, 95, 122
Klein, Melanie, 167n7, 170n20
Knapp, Liza, 186n33, 187n34, 204n28, 204n30
Koshchei the Deathless, 104
Kostalevsky, Marina, 154n10, 165n25, 190nn51–52, 192n6, 195n17
Krasnoshchekova, Elena, 199n4
Krieger, Murray, 182n16
Kristeva, Julia, 162n9

Laub, Dori, 213n2
laughter, spiritual significance of, 117, 119
Lazarus, 64–66
Leatherbarrow, W. J., 163n11, 168n14, 169n15, 181nn9–10, 187n37, 191n1, 193n7, 195n16, 196nn23–25, 198n33, 204n24
Lebiadkina, Maria Timofeevna, 23, 96, 97, 99, 100, 167n6
Lenin, V. I., 214n11
Lerner, Paul, 160n29
Levinas, Emmanuel, 4, 181n9, 186n29
liberalism, 87, 102, 192n5, 195n17
Livermore, Gordon, 193n7
Lossky, Vladimir, 158n23, 191n2
Luckhurst, Roger, 160n29
Lukács, Georg, 5
Lunde, Ingunn, 202n11

Maguire, Robert, 202n15
Manicheanism, 83
Mann, Thomas, 5
Mantzaridis, Georgios, 204n30
maps of the self, 8–9, 12, 29, 46, 78–79, 126–27, 131–32, 143. *See also* symbolic vocabulary of selfhood; tripartite self
Marmeladova, Sonya, 46, 48–50, 64, 83
Martin, Raymond, 151n4
Martinsen, Deborah A., 166n3, 194n9, 194n11, 197n27, 210n29, 211n36

Marullo, Thomas G., 161n34, 165n26, 170n25
Marx, Karl, 108, 202n12,
materialism, 52, 108
Matich, Olga, 214n15
Mazurek, Slawomir, 192n2
McReynolds, Susan, 175 n19, 178n31
medieval morality play, 5
Meerson, Olga, 165n27, 187n35,
memory, 6, 8, 9, 20, 26, 28, 30–31, 33–34, 37–38, 47, 80–83, 122, 146–48; carrier of, 38, 42, 48–50, 63–65, 70–73, 133–135 (*see also* external soul); collective memory, 64, 147–148; distressing memory, 51–53 (*see also* trauma); as fortifying, 52, 64, 149–150, 213n5; as leading beyond itself, 66, 79–80, 141, 145–148; revelatory memory, 49, 65. *See also* amnesia; Lazarus
Mephistopheles, 34, 165n12
Mesmer, Franz, 32
Mestergazi, Elena, 182n16
metaphysical psychology, 6, 65, 67, 83, 86–88, 102
Micale, Mark, 160n29
Miller, Robin Feuer, 173n3, 174n11, 181n11, 187n34, 187n36, 193n7, 194n13, 197n28, 206n8, 211n37, 213n6, 214n8
mind, 12. *See also* external mind; interiority; reason; tripartite self
Mochulsky, Konstantin, 112, 153n8, 154n10, 166n5, 170n21, 171n26, 173n5, 174n11, 176n22, 178n1, 179n3, 179n6, 185n28, 190n51, 191n2, 194n9, 197n29, 200n7, 201n8, 201n11, 203n20, 209n25, 211n33, 212n41
modernity, malaise of, 10, 36, 189n46
money (as symbol of selfhood), 71, 107–9, 137, 202n12
Moretti, Franco, 200n5
Morson, Gary Saul, 155n16, 156n18, 178n32, 203n23, 205n6, 206n9, 206n11, 213n3, 213n7
Moser, Charles, 192n5, 193n8
Murav, Harriet, 179n4, 188n40, 196n23
Myshkin, Lev, 9, 11, 39, 45, 60, 63, 68–85, 125, 133, 145
mysticism, 12–13. *See also* journey inward; indwelling divinity

Index

Naiman, Eric, 172n31
Naginski, Erika, 160n28
nationalism, 7
natural law, 25
Nechaev, 101
Nekrasov, Nikolai, 51–52, 66
Neoplatonism, 17, 32, 79–80, 116, 167n6, 206n12
Neuhauser, Rudolf, 169nn15–16
neurology, 13
"new man," 102
Nietzsche, Friedrich, 4, 162n5
nihilism, 87, 145, 192n5, 195n17

object-relations theory, 32, 167n7, 170n20
Offord, Derek, 152n5, 157n20, 197n30
Orwin, Donna, 184n24, 191n57
Otverzhennyj, N., 173n6

Paperno, Irina, 214n14
"paradox" of selfhood (as collective and individual), 3–5, 102–3, 121, 144, 147–48, 152n6
Passage, Charles E., 167n5, 170n17, 195n15
pathogenic secrecy, 58–59, 66, 175n17
Paul, Jean, 163n17
Peace, Richard, 165n23, 171n26, 184n23, 186n33, 191n2, 192n4, 193n7, 208n18, 209n22, 212n41
pedagogy. *See* education
personality (*lichnost'*), 11–13, 157nn20–21. *See also* selfhood
Petrashevsky circle, 173nn5–6
Pevear, Richard, 101, 198n34
Pirog, Gerald, 159nn25–26
Plato, 151n4, 180n7, 182n12, 188n41, 209n25. *See also* Neoplatonism
Platonov, Andrei, 16
Plotnikov, Nikolai, 157n20
pochvennichestvo (return to the soil), 7
Pomar, Mark G., 205n3
Pope, Richard, 194n10, 194n12
possession, 84–85, 87, 95–96, 101–3, 112–13, 114–15, 135–36. *See also* demonism
postmodernism, 5, 17
prayer, 22, 37, 41, 80, 100, 125, 130
pretend sleep (as motif of collective self), 21–23, 27–28, 45, 99–101
privacy, 21, 49, 55, 94–96

projection, 8, 27–28, 35–40, 63, 76, 78–79, 89, 134, 145–46; projective identification, 6, 28, 32, 78, 167n7, 170n20. *See also* anima; external soul; memory, carrier of; self-consciousness, as externalized; shadow
Proust, Marcel, 5
psyche, structure of. *See* maps of the self; unconscious
psychiatry, 8, 31, 122
psychic wound. *See* trauma
psychoanalysis, 5, 6, 8, 14, 32, 58–59, 153n9
psychological realism, 3, 5–6, 17, 46, 86–87, 152n7, 153n9
psychology, 8, 32. *See also* metaphysical psychology
Pushkin, Alexander, 149, 193n8; *The Covetous Knight*, 108–9, 186n32

Quinton, Anthony, 157n23

Rassin, Eric, 166n4
rational egoism, 173n7
realism. *See* psychological realism
reason, 25, 36, 37
repetition compulsion, 46–47, 196n21
repression, 8, 14, 36, 166n4
Rice, James, 122, 154n11, 161n34, 179n4, 205n2, 207n13
romanticism, 12–13, 17, 32, 36, 37–38, 108–9, 128, 140–41, 161n4, 163n13, 208n19. *See also* expressivism
Rosen, Nathan, 201nn8–9, 204n33, 207n16, 208n17
Rosenthal, Richard J., 165n26, 167m7, 170n20
Rothschild, as "idea," 106–8, 111
Rousseau, Jean-Jacques, 51, 55, 56, 173n4, 174n12, 174n14, 176n21, 193n7, 197n28
Rowling, J. K., 199n2
Rozanov, Vasilii, 153n8, 214n9
Russia: and civil service, 18; and concept of selfhood, 11–13; controversy over "inner life" (*Vekhi*), 7, 148–49; and intelligentsia, 102; and messianic mission, 10; and modernity, 10, 101, 189n46; and political fate, 87; and religious past, 81–82; and rise of materialism, positivism, 52; "Russian soul," 74,

236

Index

87; and transition from liberalism to nihilism, 87
Russian orthodoxy, 7, 116, 121, 122, 158n23, 175n17, 188n39, 198n34, 203n19, 208n21
Rzhevsky, 200n7, 201n10

Sade, Marquis de, 174n12
Saint Petersburg (as modern capital), 10, 18, 23–24, 35, 144, 164n18
Sandomirskaia, Irina, 162n8
Saraskina, Liudmilla, 197n31
Sartre, Jean-Paul, 4
Scanlan, James P., 155n15, 175n16, 175n19
Schelling, F. W. J., 161n4, 190n51
Schiller, Friedrich, 30
schizoid disorder, 6, 32
Schmid, Ulrich, 190n53
Seeley, F. F., 210n30
seemliness (*blagoobrazie*), 116–18, 204n32
Seigel, Jerold, 151n4
self. *See* selfhood
self-consciousness, 10, 90, 145, 156n19, 172n2; as externalized, 32–35, 36, 39–40, 43–45; Hegelian dialectic of, 167n8
self-destruction, 10
selfhood, 11–13; as activity, 17, 29, 133; "becoming a personality," 4, 6; as dialogical, 18, 24–25; as divided, 10; in Dostoevsky criticism, 5–6, 16–17; as dramatized externally, 5–6, 8, 31–40, 42–50, 63, 83–84, 86–87, 153n8, 203n20; as embodied, 25, 33; as essentialist, 16–18, 56–57, 116–19, 128, 158n25, 162n8; as indwelling, 5, 16–18; as inviolate, 4, 110–11; as microcosm, 153n8; in negative sense (*samost'*), 3–4, 12, 60; as intersubjective, relational, 5, 16–18, 24–25, 111–15, 147–48; romantic landscape of, 12–13; in scholarship, 5, 177n29. *See also* collective selfhood; ego (the "I"); maps of the self; "paradox" of selfhood (as collective and individual); selflessness; symbolic vocabulary of selfhood
selflessness (*samootverzhenie*), 12, 60, 152n5
Semenov, E. I., 199n4, 201n8, 202n12, 202n14
Serno-Solov'evich, 101

sexuality, 28, 44, 91, 124, 129, 163n14, 174n13, 177n28, 179n2, 183n21, 185n28, 195nn13–14, 196n22, 199n4, 204n27
shadow, 8
Shay, Jonathan, 160n28
Shelley, Percy, 202n14
Shestov, Lev, 4
Shigalyov-ism, 101
Shklovsky, Viktor, 168n11
slavophiles, 6, 114, 202n12
Smith, Jeremiah, 34–35, 61–62, 74
sobornost', 6, 7, 111–14, 203n19
socialism, 55, 57, 87, 163n11, 169n15, 192n5
solipsism, 10, 35–36, 44, 145, 213n3
Solovyov, Sergei, 76
Solovyov, Vladimir, 4, 17, 147, 157n21, 161n2, 190n51
Sorabji, Richard, 161n4
soul, 17, 36, 38, 107–11, 128; definition of, 11–13, 157n23; as immortal, 29, 98, 104; as indwelling, 107–8, 116–18, 126–27, 131–32; as intersubjective, 12–13, 112; as unconscious, 32–33, 159n25. *See also* external soul; interiority; selfhood; unconscious
source (indwelling), 6, 8, 17, 24–25, 66, 80, 82–83, 96–97, 102–3, 125–28, 131–32, 138, 142. *See also* indwelling divinity
Spektor, Sasha, 164n21, 180n8, 181n9
Starobinski, Jean, 173n4, 176n21
Stavrogin, Nikolai, 23, 86–87, 90–94, 99–100, 102
Stavrogina, Varvara, 23, 87, 89–90, 96–99, 129
Steinberg, Mark, 214n15
Steiner, Lina, 199n4
Stepun, Fyodor, 164n18, 171n26, 191n2, 192n5
Stirner, Max, 56, 165n28, 173n6, 173n7, 174nn8–10, 174n12
Stolypin, A., 214n11
Strelsky, Katherine, 163n14
subconscious. *See* unconscious
subjectivity. *See* selfhood
suppression (of thought, memory, emotion), 31, 37, 40–50, 53, 59–62, 63, 66, 71, 73, 75, 78–79, 81, 84, 93, 127, 133–36, 142, 143, 166n4
Suvorin, Alexei, 14
Swales, Martin, 200n4

237

Index

Swoboda, Philip J., 158n23
symbolic vocabulary of selfhood, 7, 45, 61–63, 66. *See also* apartment edifice; corpse; dog; maps of the self; money; pretend sleep; tears, weeping onto the other; tripartite self; "whirlwind"
Szczepanska, Kathryn, 167n8

Taylor, Charles, 151n4, 161n1, 197n29
tears, weeping onto the other (as motif of collective self), 38–39, 45, 170n18
Terras, Victor, 163n10, 168n11, 169n15, 170n17, 170n23
Theodora, Saint, 208n21
theology, 6; as inextricable from psychology in Dostoevsky's writing, 6, 65, 67, 87–88, 154n14
Thompson, Diane O., 209n25
Todorov, Tsvetan, 17, 156n19, 162n6
Tolstoy, Lev, 149, 166n1, 214n9, 214nn13–14
topography of the self. *See* maps of the self
transcendent ideal, 76–78, 100
transparency (of personality), 9, 52–53, 53–58, 59–60, 66, 204n32; as Enlightenment virtue, 9, 60, 173n4, 176n21; and opacity, 53, 58–59
trauma, 8, 13–15, 36, 37–38, 40–42, 43, 46–50, 51–53, 55, 60, 69–71, 90–94, 121, 124, 142, 159n27, 196n21, 213n2; in Dostoevsky's life, 14–15; genealogy of, 14, 160n29; prehistory of, 13–15, 51–53, 58–59, 160nn28–29; post-traumatic stress disorder, 46, 159n27. *See also* amnesia; child abuse; memory; pathogenic secrecy
Trinity, 141
tripartite self, 29, 35, 39–40, 47, 49–50, 82, 126, 131–32, 139–40, 171n30; mind-body-consciousness, 82; mind-soul-consciousness, 49, 75, 126; watchman-prisoner-redeemer, 47, 49–50, 73–76, 132, 143; self-soul-spirit (*ia-dusha-dukh*), 12–13
tsel'nost', 6. *See also* wholeness (of personality)

Turgenev, Ivan, 166n1
Turner, Denys, 187n38, 207n12
Turner, Judy, 194n10, 194n12
Turner, Léon, 155n14
Tymms, Ralph, 163n13, 166n5, 168n12

unconscious, 5, 6, 28, 31, 32–35, 36–40, 63, 73, 79, 123, 126–28, 130–32, 159n25. *See also* collective unconscious; maps of the self; soul
unhappy consciousness, 10

vampirism, 9, 90–91
Vekhi (*Landmarks*), 148–49, 214nn10–11
Vetlovskaia, Valentina A., 205n3
Vinokurov (Vinokur), Val, 180n9
Vitz, Paul C., 152n4
Volgin, I., 160n32
Volokhonsky, Larissa, 101

Wasiolek, Edward, 176n20, 177n26, 191n2, 192n4
Weil, Simone, 120
Westernizers, 102, 192n5, 197n30
"whirlwind" (as symbol of collective self), 5, 105, 111–15, 117, 142, 148, 153n8, 203n20
Whitman, Walt, 68
wholeness (of personality), 6, 98–99, 142
Williams, John S., 195n13, 196n21
Woloch, Alex, 156n17, 168n11
Wood, James, 156n17
Woolf, Virginia, 5
world soul, 147, 167n6, 184n24. *See also* collective unconscious
wounds of the mind. *See* trauma
Wyman, Alina, 164n21

Yanovsky, Stepan, 14, 161n34
Young, Allan, 160nn28–30, 175n17
Young, Sarah, 180n9, 183n17, 183nn20–21, 184n26, 185n27, 189n45, 190n55

Zander, L. A., 152n6, 152n7, 153n8, 167n6
Ziolkowski, Theodore, 208n19